á maman

et papa.

Without whose unfailing and unconditional love, friendship, advice, and support

so much would have been simply impossible.

Je t'embrasse bien fort.

A comprehensive, non-technical guide to modern audio post-production techniques <u>for film and video</u>, starting with the beginner's guide to the fundamentals of audio, step by step explanations of microphones, consoles, tape decks, editing, effects, patching, connecting equipment, and culminating with voice overs, location sound procedure, film sound transfers, ADR, Foley, conventional and modern film and video sound mixing, audio/video interlock, MIDI, SMPTE time code, synchronization, computer sequencing, sampling, digital audio, and modern post production techniques. Fully illustrated by the author.

The Cutting Edge of Audio Production and Audio Post-Production

Theory, Equipment and Techniques

Mico Nelson

Knowledge Industry Publications, Inc.

The Cutting Edge of Audio Production and Audio Post-Production

Mico Nelson

ISBN 305-5-KC

FOREWORD

In recent years, the technology available for audio post-production has become both staggering in the opportunities it provides and intimidating to the novice.

When I began teaching in New York I searched for reading materials to assign. Almost all the books I found dealing with audio and post-production — though of high quality — seemed to require an engineering degree to understand. Nothing I found was geared for the beginner.

Therefore, during my first year of teaching, I compiled a series of notes, which, over the course of five years, grew into a prepared text with illustrations. This I handed out to my students. As I continued teaching, the text evolved into this book.

I have tried to limit the contents of this book to the practical and aesthetic matters of audio production and post-production. In other words, this is not meant as a general reference book in which to look up, for example, technical details about the relative sizes of audio head gaps. Nor have I ever, in my 15 years as an audio professional, believed that that level of technical detail had any bearing on the use of the equipment or the process of learning the fundamental aspects of audio.

This book is meant to introduce you to the fundamentals of audio and post-production and deliberately excludes as much technological jargon as possible. No law or rule says that you must apply the techniques presented. The only goal of the text is to introduce you to the options available.

Film and video are both visual media supported by audio. Strangely, people rarely notice the audio until its quality is poor enough to detract from the visual material. This book, then, is geared toward providing the basic skills to produce a high-quality soundtrack and increase your understanding of the opportunities provided by the technology.

As in any creative endeavor, the integration of technique and production can be achieved only through long hours of study and practice. It is hoped that you will apply the material and techniques presented in this text to the projects you are currently working on, as well as to future projects.

In addition, a goal of this book is to provide you with new direction. Should you gain an interest, for example, in MIDI, SMPTE interlock or other subjects touched upon, you will undoubtedly find yourself at an advantage having gained some familiarity with it in this book.

ACKNOWLEDGMENTS

The author wishes to express his deepest gratitude to Gil Bassak, who combines the very best qualities of editor, technician and ally. Without his steadfast dedication, this project would never have reached its conclusion. The author also wishes to thank with equal acknowledgment and gratitude the untiring efforts of Janet Moore, whose efforts kept this project alive. Only a publisher with Janet's vision and understanding of the ever changing aspects of this field could be qualified to support this text.

Thanks to Mr. David Rhodes, who (on the basis of an acerbic opinion made by the author regarding wiring) hired the author from a continuing education class to teach audio production and post-production courses to film and video students. Mr. Rhodes has also supported the author's efforts in many other ways, and this book could not have been written without his auspices.

To Bruce Teed, who, along with considerable friendship, support and other warm considerations, introduced me to Mr. Rhodes. We miss you.

And, finally, my warmest thanks to David Tung, Rifka Althaus and the staff of the Computer Center for their cheerful cooperation and help during the countless hours when I laser-printed mountains of drafts for this book.

It is indeed rare in this industry to find individuals who are as generous with their time and resources as Mr. John Dowdell, vice-president of The Tape House in New York City. The author expresses his gratitude for Mr. Dowdell's literally invaluable help.

The following people and companies lent inestimable assistance during the writing of this book. Without their help it is doubtful that this text would have been completed as it was:

Marie Berardino, CRN Inc.; Vincent Stancarone, Devlin Video Services, New York City; Peter Goetcher, Digidesign; Tim Spitzer and Alan Gus, DuArt Film Labs, Inc., New York City; Paul DeBenedictis, Opcode Electronics; Barbara Flyntz-Bradley, Teletronics; Larry Spotts, Todd A-O, Hollywood, California; and Tony Romano and Rosanne Schaffer, vice-president, TVC, Inc., New York City.

The author would also like to thank the following people and companies for sending the photographic and technical materials that were vital to the creation of this book:

Andrew Simon and Henry Adams, Adams-Smith; Carol Himmelman-Chistopher, ADC Telecommunications, Inc.; Mindy Williams, Akai; Spence Burton, Alpha Audio Automation Systems; Applied Research and Technology, Inc.; Mark Overington and Scott Greenburg, Avid; Julie Pelz, Bruel & Kjaer; Patti Carpenter, BTS Broadcast Television Systems, Inc.; Anthony Mattia, Cipher Digital; Linda Petrauskas and Jim Rosenberg, E-Mu Systems, Inc.; Maddie Nardella, Elmo; Gil Griffith, Ventide, Inc.; Fast Forward; Hagai Gefen, Gefen Systems; Marjory Miller, Gold Line, Inc.; Jerry Graham, Gotham Audio Corporation; Theresa Parsley, Harrison by GLW, Inc.; Becky David, J.L. Cooper; Rita Vix, JBL; Sam Spinnachio, Klark-Teknik; Mike Malizola, Kurzweil Music Systems, Inc.; Will Egleston and Leah Holsten, Lexicon, Inc.; Bob Eberenz, Magna-Tech Electronic Co.; Bob Schluter, Middle Atlantic Audio; Ken Berkowitz and Bruce Tucker, Network Production Music, Inc.; Lisa Vogel, Neve; Carla Posgate, Orban; Sally Saubolle, Otari; Martin Porter, Porter Associates; Trevor Boyer, Saki Magnetics, Inc.; Sara Hornbacher and Richard Pepperman, School of Visual Arts; Davida Rochman, Shure; Nick DeLello, Bruce Lily, Trevor Donovan and Jim Streeter, Sony Corporation; Larry Newlon, Studer Revox America, Inc.; Bill Mohrhoff, Tascam/Teac Inc.; Tektronix Personal Test Instruments Division; Fred Ridder and Josanne Block, Timeline Inc.; Peggy Brooks, WaveFrame Corp.; and Jeffrey Hodgson, Fredy Atcheson, Bob Davis and Phil Moon, Yamaha Corp. of America.

CONTENTS

PART ONE: PRODUCTION

1
BASIC WAVE THEORY

A. INTRODUCTION

Imagine a stone dropping into a pool of water...

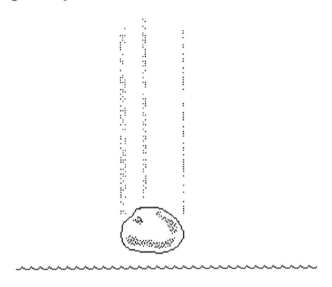

Fig. 1.1 Drop a stone into water.

After the impact, waves fan out over the water. From above, they might look something like this:

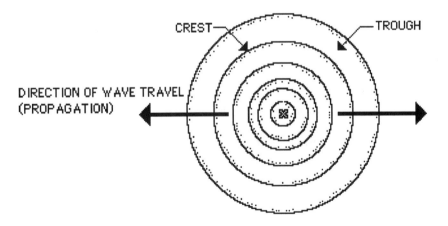

Fig. 1.2 The motion of waves in water.

Note that the waves in Fig. 1.2 consist of crests and troughs; the high and low points in the waves. These same waves, seen from the side, might look like this (Fig. 1.3):

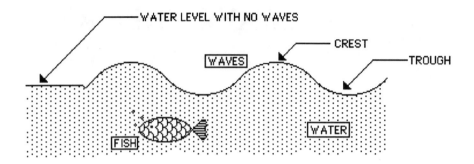

Fig. 1.3 Crests and troughs in waves.

Waves occur when energy in a medium is transmitted from one molecule of that material to the other. Simply put, sets of molecules smack into one another like billiard balls, starting a chain reaction (Fig. 1.4):

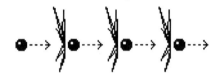

Fig. 1.4 Waves form when molecules collide.

The same waves shown in Fig. 1.3, if seen in terms of molecular action, would look like this (Fig. 1.5):

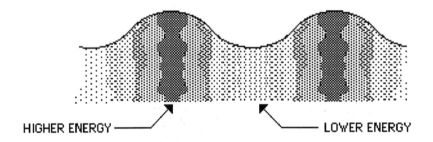

Fig. 1.5 Waves seen as the transmission of molecular energy.

One can see that the energy is most concentrated at the crests of each wave, and most diffused at the troughs. For this reason, the crests are called **positive peaks**, and the troughs are called **negative peaks**.

Sound waves are transmitted through air in exactly the same way. The distance between air molecules is alternately compressed and expanded at a rate that depends on the source of the sound. Like the rock displacing the water, the source that dislocates the air could be a plucked string, scraping surfaces, the impact of objects, or other air in motion. In each case, the action starts a vibration.

When any kind of sound wave or vibration is discussed throughout this book, a linear pictogram is almost always used to represent the changes of that wave in time. Thus, Figs. 1.3 and 1.5 could each be represented as:

4

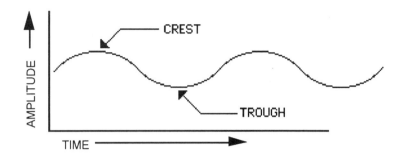

Fig. 1.6 Representing a wave as amplitude changes in time.

B. FREQUENCY AND PITCH

Sounds have individual characteristics like frequency and amplitude that impart unique qualities. These characteristics become most apparent when comparing different sounds, like a fog horn and a flute.

When an object vibrates in air, it does so at a specific rate, or **frequency**. For example, when a guitar string is plucked, it takes specific amount of time for the string to bounce back past — and then return to — its original position (Fig. 1.7):

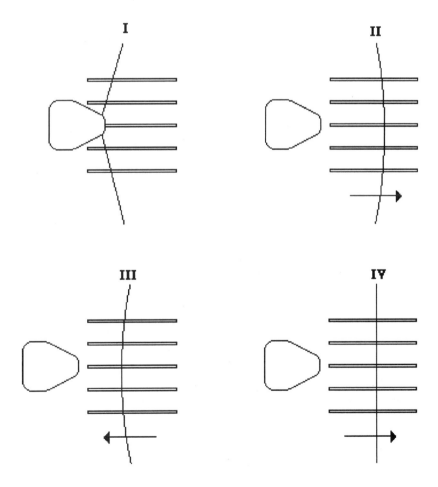

Fig. 1.7 One cycle of a vibration guitar string.

This movement of the string through the to and fro motion and returning to its original starting point is called a **cycle**. The number of cycles occurring within one second determines a given sound's frequency. Conversely, **wavelength** describes the distance between two adjacent cycles in a wave. If the guitar string shown in Fig. 1.7 were to vibrate 120 times in one second, the frequency of the sound it produced would be said to vibrate at 120 **cycles per second**; a characteristic that is expressed in **Hertz,** abbreviated **Hz.** If the same string were to vibrate 500 times per second, its frequency would be 500 Hz; frequencies of 1,000 Hz and above are abbreviated as K. For example: 1,500 Hz = 1.5 KHz; 10,000 Hz = 10 KHz, and so on.

A cycle can be measured from any two identical points on a wave (Fig. 1.8):

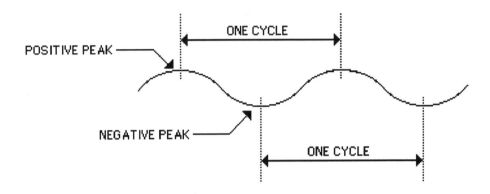

Fig. 1.8 Measuring one cycle of a wave.

However, for our purposes, a cycle is always measured from the beginning of the rise to the positive peak (Fig. 1.9):

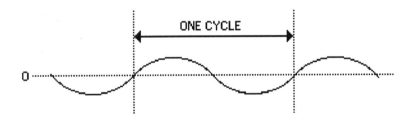

Fig. 1.9 One cycle of a wave.

We perceive the frequency of any sound as **pitch**. For example, the pitch of a train whistle is higher than the rumbling of a bulldozer. The difference is that air escaping from the train's steam whistle is vibrating much faster than the vibrations caused by the bulldozer's engine and parts. Faster vibrations of air, and thus higher frequencies, are perceived as progressively higher pitches of sound.

Examples in the following frequency chart illustrate the differences in pitch between certain voices and instruments in relation to the piano (Fig. 1.10).

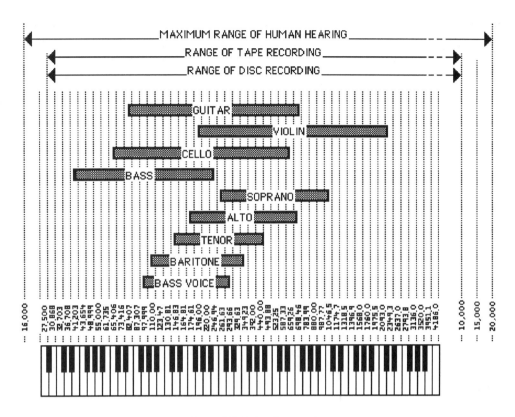

Fig. 1.10 Relative frequencies.

C. THE FREQUENCY SPECTRUM

Variations in the range of perceived pitch determines an individual's response to the tonal characteristics of that sound. The differences between boominess, brilliance, muffled, tinniness and other qualities of a sound can be attributed to the sound's **frequency spectrum**. This spectrum can be subdivided into several sections, each of which lend a unique disposition to the sound, and is limited by the range of human hearing. That range is generally from 20 Hz to 16 KHz, but differs among individuals:

Bass

The lower frequencies of the spectrum are those between 16 Hz and 256 Hz, and are called the bass frequencies. These are associated with boominess, power, "roar" and "bottom". The lowest tones in this range can be found in earthquakes, thunder, explosions, rocket launchings, and so on. Too little emphasis in this range will result in a "thin" quality of sound; too much will "muffle" or "muddy" the overall sound, resulting in a loss of clarity and intelligibility.

Lower Midrange

The midrange frequencies lie between 256 Hz and 2,048 Hz. These determine a sound's substance, as most of the origins of sounds lie in this range. Excessive boosting of this range will result in a "telephone" quality. Too little emphasis in this range will result in a loss of basic sound quality.

7

Upper Midrange

The upper midrange consists of frequencies between 2,048 Hz and 4,096 Hz. These are responsible, in part, for the intelligibility and presence of sound. Too many of the frequencies in this range will lend a harsh, aggravating quality; too few will diminish the overall prominence.

Treble

The treble frequencies fall between 4,096 Hz and 16,384 Hz, and establish the brilliance, sparkle and clarity of sound. Any excessive increases in this range boosts electronic noise and hiss. Too little emphasis in this range gives a dull, lifeless quality to the sound.

D. AMPLITUDE

The vibration of a sound source can be characterized not only its frequency but also its perceived volume. As sets of molecules vibrate at certain rates, the distance that the molecules vibrate is also determined by the sound source. A flute will displace molecules less than a jackhammer, and it is for this reason that a flute is the softer of the two. It is displacement of the air pressure that determines a sound's **amplitude**. In terms of the sound wave, the amplitude is the difference in height between the negative and positive peaks, and this determines the loudness or volume of a particular sound (Fig. 1.11):

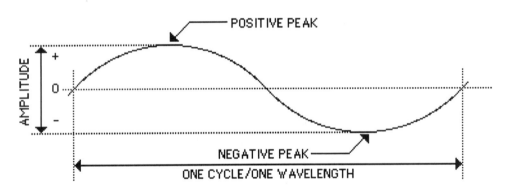

Fig. 1.11 Amplitude is the distance between peaks.

<u>Again, as amplitude increases, volume increases</u>. Amplitude is expressed in **decibels**, abbreviated **dB.** Generally speaking, a decibel is the smallest change in volume the human ear can detect. The relative levels of acoustic pressure are referred to as **sound pressure level**, or **SPL.**

The range of sounds, from inaudible (zero dB) to unbearably painful sound levels (120 dB), is called the **dynamic range**. To relates decibel counts to common sounds, refer to the following decibel chart, which illustrates relative units of volume (Fig. 1.12):

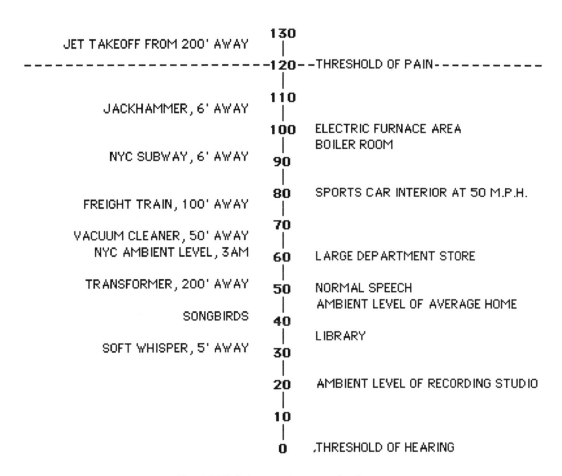

Fig. 1.12 Relative sound pressure levels.

E. WAVEFORM & TIMBRE

Just as the frequency of a sound source determines its perceived pitch, and amplitude determines its relative SPL or volume, the actual tonal quality or color of a particular sound is determined by its **timbre**. The timbre of a sound is determined by its **waveform**. For illustration, the waves depicted thus far have had simple and smooth waveforms. This type of wave is called a sine wave and has only one frequency. However, most sounds consist not of one frequency, but of several different frequencies that may each vary in amplitude. These combinations of frequencies produce complex waveforms, which when displayed on an oscilloscope, appear radically different in shape from the sine wave. It is the frequency content, called the harmonic structure, of these waves, and thus their waveforms, that produce various timbres.

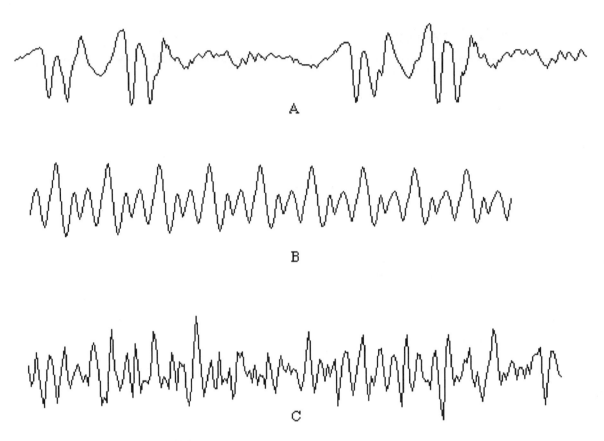

Fig. 1.13 The waveforms of a saxophone (A), pipe organ (B) and crash cymbal (C).

The waveforms shown in Fig. 1.13 are taken from single notes of three instruments. Example "A" illustrates the waveform of a saxophone; example "B" depicts the waveform of a pipe organ. Note the repetition of each waveform in comparison with example "C", which shows the waveform of a crash cymbal, and which is largely composed of irregular frequencies. The notes played on the sax and organ contain mostly lower and midrange frequencies, producing a full, mellow sound, while the crash cymbal contains mostly upper midrange and treble frequencies which yield a harsh, grating sound.

F. ENVELOPES

Timbre is also affected by the way the **envelope** of a particular sound progresses. The envelope of a waveform describes the overall way in which the loudness, or amplitude, of a sound waveform varies from its beginning to its end.

Understanding the concept of an envelope is crucial to the art of signal mixing and processing. Generally speaking, no two sound sources have exactly the same envelope. For example, the envelopes of both a cymbal crash and snare drum hit will differ . Thus, one may consider an envelope to represent an auditory "fingerprint".

All envelopes have the following characteristics (Fig. 1.14):

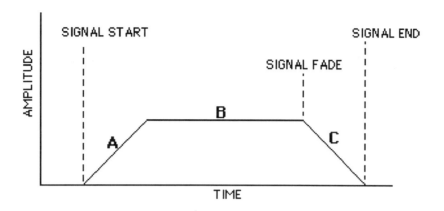

Fig. 1.14 The characteristics of an envelope showing the attack (A), sustain (B) and release (C).

Section A of Fig. 1.16 is called the attack or the portion of the sound emitted after the initial action producing the vibration. Section B depicts how long the sound remains at full amplitude, and is called the sustain of the envelope; section C, is the release, or the amount of time required for a sound to go from full volume to silence. Bear in mind that this diagram represents the overall amplitude of one sound as heard from its beginning to end.

To describe individual envelopes in greater detail, one must add additional components to the envelope. The standard method of describing an envelope in analog synthesis is called **ADSR**, which stands for Attack-Decay-Sustain-Release:

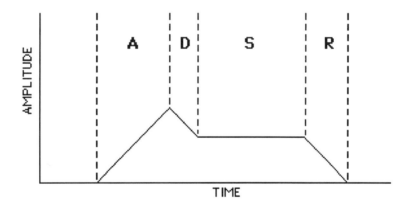

Fig. 1.15 Adding a decay stage (D) to the envelope diagram.

Note that the additional stage of the envelope, the decay, has been added between the attack and the sustain. This describes the initial loss in volume after the attack prior to sustaining its full volume. This method of depicting an envelope is more accurate than the three stage envelope, as it adds another factor for analyzing the overall sound.

Some actual envelopes are shown in the following diagrams. These figures were derived from computer software that stores instrument sounds in the form of digital information and visually displays the envelope shape (Figs 1.16, 1.17, 1.18):

Fig. 1.16 Crash cymbal envelope.

Fig. 1.17 Plucked hard envelope.

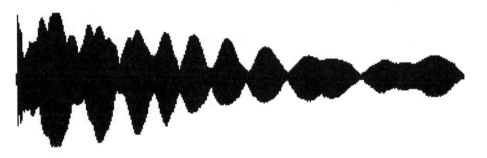

Fig. 1.18 Electric guitar envelope.

G. MEASURING DEVICES

There are four basic devices used for measuring or generating an audio signal. These are specialized instruments, and are mentioned now because they help in understanding the fundamental properties of sound.

An **oscilloscope** lets one see how a signal looks by measuring changes in voltage and displaying these changes on a tube similar to a television screen. The display appears similar to the wave diagrams in this book (Fig. 1.18).

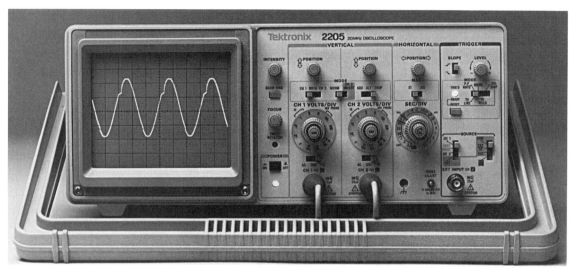

Fig. 1.18. An oscilloscope displaying a sine wave.
(Photo courtesy of Tektronix, Inc.)

Another type of device called an **oscillator** generates signals of different types and frequency. These signals are sometimes put through various signal paths in an audio environment and can be, if required, observed by an oscilloscope. An oscillator is sometimes found built into audio consoles, or may be a separate unit; the frequency of the signals produced can be altered in pre-set increments and are used to put tones on the portion of a videotape; this is the audio equivalent of color bars in television. Using tones allows an operator to determine if the equipment is playing back at the same levels it recorded, and is used as a standard for referencing tapes and machines.

A **spectrum analyzer**. breaks an audio signal into specific frequency bands, and shows the SPL of each band. Using a spectrum analyzer, one can determine how a room sounds. The frequency bands are displayed in pre-set increments, and each band will display the relative volume of a specific frequency range. The display is commonly a sequentially illuminating series of light emitting diodes (LED's) arranged in vertical columns. The loudness of a specific frequency band will be reflected by the number of LED's lit in that particular band; the louder the range, the more LED's will illuminate (Fig. 1.19).

Fig. 1.19. A spectrum analyzer. The dots over most of the unit are lights, and each vertical strip represents a frequency band. The more that the lights become lit in a vertical column from bottom to top, the louder the sounds in that particular frequency band. (Photo courtesy of Gold Line, Inc.)

13

A **sound pressure level meter** determines the relative loudness of sound in an area or environment. It is usually hand-held and consists of a calibrated microphone, a range selection switch, processors and a display, usually a VU meter or digital numerical readout. The meter is placed in the area where a reading is to be taken, and the measurement reflects the actual sound pressure level at that location (Fig. 1.20).

Fig. 1.20. An SPL meter. The cylindrical protrusion at the top is a calibrated microphone. This particular model has a numerical readout.
(Photo courtesy of Gold Line, Inc.)

2
MICROPHONES AND SIGNALS

A. INTRODUCTION

Audio quality, be it in a radio station, recording studio or in the field, is only as high as its weakest link. If, for example, high-quality microphones, tape decks, recording media and headphones are used to make a recording, the final recording will likely be of a high caliber. Noise introduced by any element in the audio chain will degrade the signal. We start the recording chain with microphone, which converts acoustic energy from the sound source into electrical energy that is processed by all the other recording and processing devices in the chain. A working knowledge of microphones and their properties is essential to any audio production work; learning to choose the best microphone for a given application may take years of practice, and often separates good engineers from mediocre ones.

B. IMPEDANCE

Impedance is the term for the resistance to the flow of electrical energy in a circuit; more resistance means higher impedance. Microphones come in two impedance types: high and low impedance. Because there is less resistance to the flow of current in a low-impedance circuit, low-impedance microphones are less susceptible to hum and noise induced by motors, electric lights and other electrical equipment. In addition, low-impedance microphones and equipment can better tolerate long cable lengths. For these reasons, low-impedance microphones and equipment are what professionals use most often. High-impedance microphones have the opposite characteristics, and are generally restricted to non-professional use. The main differences between high- and low-impedance microphones are sound quality and price; low-impedance microphones are more expensive, ranging from $50 to over $3,000, and yield significantly better results.

C. TYPES OF MICROPHONES

There are three basic types of low-impedance microphones, each distinct in its construction. In every microphone, however, the component that converts acoustical to electric energy is called the **element**. It is (in part) the manufacture of the element that determines how the microphone responds to sound and, therefore, the quality of the signal it produces.

Dynamic

The **dynamic** microphone utilizes a principle called EMI, or **electro-magnetic induction**, to generate its signal. EMI is a phenomena which occurs under the following conditions (Fig. 2.1):

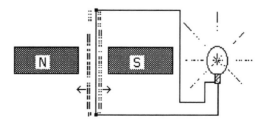

Fig. 2.1 The principle of electromagnetic induction.

When a wire is put in motion between two permanent magnets, voltage is caused to appear within the wire. The same effect works in reverse, and this is the basic operating principle for motors, generators, tape heads, most loudspeakers, and some microphones (Fig. 2.2).

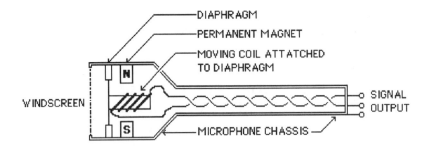

Fig. 2.2 Cut away view of a dynamic microphone.

Fig. 2.2 illustrates a simplified cut away view of a generic dynamic microphone As air hits the diaphragm, the moving coil moves back and forth between the magnets, and this produces a voltage to appear at the signal output. The response of the diaphragm is in direct proportion to the acoustic energy received; the greater the SPL of the sound source, the greater the movement of the diaphragm, and the greater the voltage appearing at the signal output.

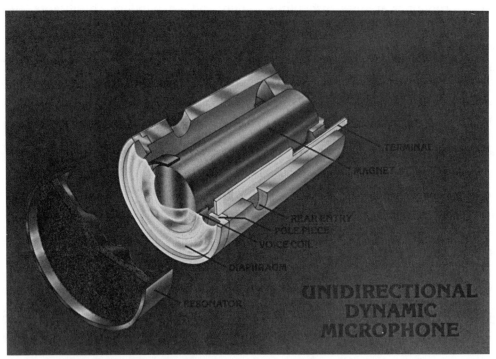

Fig. 2.3. An exploded view of a unidirectional dynamic microphone assembly.
(Photo Courtesy of Shure Brothers, Inc.)

The dynamic microphone is the most common and usually the least expensive of the low-impedance microphones. In addition, the dynamic microphone is rugged, less receptive to overloads from high volume levels, less sensitive to wind noise and is used in many field applications. However, its **frequency response** is usually not as expensive as other types. Consequently, it is less responsive to the higher frequencies and, therefore, gives a duller, or darker, sound.

16

Fig. 2.4. The Shure SM58 cardiod dynamic microphone, commonly used by vocalists for live performances.
(Photo Courtesy of Shure Brothers, Inc.)

Fig. 2.5. The Shure SM63L omnidirectional dynamic microphone.
(Photo Courtesy of Shure Brothers, Inc.)

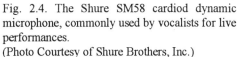

Fig. 2.6. The Shure SM63L super-cardiod dynamic microphone.
(Photo Courtesy of Shure Brothers, Inc.)

Ribbon

The **ribbon** microphone also generates its signal using EMI, and functions much like a dynamic microphone. However, the ribbon microphone replaces the diaphragm and coil with a thin metallic ribbon suspended between the poles of a magnet (Fig. 2.7).

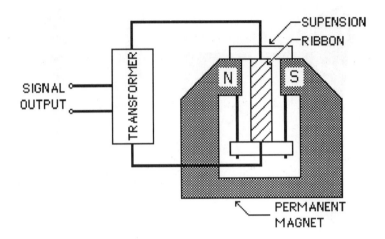

Fig. 2.7 The ribbon microphone suspends a metallic ribbon between the poles of magnet

Because the ribbon element has less mass than the element of a dynamic microphone, it is able to move faster in response to much higher frequencies, making it much more sensitive than the dynamic, and produces a brighter and clearer sound that has warmth and vitality. However, the ribbon microphone's drawback is that loud, percussive sounds or rough handling may damage the thin and fragile ribbon .

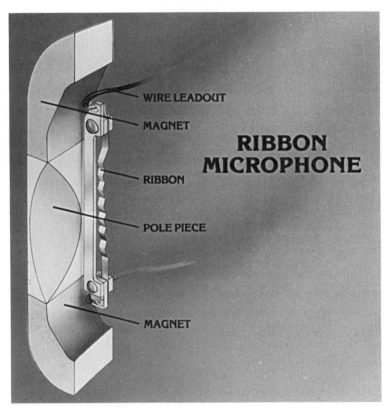

Fig. 2.8. An exploded view of a ribbon microphone assembly.
(Photo Courtesy of Shure Brothers, Inc.)

Condenser

The **condenser** microphone operates on a different principle from that of the ribbon or dynamic types. Instead of using EMI to generate a signal, the element of the condenser microphone has two miniature parallel plates separated by a small distance. One plate is fixed in position, and the other is free to vibrate under the influence of acoustic pressure. At the same time, an electric charge placed across the two plates generates a voltage that varies with the distance between the plates. The changing voltage follows the acoustic waves, producing the microphone's signal.

However, because the level of signal produced is very low, a built-in amplifier is required to boost the voltage to make it usable by equipment further down the signal path. This built-in amplifier is usually battery powered by between 1 to 48 volts DC. When supplied by a source physically outside of the microphone, this voltage is called **phantom power**, and eliminates the need for any internal battery. Phantom power may be supplied by a console or portable power supply. In any case, without this supplied voltage, the condenser microphone will not operate (Figs. 2.9 and 2.10).

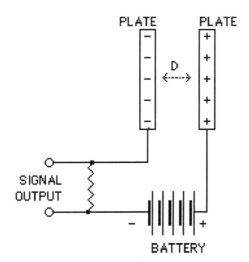

Fig. 2.9 The condenser microphone consists of two parallel plates charged by a voltage.

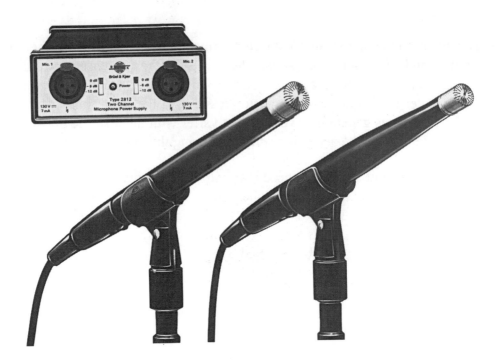

Fig. 2.10. Two Bruel & Kjaer Microphones with a phantom power supply.
(Photo Courtesy of Bruel & Kjaer Instruments, Inc.)

The condenser type microphone is the most popular for studio work, and usually the most expensive of the three. It generally has the most uniform response and the greatest clarity. However, these too are fragile. In general, HANDLE ALL MICROPHONES WITH CARE!!

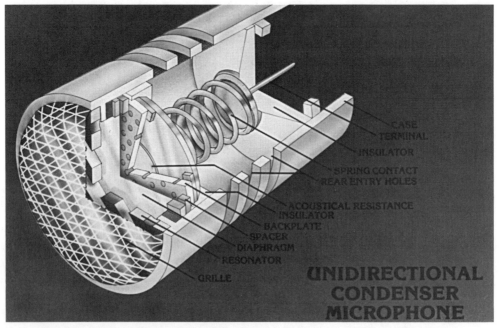

Fig. 2.11. An exploded view of a unidirectional condenser microphone assembly.
(Photo Courtesy of Shure Brothers, Inc.)

Fig. 2.12. The Neumann TLM-170, one of the most popular voice recording microphones. (Photo Courtesy of Gotham Audio Corporation)

There are many different microphone manufacturers, each of which make many different models having different sound qualities. Only with experience can a user know what to expect from a particular microphone, and which ones are best for a particular application. The following chart gives a general summary of the three types of microphones and their characteristics (Fig. 2.13):

MICROPHONE TYPE

CHARACTERISTICS		DYNAMIC	RIBBON	CONDENSER
	SOUND QUALITY	BASSIER, LESS TREBLE	MORE TREBLE, LESS BASS	ALL FREQUENCIES
	HANDLING	RUGGED	EXTREMELY FRAGILE	FRAGILE
	POWER	NONE	NONE	BATTERY OR PHANTOM

Fig. 2.13 Low-impedance microphones and their characteristics

D. PICKUP PATTERNS AND FREQUENCY RESPONSE

Microphones "hear" things differently than people do. The way a particular microphone responds to the loudness and direction of a sound is called a **pickup pattern** and is determined by its design. Specifically, the pickup pattern refers to a microphone's **directional characteristics**. Moreover, these characteristics are independent of the type of microphone being used. For example, different dynamic microphones can pick up sounds in different ways. Microphones work best at an optimum distance from the sound source and within their particular field of acceptance.

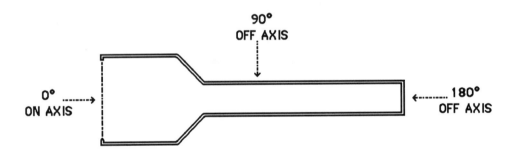

Fig. 2.14 Directional characteristics are defined by their relation to the microphone's axis

When sound enters the microphone from the front (at 0°), it is said to be **on axis** (Fig. 2.14).

Consider the most common types of pickup patterns (depicted in three-dimensional space):

A that microphone that picks up sound with equal or almost equal sensitivity from its front, back and sides has what is called an **omni-directional** or **non-directional** pattern (Fig. 2.15):

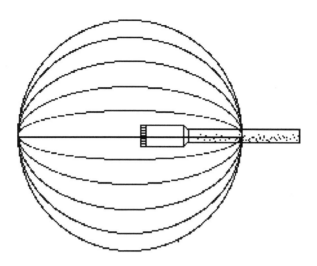

Fig. 2.15 An omni-directional pattern .

A pattern that picks up sound equally on both sides (90° off axis) or from front to back rear is said to be **bi-polar** or **bi-directional** (Fig. 2.16):

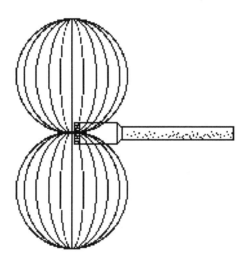

Fig. 2.16 A bi-polar or bi-directional pattern.

A microphone that picks up best from its front end, or at 0° axis, is said to have a **cardiod**, or **uni-directional** (Fig. 2.17) pattern:

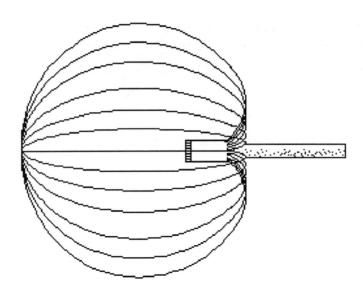

Fig. 2.17 A cardiod or uni-directional pattern.

As the directionality of a cardiod microphone increases, its pickup pattern becomes a **super-car-diod**. This type of microphone pattern is preferred when the aural focus is directly in front of the microphone, and any ambient or extraneous sounds need to be rejected (Fig. 2.18):

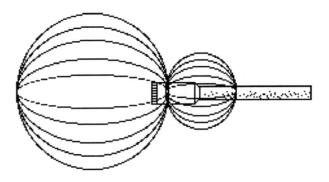

Fig. 2.18 A super-cardiod pattern.

Further increasing the directionality of a supercardiod microphone yields a **hyper-cardiod** pick-up pattern, for an even higher rejection of ambient or extraneous sound (Fig. 2.19):

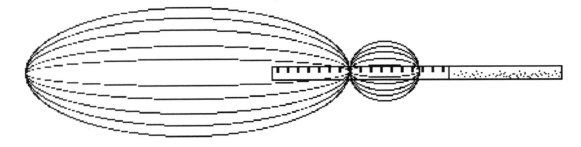

Fig. 2.19 A hyper-cardiod pickup pattern.

The **ultra-cardiod** pickup pattern is an even more extreme version of the hyper-cardiod pattern. It has a narrower angle of acceptance than the hyper-cardiod, but similar rejection characteristics at the sides (Fig. 2.20):

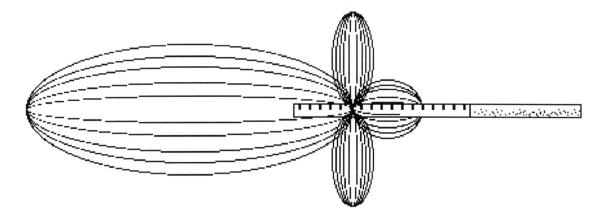

Fig. 2.20 An ultra-cardiod pickup pattern.

In addition to microphones with fixed pickup patterns, some microphones have selectable patterns — accomplished by using one or more switchable diaphragms within the element. This type of microphone is called **multidirectional** or **polydirectional**. The pickup pattern is selected by a switch on the microphone body, usually engraved with the symbols shown in Fig. 2.21, indicating (A) omnidirectional, (B) bipolar (bidirectional), (C) cardiod and (D) hypercardiod patterns.

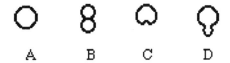

Fig. 2.21 Indicators for selecting (A) omnidirectional, (B) bipolar (bidirectional), (C) cardiod and (D) hypercardiod patterns on a multidirectional microphone.

Fig. 2.22. The Neumann U89 is one of the most popular studio microphones currently in use. Note the pickup pattern indicator in the center just below the windscreen.
(Photo Courtesy of Gotham Audio Corporation)

To describe the pickup pattern of a microphone, many manufacturers supply a **polar response chart**. This is a circular graph, plotted in fixed increments of decibels and combined with a curve to illustrate the directional characteristics. The following are examples of these charts:

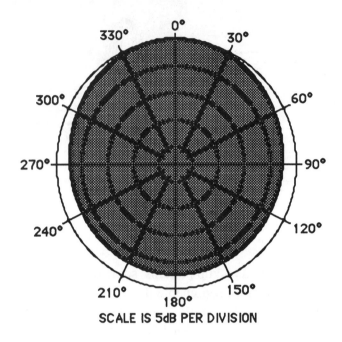

SCALE IS 5dB PER DIVISION

Fig. 2.23 Omni Directional

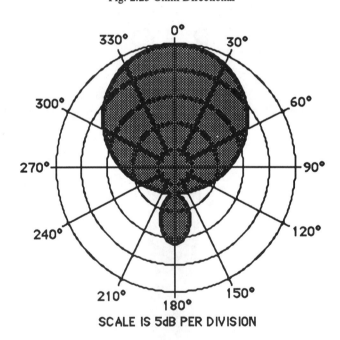

SCALE IS 5dB PER DIVISION

Fig. 2.24 A cardiod pattern.

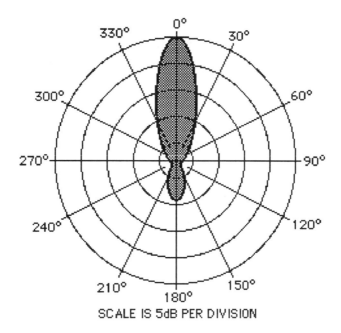

SCALE IS 5dB PER DIVISION

Fig. 2.25 A hyper-cardiod pattern.

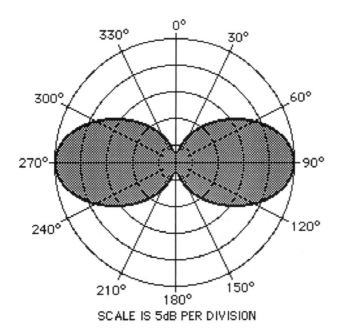

SCALE IS 5dB PER DIVISION

Fig. 2.26 A bipolar pattern.

Some manufacturers provide, in addition to polar response charts, frequency response charts. These charts show how a microphone will respond to different frequencies. Depending on its type and directional characteristics, each different make and model will provide a different response to the same sound. If a particular microphone provides greater output between the 5 KHz and 10 KHz range (as depicted in Fig. 2.27), the tonal quality of that microphone will be "brighter."

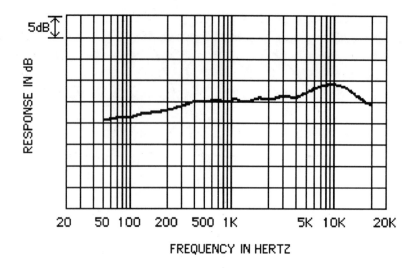

Fig. 2.27 The frequency response of a microphone that provides a greater output between 500 Hz and 10 KHz .

E. PROXIMITY EFFECT

Proximity effect occurs when a directional microphone (i.e., any microphone other than an omni-directional) is placed too close to the sound source, resulting in a relative increase of bass frequencies. (<u>Omnidirectional microphones are not subject to proximity effect</u>.) The resulting boost in bass frequencies causes "boominess". If the sound source is weak, proximity effect might lend a positive quality that would otherwise be missing. With strong sounds, however, it might drown out midrange and treble frequencies, resulting in an unintelligible wash of rumble.

To reduce proximity effect, many microphones have a built-in filter to reduce bass response; when activated, the filter will "roll-off" by several decibels all frequencies below a certain point, compensating for the increased bass. The filter is controlled by a switch on the microphone body and often marked as shown in Fig. 2.28:

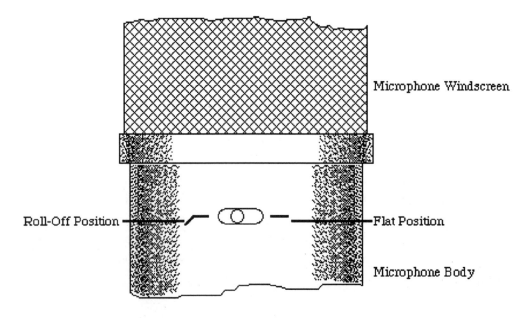

Fig. 2.28 A switch controlling a "roll off" filter for reducing "boominess."

28

Other features to boost or attenuate frequency ranges include several switchable frequency-atten-uation levels and high-frequency boost settings to extend the microphone's frequency response. Also, something like a volume control, called a pad, is used to attenuate the sound level across the entire frequency spectrum. Should excessive sound pressure level overload the microphone, the pad may be switched on to reduce the signal by a fixed amount of decibels. Because dynamic microphones are less susceptible to overload, and ribbon microphones should not be subjected to high sound pressure levels, pads are mostly found on condenser type microphones.

F. WINDSCREENS, POP FILTERS AND SHOCK MOUNTS

Occasionally a narrator may "pop" his or her "P's", and the result is an intermittent proximity effect of very short duration. Any time a word with a percussive letter is spoken, the "blast" from that one letter is enough to render the recorded word useless.

A device to reduce "pops" and wind noise is the **pop filter**. The pop filter, usually a foam rubber cover, is found either within the microphone windscreen or as an accessory made to slip over the outside of the windscreen (Fig. 2.29):

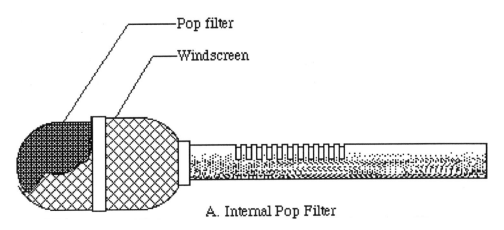

A. Internal Pop Filter

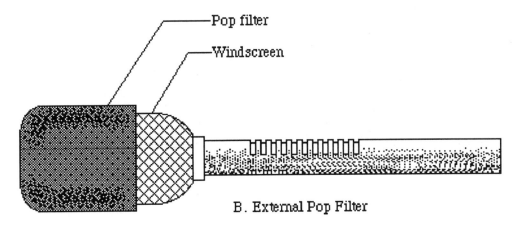

B. External Pop Filter

Fig. 2.29 Pop filters reduce the proximity effect from percussive wind blasts and wind noise.

29

Because dynamic and condenser microphones have an extended low-frequency response, they are most susceptible to wind noise. Consequently, they are more likely to have pop filters than are ribbon microphones, in which a pop filter can adversely affect the microphone's response. Also, omnidirectional microphones are less sensitive to wind noise than unidirectional types.

A common problem when recording outdoors is the interference caused by wind. Wind noise is often heard as an intermittent rumbling and/or hissing, and usually washes out the desired sound source resulting from proximity effect. The standard method for eliminating this obstacle is the use of the "zeppelin" windscreen. Fig. 2.30 shows this type of windscreen for a hyperdirectional microphone.

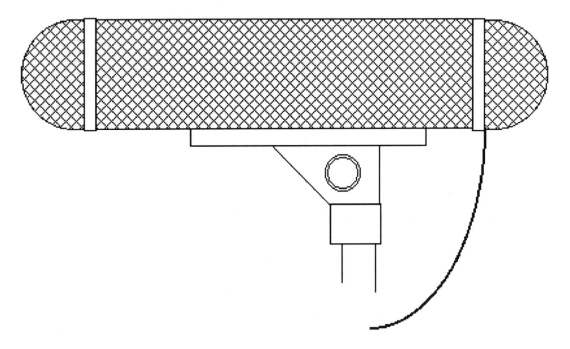

Fig. 2.30 The standard method for eliminating wind noise is the "zeppelin" windscreen.

Unwanted vibrations, such as footsteps, traffic or mechanical noise, may travel through room surfaces and up the microphone stand to the microphone itself. These noises can be picked up by the microphone and may be heard as low-frequency rumble, thuds or pops. To eliminate the transmission of these sound, a **shock mount** is often used. The shock mount physically isolates a microphone by suspending the entire body in an elastic web, often made of rubber. If any extraneous vibrations reach the mount, they are dissipated by the elastic bands suspending the microphone. Shock mounts are available from microphone manufacturers, and are usually configured for an individual model microphone. Fig. 2.31 illustrates one type of shock mount:

Fig. 2.32. A studio microphone with shock mount. The triangular pieces supporting the microphone are made of rubber to minimize induced vibrations.
(Photo Courtesy of Bruel & Kjaer Instruments, Inc.)

G. MICROPHONE TYPES, APPLICATIONS, AND TECHNIQUE

Microphones fall into categories beyond element type and pickup pattern. Many of these categories have evolved over the years from the special requirements of film and television production. This evolution has led to the development of microphones that are aurally superior and visually unobtrusive. Bear in mind that this chapter covers only the more common types of microphones; many more specialized types exist.

Shotgun

Most hyper-, ultra-, and super-directional microphones are often called **shotgun** microphones (Fig. 2.32). Their nickname is derived from the method in which they are used— aimed like a shotgun at the aural "target." The principal function of the shotgun microphone is to reject extraneous sounds from the rear and sides, and to permit only a narrow angle of acceptance at the front, making it ideal for "miking" an on-camera actor or sound source while remaining out of the picture. The shotgun may forgo sound quality for directional characteristics. Moreover, at lower frequencies, both the microphone's sound quality and its directional characteristics deteriorate. Shotgun microphones are available in 6-inch, 18-inch, 3-foot and longer lengths, and should not be used in applications where low-frequency sounds are predominant.

31

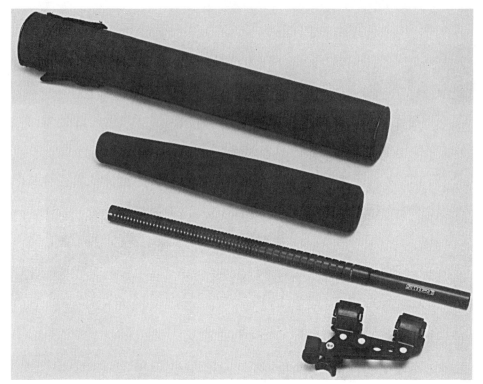

Fig. 2.323. A shotgun microphone with windscreen.
(Photo Courtesy of Shure Brothers, Inc.)

Lavalier

Another type of microphone developed to be unobtrusive is the **lavalier** (Fig. 2.33), which is clipped or pinned to an actor's lapel or tie. Lavalier microphones vary widely in size, but are generally less than one inch long. There are different types of lavaliers, although most have omnidirectional characteristics and tend to boost high-frequencies. The boost compensates for the high frequencies that are lost because of the microphone's position under the chin. Some lavaliers are made to be directional, thus isolating the speaker's voice from any unwanted sounds. Lavalier microphones can be used outdoors, and are available as dynamic or condenser types.

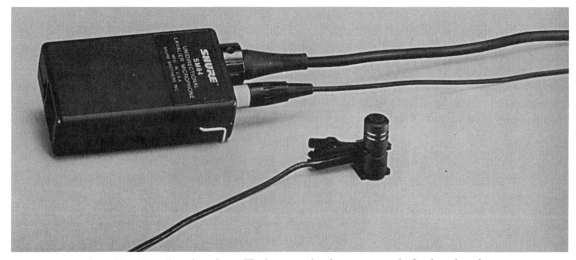

Fig. 2.33. A Lavalier microphone. The box contains the power supply for the microphone.
(Photo Courtesy of Shure Brothers, Inc.)

PZM

The **pressure zone microphone** (Fig. 2.34) is a relatively new design that arose to eliminate reflected sound waves reaching the microphone after the direct sound. It appears as a flat plate with a connector attached, and is available with either a directional or hemispherical pickup pattern.

Fig. 2.34. Two-surface pressure zone microphones with power supply.
(Photo Courtesy of Shure Brothers, Inc.)

Transducers

Transducers, also called **contact microphones**, attach directly to the body of a musical instrument such as an acoustic guitar, piano or violin. Rather than responding to sound pressure transmitted through the air, transducer microphones transform the mechanical vibration of the instrument directly into electrical energy. For that reason, they are do not respond to sound reflections.

Wireless

Wireless microphones are useful where the microphone needs to be concealed or unconstrained by a cable. A wireless microphone utilizes a radio transmitter and receiver in lieu of a standard cable to carry the signal.

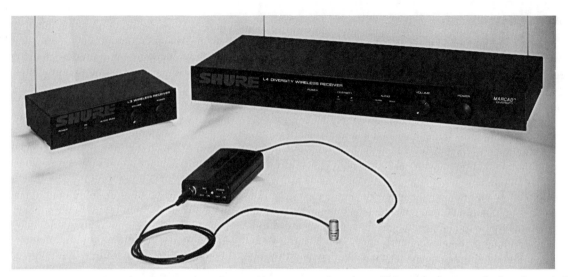

Fig. 2.35. A wireless lavalier microphone, center, shown with two types of receivers. This particular type of microphone is ideal for picking up actors during medium or long shots, as the entire assembly is unobtrusive and may be concealed under clothing. (Photo Courtesy of Shure Brothers, Inc.)

H. ENVIRONMENT

The factors crucial for good sound lie as much with the acoustic properties of the room or environment as with the quality of equipment. If necessary, steps should be taken to correct the acoustic properties of an environment before recording.

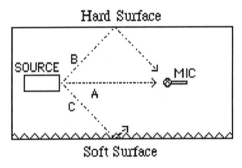

Fig. 2.36 Environment affects the sound reaching a microphone.

In Figure 2.36, **A** is the shortest distance between the sound source and the microphone. Thus, sound traveling along route **A** is called **direct sound**; the sound reaches the microphone by following a straight path. Sound passing along route **B** is reflected from the hard surface of the wall and is called **reflected sound**. A third wall, covered with soft material such as foam rubber, drapes or acoustic tile has negligible reflective qualities, and consequently little or no sound following route **C** reaches the microphone.

Sound waves traveling along route **B**, because they take a longer path, reach the microphone later than sounds following route **A**. This delayed sound will produce a hollow, echoing, or "empty" feel.

One solution to this effect might be to move the microphone closer to the sound source, which, depending on the nature of the source, may cause a proximity effect (Fig. 2.37, Example "A").

Placing a portable acoustic baffle, called a **gobo** (Fig. 2.38), between the reflective surface and the microphone (Fig. 2.37, Example "B"). could possibly eliminate any unwanted reflections. Locating both the sound source and microphone nearer to the non-reflective wall (Fig. 2.37, Example "C") or a combination of all three techniques (Fig. 2.37, Example "D") might be necessary. Varying the pickup pattern of the microphone or using a different type could factor into obtaining a solution.

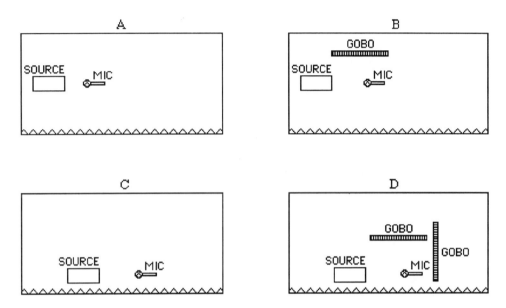

Fig. 2.37 To eliminate the effect of reflected sounds (A) move the microphone closer to the sound source, (B) place a portable acoustic baffle between the reflective surface and the microphone, (C) locate both the sound source and microphone nearer to the non-reflective wall or (D) a combine all three techniques.

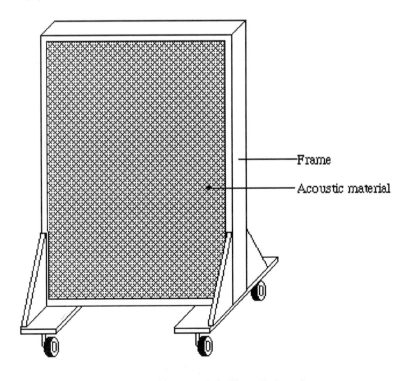

Fig. 2.38 A portable acoustic baffle, called a gobo.

Experimentation is usually required to achieve the correct results, and may take a balance between varying the microphone and local acoustics.

I. STEREO IMAGING THEORY

Because we have two ears, we hear in stereo. And when recording in stereo, we want to reproduce a sound the way we would hear it in the real world. Reproducing sound this way depends on the placement of sound sources between left and right, and is called **imaging** (Fig. 2.39). The goal of proper imaging is to ensure that each sound source is reproduced in its original location, and to accurately capture the ambiance in which the recording was made.

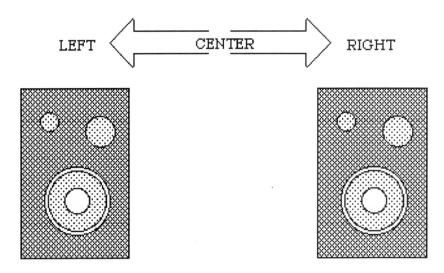

Fig. 2.39 The placement of sound sources between left and right is called imaging.

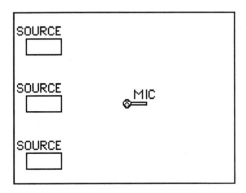

Fig. 2.40 A monaural set-up.

Fig. 2.40 shows a monaural set-up. With only one microphone, only one output signal is produced. In this situation the control over the balance between the microphone and sound sources is, at best, limited. Any recording made in this way will not reproduce the original locations of the sources, but only the relative levels of the sources.

The center source in the left diagram of Fig. 2.41 is closest to the mike, and will therefore be the loudest of the three. In the right diagram, all sources are an equal distance from the microphone, and will be about equal in volume:

36

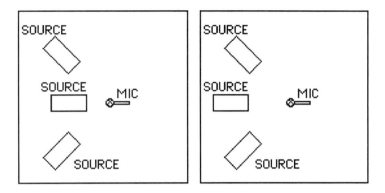

Fig. 2.41 In the left diagram the center source is closest to the mike, and will be the loudest of the three. The right diagram shows all sources at equal distance from the microphone, putting each at about equal volume.

Stereo imaging is quite another matter. There are two specific techniques used to record in stereo, and the technique employed depends upon the result desired. The two categories for recording in stereo are **spaced miking** and **coincident miking**.

Spaced Miking

There are several variations of this technique, but in general, two microphones, usually directional types, are placed parallel to each other and pointed toward the sound source (Fig. 2.42). The distance between the microphones may be from several inches to several feet, depending on the situation. If the distance between microphones exceeds several feet, however, the result will be an unfocused, blended mix of sound. Distances of over ten feet will result in a widely spaced blend of sound with a "dead spot" in the center, requiring a third "fill" microphone (Fig. 2.43).

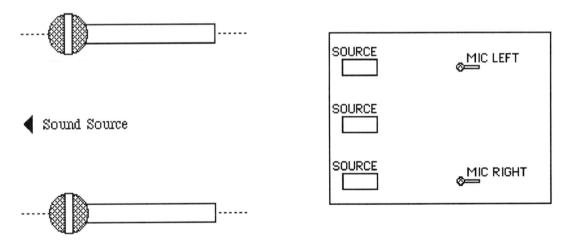

Fig. 2.42 In spaced miking, two directional microphones are placed parallel to each other and pointed toward the sound source.

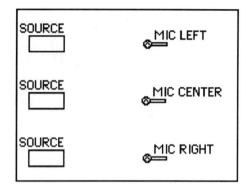

Fig. 2.43 Distances of over ten feet between the microphones will cause a "dead spot" in the center, requiring a third "fill" microphone.

Coincident Miking

In coincident miking, two microphones are placed at an angle with their elements above one another (Fig. 2.44). Again, the microphones used are usually directional and the angle at which they are placed varies. The four accepted angles are 90°, 120°, 135°, and 180°. Each angle of miking gives a different result. A 90° angle will yield a tight, un-spacious blend; at 180° the center of the sources might not sound as loud as the sides.

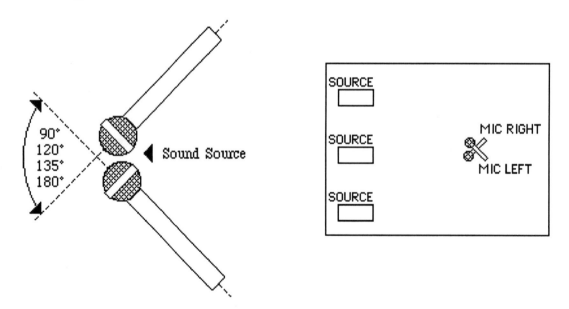

Fig. 2.44 In coincident miking, two microphones are placed at an angle with their elements above one another.

Recording these signals leads to the next step in the audio chain. Whether these separate signals are combined at the time of recording or later depends upon several factors. In the case of multiple signal sources, specialized equipment has evolved over the years to cope with the complexities of handling these applications.

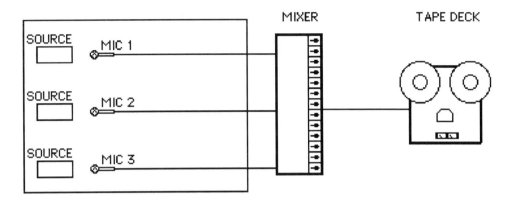

Fig. 2.45 All three microphones being combined, or mixed, onto one track of an audio recording deck.

Fig. 2.45 shows all three microphones being combined, or **mixed,** onto one track of an audio recording deck. The signals are combined through a device known as a **mixer**; recording while mixing in this fashion is called **live mixing.** The balance among all three microphones is obtained physically by their positioning and the location of the sources, and electronically within the mixer.

Note that any stereo imaging is lost, because all three signals have been combined into one channel of the tape deck. Because these signals are combined and recorded at the same time, any subsequent control over the balance between sources is lost.

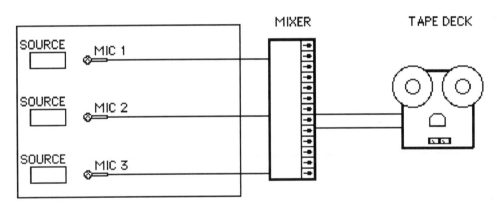

Fig. 2.46 Three microphones being mixed onto both tracks of a stereo tape deck.

Fig. 2.46 depicts the three microphones being mixed onto both tracks of a stereo tape deck; again, the balance of all three microphones is obtained by their positioning, the location of the sources, and electronically within the mixer. Unlike the previous example, however, this will result in a stereo mix of all sound sources. But as before, the balance between sources cannot be altered once the recording has been made.

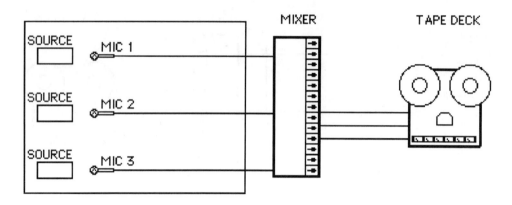

Fig. 2.47 All three microphones being recorded individually onto separate tracks of a multitrack deck.

Finally, Fig. 2.47 shows all three microphones being recorded individually onto separate tracks of a **multitrack** deck. This type of recorder is capable of recording on separate, individual tracks, and these tracks may later be played back, combined and recorded onto a stereo tape deck called a **mastering deck** during the **remix** or **re-recording**. Full spatial control is retained and can be manipulated, and imaging can be controlled or altered in the studio. This is the basic principle of multitrack recording.

J. LINE VALUES

As previously mentioned, analog audio signals appear as voltages traveling along wires or cables. Two distinct systems for describing these signals have evolved, both of which are currently in use. The measure of these voltages and the impedances involved in each system have become standard. These systems are used to describe **line values**, or the electrical measurement of a given audio system.

Audio cable is subject to electrostatic and electromagnetic interference, such as radio signals and proximity to electrical conductors. Proximity of a cable to a source of interference will cause the cable to act like an antenna, which is basically just a piece of wire. For that reason, any audio cable is subject to picking up the same signals. When this occurs, radio signals are transmitted through the cables to the equipment, and interfere with the desired audio signals. This is called radio frequency interference, or **RFI**. To prevent RFI, a wire shield is wrapped around the leads carrying the audio signals, separated by insulation and electrically connected to ground. Radio waves that hit the shield are carried to "ground" and disperse, much like a lightning rod carries an electrical charge to the earth. This arrangement of shield, conductor and insulation is called **coaxial cable** (Fig. 2.48).

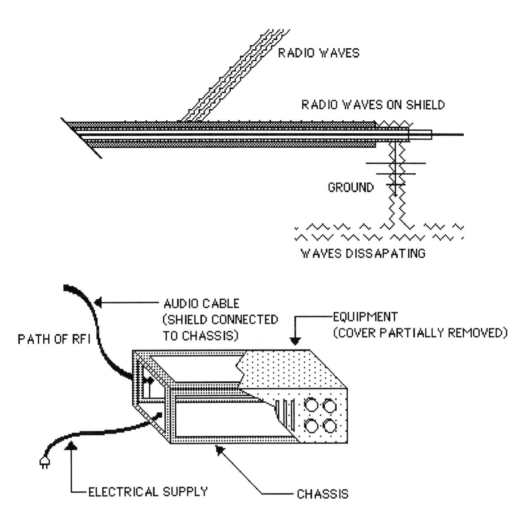

Fig. 2.48 (Top Diagram) In coaxial cable, a wire shield is wrapped around the leads carrying the audio signals, separated by insulation and electrically connected to ground. (Bottom Diagram) One arrangement is shown above: The shield of the cable is connected to the chassis of the equipment, which is in turn grounded through the power supply.

An audio signal has positive and negative values. To be carried by an audio cable, the signal requires at least two conductors. One serves as a reference or ground, compared to which the signal on the other conductor is positive or negative. Fig. 2.49 shows the basic components of a cable. Because there are only two conductors, the signal is carried by both the center conductor and the shield. Note that the shield acts as both the shield and a conductor. This type of cable is called **unbalanced**.

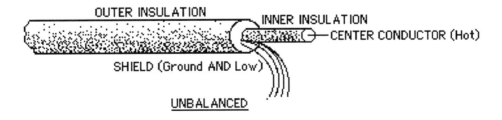

Fig. 2.49 When the shield acts as both the shield and a conductor, the cable is said to be unbalanced.

Fig. 2.50 shows a cable with two conductors that are electrically separate from the shield, which acts only as the ground. This type of cable is called **balanced**.

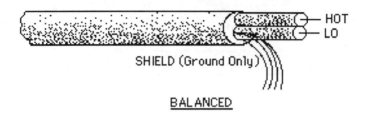

Fig. 2.50 A cable that has two conductors that are electrically separate from the shield, which acts only as the ground, is called balanced.

Balanced cable is usually found on microphone cables, and is used in professional studios and equipment. A home stereo, on the other hand, uses only unbalanced cable. Balanced cables can be run for several hundred feet without problems; unbalanced cables can only be run for 25 to 50 feet before signals become attenuated and subject to RFI. Another reason that different cable types and operating systems are used is that not all signals are of equal voltage and impedance. Voltages, in this case, are measured in units of dBm.

The professional operating standard is described as balanced and having an impedance of 600 ohms (600 Ω) and a voltage level of +4 dBm; this standard is called **line level**. The second operating standard is considered to be a "consumer" level, and has evolved over recent years to meet the demands for less expensive audio equipment. "Consumer" systems are generally unbalanced, have an impedance of 10,000 ohms (10K Ω) and a voltage level of -10 dBm.

Fig. 2.41 is a graph illustrating several different types of operating levels; "mic level" is the output obtained from a microphone. By necessity, this level is boosted to line level by a preamplifier (preamp) at the input section of a console (Fig. 2.51).

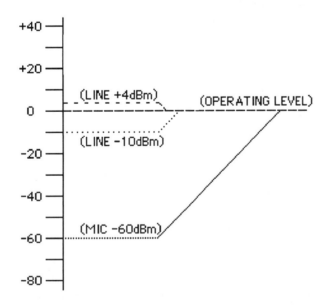

Fig. 2.51 Graph illustrating several operating levels. The "mic level" is the output from a microphone.

The following chart is intended to serve as a summary of various signal levels (Fig. 2.52):

CABLE TYPE	APPLICATION	SIGNAL LEVEL	IMPEDANCE
UNBALANCED	SEMI-PRO/ CONSUMER	–10dBm	10K OHM
BALANCED	PROFESSIONAL	+4dBm	600 OHM
BALANCED	MICROPHONE	–60dBm	600 OHM

Fig. 2.52 Summary of Signal Levels

There are a few useful tricks to memorizing the chart in Fig. 2.52:

• A table (cable) with 2 legs (conductors) is <u>unbalanced</u>; a table (cable) with 3 legs (conductors) is <u>balanced</u>.

• The impedance of a balanced line is *always* 600 Ohms.

• The specifications for unbalanced audio can be remembered as: <u>U-2-10-minus 10</u>. Unbalanced, **2** conductors, **10 K** Ohms, **minus 10** dBm.

K. CONNECTOR TYPES AND USES

An assortment of connectors are used for plugging the different kinds of cables into various pieces of audio equipment. The male 1/4-in. phone plug (Fig. 2.53) is a two-conductor plug, and is therefore used only with unbalanced lines; it is found on guitar cords, unbalanced microphone cords and so on.

Fig. 2.53 A male 1/4-in. phone plug (monaural)

The stereo male 1/4-in. phone plug (Fig. 2.54) is a three-conductor plug, and can therefore be used with either balanced or unbalanced lines. It is also found on headphone cords.

Fig. 2.54 A male 1/4-in. phone plug (stereo).

43

The RCA phone plug (Fig. 2.55) was developed as an inexpensive alternative to the male 1/4-in. phone plug. This is one of the most economical connectors, and is found on sub-professional recording equipment and home stereos. Because it has only two conductors, it can only be used with unbalanced lines.

Fig. 2.55 An RCA phone plug.

The XLR, or Cannon, connector is used in conjunction with microphone lines and professional audio equipment; it has three conductors and is almost always used exclusively with balanced lines. This connector comes in both female and male versions, and the pins nearly always point in the direction of signal flow (Figs. 2.56 and 2.57).

Fig. 2.56 A male XLR connector.

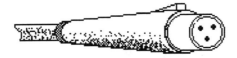

Fig. 2.57 A female XLR Connector

Finally, 1/8-in. mini-phone plugs (Fig. 2.58) are almost never found an anything but consumer equipment. These may be configured for either two or three conductors, and are chiefly found on Walkman-type headphones.

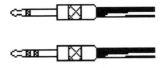

Fig. 2.58 1/8-in. mini-phone plugs

L. SIGNAL -VALUE CONVERTING DEVICES

Because of the differences in impedances and signal levels, **transformers** or **impedance matching devices** have been developed to match signals from various equipment. These devices are available in several forms, but all have it as their primary purpose to convert signal values from one standard to another. Transformers may either be active (requiring a power source) or passive (requiring no power). Multi-channel transformers are useful in situations where several lines have to be converted. In any case, the sole function of any transformer is to convert signal's +4 dBm, 600 ohms balanced and -10 dBm, 10K ohms unbalanced.

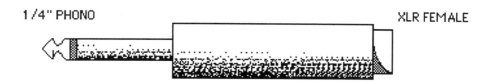

1/4" PHONO   XLR FEMALE

Fig. 2.59 Passive single -channel line transformer.

Yet another device to transform line values is the **direct box** (Fig. 2.60). The direct box matches the output of an electric guitar or bass to microphone level, allowing for **direct insertion** of the instrument into the recording system and bypassing the microphone. Direct insertion has four advantages over putting a microphone in front of an amplifier to capture the sound:

• It provides a fuller range of frequencies from the instrument

• The sound quality is much cleaner

• It blocks out sound from other sources ("leakage"),

• It allows more control of the signal at the console.

Direct boxes are either passive or active, and some models allow for phantom powering of the box's circuitry.

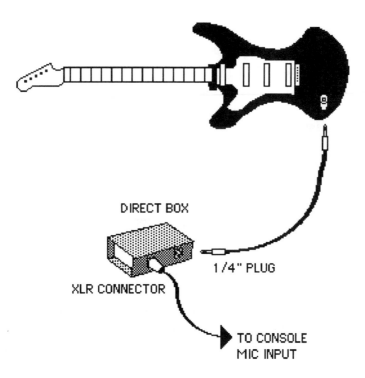

DIRECT BOX

1/4" PLUG

XLR CONNECTOR

TO CONSOLE
MIC INPUT

Fig. 2.60 A direct box matches the output of an electric guitar or bass to microphone level, allowing for direct insertion of the instrument into the recording system.

45

M. SIGNAL INTERFERENCE AND DISTORTION

In addition to RFI, other factors can adversely affect the quality of a signal. Interference with unwanted signals is as much a part of recording as any other factor. In part, the ability to obtain the best possible recording stems from being able to recognize and cope with these interferences to the best of one's ability.

Noise

Noise is any unwanted audio signal. Typically, it may be a hissing sound with frequencies ranging from about 8 to 12 kHz. It is unavoidably produced by electronic equipment or magnetic recording tape in varying degrees; logically, it falls under the two categories of **equipment noise** and **tape noise**. In general, the higher the quality of the equipment, the less noise it produces. If a signal passes through many pieces of equipment, the sum total of all the noise generated by each piece of equipment becomes intolerable. The methods for reducing tape noise are discussed in chapter VI.

Fluorescent lights, generators, motors, high voltage lines and other types of electrical appliances can all introduce noise into an audio system. Interference of this type, unlike noise produced by tape or equipment, sounds more like crackling, humming or buzzing. It is carried through the air or over the electrical lines that power the audio equipment. Solutions may include rewiring the electrical system, eliminating all fluorescent lights, installing special noise suppression filters in the electrical system or a combination of the three.

Signal-to-Noise Ratio

A standard of measuring equipment and tape noise was established to provide a common reference for both the users and manufacturers of equipment. This standard is called the **signal-to-noise ratio**, abbreviated as **S/N**, and describes the difference between the loudest sound a piece of equipment will record or play back, and the noise generated by that equipment. This ratio is expressed in dB, and the greater that ratio, the less noticeable the noise will be. If a piece of equipment produces 1 dB of noise while it records or reproduces 70 dB of signal, then the S/N ratio is 70 to 1. This figure is frequently expressed as a negative number, for example -70 dB, to indicate noise suppression. Since a S/N ratio of 80 is better than one of 70, an increase in a negative number indicates progressively higher quality. The lowest generally accepted standard for a S/N ratio is about -50 dB; it isn't uncommon for professional recording equipment to meet or exceed ratios of -85 dB.

Distortion

There are many types of **distortion**, but the most common type is called **overload** or **peaking** and is caused by the signal level being set too high. The sound quality produced by this condition is exactly like the sound of a "boom box" or radio being played too loudly. The signal level exceeds the equipment's ability to handle it, and the tops of the signal cycles are actually cut off (Fig. 2.61):

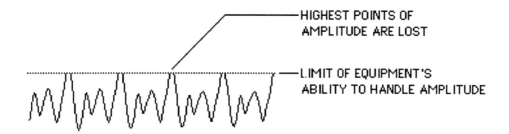

Fig. 2.61 Overload is caused by the signal level being too high and is sometimes referred to as clipping.

Since the highest points of signal amplitude are lost, or "clipped off", this type of distortion is sometimes also referred to as **clipping**.

Phasing

Phasing occurs when cycles of the same signals arrive at one point; the resulting sound quality may suffer from a decreased bass or from stereo imaging with a drifting center. Fig. 2.62 illustrates two different signals arriving in phase at one point; their amplitudes are equal at any given time, and the result is the sum of both.

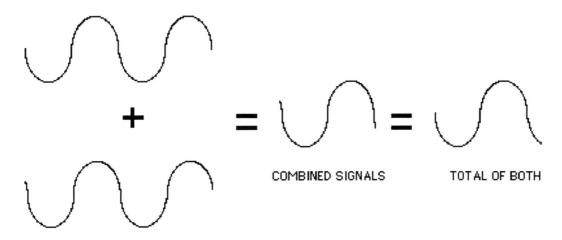

Fig. 2.62 When two different signals arrive at one point in phase; their amplitudes are equal at any given times, and the result is the sum of both.

Fig. 2.63 illustrates two different signals arriving at one point, but out of phase; their amplitudes are exactly opposite at any given time. The result is that the sum of their amplitudes equals zero at any given point.

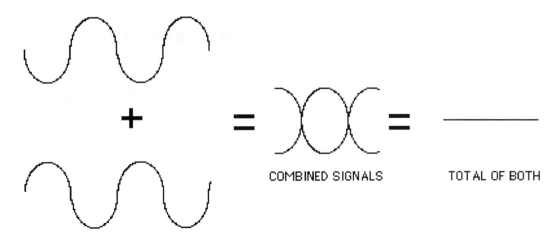

Fig. 2.63 When two out-of-phase signals arrive at one point the sum of their amplitudes equals zero.

Incorrect phasing may occur when microphones are placed equidistant from a sound source or if sound monitors (speakers) are miswired. Each condition is relatively easy to correct. In the case of microphones, the signal leads (NOT the ground) are reversed on one microphone cable. Some consoles have switches to do this. If a particular console is lacking this feature, an adapter with an XLR male and an XLR female connector in which the wires have been reversed is used. This device is known as a **phase inverter** (Fig. 2.64).

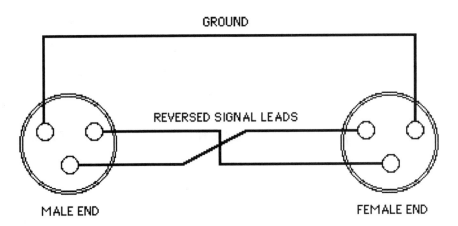

Fig. 2.64 An adapter in which the wires have been reversed is known as a phase inverter

Phasing problems occur in monitors when they are improperly wired to an amplifier. Fig. 2.65 illustrates two monitors correctly wired and phased to the outputs of the amplifier. Note that the monitors' positive (+) and the negative (-) leads are wired to the respective positive and the negative amplifier outputs.

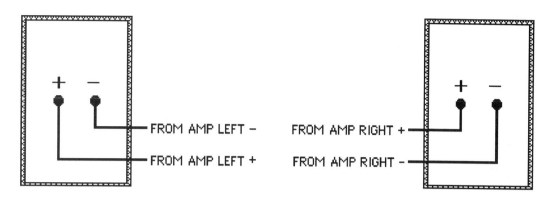

Fig. 2.65 Correctly wired monitors have positive and the negative leads wired to the respective positive and the negative amplifier outputs.

Fig. 2.66 shows the left monitor's leads being reversed; the amplifier's positive output is connected to the left monitor's negative terminal. As a result, signals will arrive at each monitor out of phase, and partial cancellation of sound is sure to occur.

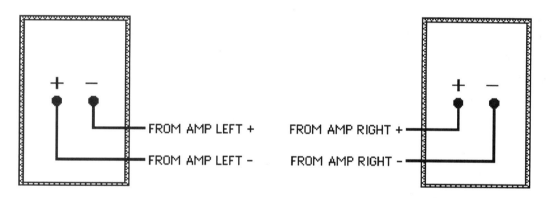

Fig. 2.66 When one monitor's leads are reversed, signals arrive at each monitor out of phase, and a partial cancellation of sound will occur.

All speaker cable is marked on one side; one lead may be copper and the other silver colored. Incidentally, "zip" cord, used in the wiring of lamps, makes excellent speaker wire. It is available at any hardware store, and close inspection of the cord will reveal that one side of the jacket is ribbed, and the other smooth. This makes it easy to trace connections between the monitors and amplifier, and verify that all components have been correctly wired.

3
CONSOLES AND SIGNAL PATHS

A. TYPES OF CONSOLES

The most intimidating sight on walking into an audio studio is often the console, with its seemingly infinite rows of buttons, knobs, meters, lights and switches.

Fig. 3.1. A Harrison PP-1 post-production console installed at Walt Disney Productions in Burbank, CA. (Photo Courtesy of Harrison by GLW, Inc.)

The basic operating principles behind all consoles, however, are essentially the same. Once you become familiar with these principles, learning to use any console is relatively easy.

Fig. 3.2. The DDA AMR-24 split format recording console.
(Photo Courtesy of Klark-Teknik Electronics, Inc.)

An audio console is the nerve center of any audio studio. The routing and combining of signals takes place within the console, and its complexity is determined by the requirements of the facility. By comparison, a console in a radio station, called a **broadcast** or **on air console**, is simple next to one found in a production studio. That is because material for broadcast is complete by the time it reaches the station. Before that stage, however, the same material must first be created in a studio with a **production** or **post-production console**; this is the type of console that we are primarily concerned with.

Fig. 3.3. A six channel mixer. Although much smaller than the console in Fig. 3.1, both operate on the same principles. (Photo Courtesy of Tascam/Teac Professional Division)

B. CONSOLE SECTIONS

Any console has three basic functions:

1. To control the input being supplied to it,

2. To control it's outputs,

3. To provide a way of listening to signals at various points within it.

We will use the following diagram to represent a typical audio production console (Fig. 3.4):

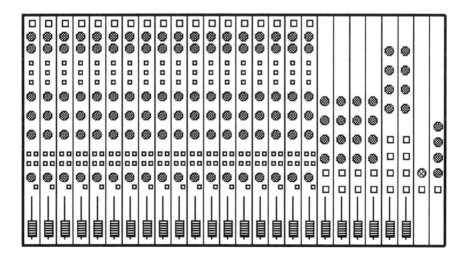

Fig. 3.4 Representation of a typical audio production console.

The console is composed of strips, or **modules**. In most cases consoles only have three or four different types of modules, some of which appear repeatedly. To better visualize this arrangement, imagine a console grouped by its different module types (Fig. 3.5):

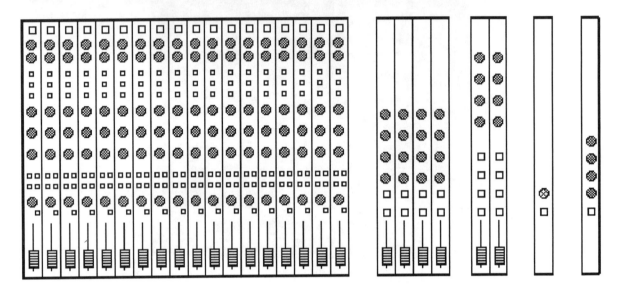

Fig. 3.5 Imagine a console grouped according to its different module types.

To make it simple to maintain or modify a console, individual modules are frequently removable (Fig. 3.6):

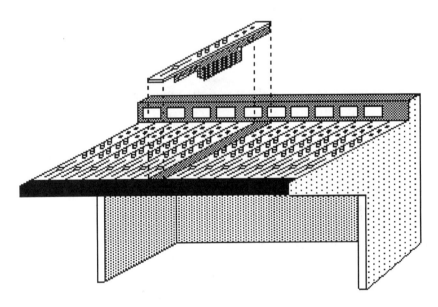

Fig. 3.6 Depending on their design, the modules of a console may be removable.

Input Section

The different types of modules found in a console vary by <u>function</u>. The modules types reflect that a console has three basic purposes: **input**, **output** and **monitor**

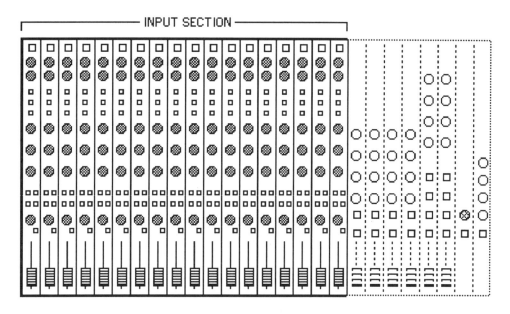

Fig. 3.7 The input modules comprise the section that receives all the audio inputs.

The input modules (Fig. 3.7) comprise the section that receives all the signals from microphones, turntables, tape recorders and all other types of audio equipment. Its basic functions include:

1. <u>Input source selection</u>: Most input module can accept signals from two or more sources, eliminating the need to re-connect cables to select an alternate source. The source is selected by an **input select switch**. Although the different inputs may vary in signal level, the different levels are adjusted by preamps within the console. These preamps boost, for example, the microphone level and phono level signals up to line level (Fig. 3.8). Therefore, a microphone, line-level, or phonographic input can all be connected directly to the module.

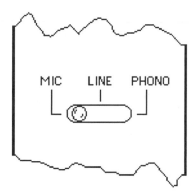

Fig. 3.8 An input select switch.

2. <u>Input level control</u>: Since the preamp outputs from the mike and phono inputs are fixed at one level, the signal level <u>entering</u> the input module is controlled by means of the **trim and pad controls**. The trim (also called **attenuation**, **att**, or **gain**) usually appears as a knob on the face of the module. Rotated to the maximum clockwise position, the trim control allows the full output of the preamps to continue through the module. As the knob is rotated progressively to the counterclockwise, the preamp signal output is proportionately decreased.

Because this control only decreases (never amplifies) the signal level , this method of signal reduction is called **attenuation**. In general, most trim controls affect only the microphone signal preamp output; in some cases, however, these may also act on any signal source. The **pad**, unlike the trim control, is not variable. Instead, it reduces the incoming level by a fixed amount. The amount of level reduction it provides can vary between -10 and -20 decibels or more, depending on the design of the console. Both pad and trim are used in conjunction with each other; it is essential to provide the proper signal operating level to the input module. Too high a signal level will result in the lighting up of the **peak LED** (light emitting diode). This is a small light, usually red, located on the input module, usually near the fader.(Fig. 3.9).

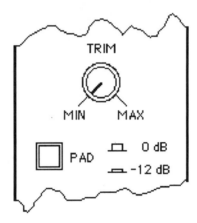

Fig. 3.9 Pad and Trim controls on an input module.

3. EQ (tone) controls: The **EQ**, or **equalization**, section of the input module lets the operator change the tonal quality (see chapter 1) of the incoming signal. The complexity and specifics of this portion of the module vary widely among the different makes and models of consoles. More expensive models generally have elaborate sets of controls split into specific frequency divisions. Thus, any signal passing through the EQ section is divided into as many separate frequency bands as there are controls per band. Each independent frequency band of the original signal then passes through an amplifier within the module. Before leaving the EQ section, the separate bands are re-combined. In addition, the output level of each amplifier is either increased or decreased by turning the knob dedicated to that specific frequency band. Clockwise rotation increases the level of an individual frequency band; counterclockwise rotation left decreases its level. When provided, a **bypass switch** lets the console operator re-route the signal, completely circumventing the equalization section. Using the bypass switch, the operator can compare the signal with and without equalization (Fig. 3.10).

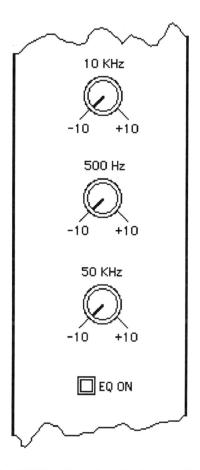

Fig. 3.10 The EQ section of an input module.

In some cases, the level and frequency controls are placed as concentric knobs (Fig. 3.11), allowing for the selection of various frequencies. Because the knobs are continuously variable, this arrangement is known as **variable** or **sweep** equalization. When control of the frequency is predetermined and the only variable control is the level of that frequency, this type of equalization is known as **fixed** (Fig. 3.11).

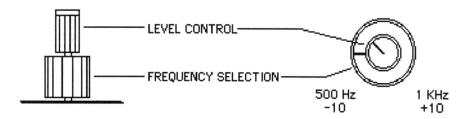

Fig. 3.11 A variable EQ control.

4. <u>Output level control</u>: The overall level of the signal leaving the console must be variable, letting the operator fade and boost various signals. This type of control is done with a **fader** which, unlike an attenuator, can both decrease *and* increase the signal level it receives. For this reason the fader is also called a **gain control**. When the fader is in the down position, the signal level is cut off; in the uppermost position, the signal level is at maximum. The "zero" position on the fader, in which the signal is neither increased nor reduced, is usually located about

2/3 from the bottom of the fader, and may be marked with a zero (as shown in Fig. 3.12) or as a gray zone. This position on the fader is known as the **benchmark**, and it is significant because at this point a signal's input amplitude at the fader equals its output leaving the fader. This is level is considered to yield the best possible signal quality. (Fig. 3.12).

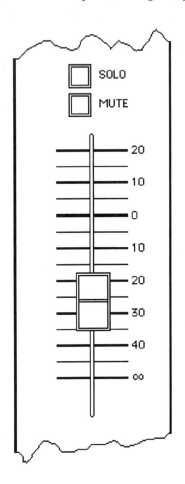

Fig. 3.12 An input module Fader, shown with Solo and Mute buttons.

Control of a signal's level can also be achieved with a **mute** or **channel on/off** switch. This switch halts the signal through the input module, which may be needed should the operator wish to temporarily shut off signal flow without disturbing a pre-set level..

The **solo** switch (sometimes called **PFL** or **Pre-fade Listen**) lets the operator monitor individual channels without changing signal flow or level. It is useful if, for example, extraneous sounds are heard during a session. Then the solo function on each module can be engaged one at a time to isolate the noise.

5. Output assignment: Once a signal is processed, it is sent to the output section of the console. Control of this section is usually through a group of pushbuttons called the **matrix** or **bus assign**. This section determines the destination of the signal leaving the input module. Outputs can be selected in any configuration. If, for example, the buttons for bus 1, bus 3 and bus 4 are pressed, the signal leaving the module is be sent to those three locations (Figs. 3.13 and 3.14). The signal on the input module is said to be **assigned** to its respective destinations.

58

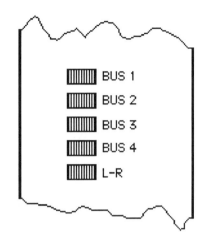

Fig. 3.13 The Matrix of a four group console.

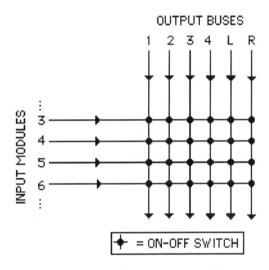

Fig. 3.14 Signal flow diagram of the Matrix.

6. Stereo Imaging: In addition to the imaging made possible by balancing the microphones and sound sources (see chapter 2), balances can be enhanced or created with the **pan control** (Fig. 3.15). The pan control is similar to the balance control on a home stereo system and works in conjunction with the matrix. If the output of a module is assigned to left and right (see Fig. 3.13), rotating the pan control to the right will increase the amount of signal being sent right, while proportionately decreasing the amount of signal being sent left. In the full right clockwise position, no signal is sent left (and vice-versa).

59

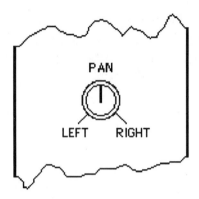

Fig. 3.15 The Pan control of an input module.

If, as in the previous example, bus 1, bus 3, and bus 4 are selected, the pan control acts as if bus 1 and 3 are left, and bus 4 is right; left rotation of the pan control will send more signals to bus 1 and 3, and less to bus 4 (and vice-versa). This method of panning is called **odd-even panning**.

7. The provision of additional mix outputs: In many cases additional outputs from the input module are required for supplemental mixes. These mixes can be processed for special effects and later re-introduced into the console, or sent to a performer's headphones in another room. These controls are called **auxiliary sends**, and do not affect the signal in the input module in any way. The number of sends for each input module of a console are the same and may number between one to eight or more depending on the console. Rotating the send (on any particular input module) clockwise sends more signal from that module.

If a mix derived from an auxiliary send is used in conjunction with an effect, the mix is called an **effects mix**. An auxiliary mix used for performer's headphones is called a **cue mix**.

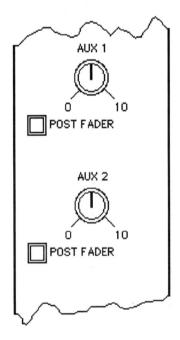

Fig. 3.16 Two Aux Send controls on an input module.

Some consoles have a **pre-** or **post-fader** switch for one or more sends (Fig. 3.16). If the switch is in the pre-fader position, the signal sent from the aux send originates before the fader and any level changes made by the fader do not affect the aux send signal level. Conversely, signals sent "post-fader" are affected by the fader's position.

Fig. 3.17 illustrates signals from consecutive modules being combined in different amounts and sent out from the console. Heavier lines represent more signal being sent from each module, determined by the position of each aux send knob.

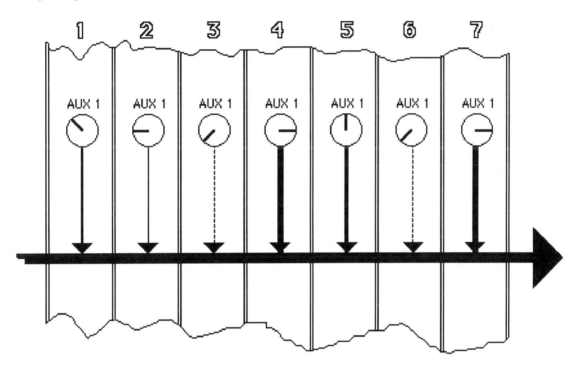

Fig. 3.17 Graphic depiction of an Aux Send mix.

Refer to the following diagram for a full summarized explanation of the controls normally found on any input module.

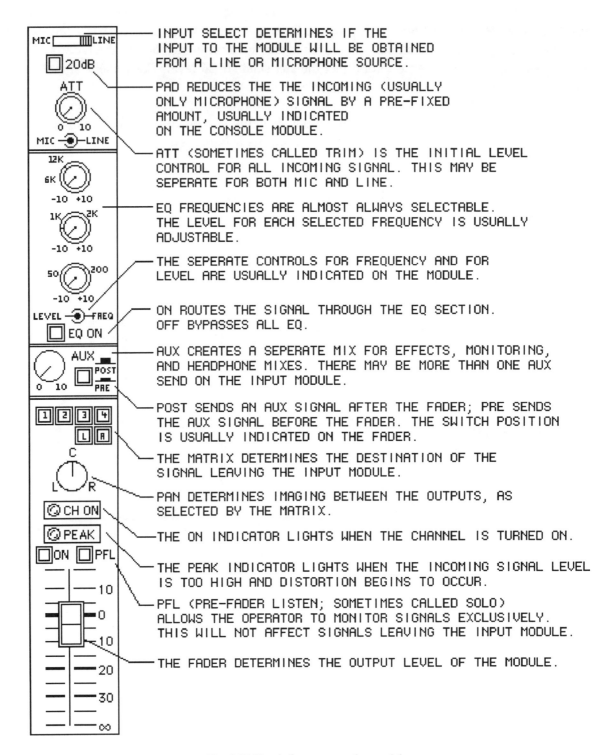

INPUT SELECT DETERMINES IF THE INPUT TO THE MODULE WILL BE OBTAINED FROM A LINE OR MICROPHONE SOURCE.

PAD REDUCES THE THE INCOMING (USUALLY ONLY MICROPHONE) SIGNAL BY A PRE-FIXED AMOUNT, USUALLY INDICATED ON THE CONSOLE MODULE.

ATT (SOMETIMES CALLED TRIM) IS THE INITIAL LEVEL CONTROL FOR ALL INCOMING SIGNAL. THIS MAY BE SEPERATE FOR BOTH MIC AND LINE.

EQ FREQUENCIES ARE ALMOST ALWAYS SELECTABLE. THE LEVEL FOR EACH SELECTED FREQUENCY IS USUALLY ADJUSTABLE.

THE SEPERATE CONTROLS FOR FREQUENCY AND FOR LEVEL ARE USUALLY INDICATED ON THE MODULE.

ON ROUTES THE SIGNAL THROUGH THE EQ SECTION. OFF BYPASSES ALL EQ.

AUX CREATES A SEPERATE MIX FOR EFFECTS, MONITORING, AND HEADPHONE MIXES. THERE MAY BE MORE THAN ONE AUX SEND ON THE INPUT MODULE.

POST SENDS AN AUX SIGNAL AFTER THE FADER; PRE SENDS THE AUX SIGNAL BEFORE THE FADER. THE SWITCH POSITION IS USUALLY INDICATED ON THE FADER.

THE MATRIX DETERMINES THE DESTINATION OF THE SIGNAL LEAVING THE INPUT MODULE.

PAN DETERMINES IMAGING BETWEEN THE OUTPUTS, AS SELECTED BY THE MATRIX.

THE ON INDICATOR LIGHTS WHEN THE CHANNEL IS TURNED ON.

THE PEAK INDICATOR LIGHTS WHEN THE INCOMING SIGNAL LEVEL IS TOO HIGH AND DISTORTION BEGINS TO OCCUR.

PFL (PRE-FADER LISTEN; SOMETIMES CALLED SOLO) ALLOWS THE OPERATOR TO MONITOR SIGNALS EXCLUSIVELY. THIS WILL NOT AFFECT SIGNALS LEAVING THE INPUT MODULE.

THE FADER DETERMINES THE OUTPUT LEVEL OF THE MODULE.

Fig. 3.17 Signals from consecutive modules

Output Sections

There are two types of output modules, the **group bus** and the **master bus**, each of which serve a specific function. The output section sums (combines) all the effects monitor signals and output mixes assigned by the input section. Thus, all modules which comprise the output section are referred to as **summing buses**. Using faders, it controls the final output levels sent from the board (Fig. 3.18).

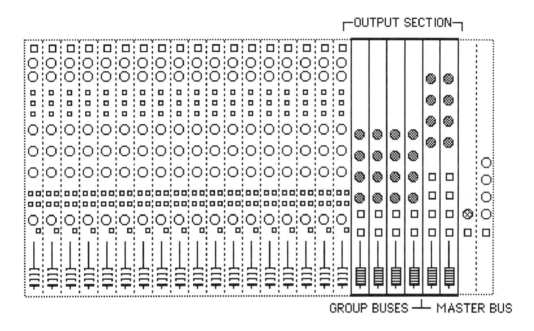

Fig. 3.18 A usual arrangement of both types of output modules.

Two types of output modules are supplied because the typical layout of an audio production or post-production studio requires two types of audio tape recorders: As discussed in chapter 2, <u>the multitrack recorder records signals on individual, separate tracks; the mastering deck records the mix of the individual signals</u>.

Because any of the input modules can be assigned to any individual group or master bus, it is possible to record on either deck by connecting the multitrack recorder's inputs to the group buses, and the mastering deck to the master buses. The group outputs are usually connected to the multitrack deck in sequence, that is, group one is connected to track one, group two to track two and so on. In this way, any input module may be assigned to any track on the multitrack deck and recorded by using the matrix (Fig. 3.19).

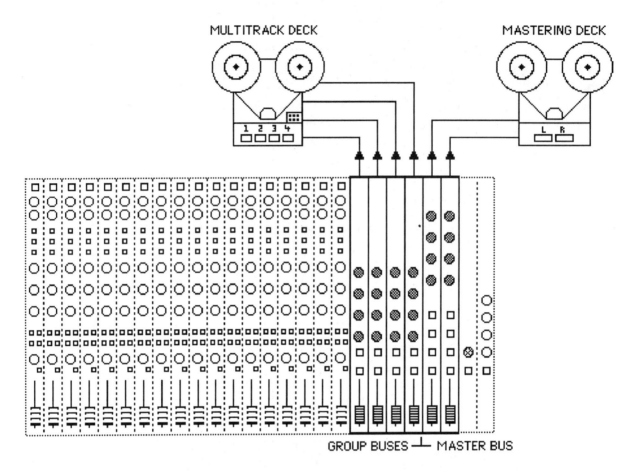

Fig. 3.19 Typical ATR (tape deck) connections to the outputs of a console. The multitrack deck is connected to the group outputs, while the mastering deck is connected to the stereo outputs.

Consoles come in many different configurations, depending on their intended use. A particular configuration is described by the number of inputs and outputs available. For example, a model described as a 16x4x2 console is one that has 16 input channels, 4 group output modules, and is equipped with a stereo (hence the "2"), or master bus output. In general, this type of description is given in the order of (number of inputs) x (number of group outputs) x (stereo output).

The number of group outputs on a console usually equals the number of tracks available on the multitrack deck. If an eight track recorder is used, the console should have eight group outputs; a sixteen track deck would imply sixteen group outputs and so on.

In addition to the differences already described, the master left and right modules differ from the group outputs in another way: Usually, all of the auxiliary sends from the input modules arrive at a master send, which controls the overall level of the send leaving the console. This is called the **auxiliary send master**. Should the signal level arriving at the effect or performer's headphone exceed an acceptable amounts, the level of the entire mix can be decreased by using this control.

If the aux send is used for a cue mix, the signal leaves the board and winds up in one or more sets of headphones and does not re-enter the console (Fig. 3.20).

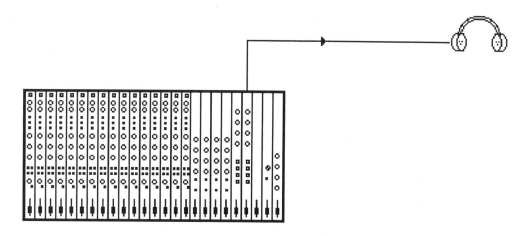

Fig. 3.20 Headphones supplied by an aux send.

However, an aux mix sent to an audio effects *must* re-enter the console to be combined with the mix appearing on the left and right modules (Fig. 3.21).

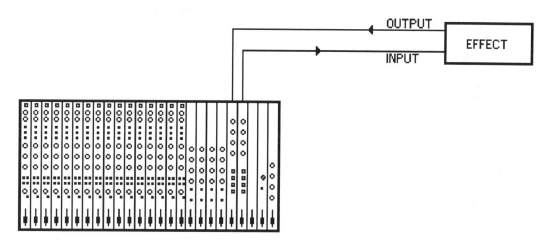

Fig. 3.21 Connection of a signal processing device to an aux send and effects return.

An **effects return** is provided for this purpose, and can vary the signal level returned back an effect or other device. The return is then combined with the master left and right outputs of the console (Fig. 3.22).

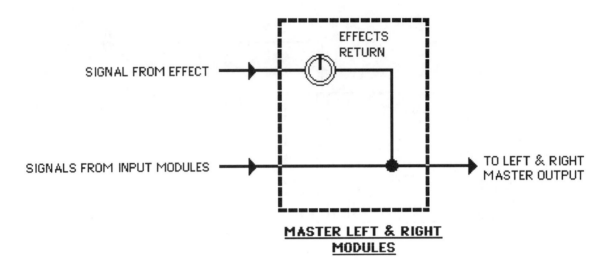

Fig. 3.22 Signal flow diagram of the effects return control.

Monitor Section

So far we've looked at ways in which consoles route signals. However, until now all signal paths have led to recording or effects devices. We still need a way to listen to these signals, and that function is handled by the console's **monitor section**.

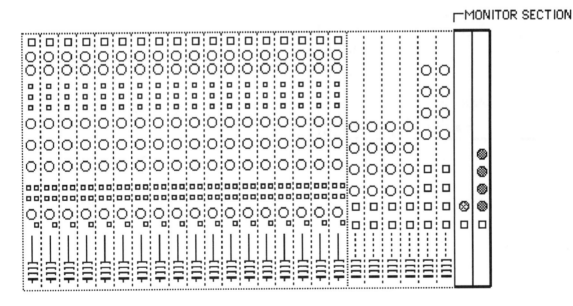

Fig. 3.23 Monitor sections of a console.

Control of the monitor section centers on a knob that regulates the overall volume of the monitored signal. In addition, a series of switches select which source is listened to, as illustrated by Fig. 3.24:

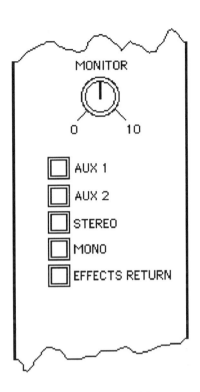

Fig. 3.24 Typical monitor control with source selection.

The output of the monitor module is sent to one or more amplifiers and one or more pairs of loud-speakers called **audio monitors**. When the Aux 1 button (Fig. 3.24) is pressed, the console operator hears the output of the aux 1 send. The Stereo button connects the monitor section to the master left and right outputs, and Mono combines left and right master outputs, letting the operator verify compatibility of the mix in mono.

Also frequently found on this module is a master PFL level control, which acts like an overall level control for any module on which the PFL function is engaged. Pushing the PFL button overrides the normal monitor mode and the operator hears only those modules selected. Normal group and master outputs from the console are unaffected. The PFL or solo level control is usually accompanied by a light that comes on when any PFL button is pressed (Fig. 3.25).

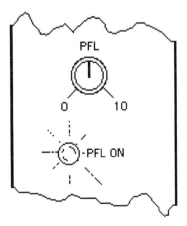

Fig. 3.25 PFL control with indicator.

The Tape Return Section

The tape return section is used to monitor the audio tracks being recorded and played back. This is a simple section, usually consisting simply of pan and level controls. The tape returns are used to:

• Free up console input modules

• Simplify the monitoring of the audio deck by reducing the amount of controls

• Reduce the chance of feedback loops or the unintentional assignment of signal to a track being recorded.

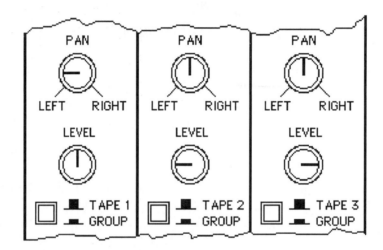

Fig. 3.26 Three modules of a Tape Return section. The "Tape/Group" buttons determine the source of the signal; in this case, signals will originate either from the group output or the multitrack tape deck, depending on their position.

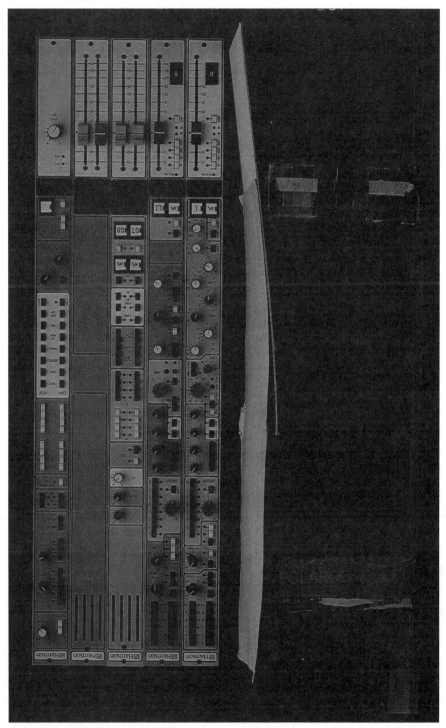

3.27. The different modules used in a Harrison TV-3 Console. Compare the controls shown with those discussed in this chapter. (Photo Courtesy of Harrison by GLW, Inc.)

C. ADDITIONAL CONSOLE FEATURES

Because consoles vary in complexity, they also vary in cost. In general, the more expensive models have more complex and useful features.

Oscillators

Some manufacturers provide an oscillator (refer to chapter 1) for setting recording levels, testing signal paths, and for matching console and tape levels. The oscillator may have a switch to select the frequency (Fig. 3.28).

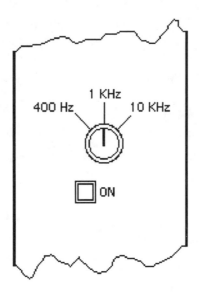

Fig. 3.28 A variable oscillator with on/off.

Talk-back Modules

A talk-back module lets the engineer communicate with performers in acoustically isolated and separate rooms located in the studio. This module usually consists of a built-in microphone, a control to vary the output of the module and several pushbuttons (Fig. 3.29). A momentary pushbutton ("talk-back") controls the output of the microphone, allowing the microphone to remain switched off when not in use. In addition, a **slate** button routes the output of the talk-back module to the group and master outputs, letting the operator record announcements of take numbers on tape. "Aux 1" and "Aux 2" direct the output of this module to the outputs of each aux send; if performers' headphones are being fed by either or both aux send, the operator can communicate by pressing the appropriate button(s).

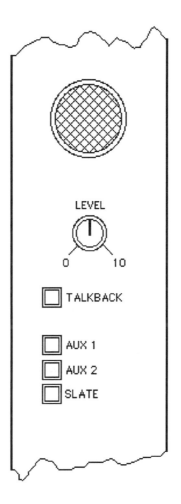

Fig. 3.29 A Talkback section, showing microphone, level, and destination controls.

Occasionally, a console will have a button that lets the operator control phantom power for microphones. This control may be one button that applies power to all input module microphones or it may have separate buttons, one on each input module.

VU Meters

Almost all consoles are equipped with VU (volume unit) meters (Fig. 3.30).

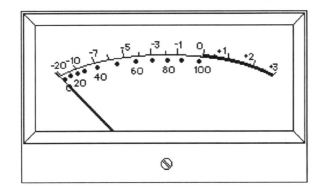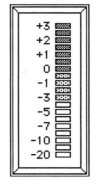

Fig. 3.30 Two types of VU meters.

In the figure, the meter on the left is a conventional design; the one on the right is called an LED (light emitting diode), bar graph or plasma style. Consoles may use either or both types.

All VU meter serve the same function: They indicate the strength of the signals passing through various points of the console. Accurate readings of signal strength is a crucial factor in recording. A signal that is too strong will cause distortion; one that is too weak will decrease the signal-to-noise ratio. Simply listening to signals to determine their level is inadequate because judging sound level and quality is subjective.

VU meters measure the electrical flow through the console. As the amplitude of the signal being measured increases, the needle of the meter swings further to the right. In the case of the bar graph style, the LEDs illuminate toward the top. In either case, if the signal is excessively strong, both types will show this. In addition, for very strong signals the VU meter's needle will hit the right side of the meter, pinning the needle against it and possibly damaging the meter.

Proper recording levels vary among different makes of equipment. <u>In general, levels should not exceed 0 to 3 VU nor fall below -5 to -7 VU</u>. If the sound being recorded has a wide **dynamic range** (varies between very high and very low volumes), it may be necessary to **ride the gain**, a term that describes the occasional adjustment of the faders to keep the average signal level within acceptable limits.

Generally, the meters are wired only to the console outputs. Some consoles may have one meter per output; some may switch one meter among various signal paths. Additional meters may be provided to monitor auxiliary outputs.

Summary: Input Module Signal Paths

Block diagrams are commonly used to describe the signal paths of a given piece of equipment. The ability to read this type of diagram will greatly help in understanding a console's functions. Fig. 3.31 illustrates, in block diagram form, the generic input module used in this book.

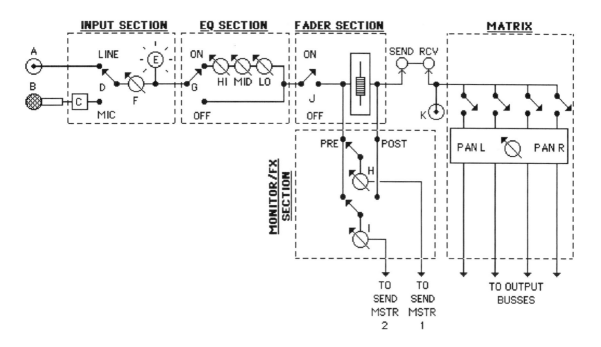

Fig. 3.31 Block diagram of a typical input module signal path. Compare this diagram with the illustration of an input module shown earlier in this chapter.

In figure 3.31, (A) is a line-level input, (B) is a microphone input and (C) is a **pad** that attenuates (lowers) the incoming microphone signal by a fixed amount. This amount will vary with different consoles. The input to the module (line or microphone) is selected by the **input select switch** (D). An LED (E), called a **peak indicator**, lights if the incoming signal is too high. The signal can be lowered by rotating the **trim control** (F). *The trim control attenuates the signal, and is therefore the first level control to adjust.* The signal then passes to the **EQ section**. EQ can be completely bypassed with the **EQ on-off** (sometimes called in-out or bypass) switch (G). The signal then goes to a **mute** switch (J). Turning off this switch prevents the signal from leaving the module. The **fader** is the master level control for signals leaving input the module. (H) and (I) are **auxiliary sends**. In this case, (H) is the cue send because it feeds headphones in another room for monitoring. The effects send (I) is connected to an external device, such as a reverb unit, the output of which is re-mixed with the main signals leaving the board. Note that the input to either send can be selected before the fader (PRE) or after (POST). If a send obtains its input pre-fader, the level of signal carried on that send is unaffected by changes made to the fader. The signal then goes to a patch bay (discussed in chapter 6) where the path can be interrupted for signal processing (at the SEND jack) and re-introduced (at the RCV jack). A separate line-level output can be obtained at (K). This is usually called a **direct out** or **line out**. Next, the signal is sent to the **matrix**, where it can be sent to any or all of the console outputs. The **pan** control determines the stereo imaging. Odd-even panning indicates the type of pan. For example, by selecting buses one, three and four, panning left would send the signal to the odd-numbered buses (one and three). Panning right would send the signal to the even-numbered buses (four).

D. STUDIO SIGNAL PATHS AND BASIC MULTITRACK RECORDING

The minimum requirement for a small multitrack studio are shown in Fig. 3.32.

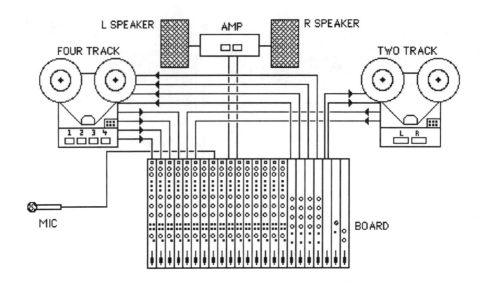

Fig. 3.32 Basic setup of a multitrack studio.

Although it looks confusing, it isn't. The inputs of the four track recorder are connected to the group outputs of the board. The four-track outputs are connected to four input modules of the board and to the tape returns. Also shown is a two-track recorder and a monitoring system. In the following diagrams, the monitoring system is omitted because it is always connected and its role never varies.

Recalling that consoles have two types of outputs — those used for recording on a tape deck and those used for monitoring — makes it easier to understand how equipment is connected and how studios work. As with consoles, the layout of audio production or post-production studios are similar. The following chart reviews the connections between consoles, monitors and tape decks:

Principle Connections Between Consoles and Tape Decks

Outputs	*Inputs*
Console Group Outputs............Multitrack Deck Inputs	
Multitrack Deck Outputs..........Console Line Inputs *and* Tape Returns	
Console L/R Outputs...............Mastering Deck Inputs	
Mastering Deck Input..............Console Line or 2-Track Monitor Inputs	
Console Monitor Outputs.........Amplifier and Audio Monitors	

Stages of Recording

To grasp the concept of multitrack recording, consider an imaginary recording session. Multitrack recording is done in three stages:

1 The initial or **basic tracks** are first recorded (individually or all at once);

2 One or more **overdubs** may be performed, where additional sound is recorded while simultaneously monitoring the basic tracks;

3. A **mix** is made at the end of the session, where all the recorded tracks are played, combined, and re-recorded onto a separate deck having one or two tracks.

Our imaginary session will take place in a four-track recording studio, but the basic principles are the same for multitrack recording.

As illustrated in Fig. 3.33, the console's group outs are connected to the four track's inputs, and microphones and instruments are connected to various input modules. For simplicity, assume that an electric guitar is recorded on track two, an electric bass on track three and drums on track four. These will constitute the basic tracks.

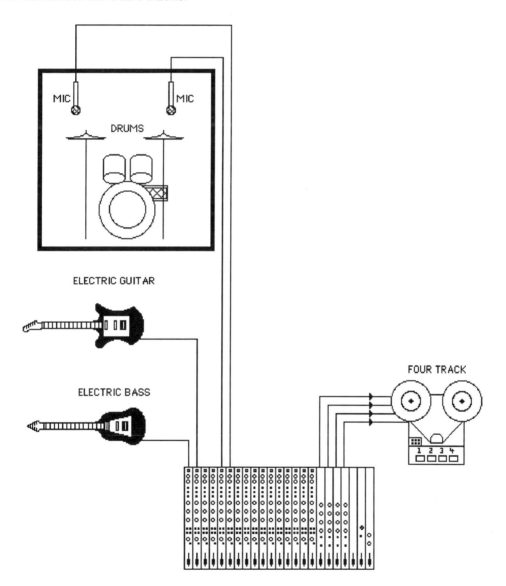

Fig. 3.33 Recording basic tracks: The drum microphones, guitar, and bass are separately connected to various input modules of the console.

The guitar is plugged into the microphone input of input module one through a **direct box.** The direct box converts the level of some electric instruments, such as guitar and bass, to that of microphone level. The bass is connected to the microphone input of input module two, also through a direct box. The two microphones on the drums are plugged into the microphone inputs of input modules five and six.

Since all input signals are microphone level, input modules one, two, five and six must be switched to accept those signals by using the input select.

To play in time and in tune, the performers must hear each other. Consequently, all three are supplied with headphones (not shown), which are fed by the auxiliary send on input modules one, two, five and six.

To record each instrument on separate tracks, input module one (guitar) is assigned to group two, input module two (bass) is assigned to group three, and input modules five and six (drums) are assigned to group four. Some time is spent adjusting EQ for each module, altering microphone placement, adjusting aux send and recording levels, and so on. At this time only the tape returns are used to monitor the four track deck; the input modules to which the four track is connected will be used only during the mix.

When the basic tracks have been recorded, the overdub begins. In this case, the overdub consists of one vocalist (Fig. 3.34).

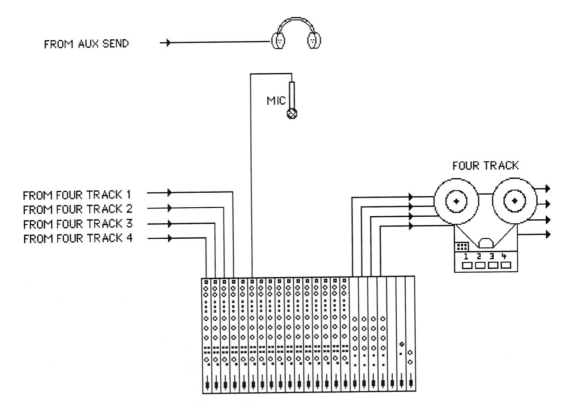

Fig. 3.34 Overdub: The vocalist is supplied with an aux send (cue mix) of the pre-recorded tracks while being recorded in sync.

The vocalist's microphone is connected to input module six and his or her headphones are fed signals from the auxiliary sends. Input six is switched to receive the microphone signal, and assigned to group one.

When the overdub is completed, the four track is played back and the tape returns are shut off. The outputs of the four track, in this case, are connected to inputs one through four. Having the four track supply signal without shutting off the tape returns would result in each track playing through two separate sources (i.e., one tape return and one input module for each track). This would make it impossible to correctly control the signal levels. These inputs are switched to line and assigned to the left and right master outputs. (Note that if these were not reassigned, a feedback loop could be created by having the four track's inputs and outputs connected together through the console.)

The four track is repeatedly played back while adjustments to EQ, panning, level, and processing are made. Note that the auxiliary send may be used at this time to introduce an effect to be recorded onto the two track. When the adjustments have been made, the two track mastering deck is put into record, and all four separate tracks are re-recorded, or mixed (Fig. 3.35).

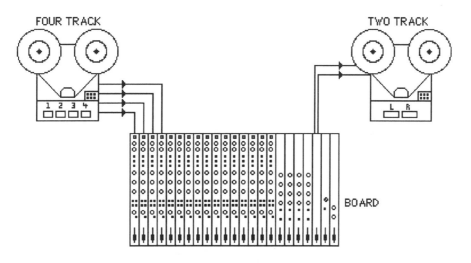

Fig. 3.35 Basic connections for a mix.

This example is extremely simplistic, but introduces the fundamental principles of multitrack recording.

Fig. 3.36. Tascam's MM-1 Keyboard Mixer. This is a line-level-only mixer intended for semiprofessional applications where the mixing of electronic instruments is required.
(Photo Courtesy of Teac/Tascam Professional Division)

Fig. 3.37. Tascam's M-600 Console; a good example of a medium -sized production console.
(Photo Courtesy of Teac/Tascam Professional Division)

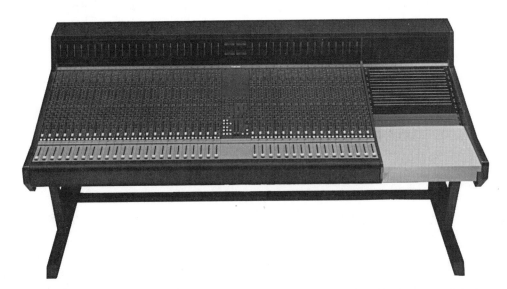

Fig. 3.38. Tascam's M-700 Console, a large format production console. Note the placement of the input
and output sections and the use of flouroscan meters.
(Photo Courtesy of Teac/Tascam Professional Division)

E. PRODUCTION TECHNIQUES: SETTING UP A CONSOLE

The following steps should be followed in sequence when setting up a console before and during
a session:

1. Tape should be placed on the console's designation strip in preparation for the labeling of
   channel inputs

2. Make ABSOLUTELY sure that the monitor and solo volumes are turned all the way down. If
   possible, the control room speakers should be turned off.

3. Remove all cords left on the patch bay from any previous sessions. If any preliminary patching is required for your session, do it now.

4. Switch all input selectors on every input channel to be used to either mic or line, depending on the types of signals being fed to the console

5. Switch every EQ section on the console off.

6. Rotate all the trim controls to about 1:00 o'clock position.

7. Turn all the pan controls to center.

8. Slide all input and bus faders about 2/3 of the way up to zero or into the "gray area" (i.e., the benchmark). The actual location will vary with the console.

9. Turn on only those input channels to be used; this reduces the amount of noise generated by analog equipment.

10. Turn the control room monitor to about the 9:00 o'clock position.

11. An oscillator must be patched into an input module. If any input modules have already been set, use another module. The module is assigned to all group outputs, and the group faders are set so that their respective VU meters read 0 VU. The multitrack deck is also adjusted to read 0 VU so that the console and multitrack meters read the same.

12. Record 30 seconds of tone, usually a 1-KHz sine wave, on all tracks of the deck. Play back the tone to verify that both record and playback levels are the same (more about this procedure in chapter 4).

13. Assign the input modules to the desired buses.

14. Put the first input module into solo and rotate the solo monitor volume to about the 9:00 o'clock position. Verify that the signal is present. If it is, label that input by marking the tape. If the signal is not present, check the following:

    a. Verify that the proper connections have been made to the console;

    b. Check to see that the input select has been properly set;

    c. Make sure that the signal is not interrupted at the patch bay;

    d. Check the trim control;

    e. Check the matrix section to see if you have properly routed the signal;

    f. Check that the monitor volumes are properly set.

15. Repeat step 11 for each input module.

16. When all inputs have been labeled and solo has been disengaged, patch in any outboard effects you might need.

17. Make preliminary settings of the pan controls to obtain stereo imaging.

18. Put the basic rhythm channel (e.g., bass drum, bass guitar, etc.) into solo, turn the EQ section on and adjust the EQ settings as desired. *If the level increases on that channel, adjust only the trim.*

19. Repeat step 16 for every channel.

20. When solo has once again been disengaged, it is possible to make comparisons between groups of signals. Continue to adjust levels, EQ, and pan as desired.

4
AUDIO DECKS

A. HEADS AND TAPE

Audio decks are commonly referred to as **ATR**'s (<u>audio</u> <u>tape</u> <u>recorders</u>).

Sound for audio, video and film is recorded on **magnetic media**, or magnetic tape. Magnetic media are not limited to recording tape, however. This book, for example, was originally written on a computer and stored as magnetic impulses on floppy disks, which are also made of magnetic media. No invention, except perhaps the transistor or silicon chip, has so profoundly affected our lives as magnetic media for recording.

All magnetic recording tape works on essentially the same principle: Microscopic ferrite particles (magnetic material) are bonded to a layer of plastic, which in turn is bonded to another layer of plastic (Fig. 4.1):

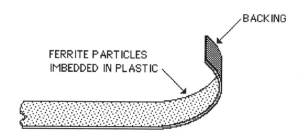

Fig. 4.1. Magnetic tape is composed of microscopic ferrite particles imbedded in plastic which is bonded to a second layer of plastic called a backing.

During sound recording, the tape passes over an **audio head** at a fixed speed, which magnetizes the particles in the tape. An audio head operates on the principles of **EMI**, or **electro-magnetic induction** (refer to chapter 2): A metal core is wrapped with a coil of wire. When current passes through the wire, the core becomes magnetic. As more current passes through the wire, the magnetism in the head increases. As the current decreases, so does the magnetic field in the tape head. In short, the magnetic field strength follows the strength of the electric current.

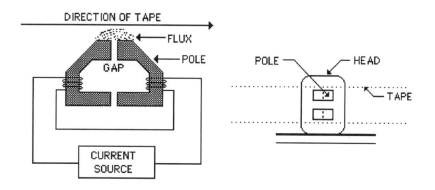

Fig. 4.2. The operating principle of a magnetic audio tape head.

81

The diagram on the left in Fig. 4.2 is a schematic representation of an audio recording head; on the right is shown a head as seen from the front.

The magnetic field, or **flux**, across the gap of the head serves as a magnetic force that aligns the particles in the tape. Particles are aligned in groups called **domains** (Fig. 4.3):

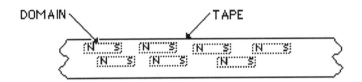

Fig. 4.3. Domains, or particles which are aligned in groups on audio tape.

In this way, the magnetic fluctuations at the head are captured by the tape passing across it. During playback, the tape passes over another head called the playback head. Moving at the same speed as when the recording was made, the tape exposes the playback head to its magnetic variations. These duplicate fluctuations across the head's gap induce a current in the playback head's wire coil. The current is amplified by the tape deck into line level signals.

B. TAPE FORMATS

Magnetic recording tape comes in a different shapes and sizes. The size of the tape, its width, the way it is packaged and the type of recording machine it is for comprise the most important aspects of the tape **format**.

Tape formats fall under two basic categories: **open reel** and **closed reel** systems. Open reel system allow you to handle the tape because it is wound on a metal or plastic reel, not unlike film. Open reel systems are available on some consumer decks, but are always found in audio production and post-production studios in the form of multitrack and mastering decks.

Closed reel systems are, in effect, small open-reel systems mounted within plastic enclosures, or shells. The shells are made to a standard specification and are intended for specific types of machines (Fig. 4.4).

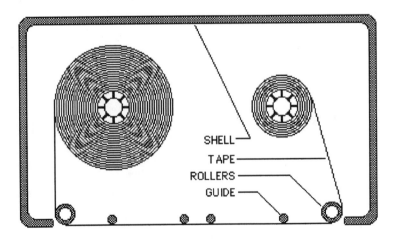

Fig. 4.4 Simplified cutaway view of an ordinary audio cassette.

Closed reel tapes are commonly known as audio and video cassettes. The specific size of the shell, and size and type of tape determine the tape's application.

Head Configurations

The way that a tape head records sound patterns onto the tape is a mostly function of **head configuration**. Head configuration is determined by the number of magnetic coils in the tape head and the way those coils are arranged (Fig. 4.5).

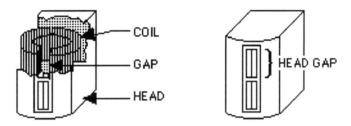

Fig. 4.5 A head gap on an audio head, used to record or play back a separate track on an audio tape. The diagram on the left shows the basic idea behind the relationship of coil to head gap.

The **head gap** is the space on the head's surface where the magnetic flux is generated. Its length is set by the size of the gap in the magnetic coil. The wider the tape, the fewer coils in the head and the longer the head gap. A longer gap uses more magnetic material to record and reproduce the signal, thus increasing sound quality.

The arrangement of the head gap also determines the format of the tape. Because the audio head in Fig. 4.6 has only two gaps, two channels, or **tracks**, of audio information can be recorded on the tape. Note that the width of tape corresponds directly to the length of the head gaps.

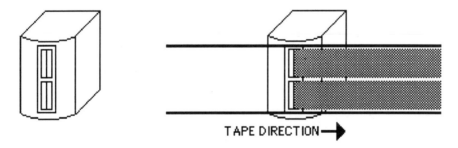

Fig. 4.6 The same audio head shown recording two tracks.

Fig. 4.7 illustrates the same width tape being recorded on by a head with four separate gaps. As a result, up to four tracks of audio information may be recorded on the tape. Again, the width of tape used for recording corresponds directly with the length of the head gaps.

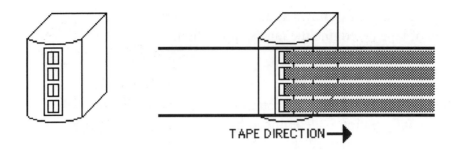

Fig. 4.7 A tape head with four gaps recording four separate tracks.

If we halve the gap length (Fig. 4.8), we double the amount of separate channels of audio information available. But this also halves the width of tape for each channel. As a result, there is a limit as to how many separate tracks may be recorded on one tape. If the tracks become too narrow, the signal becomes weak and unstable. If more channels are required, a wider tape must be used.

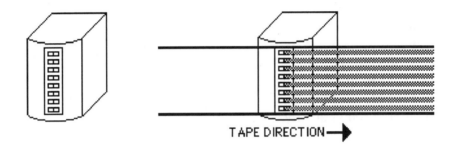

Fig. 4.8 A tape head with eight gaps recording eight separate tracks.

Fig. 4.9. Various audio heads illustrating the gap placements. Clockwise from upper left: A stereo cartridge format known as Tom-Cat; A pair of stereo film recorder heads; A half inch eight track head stack; A one inch sixteen track head stack. (Photo Courtesy of Saki Magnetics, Inc.)

Tape Width, Speed, and Noise

All analog equipment generates noise. If you turn off all sources to your home stereo system and turn the volume to maximum you will hear a hissing sound; this is the normal noise that is constantly generated. Hopefully, the level of whatever is playing (tape, record, CD, etc.) will "drown out" the noise.

The more expensive a piece of equipment is, the less noise is produced. Tape width, tape speed, and the width of each track all have a profound effect on equipment generated noise.

Assume that you have an unusually long piece of toast:

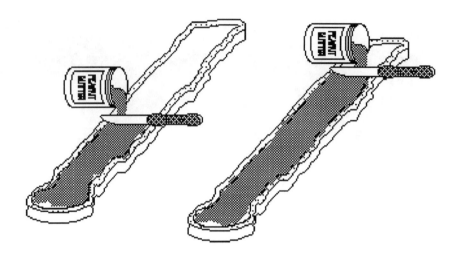

Fig. 4.10 The same piece of toast receives the same amount of peanut butter. However, the toast on the right gets the same amount over twice the distance and the peanut butter is spread half as thick.

As shown in Fig. 4.10, each piece of toast is receiving the same amount of peanut butter; let's assume that this is one gram per second. However, let's have the toast on the left travel at one foot per second, and the toast on the right at two feet per second. Since the peanut butter is being applied at the same rate, each piece of toast is spread with the same amount at any given time. However, since the toast on the right is moving at double the speed, *the peanut butter is spread only half as thick*. Similarly, if both pieces of toast were moving at the same rate, but the piece on the right was twice as wide, the same results would be obtained.

If we substitute the toast for tape, and the peanut butter for noise, we can see the relationships between tape speed, tape width, track width, and noise. If the tape or track width is increased, noise decreases. The same is true for tape speed: As speed increases, noise decreases.

Crosstalk

Crosstalk occurs when the signals on adjacent tracks interfere with each other. This happens when a signal being recorded on a given track exceeds a certain amplitude and "spills over" to an adjacent track. This amplitude limit is lower on less expensive decks, which often operate near the critical number of tracks and have areas separating the gaps, called **guard bands**, that are too thin. On professional decks, the gaps, guard bands and tape width are wider.

Let's imagine that we are recording something on track one, and are listening simultaneously on track two. At some point, the signal level being recorded exceeds the acceptable limits, and track two begins to pick up and play the signals being recorded on track one (Fig. 4.11). Needless to say, this can cause serious technical problems, not to mention emotional turmoil. The only ways to solve crosstalk problems are to:

• Use noise reduction (discussed later)

• Reduce the level of the signal being recorded

• Buy a better recording machine.

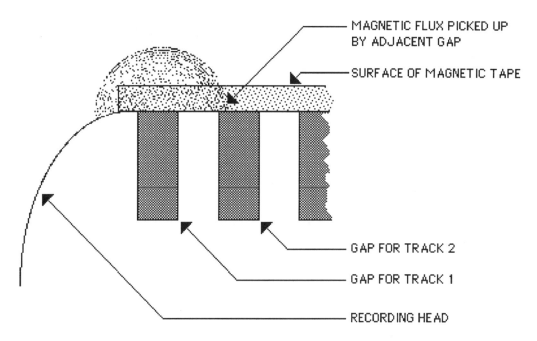

Fig. 4.11 A head-on view of what happens during crosstalk: The magnetism one from one track physically crosses the guard band and is picked up by the adjacent gap.

Mastering Deck Tape Formats

"Mastering" decks are ATR's used for recording the mix of separate channels originally recorded on a multitrack deck. They tend to have, among other features, fewer tracks and wider head gaps. Most multitrack mixes are either mono or stereo. Hence, only one track is required for mono; two for stereo. Because only one or two tracks are required, the head gap width, and thus the quality of the recorded signal, are increased.

The quality of the **mixed master** tape is crucial. It is this tape that will be used for the material's ultimate format. The audio on the mixed master is used to create records, cassette copies, compact disks, film soundtracks, and a variety of other formats for almost any audio use.

The format of the mix depends again on the head configuration of the deck, the speed at which the tape was recorded, the width of the tape, the way it was wound, and whether or not noise reduction was used. (Noise reduction is discussed later.)

The most common tape widths used for mixing are 1/4 inch and 1/2 inch, the latter being used almost exclusively in professional studios. The following illustrations depict the more common formats.

Fig. 4.12 illustrates a professional mono format called **full track**. Because almost the entire width of the tape is used for one channel, full track tends to yield the best possible signal quality. In addition, full track is almost always used with 1/4-inch tape, although a few 1/2-inch full track machines exist.

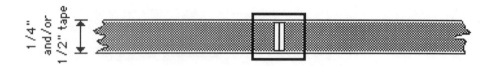

Fig. 4.12. The full track format.

The standard professional stereo format is called **half track** (Fig. 4.13). Half track provides two independent tracks, so the operator can mix in stereo. Again, the head gap lengths are greater and, like its mono counterpart, full track, half track yields excellent signal quality.

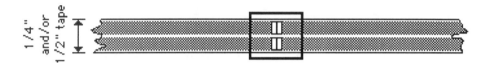

Fig. 4.13. Half track two channel format.

Fig. 4.14. A 1/4-inch, half track recorder.
(Photo Courtesy of Otari, Inc.)

Fig. 4.15. A typical mastering recorder.
(Photo Courtesy of Tascam/Teac Professional Division)

A more recent variation of half track adds a thin center track of time code between the two audio tracks. This format is called **center stripe** (Fig. 4.16). (Time code and its use are discussed in chapter 8.)

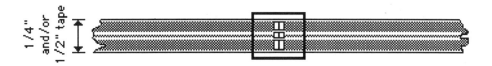

Fig. 4.16. The center stripe half track two channel format.

Quarter track, or four-channel stereo, is considered a consumer format. It uses less tape per track, and the quality is less than that of half track. The advantage of this format, however, is that tapes recorded in this manner have two sides (the tape must be flipped over to play side B), like an audio cassette. (Fig. 4.16)

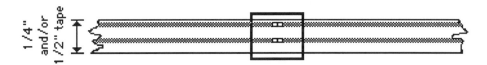

Fig. 4.17. Quarter track, or four-channel stereo.

Multitrack Deck Tape Formats

Multitrack decks, as mentioned, record a number of tracks individually. These tracks are independent of each other and can be re-recorded, played back or erased separately.

The costs and features associated with multitrack decks depend upon their intended function. Smaller decks tend to be less expensive provider for fewer recording tracks. The names of various decks reflect their track capacity; a "four track" has only four tracks, an "eight track" has eight and so on.

Overall, multitrack decks are available in multiples of four tracks. The standard formats are 4, 8, 16, 24 and 32 tracks. The tape widths associated with these decks can vary, but the greater width tapes are associated with professional decks. (Remember that greater tape width allows for greater head gap length and thus higher signal quality.)

Equipment quality is generally graded along three categories. "Pro" or professional equipment is the highest quality and is used only in professional recording and mixing facilities. "Semi-pro" is equipment that meets the demands of modestly-priced recording studios, and falls between professional grade and the next grade down, "consumer." Consumer equipment is considered lowest grade of equipment and is usually designed to meet the needs of individuals who require inexpensive recording equipment for their homes.

The Fig. 4.18 illustrates the most common analog multitrack tape deck formats, their intended application and respective tape widths.

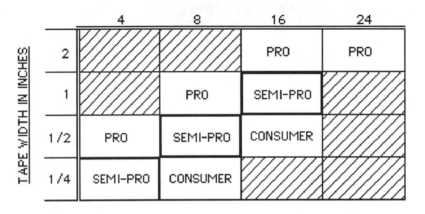

Fig. 4.18. Comparison of various multitrack formats and tape widths.

As with any deck, it is the head configuration and tape width that determines a multitrack deck's format. Note that on a multitrack deck, the heads are called **head stacks**, because they are literally composed of magnetic coils stacked upon one another.

Four track is the smallest multitrack format, and is a variation of quarter-track, four-channel stereo. The difference is that the four four track can play all the tracks simultaneously and can record on each or all tracks in any configuration (Fig. 4.19).

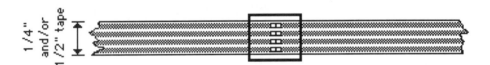

Fig. 4.19. Quarter track four track.

Fig. 4.20. A 1/4 inch four track recorder. (Photo Courtesy of Tascam/Teac Professional Division)

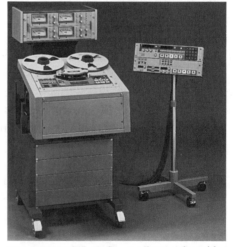

Fig. 4.21.A 1/2 inch four track recorder with autolocator. (Photo Courtesy of Tascam/Teac Professional Division)

90

Eight track is the most popular home studio format. Recently, it has also seen a resurgence for audio post-production work (Fig. 4.22).

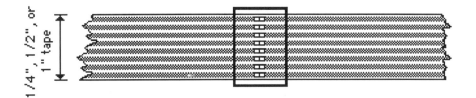

Fig. 4.22

Fig. 4.23. A 1/2-inch, eight-track ATR. This is the most popular eight-track format. (Photo Courtesy of Otari, Inc.)

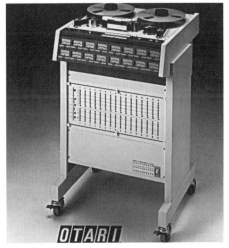

Fig. 4.24. A one-inch ATR. It can be used either as an eight- or sixteen-track recorder. (Photo Courtesy of Otari, Inc.)

Sixteen and 24-track machines using two-inch wide tape are nearly interchangeable. Often all that is needed is to replace the head block and add of some electronics. (Fig. 4.25). These machines are also available in models using one-inch tape.

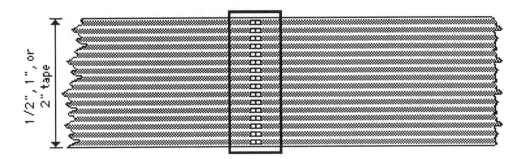

Fig. 4.25 Sixteen or twenty four track format.

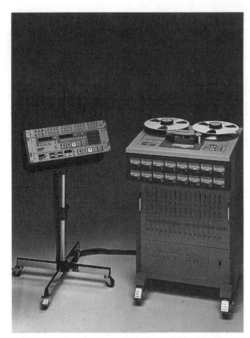

Fig. 4.26. A one-inch, 16-track ATR.
(Photo Courtesy of Tascam/Teac Professional
Division)

Fig. 4.27. A one-inch, 24-track ATR.
(Photo Courtesy of Tascam/Teac Professional
Division)

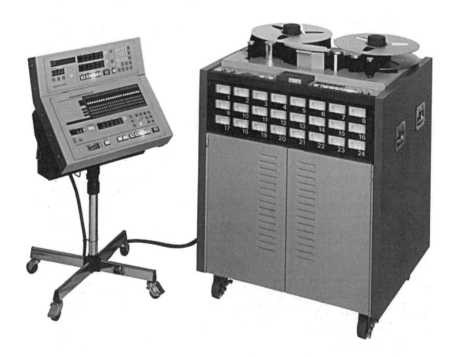

Fig. 4.28. A two-inch, 24-track ATR. Note the autolocator to the left.
(Photo Courtesy of Tascam/Teac Professional Division)

Fig. 4.29. A close view of another 2 inch 24 track ATR. (Photo Courtesy of Otari, Inc.)

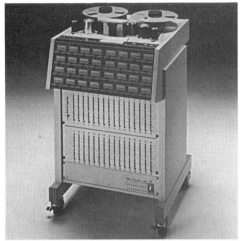

Fig. 4.30. A 1 inch 48 track ATR. (Photo Courtesy of Otari, Inc.)

Consumer Multitrack Decks

Consumer multitrack decks are not meant for use in the professional environment. However, they are mentioned because technology has fueled the mass introduction of exceptional consumer-grade equipment. Consumers with modest financial means can now produce their own demo tapes at home. In addition, the formats discussed in the proceeding chapter are increasingly used in consumer equipement, letting the amateur recording engineer copy the basic tracks to a multitrack tape in a studio and have them overdubbed and mixed.

Four-track Cassette

The first type of consumer multitrack deck was the four-track cassette deck. Although it resembles a conventional cassette deck, it acts exactly as a standard four-track deck.

Because the width of cassette tape is only 1/8 inch, several factors compensate for the reduced head gap width. First, the tape speed is double that of conventional cassettes. Second, the deck uses noise reduction to increase the S/N ratio and limit the dynamic range — and therefore the crosstalk — of the material being recorded.

Some of these decks are battery operated and portable. Some are integrated with small mixing consoles, making them ideal for home recording sessions.

Eight-track Cassette

The ideal number of tracks is like a bank balance: There's no such thing as too much. Thus, at least one manufacturer makes an eight-track cassette recorder. At one time, such a format was thought to be physically impossible: The crosstalk problems created by exceeding the physical limit of gap length and distance were unacceptable. One manufacturer solved the problem ingeniously by physically splitting the record head in two. One head records and plays even-numbered tracks; the other records and plays odd-numbered tracks (Fig. 4.31). With the two heads are physically separated, crosstalk problems are eliminated.

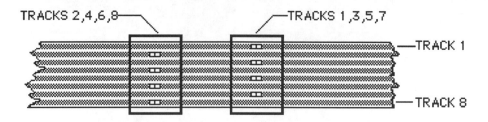

Fig. 4.31. An eight track multitrack cassette tape format. Note the "splitting" of heads.

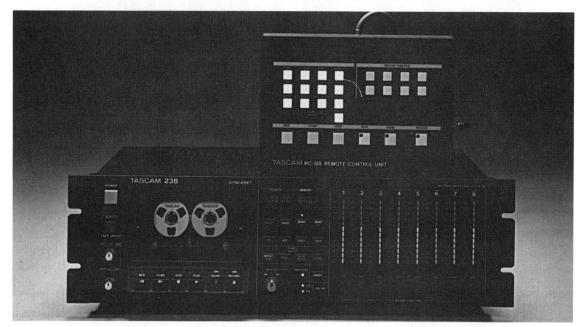

Fig. 4.32. This eight-track tape recorder, shown here with its remote control, uses standard audio cassettes. (Photo Courtesy of Tascam/Teac Professional Division)

Low-Width Open Reel

To date, the limit for audio cassette multitrack decks seems to be eight tracks. Demands for low-priced decks with greater capacity do exist however, and in response to this demand manufacturers offer eight-track decks using 1/4-inch tape, as well as 16-track decks using 1/4-inch and 1/2-inch tape. These formats are called **low-width open reel** formats. Because they are subject to more crosstalk and have lower S/N ratios, however, they are intended only for small or semi-professional studios.

Integrated Systems

Another recent development is that of the **integrated system** that combines a multitrack deck and mixer in one package. This combination is ideal for the consumer that doesn't want to be bothered— after buying an tape deck — with the trouble and expense of selecting and connecting a console. The formats of integrated systems include 1/4-inch eight-track open reel and four-track cassette.

Video Decks

To acquaint the reader with the most current methods of post-production, it is necessary to cover the basics of videotape formats and decks. Video decks are commonly referred to as **VTR**s (for video tape recorders).

The principle behind the video deck requires two separate heads; one for video, the other for audio (Fig. 4.33). The videotape moves from left to right, and the video head rotates rapidly in the same direction in which the tape is traveling. Physically separate from the video head is the audio head, which remains stationary.

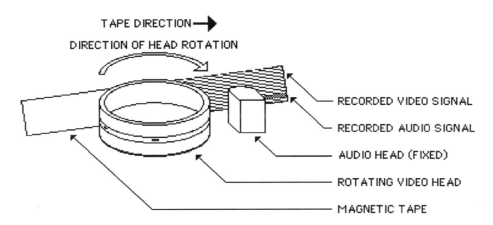

Fig. 4.33. Basic heads in the tape path of a VTR.

The basic components of a typical videotape format are shown in Fig. 4.33. Note that, in addition to the video and the audio tracks, there is often a **cue**, **auxiliary** or **address track**, and a **control track**. The cue track is essentially a third audio track used for time code (discussed in chapter 9). The control track is analogous to sprocket holes on film. When a video deck records a video signal, the deck adds a series of evenly spaced electronic pulses on the tape. These pulses are counted by video decks and editing systems to recognize a complete frame, or picture, of video.

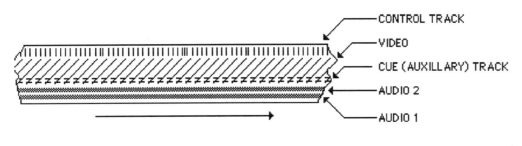

Fig. 4.34

The different video tape formats are called **digital**, **one inch**, **Betacam**, **3/4 inch**, **Super VHS**, **VHS**, and **eight mm**. Of these, one-inch video is the only format that is open reel; the others are enclosed in cassettes. The formats reflect the tape width employed: S-VHS, VHS, and beta all utilize 1/2-inch-wide tape. The 8-mm format uses a 3/8-inch wide tape. Digital and 1-inch fomats yield the highest audio and video signal quality respectively. Signal quality decreases slightly from 1 inch to Betacam, and 8-mm signal quality is a judgement best left to the individual: A controversy regarding its appropriate use as a viable production quality format has been raging since its introduction several years ago.

The basic uses of the different video formats are covered below. Moreover, details of the actual track configurations and aspects of each are covered in chapter 9. All these formats are used today. However, some are inappropriate for audio post-production.

Digital

Digital decks fall into two categories, D-1 and D-2. The two formats are incompatible, but can exchange audio and video information between each other. D-1 is generally used for film-to-videotape transfers, mastering and on-line editing; D-2 was intended to replace one-inch VTRs.

One Inch

One-inch machines are referred to as Type C VTRs and are commonly used for mastering and on-line editing. Until the advent of digital decks, one-inch VTRs were considered *the* production standard. However, at $50,000 each, they make alternative formats look very attractive.

Betacam SP

Betacam SP yields extremely high signal quality and is used for field recording in production and news situations. In some cases, it can be used for mastering and on-line or off-line editing.

3/4 inch

The 3/4-inch format falls into two categories: broadcast and industrial. In general, broadcast decks are considered superior in quality to their industrial cousins. The majority of what is seen on television is broadcast from material played on a 3/4-inch video deck. Because one-inch video decks are so expensive, many smaller video editing and audio post-production facilities use 3/4-inch video as work copies of the tapes to be edited. Work copies are dubs of master tapes and are used in lieu of the master, which allows the master to be safely stored until it is needed for the final editing session. As we'll discuss in chapter 9, these copies are also used extensively in audio post-production work. The 3/4-inch format has also been supplemented by a modified version called 3/4-inch SP.

VHS and S-VHS

Super VHS, also called S-VHS, is a relatively new, high-quality format. Some observers contend that it will eventually replace 3/4-inch tape, but others disagree. In any case, the quality of this format is irrefutably high, but is rarely used in audio post-production.

VHS is the consumer standard and is most likely the format used for the last movie you rented. The quality of the reproduced sound and image is largely a function of the deck. This format is never used in audio post-production.

8 mm

One of the most remarkable developments in video has been that of 8-mm video. The 8-mm video cassette is similar in size and appearance to a standard audio cassette, yet the picture quality is remarkably high. The audio quality, however, is not acceptable for post-production, broadcast or mastering because the tape width and gap distance are reduced considerably.

Jog and Shuttle

Like professional ATR's, video decks are equipped with the normal transport functions like rewind, fast forward, stop, pause, play and record. In addition, VTRs used in audio post-production must have other capabilities. First, each VTR must be able to freeze frames while holding a stable picture. Stability lets the viewer identify specific aspects of the picture. Second, the VTR must let the operator "scan" the images faster or slower than normal playing speed and in either direction. For these two reasons two important functions are built into all professional VTRs, called **jog** and **shuttle**. Both are controlled by a **shuttle knob** (Fig. 4.35).

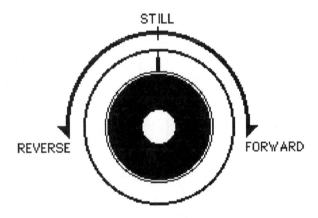

STILL

REVERSE   FORWARD

Fig. 4.35. The shuttle knob of a VTR.

In shuttle mode, rotating the knob to the left causes the tape to "search" in reverse. In this mode the picture stays on the screen, with the video and audio heads in the VTR remaining in contact with the tape. Rotating the knob counter clockwise increases the speed of the tape proportionately to the degree of rotation. In the straight up position, the picture "freezes." Rotating the knob clockwise causes the tape to search in the forward direction, with the speed again increasing as the knob is turned progressively further clockwise.

In the jog mode, a 360° rotation of the knob causes the videotape to advance or back up by one frame, depending on the direction that the knob is rotated. The important aspect of this feature is that the videotape is in contact with the heads at all times, and that all audio and video signals at that section of the tape are played.

Recording

Because videotapes are composite tapes — they contain both audio and video information — all professional VTR's will allow for the separate recording of video and audio. This is analogous to overdubbing one or more tracks on a multitrack ATR, and is explained in chapter 7. However, for now, it is enough to say that one can re-record the audio content of a tape without disturbing the video signal.

C. FILM

Film Sound Recording

As with videotape formats and decks, various film formats are used in conjunction with the new post-production methods .

There are two basic ways in which sound is recorded on film. The method used depends on the system used to originally shoot the footage, and are called **magnetic stripe** and **optical track** (Fig. 4.36). Magnetic stripe film works in a similar fashion to audiotape and, depending on the format and application, is integrated into the film stock carrying the picture or done a separate roll of film.

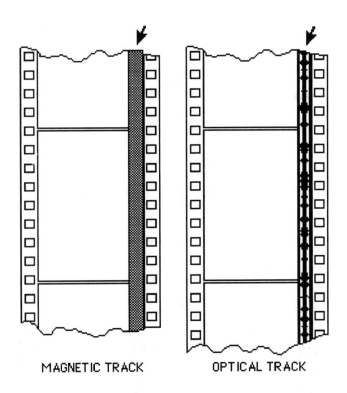

MAGNETIC TRACK   OPTICAL TRACK

Fig. 4.36. Two formats used in the projection of film.

If the magnetic material is integrated into the same stock as the picture or is placed on a separate stock in several stripes, the format is referred to as **magnetic stripe**. If the entire stock is covered with the one or more stripes of magnetic substance *without the picture*, the stock is referred to as **full coat**.

Optical track is created photographically during the development of the film at a lab, and is illuminated by an **exciter lamp** within a projector. The photoelectric pickup reads the variations of light through the track and changes them into electrical impulses. These impulses are amplified within the projector and can be heard either through the projector's internal speaker or an external sound system.

It should be noted that magnetic stripe is superior in sound quality to optical track.

Film Formats

As with audio and video tapes, film stock is available in different widths, with the larger widths being used professionally. As the size of the stock increases, so do the image and sound quality.

The formats, as with audio and video tape, are named according to their size. These are **70 mm**, **35 mm**, **16 mm**, and **super 8 mm**.

The 70-mm format is used exclusively in motion picture distribution for viewing in wide screen theaters. The 35-mm format in used for making commercials, music videos and independent productions. It is sometimes shown in smaller theaters and occasionally broadcast on television. Stock that is 16-mm wide is commonly used in film schools and low-budget independent productions. And super 8-mm is used in film schools and for "home" movies. However, super 8 mm is quickly becoming obsolete because video is cheaper, easier to handle and obtains better results — instantly.

Different formats of film may different arrangements of optical or magnetic techniques or combine the two to record sound. For example, 70 mm uses four (and sometimes six) channels of magnetic stripe to reproduce sound (Fig. 4.37). In this and the subsequent illustrations of film formats, arrows show the sound tracks.

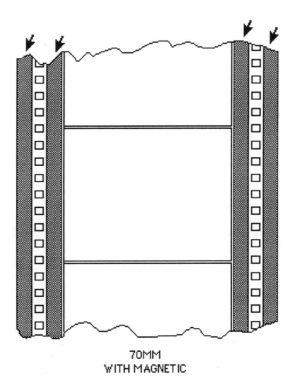

70MM
WITH MAGNETIC

Fig. 4.37. 70mm Magnetic Film with four separate audio channels.

The sound track on the 35-mm film stock is always an optical track (Fig. 4.38). The other three formats shown are magnetic stripe formats called **multistripe**. These are used to compile tracks during film mixes similar to the way that a two track is used for mixing a multitrack tape. The separate tracks on the multistripe are used for mixing narration, dialog, music and effects. This separation of tracks by category make it easy to change or update the mix. The most common format for mixing is four track. It is shown in the lower left of Fig. 4.38 and is the preferred format for mixing independent and student films.

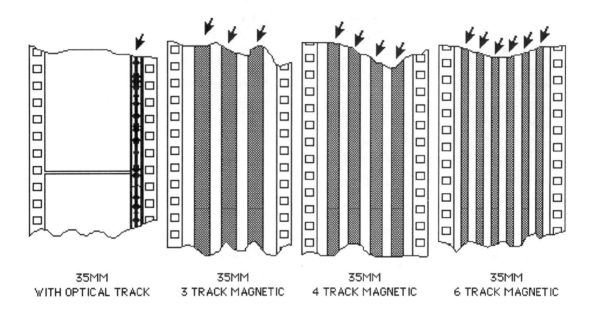

| 35MM | 35MM | 35MM | 35MM |
| WITH OPTICAL TRACK | 3 TRACK MAGNETIC | 4 TRACK MAGNETIC | 6 TRACK MAGNETIC |

Fig. 4.38. Four types of 35mm stock. The optical format is used for projection.

In contrast, 16-mm film stock is available in a variety of different configurations, as depicted in Fig. 4.39. Of these, 16-mm silent is used when no sound is required or when the sound is recorded simultaneously onto a separate deck. The 16-mm optical track is usually the final result of the 16-mm film process after all of the mixing and photographic processing has been completed. The 16-mm mag stripe is used when the sound must be recorded directly onto the film stock in the camera. Finally, 16-mm full coat, commonly called **mag stock**, is the same size as 16-mm stock, but is used for the re-recording and synchronization of sound to image (see chapter 8).

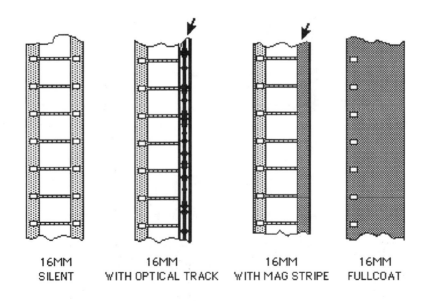

| 16MM | 16MM | 16MM | 16MM |
| SILENT | WITH OPTICAL TRACK | WITH MAG STRIPE | FULLCOAT |

Fig. 4.39 Four types of 16mm stock.

Super 8-mm film is available in both silent and magnetic stripe versions (Fig. 4.40).

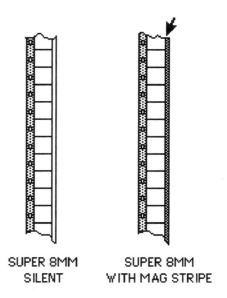

SUPER 8MM
SILENT

SUPER 8MM
WITH MAG STRIPE

Fig. 4.40. Two types of super 8mm stock.

Single System Recording

Some formats have the ability to record directly upon the stock at the same tine that the film is exposed. This is called **single system sound recording**, and requires stock with magnetic stripe. The sound is recorded directly through the camera onto the stripe simultaneously with the picture. The main disadvantages of this type of system are:

1. The sound and picture are recorded at different places on the film. This difference makes editing the picture and add sound effects, music, dialog and narration much more difficult.

2. The sound quality is inferior to the other type of recording system, discussed later.

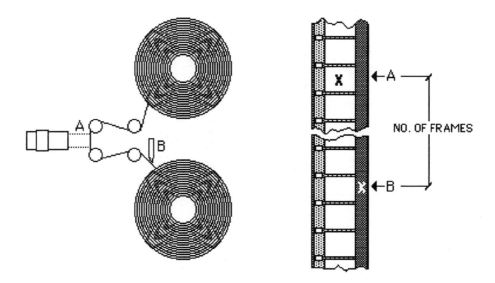

NO. OF FRAMES

Fig. 4.41. The concept behind single system recording.

Fig. 4.41 illustrates the concept behind single system recording. The diagram on the left represents a film camera, where (A) shows the placement of the image and (B) shows the location of the sound on the stock.

Double System Recording

The second way in which film sound is recorded is by a separate 1/4-inch tape recorder. The camera and the recorder are kept running in synchronization by one of two methods (discussed in Chapter 8). The separate and synchronous recording of sound and picture is called **double system sound recording**. Both sound and picture can each be manipulated and edited separately. Moreover, the sound quality is higher than can be obtained with single system recording. As a result, the double system is used exclusively in professional applications (Fig. 4.42).

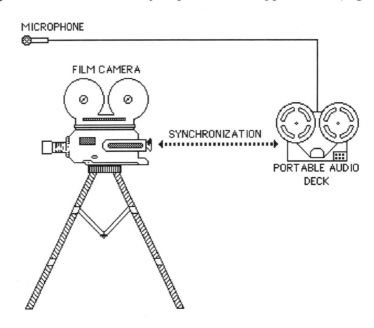

Fig. 4.42. The concept behind double system recording.

Printer's Sync

When a film is completed, the sound is placed ahead of the picture by a certain number of frames. (Frames and frame rates are explained in chapter 8.) This displacement keeps the sound track from interfering with the projection of the image. The placement of the exciter lamp for reading the sound track and the projection assembly compensates for this difference. This physical advancement of the sound to the picture is called the **printer's sync**, and the amount of frames of advance differs with each format.

Super 8-mm, the printer's sync is 18 frames, for 35 mm it's 20 frames, for 16 mm optical it's 26 frames and for 16-mm mag it's 28 frames.

D. TAPE SPEEDS

As we've seen, the speed at which an audio tape is recorded is a prime factor in determining the format of a specific tape. *The higher the speed of the tape, the better the signal quality.*

Tape speed is measured in **ips**, or **inches per second** and indicates the length of that tape pass a fixed point in one second. In practice, successively higher tape speeds are arrived at by doubling the previous speed. For example, the lowest tape speed is 1-7/8 ips. The next speed is twice that, or 3-3/4 ips, and the next four speeds are 7-1/2, 15, 30, and 60 ips:

1-7/8 ips	X2=	3-3/4 ips
3-3/4 ips	X2=	7-1/2 ips
7-1/2 ips	X2=	15 ips
15 ips	X2=	30 ips
30 ips	X2=	**60 ips**

Generally speaking, the line between professional and consumer equipment is at 15 ips Keep in mind that as the tape speed is doubled, the signal quality increases but the maximum recording time is halved.

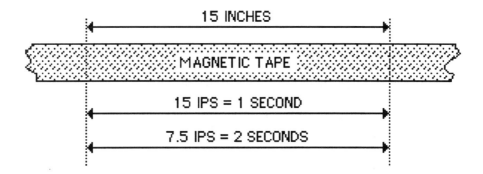

Fig. 4.43. Tape speed is measured

Shown in Fig. 4.44 is a chart that gives the common audio tape formats and their relation to tape width and speed ("LO-Q" stands for "low quality").

SPEED IN I.P.S

TAPE WIDTH IN INCHES	1 7/8	3 3/4	7 1/2	15	30
2				PRO 16 & 24 TK	PRO 16 & 24 TK
1				SEMI-PRO 16 PRO 8TK	SEMI-PRO 16 PRO 8TK
1/2			SEMI-PRO 8TK	SEMI-PRO 8 PRO 2TK	PRO 2TK
1/4	LO-Q OPEN REEL	LO-Q OPEN REEL	HOME 2, 4, 8TK	SEMI-PRO 2 TK	2TK DUBBING
1/8	AUDIO CASSETTES	AUDIO CASSETTES		AUDIO CASS DUBBING	AUDIO CASS DUBBING

Fig. 4.44. Comparison of tape speeds, tape width, and formats.

E. OPEN REEL SIZES

Other aspects of tape format are the size of the reel and the way tape is wound. Some open reel audio decks can accept a variety of reel sizes, others cannot. Audio tape intended for open reel machines, regardless of the width, is usually packaged in one of two ways. The most common method of tape packaging is called a **pancake**, which is essentially a 10-inch spool of tape wound around a plastic core, called a **hub** (Fig. 4.45).

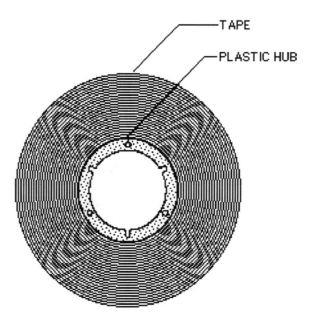

Fig. 4.45. A 10-1/2 inch pancake.

The hub has three uniformly spaced notches and holes, which we will discuss shortly (Fig. 4.46).

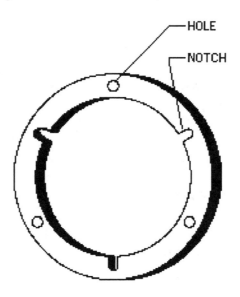

Fig. 4.46. A hub.

To place the tape on a deck for recording or playback, **flanges** are placed on either side of the tape. These are flat metal disks, usually 10-1/2 inches in diameter, which have holes and notches that correspond to those in the hub. Fig. 4.47 illustrates a pancake of tape, wound on a hub and sandwiched between two flanges.

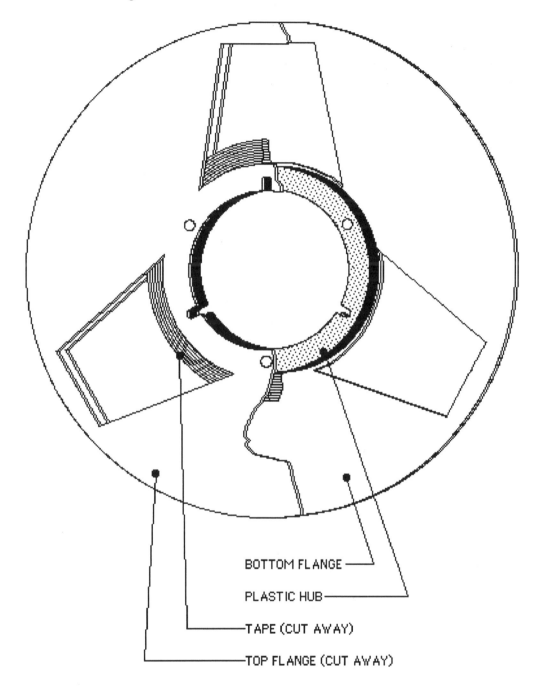

BOTTOM FLANGE

PLASTIC HUB

TAPE (CUT AWAY)

TOP FLANGE (CUT AWAY)

Fig. 4.47. View of a 10-1/2" reel.

NEVER pick up a pancake by its hub. If you do, chances are that the tape will fall off of the core and become unusable. The proper way to handle a pancake is to place a flange on top of it, match the holes and notches with those of the hub, and flip the entire affair over so that the pancake is horizontal and supported by the flange. Then place a second flange on top of the tape and immediately mount the entire package on a tape machine (Fig. 4.48).

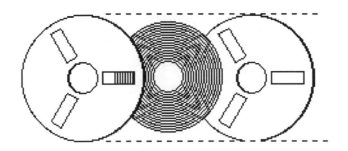

Fig. 4.48. Sandwiching a pancake between two flanges.

The holes in the flanges and hubs are made to receive special screws. When assembled, the unit forms a reel 10-1/2 inches in diameter. The 10-1/2-inch reels are an industry standard, although 14-inch reels are sometimes used in radio stations. Because the established industry tape speeds are 15 and 30 ips, smaller reels would be insufficient recording time and require frequent changing.

The reason that tapes are stored in the form of pancakes is that assembled 10-1/2-inch reels cost between $15 to $20 apiece. When you consider the volume of tape handled by a busy studio, the cost becomes prohibitive. Still, it's not unheard of for important master tapes to be stored on reels.

Smaller one-piece plastic reels are available for storing and editing (which we will discuss in the next chapter). These reels are 7 inches in diameter, and hold roughly half the tape from a pancake of 1/4-inch tape. They are not available for tape widths exceeding 1/4 inch (Fig. 4.49).

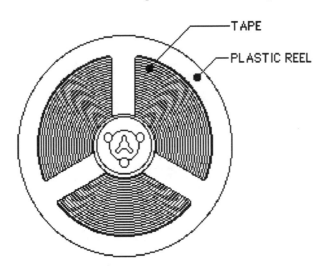

Fig. 4.49. A small hub plastic 7 inch reel.

The 7-inch plastic reels are available in two styles. Fig. 4.49 illustrates a **small hub** 7-inch reel; Fig. 4.50 depicts a **large hub** 7-inch reel. The larger hubs are used when less tape needs to be stored or worked with. The increased diameter of the center core reduces tape tension and handling problems. Compare both illustrations and take note of the difference in the size of the core in each.

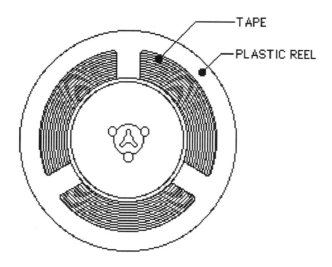

Fig. 4.50. A large hub plastic 7 inch reel.

There is yet a smaller reel that resembles both 7-inch reels but is 5 inches in diameter. This reel is generally used for film sound work on portable reel-to-reel recorders. It SHOULD NOT be used on a professional tape deck. The tensions set in professional tape decks might be too great for this size reel, and chances are good that the tape might become stretched or damaged.

Professional, semi-pro and some consumer decks that handle quarter-inch tape are made to accept both 10.5- and 7-inch reels. Notice that the reels in illustrations 4.34 and 4.35 both have a hole in the center with three equidistantl notches. These correspond to the protrusions on the **spindle** of the tape deck. The spindle can be made to lock the reel in place, preventing it from flying off the machine when in use.

The 10.5-inch reels require **hub adapters**. These have the identical size hole in their centers, and three protrusions that correspond to those on hubs and flanges. In general, the spindle locks the hub adapter to the deck, and the hub adapter locks the reel or flanges and tape (Fig. 4.51).

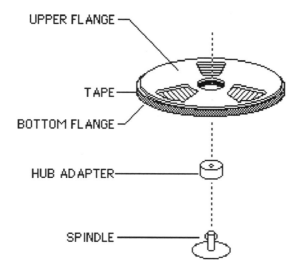

Fig. 4.51. Fitting a large reel with a hub adaptor.

F. WINDING METHODS

There are different methods for winding a tape onto 7- and 10.5-inch reels. If the tape is wound on the left (supply) reel (see The Tape Path in this chapter), the tape is said to be wound **heads out**. Tape wound on the right (take-up) reel is said to be wound **tails out**.

Professional engineers wind their tapes tails out. This helps prevent accidental damage to the tape because the recorded material will end before the tape runs out, creating a "cushion" of blank tape between the exterior of the tape and the last recorded segment.

When a tape is wound tails out, the tape is brought close to its beginning and the machine is put into "play" mode. The tape is left to wind itself slowly onto the reel. Winding the tape using the "fast forward" mode creates uneven tension in the tape, and some edges of the tape may protrude, called as **scattered wind**. Hitting them, even lightly, can damage the tape. Winding in the "play" mode creates a uniform, tight wind with no protruding edges. The left pancake in Fig. 4.52 has been wound in play mode; the right pancake was wound quickly, as evident from the scattered wind.

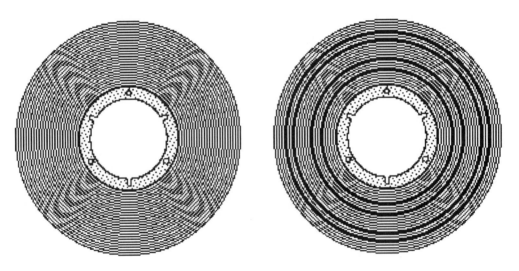

Fig. 4.52

Audio Tape Format Summary

Some studios place pre-printed stickers on the box in which the tape is to be stored. These indicate all aspects of the tape that another engineer or studio would need to know in order to work with the tape at a later date. A hypothetical example would look like the following, and serves as a good summary of tape format. Note that two different stickers might be used for the multitrack master tape and the mixed master tape (Figs. 4.53 and 4.54):

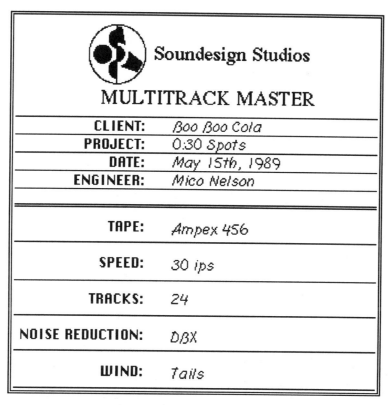

Fig. 4.53. A sticker for a multitrack tape box indicating format.

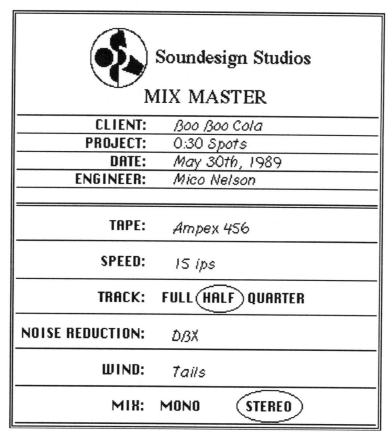

Fig. 4.54. A sticker for a mixed master tape box indicating format.

In review, tape format is determined by:

1. The head configuration (number of tracks and how they are recorded)

2. The speed at which the tape was recorded

3. The way the tape is wound

4. Noise reduction: whether it was used during the recording and, if so, what type

5. The type of tape used, which is a function of its bias. (Bias and other aspects of tape are discussed next.)

G. TAPE SPECIFICATIONS

Tape quality is directly proportional to its cost. NEVER try to save money by buying a cheaper brand of tape. Remember that audio is only as good as its weakest link, and absolutely nothing in the world — short of digital restoration, an extremely expensive process — can restore work lost because of poor quality tape.

There are several manufacturers of magnetic recording tape, and each makes different types of tape for different applications. Most tape machine makers recommend a particular brand of tape to be used with a particular model deck. This suggestion is often based on the particular properties of the tape, one of which is its response to bias.

Bias

A high-frequency current of 100 KHz or greater is combined with the audio signal during recording. This current is known as **bias current**. Bias improves the response of the tape but is too high in frequency for humans to hear or for the playback head to reproduce.

The amount of bias current generated by a tape machine is adjustable, but usually only by a technician. Too little current increases distortion; too much results in the loss of higher audio frequencies. Some types of tape work best with specific amounts of bias current, and for this reason some audio decks are sold with their bias current set for a particular brand of tape. In such cases the deck is said to be **biased** for that type of tape.

Playing Time

Knowing how much recording and playing time is available on a particular type of tape — the tape time — is always useful. Because reels are available in several different sizes, the amount of tape that can be loaded onto each one varies with the capacity of that particular reel.

Reel capacity and tape time depend on the thickness of the tape. Tape thickness is measured in thousandths of an inch, called **mils**. Tape is commonly available in thicknesses of 0.25, 0.5, 1.0 and 1.5 mils. High mil (thicker) tapes are less likely to breaking and stretching, but reduce the reel capacity and tape time. Conversely, the thinnest tape yields the highest tape time, but is much more susceptible to damage (Fig. 4.55).

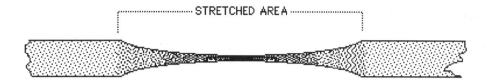

Fig. 4.55. Stretched audio tape.

Professional audio engineers tend to use 1.5 mil tape not only for its increased strength, but also to reduce the chances of **print through**. Print through refers to the transfer of magnetism from one layer of tape to the next and usually occurs when a tape has been stored for a considerable length of time. The result is two signals that play back at the same time, one much weaker than the other. In addition to using a thicker tape, winding it tails out reduces the chances of print through.

Fig. 4.56 indicates the maximum amount of tape time available using the most common tape thicknesses, reel sizes and speeds. Note the differences in the length of the tape as the thickness increases:

REEL SIZE (Inches)	TAPE THK (Mils)	TAPE LENGTH (Feet)	TAPE TIME (Minutes)			
			3.75 IPS	7.5 IPS	15 IPS	30 IPS
5	1.5	600	30	15	7.5	3.75
5	1.0	900	45	22.5	11.25	5.6
7	1.5	1,200	60	30	15	7.5
7	1.0	1,800	90	45	22.5	11.25
10.5	1.5	2,400	120	60	30	15
10.5	1.0	3,600	180	90	45	22.5

(ALL 5 AND 7 INCH REEL SIZES DENOTE SMALL HUB REELS ONLY)

Fig. 4.56. Tape specifications.

H. THE TAPE PATH

As mentioned, two main types of decks are commonly used in an audio production or post-production studio: multitrack and mastering decks. (Refer to chapters 2 and 3.) As you've seen, the multitrack acts as several independent tape recorders, each of which can record and play back at the same time. This is made possible by splitting several audio heads into separate tracks can be recorded independently of one another.

The mastering deck mixes the various tracks together into one or two tracks, which can, among other things, be broadcast; made into a phonographic record or compact disk; or copied to an audio or video cassette.

Both types of decks share some functions , and these are discussed in the following chapters.

The way audio tape passes through an audio deck is called the **tape path**. The reel on the operator's left is called the **supply reel**; the one on the operator's right is the **take-up reel**. As the tape moves from left to right, it travels through a series of tension-maintaining devices and guides. The area where all the recording and playback heads are mounted is called the **head block**.

111

The head block differs in mastering and multitrack decks in one important aspect: The middle head of a mastering deck is almost always used to record signals and is called the **record head**. On a multitrack deck, however, the middle head is called the **sync head** and can both playback and record signals. Such simultaneous recording and playback is called selective synchronization and is discussed later in this chapter. The following table gives the order in which the heads are arranged on both types of decks going from left to right:

Head Arrangements on Multitrack and Mastering Tape Decks

Mastering Decks	*Multitrack Decks*
Erase	Erase
Record	Sync
Playback	Playback

The exact tape path on an open reel deck varies from machine to machine but, aside from minor deviations, is essentially be the same. The example shown in Fig. 4.57 is the most common type of tape path and is called the **open loop transport system**.

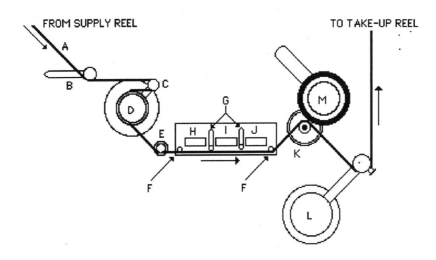

Fig. 4.57. Typical ATR tape path.

In Fig. 4.57, (A) is the tape and (B) is a **tension arm**. Tension must be maintained throughout the tape path to insure proper and consistent contact with the heads at all times. (C) is another tension arm, mounted on the **inertia idler** (D). The inertia idler is coupled to a heavy flywheel within the machine, which helps to maintain the tape's speed and tension. (E) is a **rolling guide**, which positions the tape properly over the heads and (F) refers to the **fixed guides**. The **tape lifters** (G) move in towards the head block and put the tape in contact with the heads when the machine is in play mode. In fast modes (i.e., fast forward and reverse) they lift the tape away from the heads to prevent overloads and head wear. (H) is the **erase head**, (I) is the **record or sync head** (depending on whether the machine is a multitrack or mastering deck), and (J) is the **playback head**. The **capstan** (K) is coupled to the drive motors. THe capstan spins regardless of the mode the machine is in and helps to start and drive the tape without jerking that can stretch and ruin the tape. The **puck**, or **pinch roller** (M), functions in conjunction with the lifters; only in the play mode does it move down and press the tape to the capstan's surface. The **brake arm**, or safety switch (L), maintains the tension and lets the transport function when in the up position. In the event that the tape breaks or runs out, the arm will drop and the machine will stop running. This also prevents any tape from spilling from the supply reel should the tape break.

I. ADDITIONAL FEATURES: MASTERING DECKS

Mastering and multitrack decks have many features in common. The functions that each performs and they way in which they are operated are essentially the same.

Monitor Selection

The **monitor selection** is analogous to the "source" and "tape" controls found on almost every cassette deck. In this case the monitor selection control found on most mastering decks will probably be marked in the same way (Fig. 4.58).

Fig. 4.58. An ATR source/tape switch.

When the deck is switched to "source", the signal playing back from the deck will be exactly the same signal fed into it. In other words, you are listening to the source. A simplified diagram illustrating this concept would look like this (Fig. 4.59):

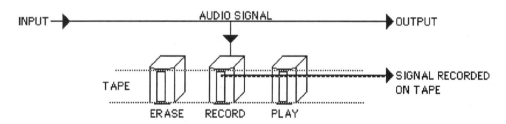

Fig. 4.59. In source mode, the listener hears the signal applied at the input of the ATR.

In principle, the incoming audio signal is "split" and goes to both the record head of the deck and to the output. Recording while in "source" will let you listen to the mix as it's being performed. You will not, however, be hearing the result of what is being recorded on the tape.

Switching the monitor selection to "tape" will let you hear the signal being played back from the tape as it is being recorded. In other words, you are listening to the tape. An illustration of this principle look like this (Fig. 4.60):

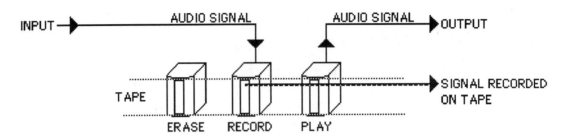

Fig. 4.60. In tape mode, the listener hears the signal as it comes from the tape via the playback head.

Note that in the "tape" mode the audio signals are fed into the deck, recorded on tape and picked up slightly later by the playback head. This will cause a slight delay between the signal being recorded and the signal heard.

In addition to switching between the monitored source, this control sometimes (depending on the deck's design) will also switch the deck's VU meters to reflect what is coming into the deck as well as what is being played from the tape. Ideally, both readings should be the same.

Transport Functions

Controlling the tape's motion through the deck is accomplished by using the **transport controls** (Fig. 4.61).

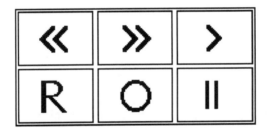

Fig. 4.61. A typical transport control for an ATR. Clockwise from the upper left: Rewind, fast forward, play; pause, stop, record.

These controls are usually marked with the standard symbols shown, although some manufacturers, for aesthetic reasons, may choose to use all, some or none of these. The symbols represent the following (Fig. 4.62):

≪ = REWIND

≫ = FAST FORWARD

❯ = PLAY

R = RECORD

O = STOP

‖ = PAUSE

Fig. 4.62

114

When in the deck is in **rewind**, the tape lifters move outwards and lift the tape away from the head block to prevent overloads and excessive head wear. Simultaneously, the pinch roller functions in conjunction with the lifters and moves away from the capstan's surface. The tape moves quickly onto the supply reel. The same action occurs during **fast forward**, except that then the tape is wound onto the take-up reel.

Pressing **play** causes the tape lifters to move in towards the head block and puts the surface of the tape in contact with all of the heads. Simultaneously, the pinch roller moves inward, pressing the tape against the capstan's surface.

The **record** button works in conjunction with the track record controls. If either or both of the track record buttons are depressed, pressing record will erase any material previously recorded on the corresponding track and record any signals being supplied to the deck. The record control works in conjunction with the play button. Both must be pressed for the tape to move and for the machine to record. When the deck is recording, an LED or light will usually turn on or flash, indicating to the operator that the deck is either recording or ready to record.

The **pause** control is usually found on older decks only. It is used most often with the record control. Pressing both record and pause will place the machine in "record ready," and pressing play will start the tape moving and the deck recording.

On some decks there is also an **edit** button (not shown in Fig. 4.61) which works either by itself or with the play control. In either case, the principle is exactly the same: The supply reel, capstan, lifters and pinch roller all work as in play mode. However, the take-up reel motor and brake arm are defeated, and the tape, after passing over the heads and through the capstan and pinch roller, falls onto the floor. This is an extremely useful feature for use when cutting and removing a large section of tape. This process, called editing, is explained in the next chapter.

Counter

The tape counter lets you find a given section of tape. Counters work in different ways, but all essentially provide a numerical display, indicating specific points on the tape.

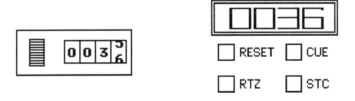

Fig. 4.63. Two types of tape counters. The one on the left is an older type of mechanical counter.

Fig. 4.63 illustrates two types of displays. The counter on the left is a mechanical version found on older machines. Its numbers are printed on interlocked rotating wheels. Pressing the button to the left of the display resets the numbers to zero. The electronic display on the right works in conjunction with newer microprocessing circuits found in more recent machines. The "reset" control again also all of the numbers to zero. The microprocessing circuits allow other functions to be integrated. Depending on its cost and sophistication, a deck may automatically return to "0000"

115

by pressing a single button. In Fig. 4.63, this is marked "RTZ" which stands for "Return To Zero." One or more "cue" points may be entered. For example, pressing "Cue" at 0036 would mark that point of the tape for the machine to return to. Pressing "STC", or "Send To Cue," would instruct the machine to go to that number. This feature is a tremendous time saver for an operator who, for whatever reason, must shuttle between two points.

Track Record

As mentioned, the **track record** controls work in conjunction with the record control (Fig. 4.64):

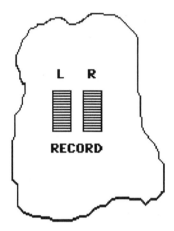

Fig. 4.64. Individual record buttons for left and right.

When either or both buttons are depressed, the corresponding track or tracks will be erased if the machine is put into record. Usually an LED or light will turn on or flash, indicating to the operator that the machine is recording.

Reel Size

All tape decks are preset for different tape tensions. Because of their reduced diameter and mass, smaller reels require less tension than larger ones. Almost all decks allow the operator to change the tension with a switch that is usually labeled **reel size**. As we've discussed, the standard reel sizes used in audio production and post-production are 7 and 10.5 inches. Using the "large" setting (i.e., 10.5 inch) with a 7-inch reel may cause the deck to stretch or break the tape. By the same token, setting the reel size switch to "small" with a 10.5-inch reel may cause the machine to stop too slowly and spill the tape (Fig. 4.65).

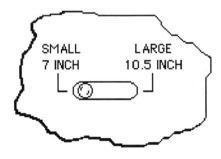

Fig. 4.65. Reel size selector on an ATR.

116

Speed Selection

As we've seen, the standard tape speeds are 7.5, 15, and 30 ips. Some manufacturers may include all three speeds, others only two. Note that on some decks "slow" may be considered 15 ips, and on others it may be considered 7.5 ips (Fig. 4.66).

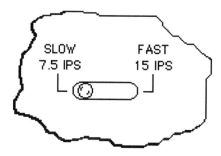

Fig. 4.66 Tape speed selector on an ATR.

Pitch Control

Some decks may include a **pitch control**. Rotating the pitch control will adjusts the speed at which the machine is set. This is a useful feature to have because, with it, you can record the same instrument twice, with one track slightly out of tune. Apart from creating effects, it is sometimes used (sparingly) to speed up or slow down a piece of music or commercial to an exact time, or to record an out-of-tune instrument with pre-recorded instruments. The pitch control may take several different forms, the simplest of which is illustrated in Fig. 4.67:

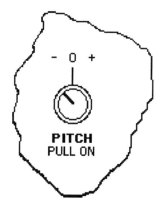

Fig. 4.67 Pitch (speed) control on an ATR.

Some pitch controls appear as shown in Fig. 4.68, but all work in much the same way:

117

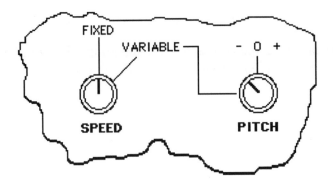

Fig. 4.68. Another type of pitch control on an ATR.

More sophisticated decks let the variations in speed be controlled by an external source by setting the speed or pitch control to "external" (this is described in Chapter 8):

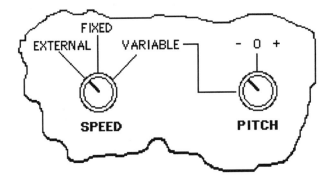

Fig. 4.69. A type of pitch control on an ATR that allows external speed control.

Remote Control

Many decks allow for some or all functions to be governed by remote control. More refined machines will allow for remote control of almost every functions. This is extremely useful, as it allows for the deck to be away from an operator, giving more physical space in which to work. The remote control is plugged into the deck via a special multi-pin plug and cable (Fig. 4.70).

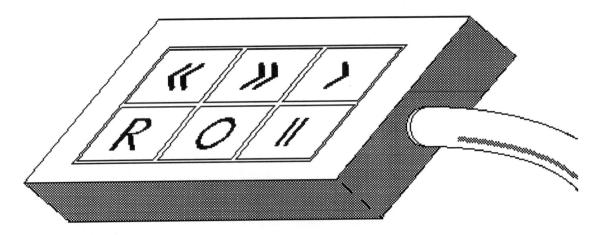

Fig. 4.70. A remote transport control for an ATR.

J. SELECTIVE SYNCHRONIZATION

As mentioned in Chapter 3, the process of adding new tracks to existing ones on a multitrack deck is called **overdubbing**. However, when overdubbing, a problem arises when trying to keep everything in time.

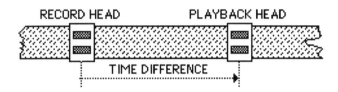

Fig. 4.71. Time difference between the record and playback heads on an ATR.

The space differential between the record and playback heads causes a time lag. For example, if an existing track, say track one, is enhanced by recording a complimentary section on track two, track one will be heard on the playback head, and at the same time track two will be recorded on the record head. This condition is called being **out of sync**. To overcome this problem, a system called **selective synchronization**, or **selsync**, was developed.

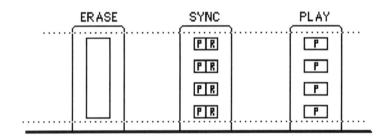

Fig. 4.72. View of the heads in a multitrak ATR's tape path.

In this system, a sync head (instead of the record head) is used on all multitrack decks. Basically, this head can switch each of its poles on individual tracks to either record or play, eliminating the time lag problem caused by the different location of play and record heads. In this way previously recorded material is heard at the same time that new material is recorded.

K. ADDITIONAL FEATURES: MULTITRACK DECKS

The three stages of recording, as described in Chapter 3, are called basic tracks, overdubbing and mixing. The most obvious differences between a mastering and multitrack deck are determined by their function. The multitrack deck "gathers" all the tracks; the mastering deck combines them. For this very reason, multitrack decks have some fundamental differences.

Monitor Selection and Record Mode

The first difference is that multitrack decks have three, not two, monitoring selections called **recording modes**. These work in conjunction with the track record switches in a similar manner to mastering decks. In some cases the record mode control may be replaced by the functions of the individual track record controls.

Each mode lets the operator listen to each head of the multitrack deck, with the exception of the first mode, called **input**. In a manner similar to mastering decks, input routes the signal both to the output of the deck and to the sync head.

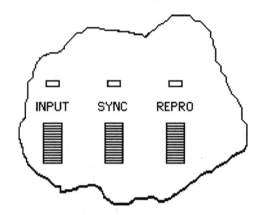

Fig. 4.73. Controls for the three monitor modes on a multitrack ATR.

When the deck is in input mode, the operator will not hear any tracks pre-recorded on the tape, but will instead hear only the incoming, or "source" signal (Fig. 4.74):

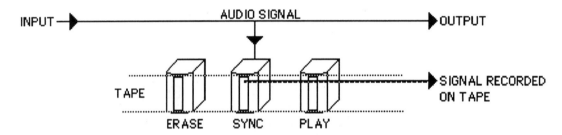

Fig. 4.74. In "input" mode the operator hears what is being applied to the ATR. (Compare this illustration with the one shown in 4.59.)

The input mode is used during the recording of basic tracks.

The next mode, **sync**, lets the operator monitor recorded signals on the tape played back through the sync head (Fig. 4.75):

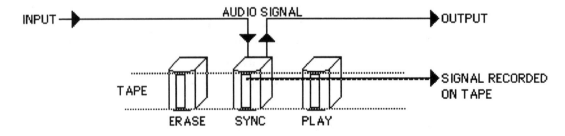

Fig. 4.75. In "sync" mode the operator hears either what is being applied to the ATR or what is being played by the sync head depending on the record status of that track. (Compare this illustration with the one shown in 4.60.)

The sync mode is used during the overdubbing process. How the tape is monitored is dependent on what tracks are being recorded. For example, let's assume that we are overdubbing on track two, and material exists on track one. In sync mode, track one will play through the sync head. However, if track two is put into record, we will listen to the *input* of track two, and the sync head will act as a *record* head for track two. When the overdub is completed, and track two is taken out of record, the sync head will act as a playback head for track two. Track one continues to be played back.

In this way the sync head allows simultaneous use of two modes at once: Track one may be considered to me in "tape" mode, while track two acts in "source" mode.

The **repro** or **play** mode routes the output of the deck to the play head (Fig. 4.76):

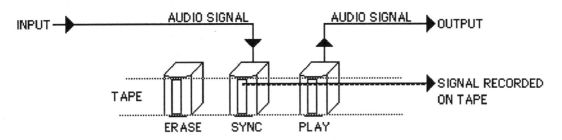

Fig. 4.76. Play mode on a multitrack ATR.

Repro mode is used to play back the multitrack tape during a mix.

Transport Functions

The transport functions of a multitrack deck are essentially the same as those of the mastering deck. Some manufacturers include the edit mode on multitrack decks as a convenient feature, but it is rarely used. For more details on this mode, refer to the transport descriptions of the mastering deck.

Counter

The counter found on multitrack decks is identical to those of mastering decks. Again, for details, refer to the counter descriptions of the mastering deck.

Track Record

On less expensive decks, the track record functions may appear as a group of on-off switches. When one or more of these switches are pressed, the main record indicator will light up or flash. Pressing both record and play will erase the corresponding track.

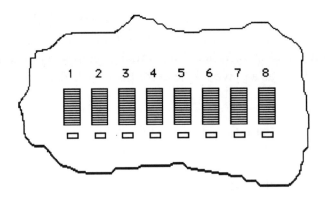

Fig. 4.77. Individual track record controls for the separate tracks of an multitrack ATR.

These controls also have an effect on the monitoring of tracks: In sync mode, the signal normally heard is the one on the tape. But pressing the track record function will monitor the input (source) signal being fed to that track. When in repro or play mode, depressing the track record will not interfere with what is being heard from the tape. However, if the deck is put into record, the signal heard will originate from either the sync head or the play head, depending on the design of the deck.

On larger and more expensive decks, the track record functions (as previously discussed) may replace the record mode control altogether. This is accomplished by allowing the operator to select the status, or record mode, of each individual track (Fig. 4.78).

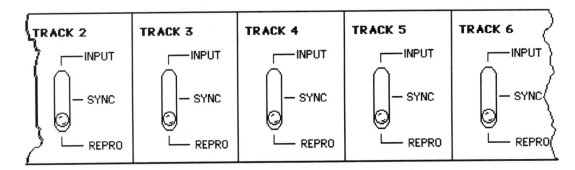

Fig. 4.78. Mode controls for individual tracks as found on a more expensive multitrack ATR.

Reel Size

On 1/4-inch multitrack decks this control works the same way as on mastering decks. Keep in mind that smaller reels hold only 1/4-inch tape and, as a result, decks using tape widths of a 1/2-inch or greater omit this control.

Speed Selection

The speed selection control works the same way as on mastering decks.

Pitch Control

Again, the pitch control also works the same way as on mastering decks.

122

Remote Control

Less expensive multitrack decks use a type of remote control that operates only the transport functions. As a deck increases in complexity and price, many have an **auto locator** that allows for the remote control of every function except (if it's included) the edit function.

L. MAINTENANCE

Cleaning

Magnetic tape passing over any surface for even a short amount of time will shed some of the oxide particles embedded in its surface. These can build up on heads and other items in the tape path that contact the tape's surface. The components, on a microscopic level, begin to deteriorate. As more particles pass over the surfaces, miniature grooves are cut into the metal. These grooves shed more magnetic particles, which trap more oxide, and a vicious cycle builds.

Oxide buildup is a natural part of the recording process. Unfortunately, it not only can destroy your decks but, at the very least, rob them of their ability to record and reproduce high frequencies.

Cleaning is an essential part of routine and preventive maintenance that will prolong the life of recording decks and the tapes they use.

Head cleaner is used to clean all metal parts of the tape path. Isopropyl (rubbing) alcohol is used to clean all plastic and rubber components. NEVER use head cleaner on any plastic and rubber parts.Formulated to dissolve oxide, it also dissolves plastic and rubber. If head cleaner is not available, then isopropyl alcohol will suffice to clean all parts of the tape path.

When cleaning the tape path, dip ordinary Q-Tips or specially made cleaning swabs into the solution. Shake off any excess liquid and rub the swab vigorously across the surfaces of the tape path that come into contact with the tape. In general, start with the heads, using one swab per head (Fig. 4.79). As a swab turns brown, replace it with a fresh one until the swab come away clean. This indicates that all the oxide has been removed. Repeat this process for each lifter, guide and roller.

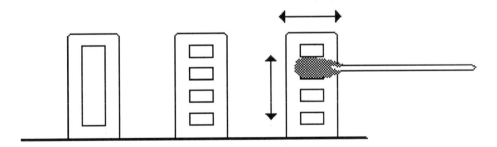

Fig. 4.79. Cleaning the heads in a tape path.

The pinch roller and capstan can be cleaned by using a slightly different technique: Any reels or tape should be removed from the deck. The brake arm is put into the "up" position so that the capstan starts rotating, and the swab is pressed against the capstan's surface. Keep using swabs until they no longer turn brown (Fig. 4.80).

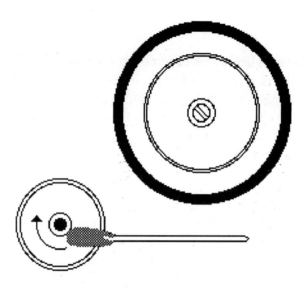

Fig. 4.80. Cleaning the capstan.

When the capstan is clean, press "play" or "edit" (with the brake arm still up), and press a swab into the area where the pinch roller and the capstan meet. Do this in such a way that you push into the direction of rotation. The idea is not to have the swab pulled into the pinch roller and capstan (Fig. 4.81).

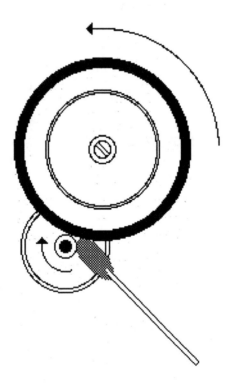

Fig. 4.81. Cleaning the pinch roller.

Clean each deck before each session, every few hours during each session and at the end of every session. There is no such thing as "over cleaning" a deck. The improvement in sound quality and the headaches you'll save make it worth taking the time to clean the equipment.

Demagnetizing

Heads will build up and store the magnetism from tapes just as they build up magnetic oxide particles. Heads that have built up enough magnetic charge can work "in reverse," partially erasing recorded tape, starting with high frequencies and erasing progressively lower frequencies as the magnetic charge increases. Magnetized heads will make a tape sound muddy, robbing it of its brilliance and "zing." Fortunately, an inexpensive device called a **demagnetizer** removes any magnetism from the heads and tape path (Fig. 4.82).

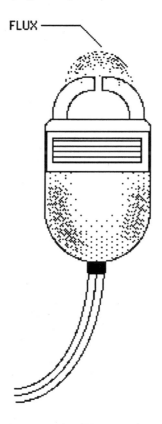

FLUX

Fig. 4.82. A head de-magnetizer.

The demagnetization procedure is simple:

1. TURN THE DECK POWER OFF!!! If the deck is on while you are demagnetizing the heads, the surge in current within the deck caused by the added magnetic flux could blow out the deck's output electronics.

2. Turn on the demagnetizer while holding it three feet or more away from the deck, and *slowly* move it in towards the head and back out (Fig. 4.83). Be careful not to touch the head or you may scratch and ruin it. Repeat the process for each head and for all metal components in the tape path.

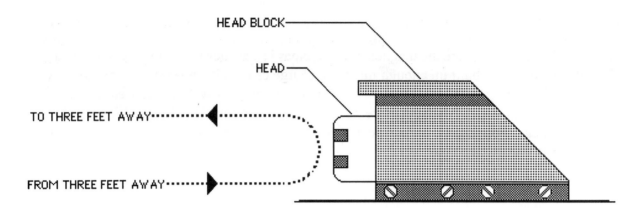

Fig. 4.83. Motion for de-magnetizing the heads of an ATR.

Calibration

Electronic components, by their nature, heat up when they are turned on. As their temperature increases, they allow more current to pass. As more current passes through them, their temperature rises.

Because of this cycle, the way a deck records and reproduces will change slightly with time. Adjustment of the controls that affect the operation of a deck is called **calibration** and is required from time to time, usually before the start of each session. In most cases the recording engineer will calibrate each deck. Larger facilities may employ technicians for whom calibration is part of their duties.

Calibration, in concept, is a relatively easy chore. Almost all decks have small openings in which a non-magnetic (for example, plastic) screwdriver is inserted to turn controls called **trimpots** (Fig. 4.84). Adjustment of these controls will change the operational characteristics of the deck.

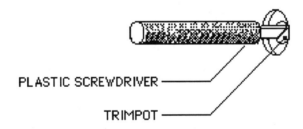

PLASTIC SCREWDRIVER

TRIMPOT

Fig. 4.84. Adjustment for calibration of an ATR.

The idea behind calibrating a deck is to first adjust it so that it plays back all frequencies at 0 VU. This is called **reproduction calibration**. Once the deck has been adjusted and is known to reproduce correctly, it must be adjusted so that it records all frequencies at 0 VU. This is called **record calibration**. Occasionally, the VU meters may also need adjusting.

A general calibration procedure follows below. However, most decks will deviate from this procedure in some way. If you're unsure of how to proceed, get detailed instructions from the dealer from whom the deck was purchased, a qualified technician or the deck's manufacturer.

1. The reproduction calibration must be done first . This requires a standard **magnetic reference tape**. This is a carefully prerecorded tape on which tones of different frequencies are recorded at a laboratory . These frequencies are recorded at exactly 0 VU and each lasts for about 15 to 60 seconds.

2. The tape path and heads should be cleaned and demagnetized to insure optimum performance. The reference tape is put onto the deck.

3. Assuming the deck is a multitrack recorder, the playback electronics for both the sync and repro (or play) modes must each be calibrated.

4. First, put the deck into sync mode and set the tape to play at the 1-KHz frequency. Then adjust the sync play-level trimpot until the meter reads 0 VU. This step should be repeated for every channel.

5. Then adjust the deck's meters, again for each channel, by patching an oscillator through the console and setting the console meter to read 0 VU. Read the line output of the console using a measuring device called a volt-ohm meter, or VOM. The reading you obtain with the VOM will depend on the line level output of the console.

6. Next plug the same console line output directly into every channel of the deck. Each meter should read 0 VU, and the reading of the VOM, again taken for each channel, should match the reading obtained from the console. If any of the deck's meter readings do not correspond, these should be adjusted with the appropriate trimpot.

7. The reference tape is played so that the frequencies played range from 8 to 10 KHz. Adjust the appropriate sync EQ trimpots, which may be labeled "sync hi EQ," until each meter reads 0 VU. This step is repeated for every channel.

8. If the deck has trimpots for other frequency ranges, play the tape so that the appropriate frequencies are heard, and adjust the corresponding trimpots. For example, if there are trimpots labeled "sync mid EQ," use the midrange frequencies on the reference tape. If there are trimpots labeled "sync lo EQ," use the low frequencies on the reference tape. This step is repeated for every channel.

9. Put the deck into repro (play) mode and repeat steps four through eight .Make the same adjustments for each trimpot labeled "repro".

10 Play the reference and wind it tails out. Remove it from the deck and carefully store it.

11. The deck is now adjusted to reproduce all frequencies at 0 VU, and we can now adjust the record calibration. The first step is to put the deck into input mode.

12. The VU meters for the input electronics are checked using the same procedure described in step five.

M. NAB EQUALIZATION

Equalization refers to a deliberate adjustment of the amplitudes of different frequencies. The equalization (EQ) process occurs in both the record and playback electronics of a tape deck. Specifically, during playback, there is a 6-dB per octave decrease of output of the reproduced frequency, while a similar decrease is imposed on progressively higher frequencies as they are recorded. The American standard of EQ is called NAB. The European standard is called IEC, and the two are incompatible. Shown below is the NAB equalization curve (Fig. 4.85).

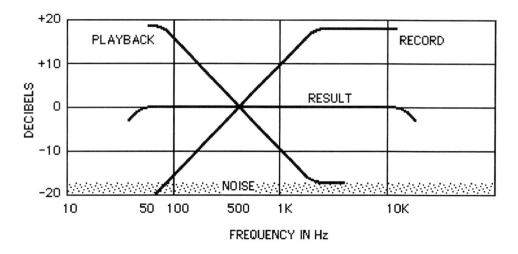

Fig. 4.85. The NAB equalization curve.

5
SIGNAL ROUTING AND PROCESSING

A. EIA STANDARD SIZES

Almost all professional audio equipment and most of the equipment discussed in this chapter can be **rack mounted**. Standard sizes have been developed for equipment and mounting hardware that let you install the equipment into a **rack cabinet** or similar enclosure. A parallel pair of **rails** mounted 19 inches apart are pre-drilled to accept screws. The spacing of the rails and the holes correspond with holes in the front panels of the equipment (Fig. 5.1).

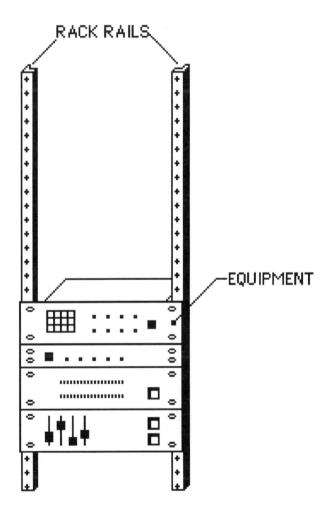

Fig. 5.1 Equipment mounted on EIA standard rails.

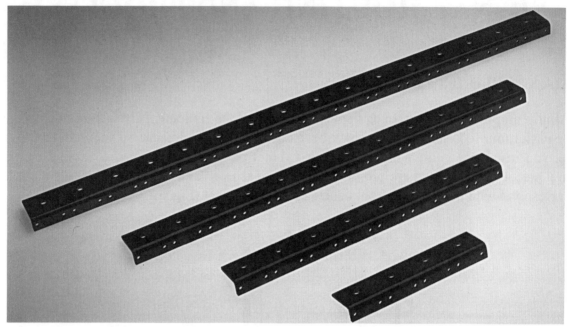

Fig. 5.2. Standard EIA rack rails cut to specific lengths. The short side of each rail with the double holes is intended for mounting equipment. The long side is attached to the interior of a cabinet or other suitable opening.
(Photo Courtesy of Middle Atlantic Audio, Inc.)

This arrangement is often called the **EIA standard** rack mounting system. Equipment made to these specifications is always 19 inches wide and multiples of 1-3/4 inches high (Fig. 5.3).

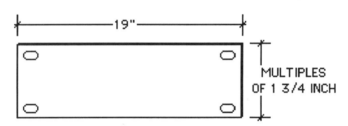

Fig. 5.3. All EIA equipment mounts in multiples of 1 3/4 inch heights.

A piece of equipment that is 1-3/4 inches high is said to be **one unit** high. Two units would equal 3-1/2 inches, three units would equal 5-1/4 inches and so on.

All signal processing devices that are physically separate from the studio's console are referred to as **outboard equipment**.

B. PATCH BAYS AND SIGNAL ROUTING

In coping with the complexities and variations of signal routing options in a studio, a device called a **patch bay** is used to help the operator or engineer easily change signal paths. This technology was adopted from telephone standards and resembles a rack-mounted version of the old-style telephone operator's switchboard. Photo Fig. 5.4 illustrates one of the more common types of patch bay known as a 1/4-inch type.

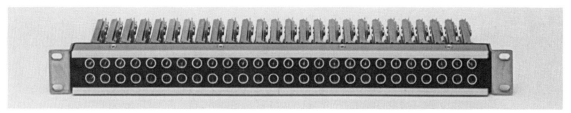

Fig. 5.4. A 1/4-inch patch bay.
(Photo Courtesy of ADC Telecommunications, Inc.)

The easiest way to envision the function of a patch bay is to imagine the rear panels of all the equipment in a studio brought to a single location, the patch bay itself. In effect, most or all of the equipment in a studio, including the console, is connected to this device:

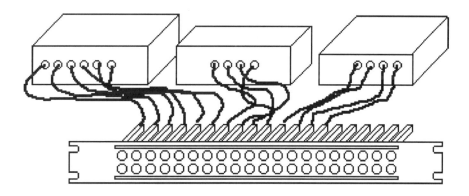

Fig. 5.5. Patch bay wired to equipment.

When components in a studio are wired directly to each other without passing through a patch bay, they are said to be **hard wired**. This arrangement makes it almost impossible to change or modify the signal path. In contrast, the patch bay allows for nearly endless variations of signal paths.

The holes seen in the front of the patch bay are jacks into which plugs are inserted. A simplified side view of the top and bottom row looks like the following (Fig. 5.6):

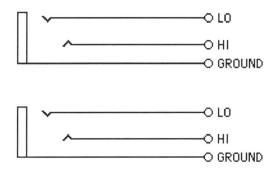

Fig. 5.6. Simplified side view of the top and bottom rows of a balanced "non-normaling" patch bay.

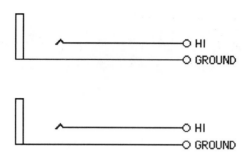

Fig. 5.7. Simplified side view of the top and bottom rows of an unbalanced non-normaling patch bay.

The example shown in Fig. 5.6 is typical of a *balanced* patch bay configuration; Fig. 5.7 is typical of an *unbalanced* patch bay configuration. The plugs inserted into the jacks are configured in the same way as the jacks so that the positions of the contacts on the jacks correspond to a matching area of each plug. Thus, each type of patch bay will have its own type of plug and **patch cord**, depending on the type of signal — balanced or unbalanced — being carried.

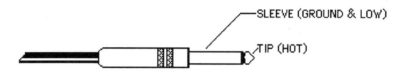

Fig. 5.8. One end of an unbalanced patch cord.

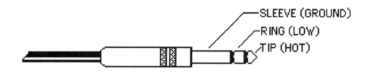

Fig. 5.9. One end of a balanced patch cord.

The example shown in Fig. 5.8 is a typical plug for an unbalanced patch-bay configuration; Fig. 5.9 shows a typical plug for a balanced patch-bay configuration. In Figs. 5.6 and 5.7, the jacks are shown like terminals; that is, terminating the signal connection. In practice, however, a signal does not terminate at just one jack but is connected to (and therefore available from) several jacks. To avoid having to manually route signals from jack to jack, spring-like prongs within each jack pass the signal from one jack to the next unless interrupted by the insertion of a plug. This type of connection is said to be **normaled**:

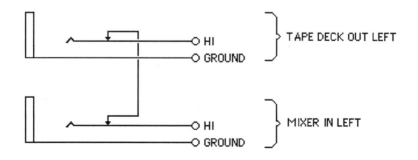

Fig. 5.10. Simplified side view of the top and bottom rows of an unbalanced normaling patch bay.

132

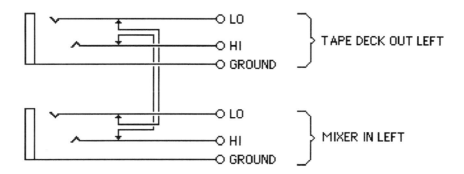

Fig. 5.11. Simplified side view of the top and bottom rows of a balanced non-normaling patch bay.

Figs. 5.10 and 5.11 show normaled configurations for unbalanced and balanced patch bays, respectively. In both cases, a signal will pass from the tape deck to the mixer through the spring contacts. When a plug is inserted, the contacts are lifted away from the spring points, and the signal path is interrupted (Figs. 5.12 and 5.13):

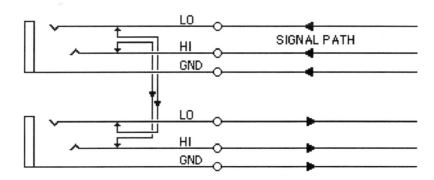

Fig. 5.12. Signal path between two normaled jacks in a balanced patch bay.

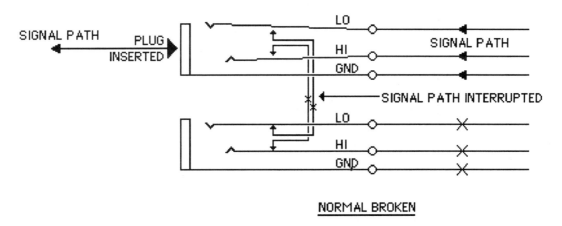

Fig. 5.13 The same signal path shown in 5.12 interrupted by the insertion of a patch cord into the top jack.

With the above explanation in mind, a **patch** between two items in a studio might look like this:

133

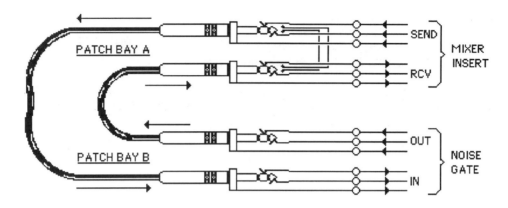

Fig. 5.14. Side view of a patch.

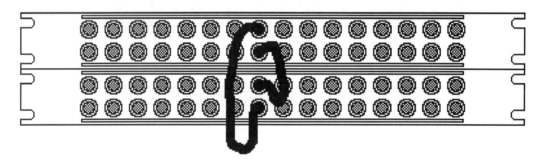

Fig. 5.15. Front view of a patch.

Other Patch Bay Features

Note that in each diagram (and in every properly configured patch bay) *the outputs always appear on the top row, and inputs always appear on the bottom row directly below the outputs.* In addition, every input and output is labeled by a slide-in paper strip called a **designation strip** (Fig. 5.16):

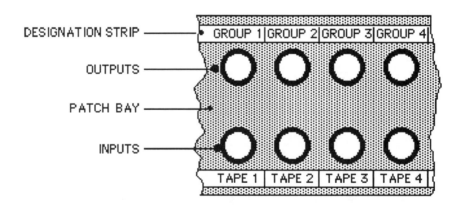

Fig. 5.16. The designation strip on a patch bay indicated where equipment is connected.

In addition, several multiple jacks may be wired together; called a **mult**. A mult allows the engineer to patch several signal sources together in much the same way that "Y" cords are used to combine signals. In some cases a mult, may be used to distribute a signal to several destinations (Fig. 5.17):

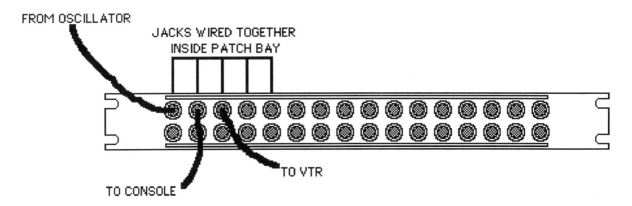

Fig. 5.17. Example of a mult.

Types of Patch Bays

There are several different types of patch bays, each designed to serve a particular kind and complexity of wiring and conform to the physical space available for installation, as well as budget. With few exceptions, patch bays can be rack mounted.

The least expensive patch bays are almost always unbalanced. They are usually one or two rack units high, and generally used in consumer installations like home studios. These might contain RCA or 1/4-inch jacks on both the front and rear panels, and let the user connect the bay into the system simply by plugging the cables into the back panel.

The most common type of professional patch bay uses a variety of 1/4-inch connectors on the front panel. Each jack terminates at the rear of the bay in a series of small terminals (Fig. 5.18), which must be soldered to the cables. The installation of this type of patch bay is best left to a technician or specialist.

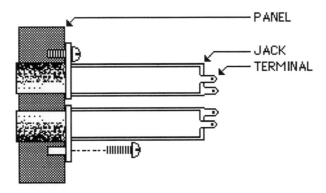

Fig. 5.18 Cross section of a 1/4-inch patch bay (not to scale).

Yet another type of professional patch bay is the **bantam**. Bantam patch bays are always balanced and are used where the physical space available for the patch bays' installation is limited (Fig. 5.19).

135

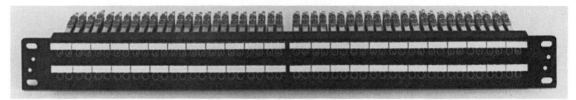

Fig. 5.19. A bantam patch bay.
(Photo Courtesy of ADC Telecommunications, Inc.)

Bantam jacks are roughly half the size of 1/4-inch jacks. Consequently one bantam bay holds twice as many connections. For example, a one-rack-unit bay holds 96 jacks for a bantam type and 48 or 52 standard professional 1/4-inch jacks (Fig. 5.20).

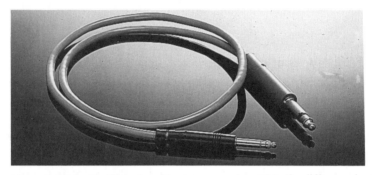

Fig. 5.20. A conversion patch cord, fitted with 1/4-inch and bantam connectors. Note the difference in size between the two. (Photo Courtesy of ADC Telecommunications, Inc.)

C. EQUALIZATION

Equalization (EQ) generally refers to the alteration of sound quality by amplifying or attenuating selected frequencies. Bear in mind that the development of good equalization techniques take years of practice. Yet, EQ is the one of the most crucial parts of engineering. Because it can be one of the weakest links in the audio chain, it can make or break an audio program. Yet the theory of EQ is simple: The audio signal is separated into different frequencies, each individually amplified or attenuated. Once processed, the frequencies are recombined to form one signal.

One equalizes a signal for usually one of two reasons: First is to *enhance* the signal, or to simply make it sound "better". The idea is much the same as when you turn up the bass and/or treble control on your stereo system. Second is to re-create a specific sound in a given situation. For example, a post-production engineer might be working on a scene in which two people are sitting in a car. To re-create the sound of music and speech as heard from a car radio, he would lower, raise, and/or eliminate specific frequencies of "normally" recorded audio until the desired result was obtained.

A signal is usually equalized for one of two reasons: The first is to *enhance* the signal, to simply make it sound better. The idea is much the same as when you adjust the bass or treble control on your stereo system. The second reason is to recreate a specific sound for a given situation. For example, a post-production engineer might be working on a scene in which two people are sitting in a car. To recreate the sound of music and speech from a car radio, the engineer would lower, raise or eliminate specific frequencies of "normally" recorded audio to reach the desired result.

To determine which frequencies must be altered, refer to Fig. 1.10. The figure shows, for example, that the upper range of bass frequencies extends to around 200 Hz. Therefore, if a bass sound must be made "brighter," the frequencies comprising the bass sounds should be amplified.

Shelving EQ

In the following examples of different EQ strategies, the vertical axes of the graphs show amplitude in units of dB, the horizontal axes show frequency in Hertz.

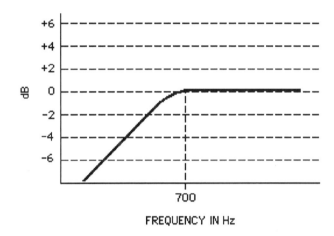

Fig. 5.21. The effect of "shelving" equalization.

The type of EQ shown in Fig. 5.21 is called **shelving**. All frequencies past a point are amplified to a uniform, preset level. In this example, 700 Hz is the **shelving** or **corner frequency.** Passing a music track through shelving equalization where the corner frequency is set to 800 Hz approximates the audio sound a car radio.

Cutoff EQ

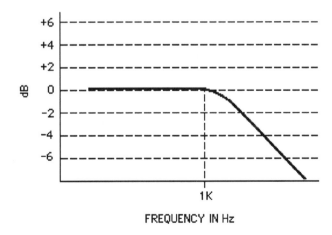

Fig. 5.22. Rolloff equalization.

Fig. 5.22 shows a type of EQ known as a **cutoff** or **rolloff**. It is essentially the reverse of shelving: All frequencies passed a predetermined point are attenuated in increasing proportion to the frequency. Passing a music track through cutoff equalization where the corner frequency is set to 200 Hz de-emphasizes the high frequencies. What you hear most is the bass.

In this case, 1 kHz is the **cutoff frequency**. Both shelving and cutoff EQ are the least flexible types of EQ and are commonly employed in consumer stereo systems.

Bandpass EQ

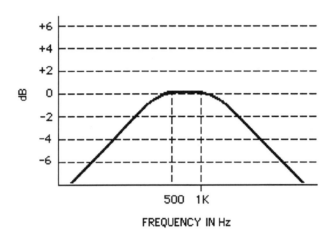

Fig. 5.23. Bandpass equalization.

Fig. 5.23 shows a type of EQ known as a **bandpass**. It is essentially a combination of shelving and cutoff: All frequencies between two predetermined points are amplified and all other frequencies before and after are attenuated.

Passing a voice track through an equalizer that is set to pass only the 700- to 800-Hz range gives the sound a "telephone" quality.

Peak EQ

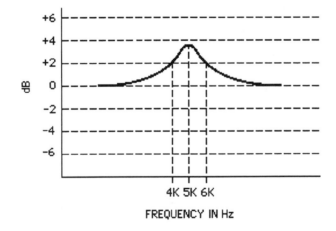

Fig. 5.24. Peak equalization.

Fig. 5.24 shows a type of EQ known as a **peak**. In this case, a central frequency is amplified and

138

a narrow range of frequencies to either side are amplified in proportion as they approach the central frequency. However, those frequencies outside the narrow range are unaffected.

Notch EQ

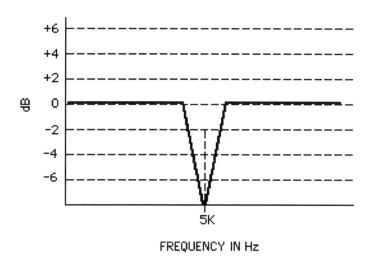

Fig. 5.25. Notch filtering.

Fig. 5.25 shows a **notch** or **dip** EQ. It is the exact opposite of a peak equalizer: A central frequency is attenuated and a narrow range of frequencies to either side is attenuated in proportion as the individual frequencies approach the central frequency. Again, all other frequencies are unaffected. Passing a voice track through a notch equalizer set to filter out only the 30 Hz range helps reduce low-frequency noise from a camera motor.

Filters

Filters are devices that are attenuate specific frequency bands. The amount of attenuation applied to that the frequency band is fixed. The names of the most common types of filters correspond to the different equalization types: **shelving, cutoff, bandpass, peak** and **notch.**

Filters and different types of EQ are found on studio equipment like consoles and microphones in addition to external equalizer units. Often the filter's type and function is indicated by a symbol that shows its affect on an audio signal. These symbols appear, with minor variations, as shown in Fig. 5.26:

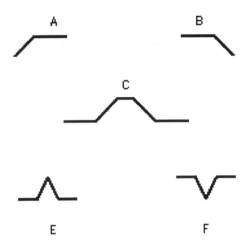

Fig. 5.26. Different filter-types are denoted by their symbols and include shelving (a), cutoff or rolloff (b), bandpass (c), peak (e) and notch or dip (f).

D. TYPES OF EQUALIZERS

Equalizers are generally available as modules on a console or as separate external units. The two main types of external equalizers are **parametric** and **graphic**. Outboard graphic equalizers generally look as shown in Fig. 5.27.

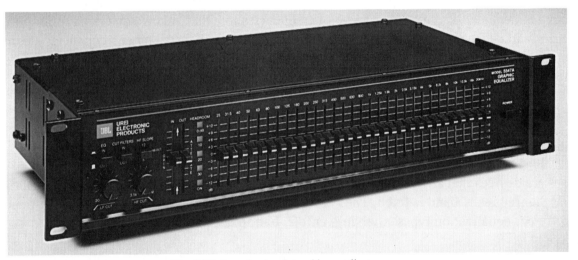

Fig. 5.27. A professional graphic equalizer.
(Photo Courtesy of JBL/UREI Electronics, Inc.)

Note that the sliders are the level controls and that each one controls a preset, fixed frequency range. Each slider is, in effect, an attenuator for its frequency range.

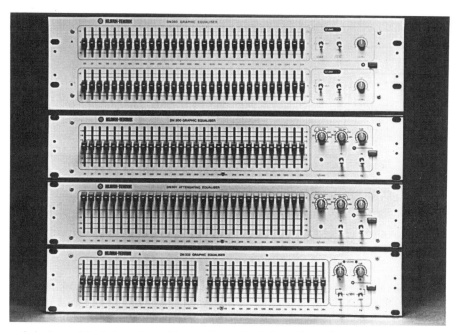

Fig. 5.28. Assorted single- and dual-channel graphic equalizers. Dual-channel equalizers can function on two different and independent signals at the same time.

The following diagram represents the action of one slider of a graphic equalizer. Note that the variable of amplitude, dB, is shown with a two-headed arrow (Fig. 5.29):

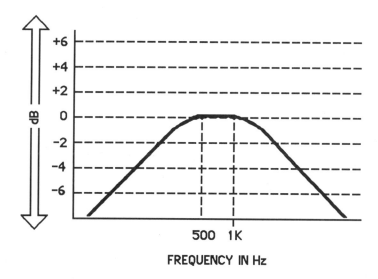

Fig. 5.29. Raising the amplitude of specific frequencies with a graphic equalizer. The range of frequencies that can be affected is fixed.

In comparison, a parametric equalizer controls not only the level for a particular band of frequencies, but also allows the *frequency intervals and the bandwidth of the selected frequency to be altered* (Fig. 5.30):

141

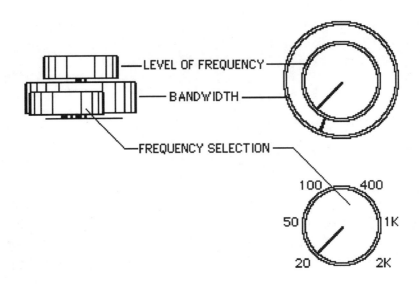

Fig. 5.30. Common configuration of controls for one band of a parametric equalizer.

Fig. 5.31. A dual-channel parametric equalizer. Note the concentric controls for bandwidth, boost and cut, and frequency. (Photo Courtesy of Orban, Inc.)

The following diagram represents one control of a parametric equalizer. Again, the variables are shown with two-headed arrows (Fig. 5.32):

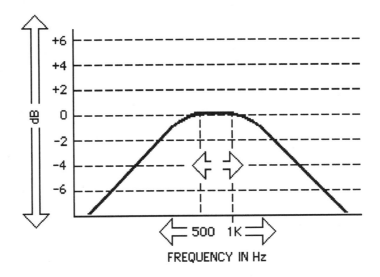

Fig. 5.32. Varying both the amplitude and range of selected frequencies.

Yet another type of equalizer is called **paragraphic** and incorporates features of both parametric and graphic types. For example, the bandwidth and frequency are independently adjustable. But

142

the boost and cut controls take the form of a graphic equalizer. This arrangement makes it easier to see the nature of the equalization being applied by simply glancing at the unit (Figs. 5.32 and 5.34).

Fig. 5.33. A single-channel paragraphic equalizer.
(Photo Courtesy of Orban, Inc.)

Fig. 5.34. A dual-channel paragraphic equalizer. Each left-hand fader controls EQ for the left channel.
(Photo Courtesy of Orban, Inc.)

When first trying to use an equalizer to obtain a specific effect, such as a telephone voice, the experience can be at best frustrating. A good approach is to try to imagine which frequencies are actually being reproduced in a given situation. This comes with practice and persistence. For example, setting an equalizer to recreate the tone of a car radio becomes easier when you realize that an inexpensive car radio does not reproduce bass particularly well. Bearing this in mind, you would eliminate progressively higher bass frequencies until you reached the desired result.

Another guideline to keep in mind is the relationship between of energy and wavelength. Simply put, the higher the frequency of a sound, the shorter its wavelength will be and the less energy it will have. The opposite is also true: The lower the frequency, the more energy it will have — and the easier it will be for that frequency to penetrate solid objects. This is why music heard from next door sounds bassy or "muffled." Only the low frequencies are able to travel through a solid wall. Therefore, a thin wall would allow more midrange sounds to pass and a thick wall would allow only the lowest frequencies through. Setting an equalizer to mimic these effects will allow you to recreate specific environmental conditions.

E. DYNAMIC RANGE

One of the greatest problems facing a recording engineer is to accurately capture wide variations in sound amplitude. For example, a classical piece can vary in loudness from the barely audible to majestic and crashing levels. Similarly, the ambient noise in a forest — rustling leaves, songbirds, light wind — can suddenly be shattered by an explosion of thunder. This range of loudness levels is referred to as **dynamic range.** (See Fig. 1.12 for the relative dB levels of sounds).

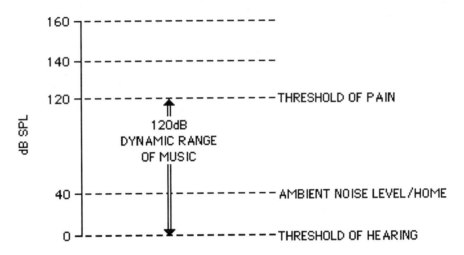

Fig. 5.35. The lowest 40 dB of sounds (in this case music) are "drowned out" by the ambient level of the average home.

As Fig. 5.34 shows, the dynamic range of live music is generally considered to be 120 dB. If a section of music having this dynamic range were to be recorded and reproduced at precisely the same range, several problems would arise. For example, the ambient noise level in most homes falls between 35 dB to 45 dB. In an average home, all passages between 0 dB and 45 dB would be drowned out by that ambient noise. At the same time, raising the volume to compensate would result in passages exceeding the 120 dB threshold of pain (Fig. 5.36):

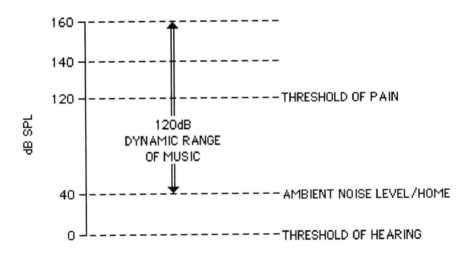

Fig. 5.36. Raising the ambient level of the music places 40dB of it above the threshold of pain.

The preceding two examples establish that an *available* dynamic range of 80 dB exists, and this range lies between the 40-dB ambient noise level and the threshold of pain:

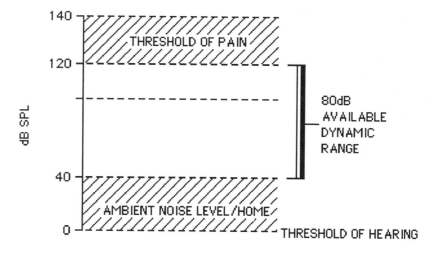

Fig. 5.37. Available dynamic range of sound is limited to 80 dB.

This 80-dB dynamic range is a theoretical one because factors other than external ones come into play. All recording media, for example, because of various electronic and mechanical characteristics, have inherent limitations on their dynamic range (Fig. 5.38):

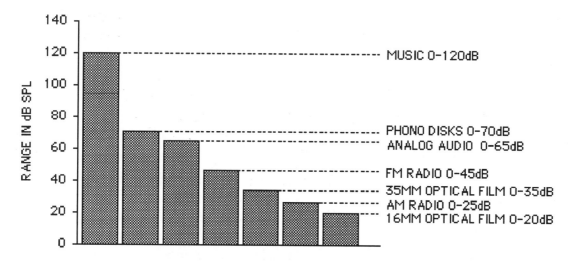

Fig. 5.38. Dynamic ranges of different media.

Figure 5.37 shows that, in fact, no recording or reproduction media meets the 120-dB dynamic range. For example, recording a musical piece on magnetic tape at a level that would capture the quietist passages would cause the recording equipment to **clip**, or **distort**, when the dynamic range of the music exceeded 65 dB. Similarly, lowering the amplification level to prevent that distortion would cause the quietist passages to be lost because the noise level inherent in the equipment would exceed the levels of signal being recorded.

When using magnetic media, clipping or distortion is caused by **tape saturation**, and occurs when the dynamic range of the recording medium is exceeded. Playing a pocket radio at full volume also causes distortion. The distortion occurs because the peaks of those signals that exceed the radio's dynamic limits are clipped off, losing that portion of the signal (Fig. 5.39).

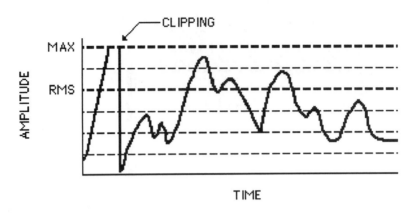

Fig. 5.39. An example of "clipping".

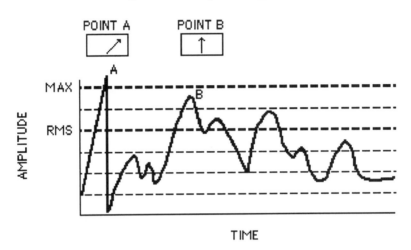

Fig. 5.40. VU measurements of two audio peaks.

Note that in Fig. 5.40 the signal amplitude at point "A" is greater than at point "B," and the meter reflects these differences in level. Personal preference and technique will determine the maximum allowable amplitude, but in all cases extremes should be avoided. If the average signal level is too low, anywhere between -20 and -5 dB, the quality of the audio will suffer. As the *average* signal level slides to the low end of the scale noise, the noise inherent in all audio equipment becomes audible. Similarly, as the *average* signal level goes beyond +20 dB, distortion — caused by the signal exceeding the dynamic capacity of the equipment — becomes apparent to the listener.

The questions most often asked about audio mixing generally have to do with selecting the signal's optimum levels. The best advice to follow is to use your ears rather than rely on or try to interpret equipment specifications. Some types of equipment may distort at +10 dB, others at +1 dB. Professional engineers will rely more on what they hear than on levels indicated by meters. The ability to distinguish correct levels by hearing, however, comes with practice and for which there is no substitute.

F. COMPRESSORS AND LIMITERS

To overcome the limitations of recording and playback media, electronic devices called **compressors** and **limiters** can be used to limit a program material's dynamic range. **Compressors** and

limiters do exactly what their names imply: They compress the dynamic range of the source material to fit within a prescribed range. The principle of compression is simple: A predetermined signal level, called a **threshold**, is established. Signals exceeding this threshold are reduced to fall within the established dynamic range (Fig. 5.41):

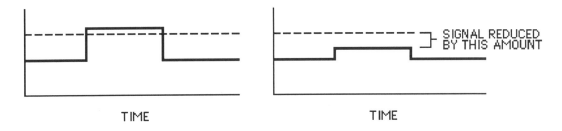

Fig. 5.41. Reducing the gain of a signal.

In essence, a compressor or limiter acts as an automatic fader. When an input signal exceeds the threshold, the device automatically reduces the gain of the amplifying equipment. The increase in input signal in dB required to cause a 1-dB increase in the output signal level is called the **compression ratio**. For example, a compression ratio set to 4:1 will convert an 8-dB increase in input level to only a 2-dB increase output level. This ratio is usually indicated on the front panel of the device and is selectable.

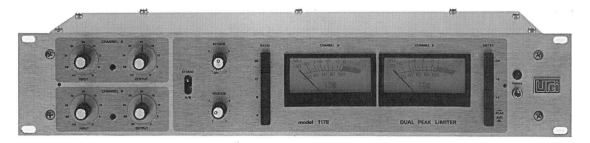

Fig. 5.42. The UREI 1178 stereo compressor and limiter, one of the most widely used models. (Photo Courtesy of JBL/UREI Electronics, Inc.)

Almost all compressors and limiters are equipped with a meter on the front panel. This meter, unlike those on consoles, indicates the gain *reduction* of the processed signal. As a result, it usually rests at zero and deflects "backwards," that is, from the right to left (Fig. 5.43):

147

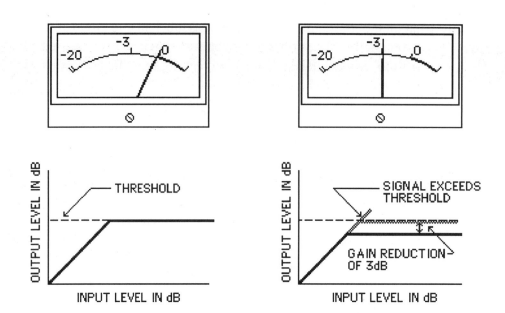

Fig. 5.43. Examples of gain reduction.

As Fig. 5.43 shows, the input signal in the left example does not exceed the threshold. As a result, the gain is not reduced and the meter does not deflect. In the case on the right, however, the input signal *does* exceed the threshold and the gain is reduced by 3 dB. To show this, the meter deflects to -3 dB.

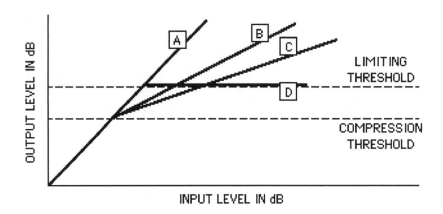

Fig. 5.44. Gain reduction becomes more active as the signal approaches and exceeds the threshold.

Other controls on a compressor are the signal **release time** and **attack time**. Release time determines the speed with which the compressor will *stop* acting on the signal. If the release time is set too short, the gain of the signal passing through the device will be altered in an unacceptable way. In such cases "pumping" or "breathing" occurs because of a rapid rise of background noise as the gain increases with the release.

The attack time of a compressor — the time it takes to act on a signal — can be set to reduce gain either instantaneously or gradually. If the attack time is too fast, the gain of the signal will be reduced too quickly, causing the signal to momentarily "drop out." With too long of an attack setting, and the signal will begin to distort because the compressor lacks enough time to reduce the gain.

Fig. 5.45. A single channel compressor-limiter. Note the threshold, ratio, attack and release controls. (Photo Courtesy of Orban, Inc.)

Fig. 5.46. A four channel compressor-limiter. Again, note the layout of controls. (Photo Courtesy of Orban, Inc.)

Again, only your ears can tell you what sounds acceptable. However, the following serves as a guide to setting up a compressor:

1. Set the compression ratio to about 4:1.

2. Turn the attack time to off.

3. Adjust the release time for the fastest setting.

4. Set the threshold should to minimum.

5. Set the meters, if switchable, to show gain reduction.

6. Feed the signal to the unit. Increase the threshold until the meter(s) on the compressor begin to deflect.

7. Increase attack time until a "thumping" is heard and then reduce the attack time.

8. Decrease the release time until "whooshing" occurs, then increase the control slightly.

9. Set the meters to show output, and then adjust the output control to an acceptable level.

10. Vary the compression ratio, if desired, to obtain further reduce gain.

11. Repeat steps 6 through10 as required.

Some compressors provide a stereo interconnection, which allows control of one signal's level by another. For example, if a narrative occurs at the same time as background music, the output of the voice track may be used to trigger the threshold of the music channel. When the narration pauses, the music will come back up.

G. DE-ESSERS

Occasionally, if a spoken or sung voice is recorded, accentuation of hissed sounds like "s" and "ch" will cause an unpleasant signal boost in the 3- to 3.5-kHz range. This phenomenon is called **sibilance** and can be counteracted by a **de-esser**, which is essentially a compressor with a 3.2-kHz filter. A de-esser will reduce the emphasis on this particular type of signal without affecting other sounds (Fig. 5.47).

Fig. 5.47. The Orban 536A sibilance controller
(Photo Courtesy of Orban, Inc.)

H. STEREO SYNTHESIZERS

It is sometimes desirable to recreate a signal recorded in mono into simulated stereo. In such cases, a **stereo synthesizer** is often used to obtain this effect. Essentially, there are two different ways to synthesize stereo. The first method is to use a delay to effect a separation between the left and right outputs. However, this may result in a "boingy" effect as the audio frequency of the increases.

The two stereo synthesizers shown in figures 5.48 and 5.49 are made by Orban, Inc., instead, use filters to simulate a stereo output. Because their filtering parameters are selectable, it is possible to send fundamental frequencies to specific stereo location while higher frequencies of the same side are sent to the opposite channel. This system simulates a clean, realistic stereo sound. The Model 245F is commonly used in audio production and post-production work. The Model 275A is designed for use with stereo television broadcasting. It can detect changes in monoaural and stereophonic sources and adjust itself accordingly. In addition, it can detect and correct the phasing problems most likely to occur in broadcast applications.

Fig. 5.48. The Orban 245F stereo synthesizer. This particular model is typically found in audio production and post-production facilities.
(Photo Courtesy of Orban, Inc.)

Fig. 5.49. The Orban 275A automatic stereo synthesizer, often used in stereo television broadcasting.
(Photo Courtesy of Orban, Inc.)

I. REVERBERATION

Reverberation occurs when both reflected and direct sounds reach a listener within closely spaced spans of time. The sound is then heard as having "depth" or echo. Consider, for example, two people at opposite ends of a gymnasium. In this case, one is dribbling a basketball (A); the other is an observer (B):

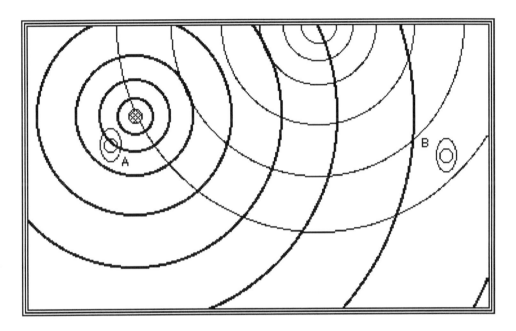

Fig. 5.50. Diagram of sound reflecting and re-reflecting.

The heavy lines shown in Fig. 5.50 represent initial, or direct, sound waves. These are waves that travel unobstructed from the source to the listener. In contrast, reflected, or indirect, sound waves are direct waves that bounce off a hard surface, in this case, a wall. These reflected sounds travel a longer distance from the source to the listener. Because the speed of sound in both cases is the same, it follows that more time is required for reflected waves to reach the listener. This effect can be recreated in the studio electronically, and is called **reverb** (short for reverberation).

Reverb and Processing

Chapter 2 discussed the reflection of sound in an environment and how it relates to imaging. In addition, you learned that the pan control on a console will control imaging, as does microphone placement. These effects, along with EQ modification and level control, give an operator several parameters with which to work. In relation to imaging of the signal in stereo, the audio signal can thus be seen as follows :

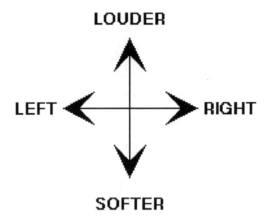

Fig. 5.51. The two dimensions of stereo imaging provided for by pan and gain.

Louder and softer, of course, are controlled by level; left and right, by pan. However, a third element can be introduced (Fig. 5.52):

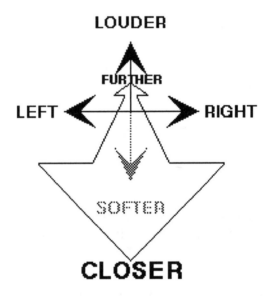

Fig. 5.52. Reverberations adds yet another dimension.

This third element is the electronic re-creation of reflected sound. As indicated in Fig. 5.52, reverberation adds a new dimension to the signal. That signal will sound further away as reverberation is added. This effect is accompanied by sending an additional mix via auxiliary send(s) on the input module (refer to chapter 3). A simplified view of this signal path appears in Fig. 5.53.

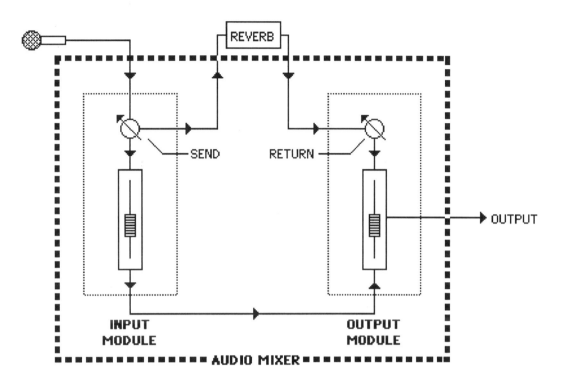

Fig. 5.53. Basic signal flow for an effects send and return.

Note which connections in Fig. 53 are external and which are internal. For example, the reverb unit is located physically outside the console. However, the signal path from the input module to the output module is internal.

As previously stated, a mix is sent through the send and remixed with the output through the return. A reverb signal returning to a console is referred to as a **wet** signal; a signal with no reverb is referred to as a **dry** signal.

Reverberation can be used to simulate a large space. If, for example, a visual scene includes one or several characters walking towards the camera through a tunnel, stock footsteps can be added to the track. Reverberation can be added to the footsteps and decreased as the camera is approached. This gives an added feeling of decreasing distance which serves to reinforce the picture.

J. TYPES OF REVERBERATION DEVICES

There are several different types of reverb units available. For the most part, selection is determined by price. In comparing the various types of reverberation devices, the main parameter to consider is the **decay time** of each effect. Decay is measure of the amount of time required for the reflections of a reverberation signal to fade. In the more sophisticated, expensive reverb units, more parameters are user-controllable and decay is one of the most crucial of those parameters.

Spring Reverb

The least expensive type of reverb is a mechanical device called a **spring reverb**. This device uses a combination of springs and transducers located within the unit to achieve reverberation. The input signal literally bounces back and forth along the springs, causing reverberation. With his type of device, percussive signals (e.g., a snare drum) send high transients through the springs, causing a "boing." In addition, it is difficult to control the decay time of a spring reverb (Fig. 5.54).

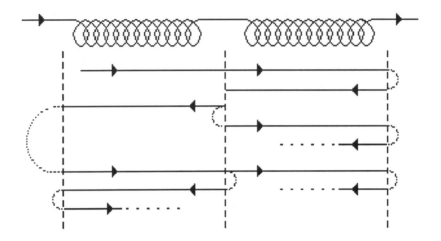

Fig. 5.54. Signal path of a spring reverb unit.

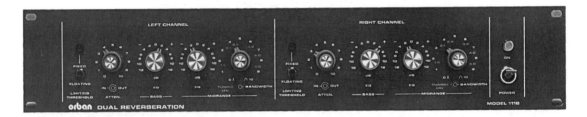

Fig. 5.55. A dual-channel spring reverb unit.
(Photo Courtesy of Orban, Inc.)

Plate Reverb

Until somewhat recently, the most common type of reverb in professional use was a type called a plate reverb. This device uses a 1/64-inch-thick rectangular steel sheet about 3 feet high and 6 feet wide. The sheet is placed under tremendous tension and encased in a frame. Reverberation is caused by inducing wave motion in the plate through a driver, which turns electrical energy into mechanical energy, as shown in Fig. 5.55. Contact microphones, shown as pickups, sense the wave motion and convert it back into electrical energy. Decay time is controlled by moving a second plate covered with damping material closer to the active plate. The quality of reverberation achieved by this type of device is almost unsurpassed. However, it is extremely expensive, very heavy and must be mechanically isolated from the floor. These constraints usually require placing it in a separate room.

154

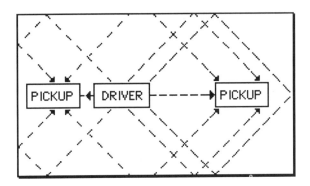

Fig. 5.56. Signal path within a plate reverb.

Dedicated Room

The most natural sounding reverb is achieved with a rectangular dedicated room having all surfaces covered with tile or similar reflective material. A loudspeaker is placed at one end and microphones located at various spots within the room. Decay time is controlled by selecting and controlling the level of the various microphones. Note that the loudspeaker faces away from the microphones to help eliminate feedback (Fig. 5.57).

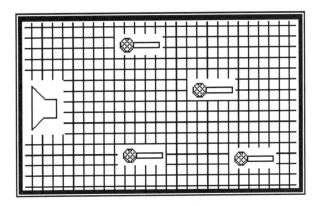

Fig. 5.57. Common set up for a reverberant room.

Digital Reverb

The most recent and by far the most common type of reverb in use today is digital reverb. This approach uses **sampling** to record signals from plate and other types of reverb devices. Sampling is a process that converts analog signals to a digital format, stores them in memory circuits and recalls them after a delay. With this approach, almost any type of reverberation can be recreated. Most parameters are user-controlled, and combinations of preset parameters can be stored and recalled at any time. Some digital reverb units can also achieve other types of effects, such as transposing pitch.

Fig. 5.58. A digital reverb unit, capable of numerous signal processing tasks including pitch transposition. (Photo Courtesy of Applied Research and Technology, Inc.)

K. DELAY EFFECTS

Another way of defining reverberation is to see it as a closely spaced series of echoes. If we increase the time between echoes, the effect is distinctly different than that of a reverberated signal. This interpretation suggests a group of effects known as delay-based effects. Generally speaking, it becomes possible to change not only the decay time of a signal, but also its rate of reverberation, the amount of time between echoes, the repeat rate of each echo and the number of repetitions.

There are several ways to achieve this level of control. Prior to the introduction of digital technology, the most common method of obtaining a delay or echo was to use a specialized tape recorder (see Chapter 4). The signal would be recorded on tape and then played through a series of playback heads. The timing of the echoes depends on the spacing of the heads and the tape speed, and the repeat rate is determined by the heads selected to play the sound back (Fig. 5. 59):

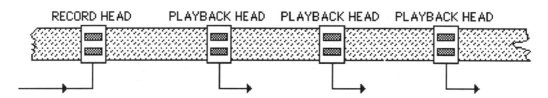

Fig. 5.59. Using multiple playback heads to obtain progressively longer delay times.

Note that a variation of this method is still in use and that a regular tape deck can serve the purpose. In much the same way, a signal is fed into a deck that is operated in the play mode. The output of is then recombined through the mixer with the original signal. This produces a single repetition, the rate of which can be controlled by varying the tape speed and, if the deck is so equipped, the pitch control of the deck. This effect is commonly referred to as **tape slap**. Tape slap is reminiscent of '50s style vocal tracks.

Tape-based delay effects have several drawbacks: The tape itself degenerates and must be replaced; the heads and tape path must be constantly cleaned, as with any machine; and the quality of signal is sometimes unacceptable. Devices using digital technology offer a more convenient method for achieving various combinations of delay. One such device is called a DDL or digital delay line. In addition to creating delays and allowing the user to control a variety of delay parameters, some DDLs can create additional effects. A DDL employs sampling, as does the digital reverb. As a result, in many cases, the capabilities of various digital effects overlap and allow for an extremely wide range of signal processing effects. One of the more popular effects created with a DDL is called doubling. Doubling adds an extremely short delay, about 1/1000 second, that produces a "fatter" sound that will stand out in a mix. Doubling is best suited for a lead vocal or instrument.

Fig. 5.60. A digital delay line. This particular model, the DN-716, has three separate outputs. Note the simplicity of controls and the readout indicating delay time in milliseconds (thousandths of a second).
(Photo Courtesy of Klark-Teknik Electronics, Inc.)

L. TAPE EFFECTS

Reverse Tape

In addition to delay, there are two other effects that can be obtained by using a tape deck. First, consider the normal tape path, shown in Fig. 5.59 (also see Chapter 4).

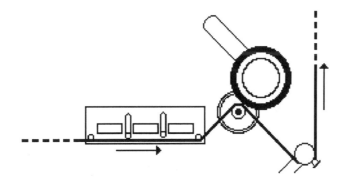

Fig. 5.67. Usual tape path for an ATR.

It is also possible to thread the machine to obtain a **reverse tape effect**, shown in Fig. 5.62.

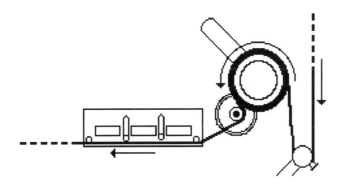

Fig. 5.62. Threading the tape as shown will make the tape run backwards during play.

By winding the tape around the capstan and idler as shown and putting the tape machine into play, the tape motion is reversed and all prerecorded signals are played backwards. This method is recommended only for 1/4-in., two- or four-track machines and only for playback. It is impossible to record in reverse using this method: The erase head will wipe out anything on the tape as it passes the head block. However, should you wish to record a reverse tape effect on a multitrack machine, you can physically remove both reels, turn them upside-down and replace them:

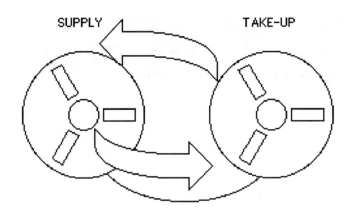

Fig. 5.63. Reversing reels to obtain a reverse tape effect.

This tactic can become a bit confusing, as the start of the song now becomes the end, and the order of tracks is reversed, with track one appearing where track eight usually is and vice-versa (see Chapter 4):

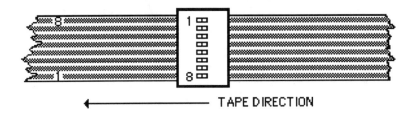

Fig. 5.64. Multitrack tape reversed.

Tape Loop

Chapter 4 discussed aspects of tape editing and one of the effects possible with editing, **tape loop**. In a tape loop, a section of the tape is recorded on a two-track machine, the desired section removed, both ends joined and then replaced on the machine. Playing back this loop results in the continuous repetition of the program material. Care should be taken, however, that the loop does not drag on the floor or become twisted. It is a good idea to physically support the loop with mic stands or equivalent items. Also, the playback machine should be horizontal.

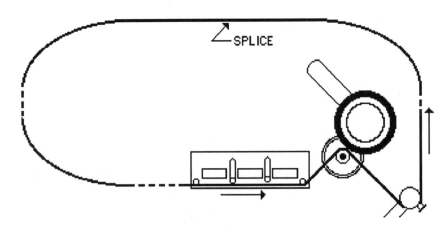

Fig. 5.65. A tape loop.

It is possible to integrate tape delay, reverse playback and loops in any combination to achieve a wide variety of effects.

M. PITCH EFFECTS

It is also possible to vary the pitch of a signal in several ways. If a tape recorder is used, changing the tape speed will also change the pitch, thus slowing down the program material. A digital device called a harmonizer can be used to overcome this problem. This harmonizer will change the pitch of a signal by a preset, user-controlled, musical interval. The analog signal is converted to digital information, processed and then returned to analog form. A possible application is to create a second melody in harmony to the original. The harmonizer is also capable of delay effects, notably doubling.

Fig. 5.66. The Eventide H3000 Ultra Harmonizer.
(Photo Courtesy of Eventide, Inc.)

N. NOISE GATES

A **noise gate** is a device that can be set to allow a signal to pass and then to shut down when no signal is present. In this way, it prevents unwanted ambient or recurring sound from being recorded.

Simply put, this device works on the principle of varying amplitude Over the course of a signal's envelope, when the level of a signal exceeds a set point, the gate opens and passes all signals fed to it. When the signal level drops, the gate closes and no signals are passed.

The point at which signal is passed is called the **threshold** and is controlled by the user. More expensive gates also allow the user to vary the attack and release time. The gate can be used if ambient noise is present throughout the program material or if unwanted noise comes before or after the desired signal:

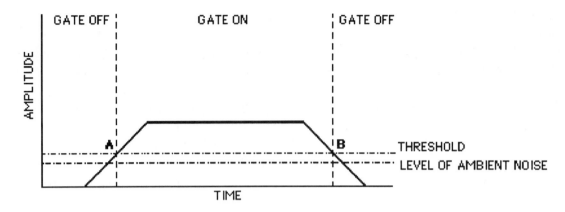

Fig. 5.67. A noise gate opening and closing.

Note that point "A" in Fig. 5.67 is where the desired signal exceeds the threshold and the gate turns on. During the time that the signal is passed, however, both the desired signal *and* the ambient noise are passed. When the desired signal falls below the threshold at point B, the gate turns off.

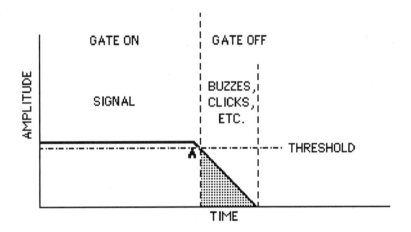

Fig. 5.68. A gate closing when the signal falls below the threshold.

Note that point "A" in Fig. 5.68 is where the desired signal falls below the threshold and where the gate turns off. The buzzes, clicks and other unwanted signals proceeding the release of the signal are not allowed to pass, but the desired signal is.

It is important to keep in mind that noise gates do not improve the signal-to-noise ratio (see below) because they pass or reject all signals together.

One possible use of a gate is in a talk-show format, where guests seated several feet from each have their own lavalier microphone. In such cases, there is a danger that the mic of one guest would pick up the sounds of another speaker. But because of its greater distance from the person speaking, the adjacent mic would pick up the other signals as lower than that of the voice of a person speaking directly into it. As a solution, gates may be applied to each mic and set to pass only the more direct signal.

O. NOISE REDUCTION

As discussed earlier in this chapter, the dynamic range of music is about 120 dB, and that of magnetic recording tape, about 60 to 65 dB. Because all electronic equipment adds noise to the signal, a measure for the amount of noise present is required. This measure is called a **signal-to-noise ratio**, or S/N ratio, and describes the amount of noise to the amount of signal present..

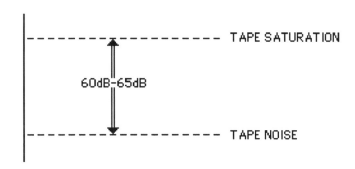

Fig. 5.69. Analog tape normally has a dynamic range of 60 to 65 dB.

Limitations imposed by recording on audio tape arise from tape noise occurring when the recorded signal level is too low or when there is distortion caused by tape saturation, that is, from a signal level that is too high (Fig. 5.69). Several noise reduction systems exist that overcome this problem. In the following, we discuss the three most common systems.

All noise reduction systems are connected before the tape deck during the recording process and after the deck during playback (Fig. 5.70).

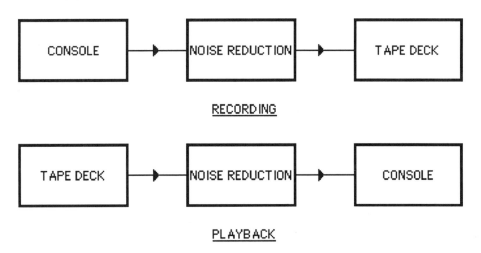

Fig. 5.70. Encoding and decoding with noise reduction.

In most cases these connections are made electronically and automatically. When the channel-record button of a multitrack deck is pressed, the noise reduction for that channel will change status automatically. The process of recording with noise reduction is called **encoding** and the process of playing back with noise reduction is called **decoding**. In all cases, the same type of noise reduction must be used during both the encoding and decoding processes. For example, if a Dolby system is used to encode a tape, the same system must be used for playback.

Dolby-A

Dolby-A is a noise reduction system that is used professionally, and is based upon splitting the signal into four separate frequency bands:

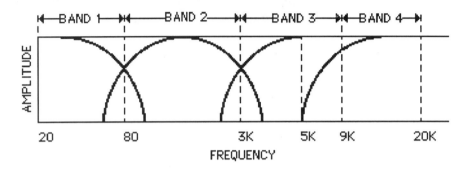

Fig. 5.71. Frequency divisions for Dolby A.

As illustrated in Fig. 5.71, the bands fall between 20 and 80 Hz, 80 and 3 kHz, 3 and 5 kHz, and 5 and 20 kHz. Each band undergoes the same post-equalization that is used for NAB equalization (Chapter 4): High frequencies are boosted during recording and then attenuated by the same amount during playback.

The Dolby-A system provides 10 dB of noise reduction below 5 kHz, increasing gradually to 15 dB at 15 kHz. This system reduces any noise introduced between record and playback. Principally, each of the four frequency bands are compressed at different ratios upon recording and then expanded by the same amount during playback.

Dolby-B

Dolby-B is strictly a consumer system, although its method of reducing tape noise is similar to the Dolby-A system. Noise is attenuated by 3 dB at 600 Hz, and that attenuation increases gradually to 10 dB at 5 kHz, where it levels off. Dolby-B has no effect on low frequency noise such as rumble, hum or pops.

dBx

dBx is a compressor-expander system that compresses all signals uniformly over the full audio frequency band of 20 Hz to 20 kHz. This method reduces noise by 20 to 30 dB, twice that of the Dolby systems.

Signals processed by the dBx unit are compressed by a 2:1 ratio when recorded and then expanded by a 1:2 ratio during playback. For example, when recording material having a 60-dB dynamic range with a tape recorder having a 60-dB signal-to-noise ratio, the noise introduced by the tape deck would be just as loud as the material during the most serene portions. If dBx is used, however, 30 dB is added to the S/N ratio, and tape noise would fall 30 dB below the lowest signal level (Fig. 5.72).

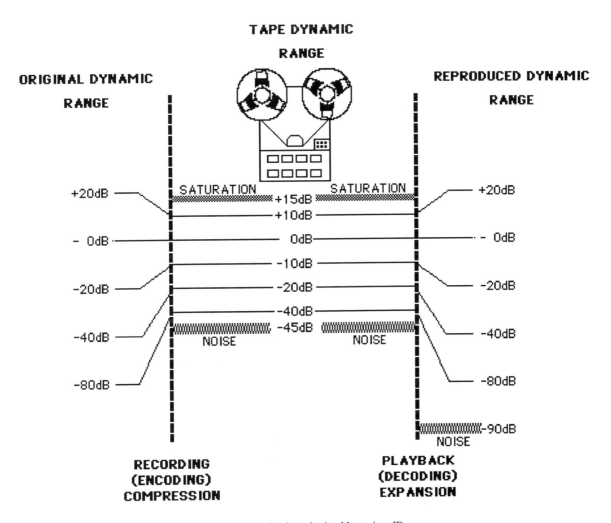

Fig. 5.72 Noise reduction obtained by using dBx.

6
MULTITRACK PRODUCTION TECHNIQUES

A. INTRODUCTION

It is impossible to describe all the ways to be creative in the production of audio. However, it is possible to introduce some standard techniques that, when put into practice, will present options not previously considered. To best understand these techniques, we recommended that, in addition to reading this chapter, you refer to Chapter 3 on how to set up the console.

B. MICROPHONE SELECTION

Selecting the best microphone for a particular application can be a frustrating experience. You should neither hesitate to explore all possible options nor be afraid to experiment. For example, try different types of microphones and bear in mind the characteristics of each. A breathy voice might be better suited to a dynamic mic; a deep voice, by a ribbon mic. When trying different mics turn off the EQ on the console input channel and remove or bypass any signal processing equipment that might alter the signal quality in any way.

In addition, consider the room and pickup pattern. Is the sound source located in a reflective environment? If so, a hyper-cardiod mic might eliminate unwanted ambient sounds. At the same time, a bipolar microphone might give greater depth to the signal. If problems in the recording environment cannot be solved electronically, consider acoustic solutions. These might include draping a moving blanket over the source and mic, using an umbrella behind the mic, placing baffles throughout the space, etc.

C. RECORDING TECHNIQUES: MULTITRACK DECKS

There are several techniques you should practice on multitrack decks. These include "punching in," "bouncing," and "live bouncing."

Punching In

The **punch in** is one in which a section of track is rerecorded while rolling the tape. For example, if a musician is dissatisfied with a section of a passage, it is possible to rerecord just that passage. To do that, be sure that the settings on the console and any mic placements are undisturbed since recording the last take. This will insure tonal and level consistency with the original pass. Also, verify that the deck is in sync mode.

The musician's headphone mix should consist of both the live signal and the deck's output. When the deck is put into record, only the live signal will be heard. Before and after recording, the musician should be able to hear both the live signal and the deck's output.

Punching in is accomplished by pressing either the track record button or the main record button while the track record control is in the "ready" mode. The exact names vary among machines and it is generally a good idea to completely understand the details of the particular model you are working with.

Practice the punch first while the musician is not wearing headphones because a feedback loop may occur if the console is not correctly set up, and the resulting squeal can hurt a person's hearing. Then practice the punch several times while the musician is wearing headphones. Be sure also that two or more people responsible for the results agree on both the "in" and "out" points on the tape.

Finally, treat the punch as if you were editing tape; that is, punch in during a quiet point on the tape, if possible. Punching in over a long, sustained note will almost always be noticeable.

Bouncing Tracks

Bouncing tracks describes the process of mixing several tracks on one multitrack deck to one or more tracks on the same deck. This process is used almost exclusively to free up tracks that are required for the recording additional instruments or voices. It is done mostly on smaller format decks, which tend to have fewer tracks than the number of signals that need to be recorded.

The principal disadvantage of bouncing is that once tracks are combined, there is no way to equalize or otherwise process the individual instruments. They are permanently combined. Other drawbacks to bouncing are that when audio signals are rerecorded from one tape to the next, noise is cumulatively added, the signal-to-noise ratio decreases, the signal is increasingly degraded and successively higher frequencies are lost. This phenomena is called **generation loss**, and it also occurs when copying from one tape to another, called **dubbing,** or when bouncing. As a result, bouncing is a process that takes place almost exclusively on smaller format decks. This is due to the fewer number of tracks available, which may exceed the number of sperarate signals that need to be recorded.

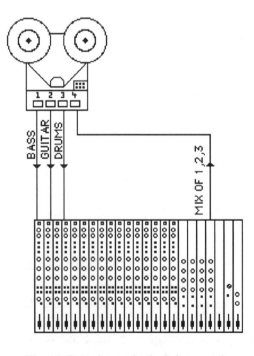

Fig. 6.1. Bouncing tracks through a console.

As seen in Fig. 6.1, bass, guitar and drums have been recorded onto tracks one, two and three, respectively. The musical passage still requires that keyboards, vocals and flute be recorded. To execute the bounce, the deck is put into sync mode and track four is put into record. Next, the input channels connected to tracks one, two and three are assigned to bus four, which is then routed to track four. Any signal processing required, including reverb and EQ, should be assigned to channels one, two or three.

The monitor mix should consist *only* of the return of track four, and as many takes as are needed should be made until the mix on track four is absolutely satisfactory. Then, tracks one, two and three are then put into record, track four is taken out of record, and tracks one, two, and three are "wiped," or erased. Be sure that all console channels connected to tracks one, two and three are turned off. This step will help to eliminate any noise and crosstalk.

In doing a bounce, there are two important factors to consider: First, on some machines it may be impossible to bounce adjacent tracks. For example, in Fig. 6.1, bouncing track three to track four may result in modulation, feedback and crosstalk. This is solely a result of the deck's design. Second, it is advisable to use noise reduction, if possible, as a bounce produces a second-generation recording, incurring generation loss that will add tape noise and decrease the S/N ratio.

Live Bouncing

Similar to bouncing, **live bouncing** is process of mixing several tracks on a multitrack deck to tracks on the same deck while also mixing in live signals.

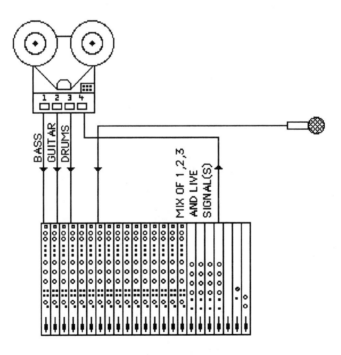

Fig. 6.2. Live bouncing.

As seen in Fig. 6.2, bass, guitar and drums have been recorded onto tracks one, two and three, respectively, and one or more live signals are mixed into the bounce. The same guidelines that apply to bouncing hold true for live bouncing.

D. RECORDING TECHNIQUES: EQ

EQ is sometimes considered a quick fix for sounds that are otherwise unacceptable. Most times this is an inappropriate approach. If recording and mixing can be considered cooking, EQ can be thought of as the spice that accentuates the flavor. In other words, do not rely on EQ and do not overdo it. EQ can just as easily destroy a mix as improve it. Here are some guidelines:

Avoid using EQ when recording basic tracks. Adding too much low-end EQ can cause distortion and crosstalk. The basic sounds should be strong enough on their own and have the needed timbre. Instead, EQ can be brought in during a mixing session to help separate sounds or instruments, or to more closely blend tones.

Equalizing too many tracks in the same range will cause frequency cancellation and may result in a shifting stereo image. For example, amplifying frequencies around 7 KHz for all keyboards and guitars will boost the overall mix and cause a shrill mix.

The lead instrument or voice should be EQ'd as required and all other instruments should avoid that frequency range, if possible. This technique will lend greater definition to the principal voice.

Remember to EQ for the particular instrument. Boosting a violin at 60 Hz will do nothing for it, but for a bass it might cause enough rumble to add a bit of excitement. Refer to Fig. 1.15 for the frequency ranges of different sources and add or cut EQ for each individual range as desired.

E. RECORDING TECHNIQUES: MONITORING

Monitoring is a deceptive aspect of recording, as a tape that sounds perfect in the studio might sound terrible outside it. To do it accurately, keep monitor levels around 60 to 65 dB, using a meter if required. That range is a good average for both quiet and loud listening. There is almost **never** a reason to blast the speakers. Rather, this is the sign of an inexperienced engineer or musician.

If possible, switch often between large monitors and small ones. The difference in sound quality is significant. Use large monitors to detect any noises and nuances that you might otherwise miss and use the smaller speakers to listen for sound clarity.

When the mix is taking place, use the smallest, cheapest, worst pair of speakers you can find. Listen to the mix on these and if, at the lowest volume possible, you can still clearly hear every voice and instrument, it is safe to assume that you have a good mix. This worst-case-scenario approach to mixing is valid because most people will listen to the material on car radios, Walkman players and TVs that use small low-cost speakers.

F. RECORDING TECHNIQUES: SIGNAL PROCESSING & SIGNAL PATHS

There are many options for processing and routing signals, some of which are described below. Bear in mind that these are only suggestions and in no way should they be considered inviolable rules:

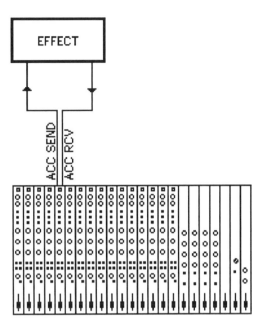

Fig. 6.3. Using an insert send and return loop on a single module.

As shown in Fig. 6.3, an effect has been patched into channel five through the effects send and receive jacks, sometimes called Acc Send and Acc Rcv or Insert Send and Receive. This is a common and straight forward method for processing a signal.

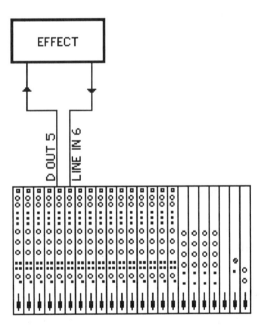

Fig. 6.4. Using the direct output of a module for signal processing.

In contrast, Fig. 6.4 shows the same effect patched out of channel five through the direct line output and returned through the line input of channel six. The same sound now appears on two channels and can be controlled in two different ways. For example, if the delay was panned right and the direct signal on channel five was panned to left of center, a wider stereo image caused by a fast sweep would occur.

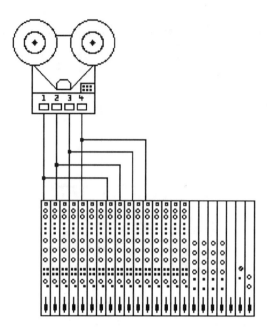

Fig. 6.5. Using two channels of the console for every track of the ATR.

Fig. 6.5 shows a four-track deck connected so that each track appears on two channels. As before, the same sound appears on two channels and can be controlled in two entirely different ways.

Also, the order in which signal processing devices are connected often creates a new effect. For example, connecting a noise gate after a reverb unit creates an effect called a gated reverb. The gate closes on the sustained portion of the envelope, cutting off the reverb. Tape effects are also possible: Placing a tape loop before a reverb unit can produce weird sounds that may be called for in some sessions.

In short, have the courage to experiment. Many people, including audio engineers, will delight in telling you that something is wrong or that something you want to try cannot be done. Pay no attention. If it works, use it.

G. KEEPING TRACK: PAPERWORK

There are several standard methods and variations for organizing takes and keeping track of tape formats, speeds and tracks. Some examples are given below:

Track Sheets

Track sheets are used to locate songs and passages on a multitrack tape. The sheets vary according to the format of the tape deck and, consequently, the tape. In all cases, however, it is a good idea to use pencil because it is likely that the status of each track will change. Initially, one track sheet per song or passage can indicate shared tracks or the changing of instrumentation from song to song. The left hand column can be used to indicate the song section (e.g., introduction, verse, chorus, etc.), or may be used to delineate time code numbers. An example of a track sheet for a song or passage recorded in an eight track studio is shown in Figure 6.6.

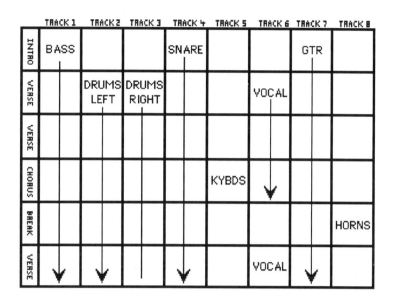

Fig. 6.6. Example of a track sheet used for one song.

The chart in Fig. 6.6 shows the bass on track one, snare drum on track four and the guitar on track seven playing continuously throughout. The drums, recorded in stereo on tracks two and three, begin during the first verse. Keyboards play only during the chorus, horns only during the break, and vocals occur only during the verses and the chorus.

A second method of keeping track sheets uses one sheet for the entire multitrack tape and reserves the left hand column to indicate the song titles.

	TRACK 1	TRACK 2	TRACK 3	TRACK 4	TRACK 5	TRACK 6	TRACK 7	TRACK 8
SONG A	BASS	DRUMS LEFT	DRUMS RIGHT	SNARE	HORNS	VOCAL	GTR	SYNTH
SONG B	BASS	DRUMS LEFT	DRUMS RIGHT	SNARE	HORNS	VOCAL	GTR	SYNTH
SONG C	BASS	DRUMS LEFT	DRUMS RIGHT	SNARE	KYBDS	VOCAL	BKND VOCAL	SYNTH
SONG D	FLUTE	PIANO L	PIANO R	CLAPS	KYBDS	VOCAL	GTR	SYNTH
SONG E	BASS	DRUMS LEFT	DRUMS RIGHT	SNARE	HORNS	VOCAL	BKND VOCAL	SYNTH

Fig. 6.7. A track sheet used to indicate the contents of a multitrack tape.

The sheet in Fig. 6.7 indicates the arrangements of instruments from one song to the next. In all cases, the instrumental track layout varies as little as possible, which saves time when remixing.

Time is saved because console settings vary less drastically from song to song. When completed, track sheets should be stored in the box — clearly labeled on its spine — containing the master tape.

On the following page is a blank track sheet that you can copy and use.

Take Sheets

Track sheets are used to keep track of the location and content of a mixed tape. Again, it is a good idea to fill the sheets out in pencil. Figure 6.9 shows what a typical take sheet looks like.

The take sheet shown in Fig. 6.9 can be used as follows:

- The column marked "Cue No." indicates the time code or tape-counter numbers.

- The column labeled "Take No." indicates the take.

- The columns marked "Title" and "Comments" indicate, respectively, the name of the passage and any comments regarding its quality and outcome.

Again, store any take sheets with the two-track master, and indicate the reel title clearly on the spine of the box.

Recording Tone

A tone produced by an internal or external oscillator, normally a 1-kHz signal, is used at the beginning of a mixing session. Passed through the console, the tone verifies that the console levels — as indicated by the left and right VU meters — are at 0. This level should, in turn, be further verified at the mixdown ATR. Note that the deck is in source mode. This is because most mixdown ATRs have input levels that can be varied by front panel knobs. In contrast, most multitrack deck levels cannot be changed from the front panel (Fig. 6.10).

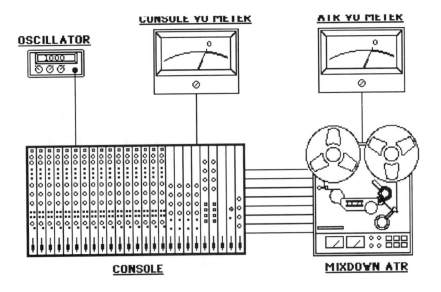

Fig. 6.10. Using an oscillator to match console and ATR levels.

ILLUSTRATION NO. VI.1

Soundesign NY

Client	Producer	Date	
Artist/Product	Engineer/Assistant	Reel __ of __	
		Page __ of __	

30 ips ☐ 15 ips ☐ 7.5 ips ☐

dolby A ☐ dBx ☐ No NR ☐

Master ☐ Safety ☐ Transfer ☐

SMPTE ☐ 29.97 DF ☐ 29.97 NDF ☐

Heads Out ☐ Tails Out ☐ Spooling ☐

Lock: MAC ☐ Lock: VTR ☐ Lock: ATR ☐

Comments:

SONG/SECT	Track 1	Track 2	Track 3	Track 4	Track 5	Track 6	Track 7	Track 8

ILLUSTRATION NO. VI.2

Soundesign NY

		Client		Producer		Date	
		Artist/Product		Engineer/Assistant		Reel __ of __	
						Page __ of __	

30 ips ☐   dolby A ☐   Master ☐   SMPTE ☐   Heads Out ☐   Mix: Auto ☐   Stereo ☐   Full Track ☐   IES EQ ☐
15 ips ☐   dBx ☐   Safety ☐   29.97 DF ☐   Tails Out ☐   Manual ☐   Mono ☐   1/2 Track ☐   NAB EQ ☐
7.5 ips ☐   No NR ☐   Transfer ☐   29.97 NDF ☐   Spooling ☐   Combined ☐   Combined ☐   1/4 Track ☐

TITLE	TAKE NO	START	STOP	TIME	COMMENTS

If the two levels show a discrepancy, then adjust the ATR levels so that its meters read 0 VU. This matches the levels read at the console to those recorded on the ATR.

The next step is to leave the settings as they are, switch the ATR into "tape" or "output" mode, and record about 10 to 20 seconds of tone. Then read the signal level from tape to verify that the deck is calibrated and functioning properly.

Another purpose for the tone is that, if the tape is played on a machine at another recording facility, it verifies that the playback levels are consistent between different machines. For this reason, the prerecorded tone is also called the **reference tone**.

H. MIXING FOR FILM AND VIDEO

Special considerations must be made when mixing for film and video because the frequency response and dynamic range of these media severely limit the characteristics of the resulting audio material (see Chapter 5). In addition to these limitations, the shortcomings imposed by the system that reproduces the program material for the ultimate audience must also be considered.

For example, the frequency response of one-inch video is about 40 Hz to 15 kHz. Although this is more than adequate for recording and reproducing most audio, chances are good that the video program will eventually be played through a television set. The speaker in the average television set — probably only two to four inches in diameter — is generally of medium to poor quality. Its inability to reproduce high and low frequencies, and the limited dynamic range imposed by the television set's internal electronics, will detract considerably from the quality of audio.

As a result, in mixing from a visual medium, limit the frequency range of audio material from 150 Hz to about 6.5 kHz. This will result in a mix that more accurately represents the final reproduced form. In addition, slightly increasing the frequencies around 700 Hz will give the bass a slightly better definition. Also, boosting around 4.5 kHz will yield greater clarity. In addition, some light compression is recommended, as portions of the audio will be lost if the dynamic range is too great (Fig. 6.11).

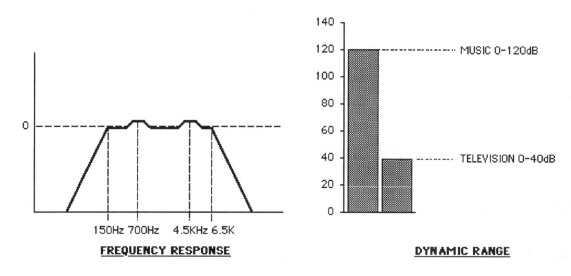

Fig. 6.11 Limiting the frequency response and dynamic range of program material for television broadcasting.

The dynamic range and frequency response of film's optical track are much lower than that of conventional magnetic recording media. As a result, high- and low-frequency sounds, although an integral portion of the original mix, will not be successfully reproduced from an optical track. As before, rolling off at around 200 Hz and 5.5 kHz will give a more accurate final mix. The dynamic range of optical film is even less than that of television, with 35 mm being slightly better than 16 mm. For that reason, the use of compression is advisable. (Fig. 6.12).

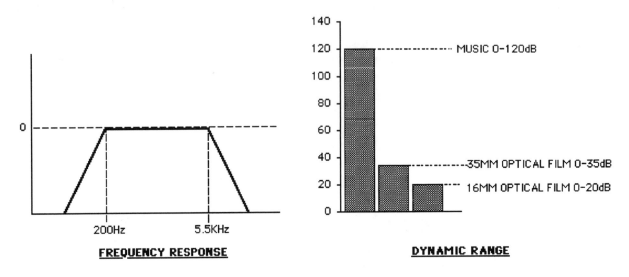

Fig. 6.12. Limiting the frequency response and dynamic range of program material for 16-mm optical playback.

In either case, consider placing a compressor and graphic equalizer between the output of the console and the input of the recording device, setting them to the values indicated in Figs. 6.11 and 6.12. Doing so will prevent the recording of frequencies that would either be lost anyway or would interfere with the final product (Fig. 6.13).

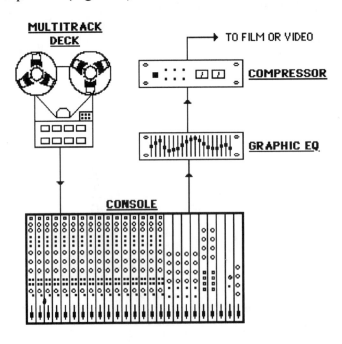

Fig. 6.13. Using a compressor and limiter on the final mix.

176

H. STEREO AND MONO COMPATIBILITY

Because most material reproduced by a video or film format may be reproduced in either stereo or mono (depending on the delivery system), it is sometimes desirable to monitor the mix in both modes. To make sure that the mix is compatible in both modes, use the stereo-mono switch on the console's monitor section (see chapter 3). In certain cases for mono, phase cancellation may occur between portions of the left and right channels. In this case readjusting the equalization, level or both may be required.

Lastly, a phenomenon called **center drift** can occur when the program-material levels alternate too rapidly or often between left and right. This too must be corrected: Center drift can create unacceptable level surges of audio when played in mono.

PART TWO:
POST-PRODUCTION

7
EDITING AND BASIC POST-PRODUCTION

A. INTRODUCTION

Editing is the process of removing, adding and rearranging sounds and images. It is an essential part of film and video, given that most footage is recorded or shot out of sequence. In fact, editing is one of the first stages of the **post-production** process. In comparison, the creation of the original or **raw footage** is called **production**.

B. ANALOG TAPE EDITING

The editing of analog audio tape is a manual process and will eventually become a lost art due to the advent of digital technology will that analog editing . Nevertheless, an understanding of the basic concepts which underlie editing is essential, since only the techniques and tools vary with different media. In many ways, analog tape editing is the most straight-forward type of editing. And, as we'll discuss later, it will help to understand the concepts behind the manipulation of digital sound effects produced with a personal computer or sampler.

To edit audio tape you need a grease pencil, straight-edged razor blade, **splicing tape**, an empty reel, **leader tape** and an **editing block**. Of these, the razor blade should be replaced often, as it quickly gets dull and also becomes magnetized. An edit made with a magnetized blade will create an audible "pop" or "click" when played. Splicing tape is specially formulated to stick to the back of magnetic tape. A **splice** is the actual connection made between two pieces of tape or leader.

An editing block is a rectangular block of aluminum with a channel down the center to hold the tape (Fig. 7.1). Editing blocks are available for every type of recording tape, although the most common blocks contain channels for 1/4-inch and 1/2-inch tape.

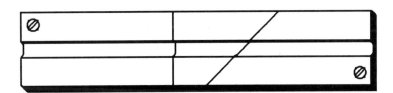

Fig. 7.1 An Editing Block

Leader tape is non-magnetic plastic or paper tape that is used for separating recorded pieces of magnetic tape. Plastic leader is stronger, but cannot be torn like paper leader; aper is easier to work with if many edits are to be made. A piece can be torn off the roll quickly, inserted, cut and spliced in.

Leader tape is also used as a visual reference to facilitate the location of the start or end of a selection as a tape is moving quickly.

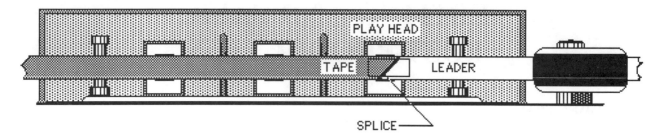

Fig. 7.2 Leader Placed At The Start Of A Recording

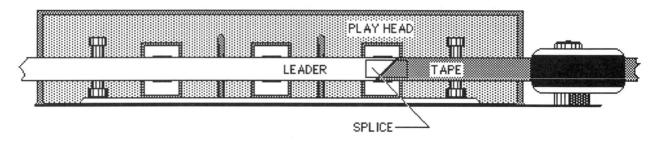

Fig. 7.3 Leader Placed At The End Of A Recording

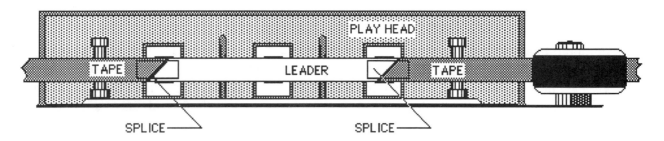

Fig. 7.4 Leader Inserted Into A Recording

Speed

The speed at which a recording is made greatly affects the ease with which it can be edited. If audio was recorded at a slow speed (e.g., 3.75 ips), less physical space will exist between sounds; s the recording speed is increased to 7.5 and 15 ips, audio passages on the tape are spread increasingly far apart.

An Editing Example

The easiest way to visualize the editing process is to visualize a hypothetical session; the simplest type of editing is that of speech. So, let's assume that a narration has been recorded and the engineer is given a copy of the script which, in part, reads: "Now is the day that we must go out and find for ourselves the meaning of editing."

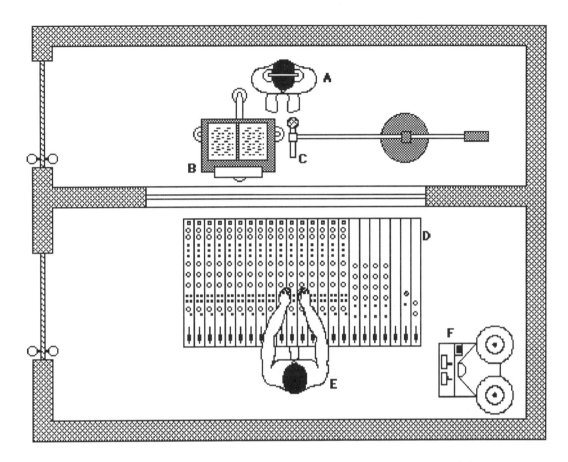

Fig. 7.5 An atypical voice over studio with console, tape deck, and two sound-proofed rooms.

The announcer (A) is in a soundproof booth and wearing headphones. He or she will read the script (B), which is placed on a stand to avoid the noise of pages being turned. The microphone (C), mounted on a stand and boom, is plugged into the console (D). The engineer (E) will operate the equipment, including a quarter inch (F) tape recorder.

The script is read and recorded several times. Each recording is called a **take**. In our example, the announcer is unable to read the script without coughing at least once. The best take, it turns out, contains a cough and a stutter (Fig. 7.6) and both must be removed by editing. In this example, the illustrations show the locations of the words and sounds recorded on the tape.

Fig. 7.6. Location of words on a piece of tape.

First, a copy of the master tape, called a **safety**, should be made and carefully stored.

The passage to be edited is located by putting the deck is put into stop, pause or edit mode; depending on the machine, the proper mode is the one in which the playback head stays "live" so that the recording will be heard when the tape is moved slightly. The reelsare then "rocked" back and forth by hand (Fig. 7.7) so that the beginning and end of each sound can be heard precisely as the tape passes over the play head.

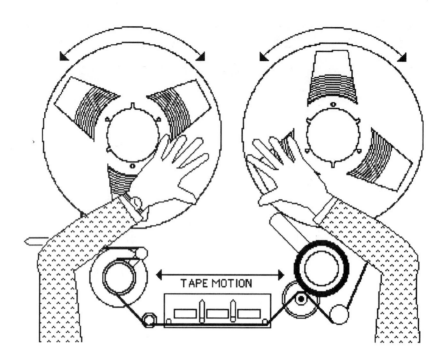

Fig. 7.7 "Rocking" reels to locate a specific passage.

Once the exact location of the sound is determined, the tape is marked with a grease pencil directly over the playback head. In this case, this will be just before the cough (Fig. 7.8).

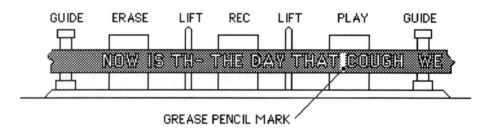

Fig. 7.8. Marking the pae with a grease pencil.

The reels are again rocked to find the beginning of the word after the cough and the tape marked; the process is repeated for the stutter. Note that not only is the unwanted sound marked out the , but *space must be left between the words twhich are o be spliced together* (Fig. 7.9). Without that space, the edit would produce a staccato jumble of unnatural speech.

Fig. 7.9 Leaving space between words.

Once the location of the cuts are marked, the take-up reel is rotated clockwise to release tension on tape. Next, the tape is lifted away from the head block, placed in the editing block and cut at the grease pencil marks (Fig. 7.10):

Fig. 7.10. Cutting the tape with the 45° cut.

The unwanted sections are removed and put aside on a clean surface (Fig. 7.11).

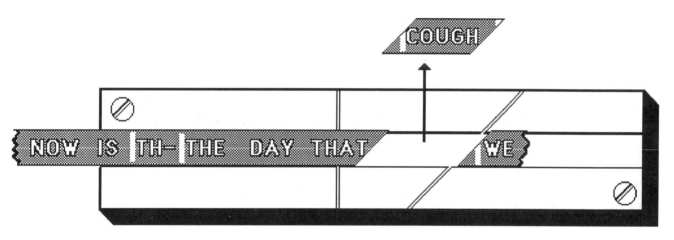

Fig. 7.11 Removing the cough from the tape.

The pieces of tape that are removed are called **outtakes**, and should be kept aside in case an error has been made in editing. Until the outtakes are discarded, one will have the option of putting them back in place and trying re-editing. If the outtakes consist of words or music that are part of the script, these should be placed on an empty reel, tails out, with leader in between each.

With the outtakes removed, the tape ends of each reel are then butted together and spliced (Fig. 7.12).

Fig. 7.12 Creating the splice.

The resulting tape will now look (and sound) like this (Fig. 7.13):

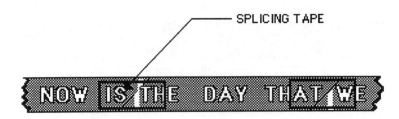

Fig. 7.13 The completed passage.

Finally, leader tape is spliced to the head and tail of the take (Fig. 7.14).

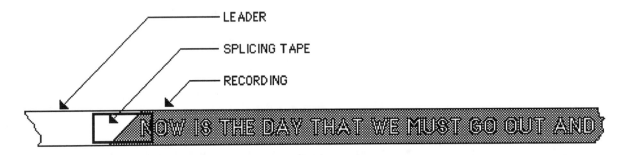

Fig. 7.14 Addition of leader at the head of the cut.

Editing, although simple in theory, is an art like any other. The ability to edit quickly and accurately comes from practice. Figure 7.15 shows some common splicing mistakes. These include mismatched splice angles (A), incorrectly butted tape ends that leave a gap (B), poorly positioned splicing tape (C), overhanding splicing tape (D) and overlapping tape ends (E). Also shown is a correct splice (F).

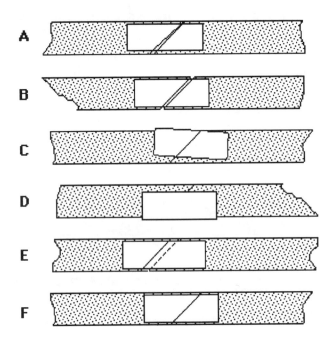

Fig. 7.15. All but the bottom example are common spicing errors.

Editing Music

Editing speech is one thing. Editing music, however, is quite another and requires a working knowledge of basic music structure. Bear in mind that the only way to *really* learn editing is to actually do it.

Before you read the next few paragraphs, listen to some music and count the pulses in the music. What you are counting is the **beat** of the music and, if you like the song, chances are good that your foot is tapping out the beats. The beat is determined by the **meter**, a musical notation for the rhythmic division of the music. For this example we'll use the easiest type of music, rhythmically speaking. The vast majority of rock and roll is written and played in what is called 4/4 time. The written notation is illustrated in Fig. 7.16.

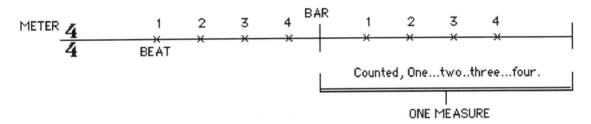

Fig. 7.16. Beats in 4/4 time.

In 4/4 time, a **measure** consists of four beats. Most drum patterns follow this structure: The snare drum plays on beats two and four, and the bass drum plays on beats one and three (Fig. 7.17).

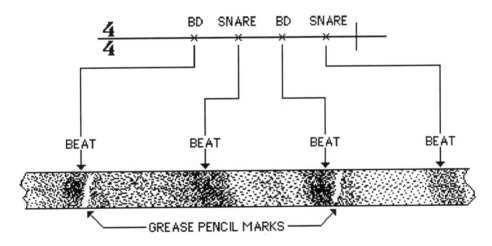

Fig. 7.17. Drum beats recorded on tape in 4/4 time.

187

If you record a piece of music and try the editing techniques we've discussed, you'll hear that rocking the reels will produce a "fwoop" as each beat passes over the play head. The general idea is to keep the rhythmic (and melodic) structure the same. To remove one bar, or measure, of music, you must cut just before the first beat of each measure. Any deviation would throw off the timing of the piece. The example shown (Fig. 7.17) shows two beats, or half a bar or measure, being removed.

In addition to maintaining the rhythmic structure of the music, the song structure has to be recognized. Again, the majority of contemporary music is structured along the guidelines shown in Fig. 7.18.

INTRO | VERSE A | VERSE B | CHORUS | VERSE A | VERSE B | CHORUS | END

Fig. 7.18. Typical song structure of contemporary music. This example is not a firm rule, and many songs may deviate slightly from the above example.

The **intro** (introduction) is usually based on the **chorus**, which is the focal point of the song. This is sometimes called the **hook** and is often the "catchy" part that people keep humming after hearing it. The verses may or may not change musically, but they might have a new set of lyrics for each one.

Assume that a mix of a song contained a verse that, for whatever reason, was unsuitable and had to be replaced. Following the guidelines above, verse "A" could be dubbed and, assuming that each is the same length and tempo, replace verse "B." In fact, the entire structure of the song could be rearranged.

C. VIDEO TAPE EDITING

To understand the concepts of modern post-production techniques, we must also discuss the ideas behind videotape editing. As this is a topic about which entire books have been written, this text will cover only the most basic aspects.

Videotape carries three basic types of signal: Video, audio and a control track (see Chapter 4 and Fig. 7.19). Without a continuous control track, a video deck has no way of recognizing frame locations on a videotape and will not stay synchronized with any other pieces of equipment.

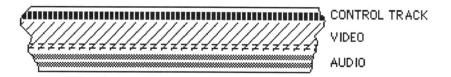

Fig. 7.19. Typical signals recorded on videotape.

Unlike analog tape editing, videotape is edited electronically; the operator never touches the tape. The simplest type of editing system, often referred to as **off line** or **A-roll**, is shown in Fig. 7.20. Note that the raw footage is put into the source deck, and that it is assembled in the desired order on the record deck.

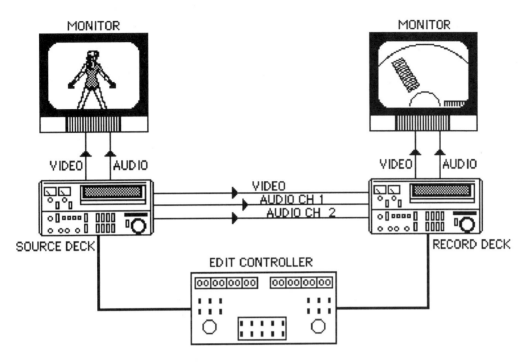

Fig. 7.20. Typical setup for off-line videotape editing.

This system is composed of an **edit controller**, two video decks and two **video monitors**. A video monitor is essentially a television without the receiver section. It displays only the image you supply to it at its video inputs. The edit controller controls the transport functions of the two video decks and remembers the location of the videotapes in each deck in one of two ways:

• By counting the pulses of control track supplied by each deck

• By reading time code (see Chapter 8) supplied by each deck.

There are specific advantages and disadvantages to using each method. Bear in mind that control track is only a series of pulses and contains no specific reference to any particular frame. Therefore, the edit controller must count these pulses and translate them into hours, minutes, seconds and frames. Once interrupted by either power failure or by ejection of a tape, the controller will have no way of knowing where any given footage is located. Time code, however, is a much more precise signal which *does* identify specific frames. A comparison of the two systems is outlined in Fig. 7.21.

	TIME CODE	CONTROL TRACK
LOCATION	WILL LOCATE SPECIFIC FRAMES	WILL NOT LOCATE SPECIFIC FRAMES
COMPATIBILITY	TAPES ARE INTERCHANGABLE BETWEEN ALL SMPTE SYSTEMS	TAPES WILL NOT WORK WITH SMPTE SYSTEMS
	CAN SYNCHRONIZE TO OTHER VIDEO AND AUDIO DECKS	CANNOT SYNCHONIZE TO AUDIO DECKS
ACCURACY	TIME REFERENCE IS PRECISE	TIME REFERENCE IS IMPRECISE. EDITS MAY SLIP BY A FEW FRAMES
SYNC	WILL NOT LOSE SYNC IF SYSTEM POWER IS LOST	WILL LOSE SYNC IF POWER IS LOST
COST	MORE EXPENSIVE	LESS EXPENSIVE
TRACKS	MAY LOSE ONE AUDIO TRACK TO RECORD CODE	NO EXTRA TRACK NEEDED; IS PART OF SIGNAL
EQUIPMENT	REQUIRES SPECIAL EQUIPMENT	NO SPECIAL EQUIPMENT REQUIRED

Fig. 7.21. Comparison of videotape editing systems which utilize control track and time code.

Assembly Editing

There are two basic methods of editing videotape. The first method is called **assembly editing** and is analogous to the assembly of an audiotape that is pieced together manually (Fig. 7.22).

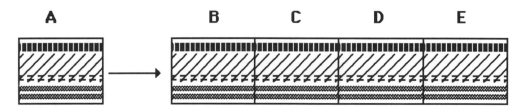

Fig. 7.22. Graphic representation of assembly editing.

Remember that the control track must be continuous and unbroken. In assembly editing, the edit controller is told which section of the raw footage in the play deck to play. The tape in the record deck is recorded sequentially from start to finish. The beginning of the sequence is called the **in point**; the end of the sequence is called the **out point**.

For example, assume that the introduction to the video (sequence "E") is recorded in the middle of the raw footage, and that the next scene (sequence "D") is recorded at its beginning. We would first play the introduction and record it at the beginning of the tape in the record deck. We would then play the next scene (located at the beginning of the raw footage), and record it after the introduction on the recorded tape. This process would continue, in sequence, until the tape was completed.

The most important concept underlying this type of editing is that the audio, video and control tracks are simultaneously recorded on the tape in the record deck, completely erasing any tracks already there.

190

Insert Editing

In **insert editing**, no control track is recorded. The tape being recorded to must first be recorded with continuous control track. This is called **blacking** or **recording black**. Because there is no high-speed system for doing this, a one-hour program takes one hour to "black." As a result, many production and post-production houses maintain a stock of prerecorded tapes.

The main advantage of insert editing, however, is that each audio channel and the video channel may be edited independently of each other, erasing only the audio or video that was previously recorded.

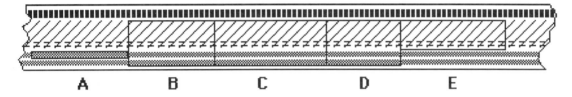

Fig. 7.23. Graphic representation of insert editing.

Using Fig. 7.23 as an example, note that sequence "E" contains only a video edit. The audio is left untouched. However, in sequences "D", "C" and "B", both the audio and video on the recorded tape have been replaced by new audio and video. In sequence "A," however, only one track of audio has been replaced.

The most important concept underlying insert editing is that each channel of audio and the video can be recorded separately of each other on the tape in the record deck, replacing or recording each in any sequence desired.

D. POST-AUDIO DURING VIDEO EDITING

Because insert editing lets you record one or both audio channels independently of the video signal, it is commonly used to add sound to the image. Consider an example in which the only system we have to work with is a simplified editing system, and the audio we want to use has been pre-recorded on video cassettes. The diagram in Fig. 7.24 and the next four illustrations represent the videotapes and their locations for this. The box on the left represents the tape in the source deck; the box on the right symbolizes the tape in the record deck. In both cases the audio channel numbers are given.

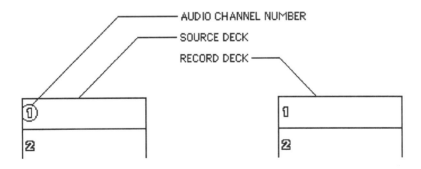

Fig. 7.24. Graphic representation of the layout of audio tracks in an off-line editing system.

For this example, presume that the original dialog was recorded with the video and that both were edited simultaneously. Music, recorded on track one of tape "A," is insert edited onto track two of the master tape (Fig. 7.25).

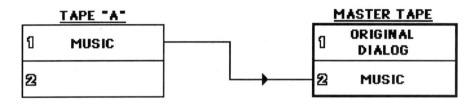

Fig. 7.25. Copying audio tracks.

However, we still need to add sound effects. Because there are no tracks open on the master tape, the master is put into the source deck, and the original dialog (track one) and music (track two) are combined through a mixer onto a new tape (tape "B"). Tape "B" is assemble edited along with picture (Fig. 7.26).

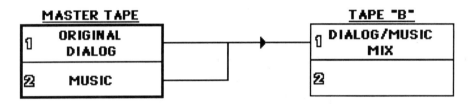

Fig. 7.26. Re-dubbing additional audio.

The master tape (source deck) is replaced with tape "C," which contains the sound effects required for the piece. These are insert edited onto track two of tape "B" (Fig. 7.27). Note that this step and the previous one are repeated as often as necessary. If there is more than one tape of sound effects, music or dialog, these must be constantly re-combined by switching tapes and mixing.

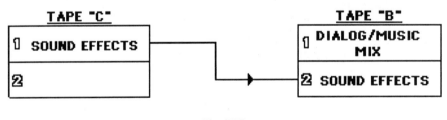

Fig. 7.27

The entire audio material, when completed, is then re-inserted onto the master tape on one or both channels (Fig. 7.28).

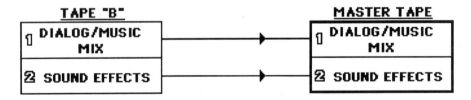

Fig. 7.28. Re-inserting the completed audio.

Yet another way to treat the audio portion of the tape is to run several decks simultaneously. But this approach often results in both less sonic control and a buildup of noise. It also requires a much more expensive and complex editing system.

E. FILM EDITING

As with audio and video editing, we must also examine the conventional methods of editing film. Since the single-system method (where sound and picture are recorded into the camera) is never used professionally, this chapter will be limited to the basic aspects of editing film that is shot and recorded on the double system.

When film is shot, the negative must be processed by a lab. A print of the raw footage is returned for projection, or **screening**. As professional shoots require a daily review of the material shot, this footage is called a **daily** or **rush**. The best **takes** (sequences of footage) are chosen, and the sound, which recorded on 1/4-inch tape, is transferred to fullcoat. The rushes and sound are then placed on a **synchronizer** to insure that the two are synchronized and to allow the labeling of both sound and picture reels. Synchronizers are available in a multitude of different configurations (Fig. 7.29).

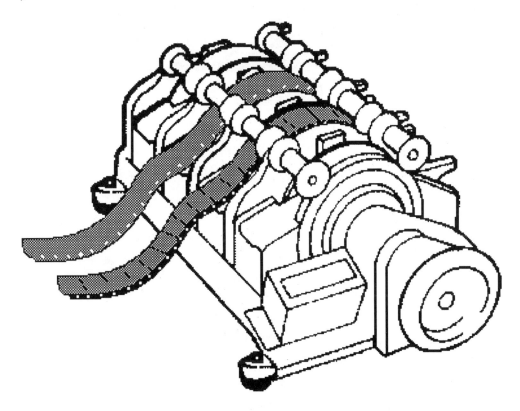

Fig. 7.29. A film synchronizer.

At the beginning and end of each take, a **clapslate** is simultaneously recorded and shot on film. The clapslate is essentially a chalkboard with a moving clapper. The individual take numbers and other information are written on the slate for each take (Fig. 7.30).

Fig. 7.30. A slate.

At the start of a shoot, an assistant holds the slate so that it is shot on film. When the director indicates to the crew and actors that the film is rolling, the clappers are struck together, creating a sharp percussive sound, and the assistant quickly gets out of **frame** (the visual area captured by the camera) (Fig. 7.31).

Fig. 7.31. Slating a shot.

194

The sound and picture are synchronized by locating the sound of the clappers and the visual frame. Both sound and picture are carefully marked, labeled and stored on spools.

The synchronized takes are then placed on a **Steenbeck** or **flatbed**. The Steenbeck is a machine that lets you display the picture in sync with sound. Units are available in a wide variety of configurations. Fig. 7.32 shows a six-plate configuration, and Fig. 7.33 shows a birds-eye view of four-plate Steenbeck. Eight- and ten-plate configurations are also available.

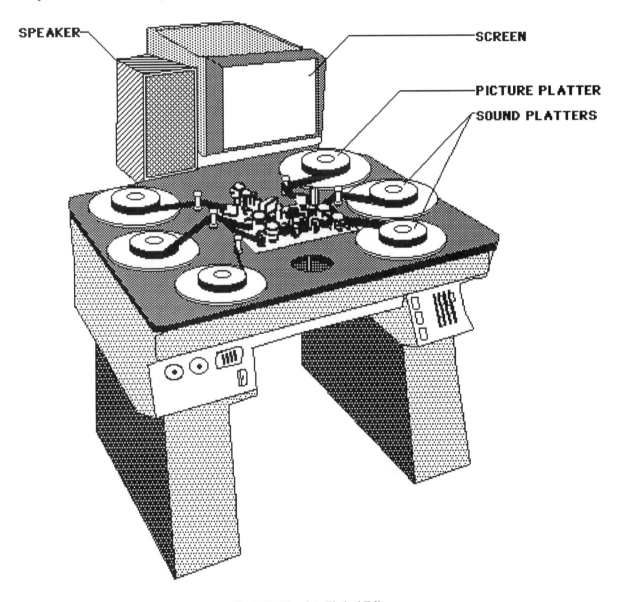

Fig. 7.32. Six-plate Flatbed Editor.

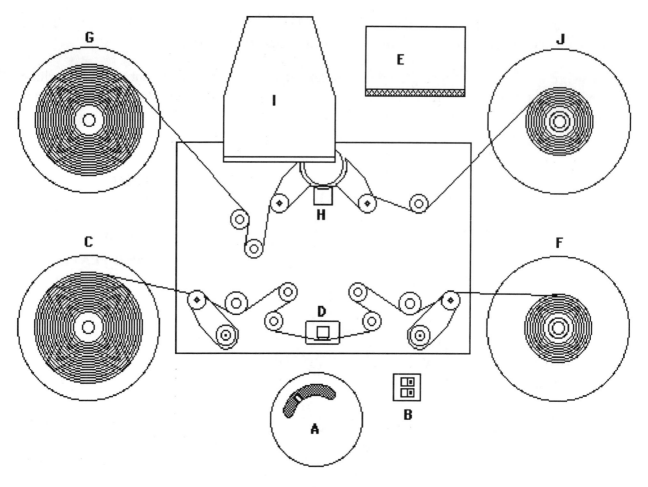

Fig. 7.33. Four plate Flatbed editor, seen from above.

"A" is the transport control lever for the plates. Its positions are (left to right) fast reverse, normal speed reverse, slow reverse, and slow forward, normal speed forward and fast forward. "B" switches each set of plates on and off; the transport control lever only affects those plates that are switched on. "C" is the feed plate for the fullcoat stock. "D" is the sound playback head, which is heard through the speaker, "E." "F" is the fullcoat take-up plate. "G" is the supply plate for the film. "H" is the lamp assembly, enabling the projection of the image onto the viewer "I." "J" is the take-up plate for the film.

The separate (and synchronized) takes are put on the Steenbeck, and the editing process begins. The piece of equipment used is called a **splicer** (Fig. 7.34).

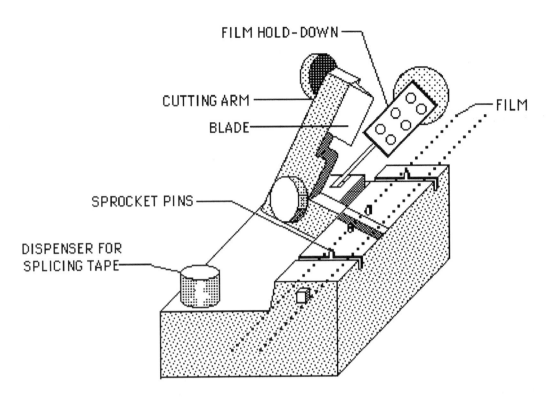

Fig. 7.34. A splicer, used in editing film.

As with audiotape, a generous amount of leader is placed before the first image, and the scenes are then assembled in their intended sequence. The frames on which the edits are to be made are identified, put in the splicer, cut and spliced to the new image. The sound is also cut so that each segment remains synchronized. Where no sound is available, leader or discarded film is spliced into the fullcoat stock so that synchronization to the picture is preserved. When used this way, the blank material is referred to as **sound fill**.

When the picture has been fully edited, the print is sent to a negative cutter who does the actual editing of the negative. Most filmmakers prefer to leave this job to an experienced professional because the negative is delicate and easily scratched. Improper handling may result in the loss of part or all of the film.

F. FILM POST-PRODUCTION AUDIO

When the negative is edited, a second print of the film is made, and additional sound effects, narration, dialog and music are added to the picture in sync using a flatbed, a **Foley Studio** (see below) or both.

Audio Transfers

Non-synchronous, or "wild" sounds (see chapter 8) such as sound effects, music and some voice can be transferred from any sound source (e.g., cassette deck, CD player, turntable, Nagra deck) to a magnetic dubbing machine, commonly referred to as a **dubber**. The process of transferring recorded dialog to mag stock is explained in Chapter 8.

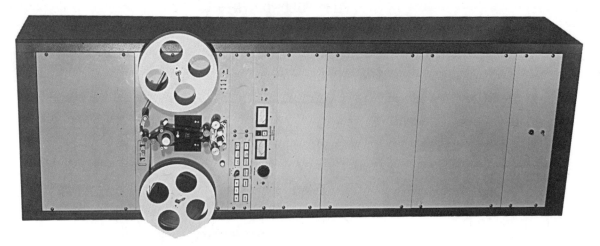

Fig. 7.35. The MRDE 4036 16mm-35mm recorder-reproducer. This type of dubber is commonly used in film post-production.
(Photo Courtesy of Magna-Tech Electronic Co., Inc.)

The dubber holds magnetic stock (see chapter 4) and operates in much the same way as a conventional audiotape recorder. The selected sounds are recorded onto the magnetic film, and later "cut to picture" on a flatbed.

Foley Studios

A **Foley Studio** is a facility where sound effects are recorded in synchronization with the picture. These studios are named after Jack Foley, the inventor of conventional film effects recording studios. Fig. 7.36 illustrates the principle behind the Foley Studio:

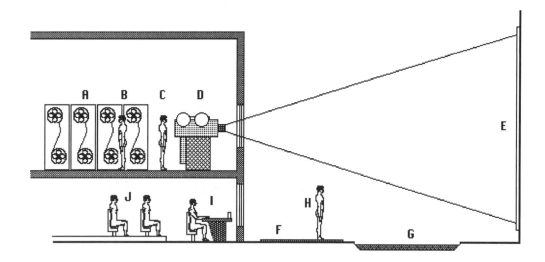

Fig. 7.36. Typical layout of a Foley Studio.

Note that the sound recording (A) and projection (D) equipment are located in a separate soundproofed room, and are running in synchronization at all times. The dubber operator (B) and projectionist (C) are each responsible for the operation of their respective machines. The projected image (E) is viewed by a performer (H) who then re-creates the desired sound(s) in sync to the picture. Microphones are placed within the studio (not shown) to capture the sounds being created. In this example, footsteps on a hardwood floor (F) and gravel pit (G) are to be recorded. The sound engineer(s) (I) will operate the console while the staff takes direction from the producer or director (J).

Foley studios are generally very large and require considerable staff and maintenance personnel. Since the objective of recording in a Foley Studio is to be able to record any sounds in synchronization to picture, some studios are capable of having cars, motorcycles and other vehicles drive into the recording area. For the most part, Foley Studios are equipped with a multitude of different floor surfaces (e.g. gravel, dried leaves, wood, etc.).

Dialogue Looping and Dubbing

In some cases dialogue recorded on location may be faulty or it may have been impossible to record dialogue at all. In either case a **looping stage** (also called a **dubbing stage**, **theater** or **studio**) must be used to record or re-record the dialogue. This process is called **looping, dialogue replacement, dubbing, post-dubbing** or **post-synchronization**. The looping stage is similar to a Foley Studio, except that the recording area is much smaller, and is used to record only an actor or actors. During the **looping session** both the film and magnetic stock are cut and spliced to form a continuous loop. The footage is viewed repeatedly until the actor or actors have achieved precise lip sync and the final take has been recorded. Recordings are generally made as the rehearsal takes place, and each pass of the magnetic loop erases the previous take.

Fig. 7.37. ELII Electronic Looping Control Console for ADR and Foley Recording. The dubbers and projector are controlled from this or a similar device during looping sessions.
(Photo Courtesy of Magna-Tech Electronic Co., Inc.)

Film Mixing

When the editing process has been completed, each spool holds its own category of sound. These categories are generally broken down into dialogue, narration, music, and sound effects (see chapter 8). Three reels might contain sound effects, two might hold music, four might be dialogue and so on. Each reel is referred to as a **track**. The studio proper (Fig. 7.38) will have a number of dubbers, all synchronized to each other and to the projector located in a separate, soundproofed room. The sound mixer (engineer) controls the operation of the projector and, consequently, all of the dubbers. Each dubber holds a separate track, and each is fed into an individual channel on the console. A footage counter located beneath the screen indicates the location of the picture at all times.

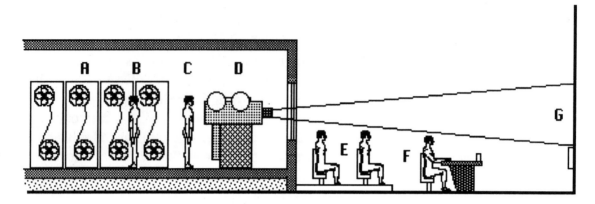

Fig. 7.38. Typical layout of a film mixing facility.

Typical film mixing studio with dubbers (A), dubber operator (B), projectionist (C), projector (D), clients (i.e., producer, director, etc.) (E), sound mixer (F) and projected image (G).

The mix is created by the combination of various dubbers (and tracks) onto the appropriate 35-mm (or 70-mm) fullcoat. For example, assume that dubbers one through four ran various dialog tracks. These might be mixed onto channel one of the 35-mm (or 70-mm) fullcoat. Dubbers five, six and seven might back music tracks, and would be mixed onto channel two. Dubbers eight through 11 could contain sound effects, and would be combined onto track three. Dubbers 12, 13 and 14 might have narrative tracks, and would be mixed onto channel four (Fig. 7.39).

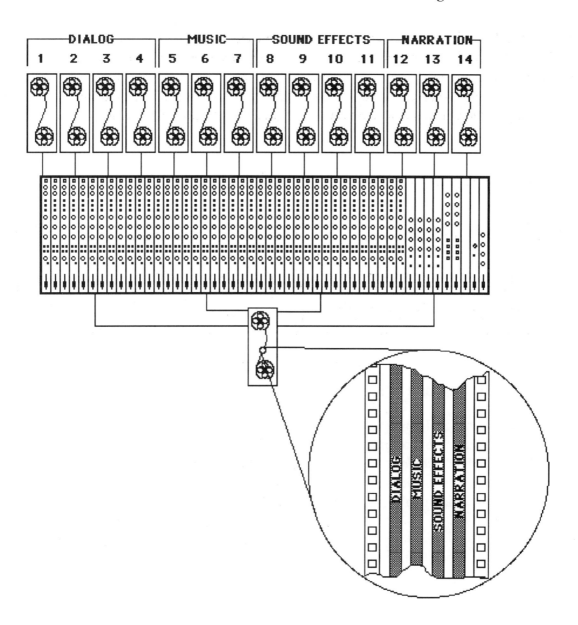

Fig. 7.39. Graphic representation of dubbers, each playing individual tracks in film; the levels, equalization, panning, and processing are controlled via the console. The end result is combined onto multistripe 35mm stock.

Unlike conventional audio mixing, film mixing is done by repeating a short sequence until the required balances among the different tracks are achieved. All of the dubbers, the projector, and the 35-mm (or 70-mm) dubber are interlocked and running in synchronization. They are rewound and played repeatedly until the sequence being mixed is completed. The next section of film is mixed in the same manner, and so on until the entire film has been mixed. This method of mixing is called **roll back**, **forward-backward** or **rock and roll** because the entire system is "rocked" back and "rolled" forward.

When the mix has been completed, the 35-mm (or 70-mm) fullcoat and picture negative may be sent to a lab and used to create an optical negative, which is in turn converted into an optical positive called an **answer print**. The answer print is the copy used for projection on optical systems.

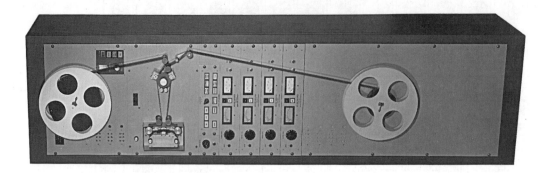

Fig. 7.40. MR-10036-4 High-speed Electronic Master Recorder. This is one type of master recorder used in film mixing. (Photo Courtesy of Magna-Tech Electronic Co., Inc.)

Preparation for Film Mixing

Studio time is expensive, and errors can cost the client dearly. To avoid any possible difficulties during a mix, each track must be properly prepared prior to the mixing session:

Leaders no less than 8 feet long must be placed at the head of every track, and at least 20 feet at each tail after the last frame of picture (including titles). *Thie leader is essential for the proper threading of the studio's dubbers.* Otherwise, should sync be lost during mixing, it will be necessary to rewind the system to the start of the film to re-establish sync. All leader should be "single perf" to avoid misthreading of the dubbers.

The leaders must identify both the head and tail ends with the position of the leader (i.e., head or tail), the title of the film, the track type and its order. Fig. 7.41 shows an example of leader markings.

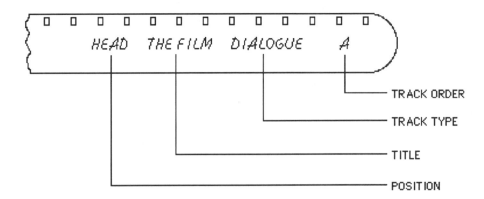

Fig. 7.41. Proper marking of a head leader.

In addition, the head leaders should all have a punch mark in the identical position at least 6 feet from the start of the leader. This will help the studio staff to verify sync as the picture starts. Also, the tail leaders should all have a punch mark in the identical position at least 5 feet after the last frame of picture to help the studio staff verify sync at the tail without rewinding.

The head leader on the film should be followed by **Academy leader** (see below). Academy leader is sometimes called **Society leader** or **SMPTE leader** (Fig. 7.42). Academy leader gives the projectionist a countdown, picture information and focusing time. The leader is also used by laboratories and mixing studios to verify proper synchronization.

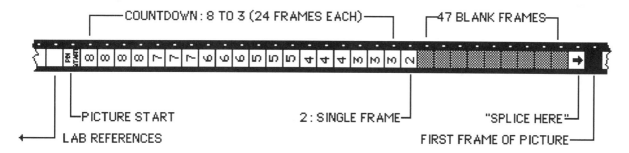

Fig. 7.42. The components of Academy Leader.

From head to tail, Academy Leader contains:

•Lab references and sound information, usually reserved for processing technicians.

•One frame indicating "PICTURE START."

•Numbers from "8" to "3" with exactly 24 frames of each.

•One single frame of the number "2."

•47 blank frames.

•One frame indicating "SPLICE HERE" with an arrow pointing down.

•The next frame is the first frame of film.

Lastly, a single frame of fullcoat containing a "beep" should be spliced into each track's head leader directly opposite the academy leader's "2" frame. This one synchronizing point will guarantee that sync is maintained to the answer print.

Film Cue Sheets

Cue sheets are written records of the positions and locations of specific sounds in each track, and are compiled by the editor and used by the sound mixer during a mixing session. Indications of sound locations are given in feet and inches. This method of counting depends on the film's format. Larger formats will have fewer frames per foot, even though almost all formats run at 24 frames per second (see Chapter 7). The **frames per foot** or **FPF** for each format is as follows:

Format	FPF
8 mm	80
Super 8 mm	72
16 mm	40
Super 16 mm	40
35 mm	16
70 mm	12-4/5

The cue sheet is drawn as a series of columns not unlike a track sheet (see chapter 6). Each column represents a given track and should be marked (from left to right) as narration, dialog, music and sound effects. (Fig. 7.43)

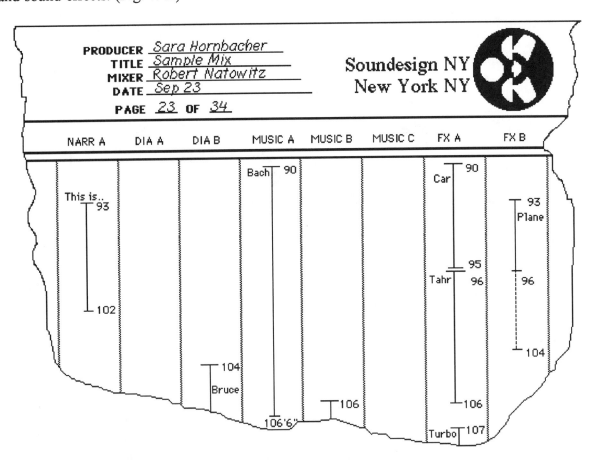

Fig. 7.43. One page of a typical cue sheet.

Vertical lines indicate that sound is playing on a specific track. The numbers at the start and end of each line represent footage counts, which is displayed by the counter below the screen (Fig. 7.38). Crossfades or sounds continuing past their intended use should be indicated by a dotted line (see Fig. 7.43, FX B track, 96 to 104 feet). Ideally, footage should be given in 35-mm or 70-mm counts, as these are the fastest frame rates and, therefore, the most accurate. If working in 16-mm, 35-mm counts can be obtained by multiplying the 16-mm count by 2.5 (e.g., 100 feet times 2.5 = 250 feet).

For narration tracks, write out the first and last few word of each narrative passage. Dialog tracks should be indicated by the character's name speaking the part. Music tracks should be indicated by the piece that's played. Finally, sound effects should be designated as simply as possible.

The principle behind the cue sheet is to be able to locate, at a glance, which tracks are playing. For this reason, the cue sheet should be cleanly written, easy to read and free of technical notes.

As a final note, it is recommended that you refer to the end of Chapter 6 for notes regarding the frequency responses involved with mixing to film.

8
TIME CODE AND
SYNCHRONIZATION

A. INTRODUCTION

To this point we've discussed different formats and media and the techniques required for dealing with each. The basic concept behind professional audio post-production is to physically isolate the audio from the film or video component, making it easier and more efficient to treat the audio portion of a given piece or project. **Synchronization** is what keeps the audio, although separated, in step with the image as if the two were physically unified. Thus, synchronization, or sync, is an essential aspect of post-production work.

Assume for a moment that you had two identical audio tape decks each having an identical audio tape set in exactly the same starting position. If both decks are connected to the same power source, set to the same speed and are started at exactly the same time, one deck will have fallen slightly behind the other by the time each reaches the end of the tape. This occurs because the error caused by even a slight variation in speed will accumulate and increase by the time the end is reached.

Synchronization is achieved differently for each media, although the concepts underlying each method are relatively simple. This book deals with the most recent trends in audio post-production, and these are derived from the merging of different technologies and practices, a merging that can cause confusion for the beginner.

Synchronization systems fall into two distinct categories: mechanical and electronic.

B. FILM SYNC

Film Sync in Production

Production in film almost always uses the double system (see Chapter 4). In this system, the camera records only the image while a separate specialized reel-to-reel tape recorder is used to record sound. Both the camera and tape recorder are specifically designed so that a common sync signal is recorded on each simultaneously. Since both sound and picture are recorded on physically separated media, this technique insures that both sound and picture can be re-synchronized later in the post-production process. The four different methods of recording the synchronizing signal, also called a **sync pulse**, are called **Pilot Tone**, **Ranger Tone**, **Perfectone**, and **Synchrotone**. Note that one commonly used brand of tape recorder, a Nagra, uses the Pilot Tone system only.

The Pilot Tone system is the most commonly used and records two tones down the center of the tape which are combined with the audio signal. Because the tones are recorded 180 degrees out of phase, they cancel each other during playback. As a result, only the recorded audio is heard (Fig. 8.1).

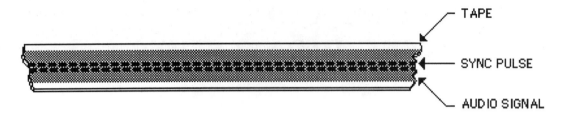

Fig. 8.1. Pilot Tone sync pulses recorded within an audio tape.

The Ranger Tone system records a single sync pulse down the center of the tape. The head used to record and play back the tone is at a different angle relative to the tape than the audio playback heads. Consequently the audio heads do not reproduce the pulse.

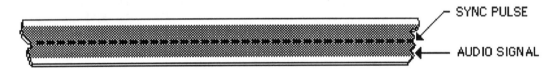

Fig. 8.2 Ranger Tone sync pulses recorded within an audio tape.

Perfectone records sync pulses on the outer edge of the tape. Because these pulses are located away from the audio signal, which is between the pulse tracks, the audio heads again do not pick up the pulse signal.

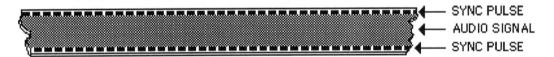

Fig. 8.3. Two Perfectone sync pulses recorded on either side of an audio tape.

The Synchrotone system is used in conjunction with stereo recording, and records a sync pulse down a center track in between the two audio tracks. This format is similar to center-stripe time code (see chapter 4).

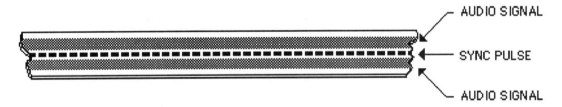

Fig. 8.4. Synchrotone sync pulses recorded down the center of an audio tape.

The synchronizing signal, regardless of the system used to record it, is essentially the same. The pulse itself consists of a 60-Hz signal generated in the camera motor. Because film runs at 24 frames per second (frame rates are explained in later in this chapter), each frame of film is indicated by 2.5 cycles of sync pulse (60 Hz divided by 24 = 2.5) recorded on the tape.

Most location productions require a portable power source for the camera. A typical portable source is battery belt holding NiCad or similarly rechargeable batteries (Fig. 8.5). Over time, the batteries will deliver less than full power, causing the camera to speed to slow down slightly. It is the sync pulse that maintains the relationship between camera and tape speeds. If, for example, the camera is running at 23 fps, the sync pulse recorded on tape will consist of a 57.5 Hz signal.

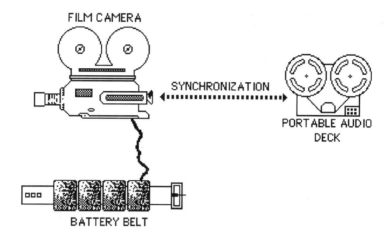

Fig. 8.5. Graphic representation of synchronization during film production.

There are two systems used to record the sync pulse signal on tape: **cable sync**, or **umbilical**, and **crystal sync**. Cable sync is the earlier of the two systems and carries a sync pulse produced by a small AC generator which is coupled to the camera motor. A cable is physically connected to both the camera and tape deck, and transmits the pulse to the deck.

Crystal sync utilizes a crystal based oscillator to generate a 60-Hz pulse, and both camera and deck have their own oscillator. The pulse from the camera's oscillator regulates the motor speed, ensuring that it runs at a constant 24 fps. The tape deck's oscillator has the dual function of regulating tape-to-camera speed and generating the tone to be recorded.

Film Sync in Post-production

When all footage and sound have been shot, the sync pulse is used in the **transfer** of 1/4-inch tape to the film's magnetic stripe (see Chapter 4). In this process, the audio is copied to the dubber through a **resolver**, which controls the speed fluctuations of the dubber's motors and, therefore, maintaining the frame-to-frame relationship between picture and sound (Fig. 8.6).

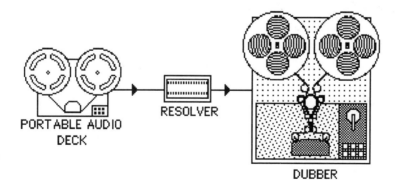

Fig. 8.6. Transferring recorded production audio to mag stock. The mag dubber is synchronized by the sync pulses on the audio tape.

At this point it's important to realize that film synchronization after production relies entirely on mechanical means. Whether on a flatbed, dubber or projector, all film media rely on mechanically coupled sprocketed wheels to ensure uniform movement between sound and image:

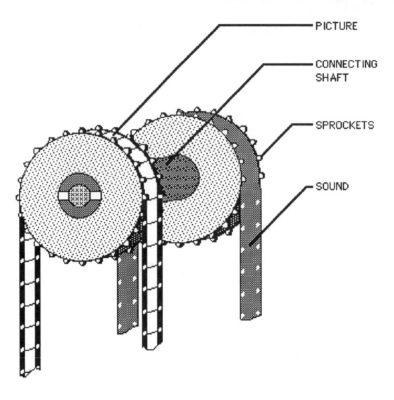

Fig. 8.7. Mechanical synchronization of sound and picture.

Bi-phase Synchronization

Film equipment also utilizes a signal known as a **bi-phase signal** in much the same way that a pilot tone is used. The bi-phase signal, usually generated by the drive motors of a magnetic dubber, varies in content and format between machines from different manufacturers. As a result, there are multiple standards in use today. Magna-Tech equipment, for example, provides a 10-pulse-per-frame, or a 240-Hz, signal (10 pulses x 24 frames per second).

This type of signal does not, however, provide any other synchronizing information other that to regulate speed. If a frame were to slip (an unlikely but possible occurrence), the film equipment would have no way of detecting or compensating for the slipped frame. The only correction possible is to stop all the equipment, return to the start of the film, re-synchronize all machines and start over.

C. SMPTE TIME CODE

In 1967, The Society of Motion Picture and Television Engineers (SMPTE), developed a system geared towards editing videotape called **time code**. This method varied considerably from other systems previously in use in that it overcame the problems created by those systems, notably slippage and loss of location information. Time code, unlike previous methods, can locate any point on a given tape, regardless of the starting point.

In comparison, the control track is only a series of pulses recorded on video tape, with no other synchronizing information. It is the electrical equivalent of sprocket holes on a piece of film. With time code, however, each frame has its own unique identification number as indicated in Fig. 8.8.

HOURS   MINUTES   SECONDS   FRAMES

Fig. 8.8. A typical time code counter.

This identification number is called a **time code address**. Because it can locate events and locations on tape, time code is used, among other things, to index or log archival and production footage.

At the same time, audio post-production benefits greatly from this system because it becomes possible to locate any given point on an audio or video tape. It lets an operator treat each medium as a separate entity, as opposed to recording unprocessed audio directly onto the tracks of a video tape. Physically separating the audiotape allows for the complete treatment of complete audio, and its subsequent assembly with video and film. The process of recording audio and video separately and later combining them in post-production is fully discussed in Chapter 9.

The recording of the longitudinal time code signal onto an audio track of an ATR or VTR is called **striping**.

D. TYPES OF TIME CODE

There are essentially two main types of time code, each with two variations. The main types are called the **longitudinal time code** andthe **vertical interval time code**.

Longitudinal Time Code

The longitudinal time code, or LTC, is the most common and least expensive time code. The LTC is recorded directly onto an audio track of an audio or video deck as if it were another audio signal. If fact, it *is* essentially an audio signal: a square wave consisting of 2,400 bits of information per second (80 bits per frame) and, if patched into a monitoring system, sounds like a tone (Fig. 8.9):

Fig. 8.9. Audio pulses of time code.

Address Track Time Code

The address track on a videotape (see Chapter 4) was developed for the recording of notes made during production by a producer or director. It is essentially a third, low-quality audio track. As such, it is frequently used for recording the longitudinal time code. Striping on the address track allows the two main audio channels to be used for stereo recording.

211

In all cases, the address-track time code must be recorded on a tape before or during the recording of the video signal. It cannot be added later. If the master videotape is to contain address track code, a tape must first be recorded with the "black" or video signal and address track code simultaneously. A common practice is to then insert edit all video and audio material onto the tape, leaving both the black and the address track code continuous and undisturbed.

Reading LTC at Shuttle Speed

Even when the LTC on a particular tape is properly recorded, difficulties in reading it can a result from tape speed variations. If an audio or videotape is shuttled at speeds above or below the correct playing speed, the time code circuitry may not be able to decode the incoming code. Some time code circuits can, however, calculate the tape's position from the transport's speed and position.

VITC

The vertical interval time code, abbreviated as VITC (pronounced VIT-CEE) carries the same information as the LTC as well as some additional synchronizing data. The primary difference between the two is that the VITC is recorded and integrated into a portion of the video signal called the vertical blanking interval. The important point is that the VITC is an integral part of the video signal. The VITC, however, is not seen when the tape is played back. Instead, the video signal is routed through a device that interprets the time code portion of the signal and then converts it to an LTC.

Because the VITC is integrated into the video signal, like the address track code it cannot be added to the later. The VITC must be recorded simultaneously with the video image.

Advantages of VITC

There are several advantages to using VITC over LTC. Primarily, these are:

1. Video heads are in constant rotation, even when the videotape is paused; audio heads are fixed in place and motionless. Consequently, the VITC can be read over speeds ranging from paused tape (i.e., stopped) to fast wind speeds.

2. The VITC does not require a dedicated audio track. Unlike the LTC, the time code signal is recorded directly into the video signal.

3. The VITC is the most accurate method of recording a time code. Again, because the code is recorded directly into the video signal, it serves as an index to each individual frame. In contrast, the relationship between the LTC and the video signal may slip by a frame.

4. The VITC can be easily converted to LTC for equipment requiring LTC.

Despite these advantages, however, use of VITC is far less common than that of LTC.

E. FRAME RATES

A frame of film or video is roughly considered to be the information it takes to construct one visual image. This is easy to visualize for film, which you can hold between your fingers and examine (Fig. 8.10):

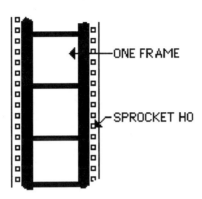

ONE FRAME

SPROCKET HO

Fig. 8.10. Film with frames and sprockets.

Video, however, is another story. To the eye, video tape appears much like 3/4-inch-wide audio tape. There are no physical distinctions between frames. The frames themselves are determined electronically by the equipment that recorded the series of images on the tape.

In the early days of video, all images were black and white (monochrome) and displayed at a rate of exactly 30 frames per second. Consequently, was comparatively easy to time program material: One second equaled 30 frames, 1 minute equaled 1,800 frames and so on.

However, when color video was introduced in the late 1940s this simplicity was lost. Because of the complexity of the color video signal, and for a variety of other technical reasons, operation of the color system required that the frame rate be altered slightly. For that reason,the National Television Standards Committee (NTSC) adopted a frame rate of 29.97 frames per second.

F. DROP AND NON-DROP FRAME TIME CODE

Because NTSC video runs at 29.97 fps, using the 30-fps SMPTE code will eventually result in a drift of 3.6 seconds every hour. This is be calculated as follows:

•30 fps - 29.97 fps = 0.03 frames drift per second, so

•0.03 frames drift per second x 60 seconds = 1.8 frames drift per minute, and

•1.8 frames drift per minute x 60 minutes = 108 frames drift per hour

To compensate for this drift, 2 frames every minute, or 108 frames per hour, of SMPTE are dropped.

This is done by dropping two frames each minute, *except for every tenth minute*. Without the tenth-minute exception this scheme would drop 120 frames every hour instead of 108.

Frame dropping occurs only at each minute's changeover point. For example, when the time code

213

changes from 01:11:59:29, the next number would be 01:12:00:02. This time code is called a **drop-frame time code**. A time code that does not drop frames is called a **non-drop-frame time code**.

Because the object of frame dropping is to match the frame rate of both the time code and NTSC video, a drop-frame time code is used in conjunction with NTSC color video. The use of this type of code ensures that the frame rate of both the video signal and the code match. If this was not the case, the two would drift apart to the extent the time code would be useless for timing or frame identification.

The drop-frame time code is used primarily in broadcast applications, where the length of a television program must correspond to an exact broadcasting time slot. However, non-drop frame code allows for direct calculations of event durations. Later in the book, we'll discuss how computers work in synchronization with post-production systems, but suffice it say that some software and time code equipment will not run properly if drop-frame code is used.

Whatever time code is used, it is essential that it be used consistently. Although some systems will allow for the use of two different types of code on two different tapes, it is generally good practice to use one type of code throughout a production or post-production project, and to use the same type of code on every audio and video tape involved.

The SMPTE time code frame rates commonly used in the United States are as follows:

- **24 Frames** .... This type of code is commonly used in conjunction with certain film applications.

- **25 Frames** .... Used when tapes conforming to European Broadcast Standards (EBU) are used. Video of this type is known as the PAL format, and is not used in the United States.

- **29.97 Non-Drop Frame** .... Used with NTSC video in conjunction with non-broadcast applications.

- **29.97 Drop Frame** .... Used with NTSC video, primarily with material intended for broadcast.

- **30 Frames** .... Early time code used with monochrome video. Sometimes used in film sound recording applications.

G. OTHER TYPES OF SYNCHRONIZING TONES

There are several other types of synchronizing tones and signals which should be mentioned.

Control Track

The control track, as mentioned in the introduction, is a series of pulses recorded on video tape, with no other synchronizing information or frame identification. It is analogous to sprocket holes on a piece of film. The control track on a videotape is required for frame counting and signal synchronization by video decks and editing systems.

FSK

FSK, or frequency shift keying, is rarely used anymore. It was introduced by some musical equipment manufacturers as an early method of synchronizing musical equipment (such as drum computers) to audio tape, permitting the user to overdub tracks on home equipment. Like the control track, it consists of a series of pulses recorded only for timing and tempo. FSK carries no other synchronizing information. It is extremely prone to tape errors, and its use was eventually discontinued because of its unreliability.

H. SYNCHRONIZATION OF TIME CODE TO VIDEO

When recording a time code to videotape, the time code must be synchronized to the video signal. If it is not, the relationship of time-code frame counts to picture frames will eventually drift, and what the code counts will have little to do with the video image.

Synchronization between the time code device and the video deck is accomplished by supplying each with the same sync information. This signal is called **black burst**, and is supplied by a **black burst generator** (Fig. 8.11). Because the VITC is automatically synchronized to image by the fact that it is embedded in the signal, this requirement applies only to the use of LTC.

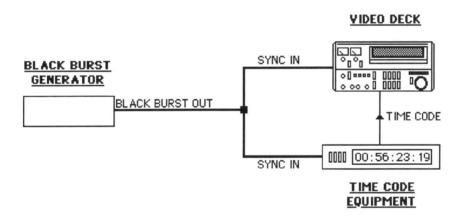

Fig. 8.11. Genlocking time code to video.

The synchronization of the video signal to a video reference is called **genlocking**, or **genlock**. In subsequent discussions black burst synchronization will be omitted from the accompanying diagrams for the sake of clarity. Moreover, some time code equipment is not supplied with an external sync input. In that case, the equipment derives its synchronization from the video signal itself.

I. TIME CODE EQUIPMENT

Before proceeding further, there are several pieces of time code equipment that you should first become familiar with.

The device that actually creates the time code signal is called a **time code generator**. Depending on the manufacturer, it may or may not display the time code numbers. A **time code reader** interprets previously recorded time code signal, and it too may or may not actually display the time code numbers.

Fig. 8.12. The Cipher Digital 710A Time Code Reader.
(Photo Courtesy of Cipher Digital, Inc.)

A **character inserter** or **window dubber** superimposes the actual time code numbers on a videotape for display (Fig. 8.13).

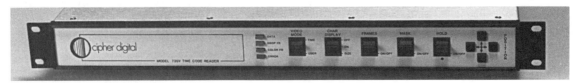

Fig. 8.13. The Cipher Digital 735V Time Code Reader and Character Inserter.
(Photo Courtesy of Cipher Digital, Inc.)

This readout is recorded onto the videotape for identifying frame when in the search modes. All of some of these devices may share a common box or enclosure. For example, a reader-generator is a character inserter that can both read and generate code.

Fig. 8.14. The Cipher Digital CDI-750 This device can read and generate LTC and character insert.
(Photo Courtesy of Cipher Digital, Inc.)

The following functions are commonly found on time code equipment:

Preset

Preset lets the user begin generating time code at any number. For example, if a generator is preset to begin producing code at 00:01:01:00, the time code will start from that point and continue sequentially.

Continuous Jam Sync

An LTC cannot be reliably recorded from one deck to another when copying tapes. That's because, by the third and even second generation, the code starts distorting to the point where it becomes unreadable by the equipment. Instead, a time code generator-reader is placed in a mode called **continuous jam sync** (also called **reshape**, **regenerate** or **transfer**), which "cleans up" the incoming code and re-generates it onto the next tape (Fig. 8.15):

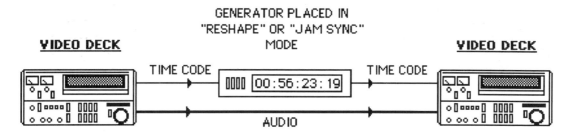

Fig. 8.15. Creating a video dub with picture, audio, and time code.

When the generator-reader no longer receives a time code, however, its ceases to produce an output. In other words, it can only regenerate a time code that it receives and cannot one on its own. Continuous jam sync is generally used for copying a tape that has no time code problems.

One-Time Jam Sync

A generator that operates in a **one-time jam sync** mode is similar to one that operates in the continuous jam sync mode, except that it does more than just regenerate the incoming code. Instead, once it receives and registers a valid time code number, the generator begins emitting a code starting with the number received. Moreover, it continues to generate code regardless of the continuity of the time code from the input device.

For example, consider a VTR that stops, halting the time code it supplies. If the time code device registers a valid number, it continues to emit a code. Thus, a one-time jam sync is used to, among other things, make a dub of a striped tape where a dropout or accidental erasure has interrupted the original code.

Drop or Non-drop Frame

Most devices will allow the user to select between drop frame or non-drop frame modes.

J. INTERLOCK SYSTEMS

One problem that has always plagued video has been poor audio quality, and the lack of suitable methods available to treat and manipulate the audio material. Admittedly, the audio quality of video decks has improved in recent years. Nevertheless, to answer the need for increased audio control and flexibility, some manufacturers have developed ways of having a multitrack deck and a video deck run together in perfect synchronization. This process is called **audio-video interlock** and is available through a number of systems.

In every type of interlock system, one deck is designated as the **master** and is the unit to which one or more **slaves** are synchronized. Furthermore, interlock systems may consist of both video and audio decks, or audio decks only. In systems using both video and audio decks, the video transport is almost invariably designated as the master.

There are two basic types of interlock systems, with some variations on each theme. These are the control synchronization system and audio chase synchronization system.

Control Synchronization System

Figure 8.12 shows a basic control synchronization interlock system.

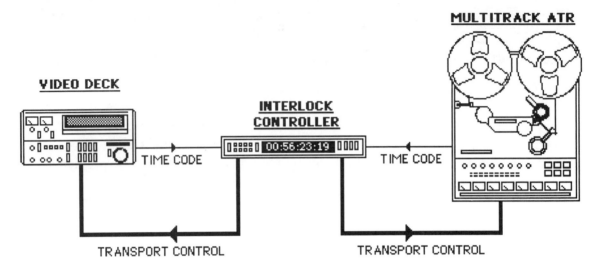

Fig. 8.16. The basic system used in audio/video interlock. Each deck supplies time code numbers to the interlock controller, which, in turn, controls the position of each deck.

The system works this way: A time code, recorded on both the videotape and on one track of the multitrack, is fed into what is called the **interlock controller.** Most contorllers display one or more sets of time code numbers. The controller determines where on the tape both the audio and video decks are playing. If, for example, the video deck is playing at a given second, and the time code number at that second is 00:00:12:23, the controller will assume the audio deck should be playing its tape at that number at the exact same time.

To achieve this, the controller sends control signals over a transport cable plugged into a connector on the back of each deck. The transport cables carry signals which instruct each machine to stop, rewind, fast forward, etc. Using this system, both the audio and video decks stay exactly synchronized from start to finish, with multitrack deck acting, in effect, as an extension of the video deck's audio capacity.

Audio Chase Synchronization System

The second type of interlock system is called an **audio chase** synchronization system (Fig. 8.17). This is exactly like the basic technique of interlocking, instead of transport control signals being sent to the video deck.to determine the audio deck's transport mode, time code numbers are fed from the video deck. For example, if "play" is pressed on the video deck, the audio deck will play. If the video deck is stopped, the audio deck stops as well. The audio deck is said to "chase" the video.

As before, the video deck is considered to be the master, and the audio deck the slave. All of the transport actions of the master determine the slave's actions.

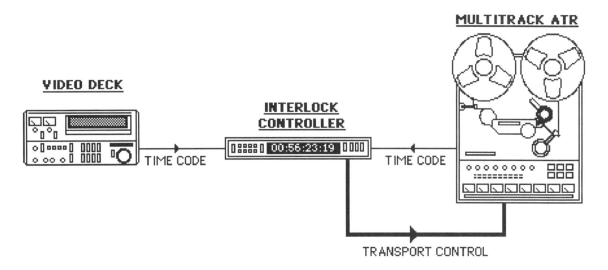

Fig. 8.17. Basic system used in audio chase-only the audio deck is controlled.

In addition to precisely matching the transport actions of two or more decks, the primary function of an interlock controller is to regulate the speed of each deck and adjust for the slight differences in speed. For that reason, all audio transports manufactured for use in interlock systems include a speed mode that is controlled by an external signal, in this case from the interlock controller (see Chapter 4). Should the video deck suddenly speed up or slow down, the audio deck will match the speed variations precisely. In this way the two machines are always in exact sync with each other.

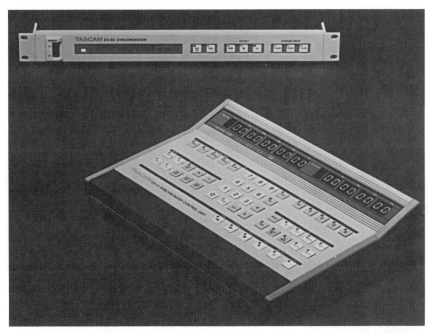

Fig. 8.18. Tascam's ES-50 and ES-51 Synchronizer. This is an excellent and synchronizing cost-effective system. (Photo Courtesy of Tascam/Teac Professional Division)

219

Fig. 8.19. The Adams-Smith Zeta 3 Interlock Controller. The Zeta 3 is capable of controlling two transports. (Photo Courtesy of Adams-Smith)

The complexity and price of any synchronization system depends, in part, on its ability to synchronize multiple decks. Some systems, like the Adams-Smith Zeta 3, are only capable of chase or control synchronization between two ATRs or one VTR and ATR. Additional synchronization may be obtained by linking two or more systems. Other systems, including the Adams-Smith 2600, Cipher Digital's Softouch, and the Timeline Lynx system, are modular. Modularity lets you configure the system to specifications and to sync multiple transports. In addition, these systems can also synchronize film equipment, an important feature that relates to modern audio post-production techniques: The ability to synchronize a time code to a bi-phase signal is the crucial link between the audio post-production processes of film and video.

Fig. 8.20. The Adams-Smith 2600 System with additional module. This system is of modular design and construction, allowing the owner the option of building the system up over a period of time. This particular system can synchronize LTC, VITC and bi-phase signals.
(Photo Courtesy of Adams-Smith)

Fig. 8.21. The Timeline Lynx system. Like the 2600, this is a modular system capable of synchronizing LTC, VITC and bi-phase signals. However, it can also synchronize to a pilot tone.
(Photo Courtesy of Timeline, Inc.)

K. INTERLOCK CONTROLLER FEATURES

The most simple and inexpensive controllers have the capacity to at least control the interlock of one deck and to provide for an offset time code. However, some manufacturers of these devices have incorporated additional useful and interesting features into their devices.

These features vary with make and model. However, the following discussion includes most of the features found on more sophisticated controllers. Keep in mind that an interlock controller is not just another "dumb" box sitting in a rack. Controllers are basically microcomputers and the more sophisticated they become, the more functions they tend to be able to perform:

Generate and Copy

A controller's usefulness is extended considerably if it has the ability to generate and copy a time code. In most cases the selection of preset numbers will be available, as will the type of code to be generated, and the copy mode (i.e., regenerated or jam sync) in which it will be running. Most controllers that generate code let the user select either a drop-frame or no-drop-frame time code.

Frame Rate Selection

Some controllers offer adjustable time code frame rates of 24, 25, 29.97 and 30.

Time Code Offset

Until now, we have assumed that both the audio deck and the video deck have exactly the same time-code numbers. If this is not the case, the controller must be "told" the difference between the two and will, from that point on, maintain a precise relationship, or offset, between the two. For example, if the numbers of each deck are:

VIDEO DECK	AUDIO DECK	DIFFERENCE (OFFSET)
00:01:34:05	00:01:35:15	00:00:01:10

The difference between the two is one second and ten frames. Almost all synchronization systems are able to cope with all least one offset entry.

Transport Type Selection

Any controller will let the user select the type of transports to be controlled, as different makes and models of decks will require variations of transport commands in order to operate properly. A multitrack audio deck made by Acme Audio might take a different set of voltages and commands for its play and stop commands than a deck made by the Butler Brothers. Not having the interlock controller properly set to the type of deck used, at the very least, cause the transport mechanism to behave erratically. At worst, both the electronic components of both the deck and controller could be damaged.

Autorecord

Some controllers allow the operator to set a time code number for an "in" point and "out" point. As soon as the controller receives the time code number designated as "in," it will instruct the deck to go into record mode. The track record functions that have been set to record will determine the tracks to be affected. When the time code number designated as "out" is received, the controller will instruct the deck to stop recording. This will occur without the transport ever stopping.

By programming the controller to carry out these instructions, an automatic punch in and out can be accomplished, recording a section of sound in conjunction with an edit. The advantages of this feature are many, the most obvious being that an exact match to a corresponding edit can be executed. Attempting this manually, no matter how fast one's reflexes may be, will not result in an exact audio to edit recording.

GoTo Commands and Memory Location Storage

A GoTo command instructs the controller to move one or more transports to an exact time code number and stop. If, for example, the beginning of a song or scene occurs at a specific point, the controller can be directed to move the tape to that exact location. This feature saves the trouble of having to watch the tape counter for a specific number.

In conjunction with the GoTo command, several controllers let you store various time code numbers into a set of memory storage numbers. For example, assume that a particular film has eighty different scenes. The beginning of each could be accessed simply by pressing several buttons on the controller. Then time code number 00:02:35:12 might be designated as memory location 01 and this location could correspond to the beginning of a specific scene. Instructing the controller to have one or more transports travel to that particular number and stop would again greatly benefit both engineer and client.

Automatic Looping, Rewind and Stop

In the same way that GoTo and Autorecord commands can be enabled, looping or cycle operations can also be programmed. Again, start and end time-code numbers may be programmed in. Then, when the end number is reached, the controller will do one of three things:

- Stop all decks under its control

- Rewind all decks under its control to the start time-code number and send a stop command, or

- Rewind all decks under its control to the start time-code number and instruct them to begin playing again, creating a loop.

The loop function selected can usually be selected by the user. Looping is an excellent way to adjust levels and other parameters associated with a mix, as well as execute dialog looping, Foley work and scoring. These techniques are discussed in the next chapter.

Remote Control

Most controllers have a remote control so that gives access to all of the controller's functions — and sometimes additional ones. Attaced to the controller by a cable, the remote can be conveniently placed on or near the console, allowing convenient access to the controller's functions, while the controller itself is out of the way in a rack mount.

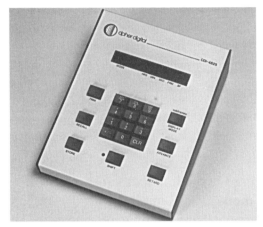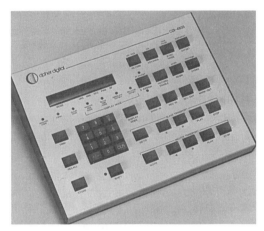

Fig. 8.22. The Cipher Digital CDI 4825 (left) and CDI 4835 (right) remote controllers. (Photo Courtesy of Cipher Digital, Inc.)

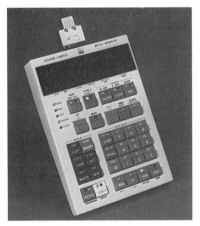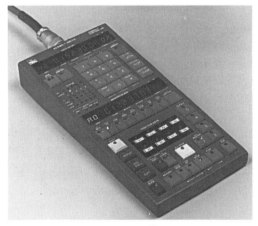

Fig. 8.23. Adams Smith's Zeta 3 (left) and 2600 remote controllers. (Photo Courtesy of Adams Smith)

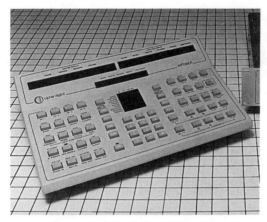 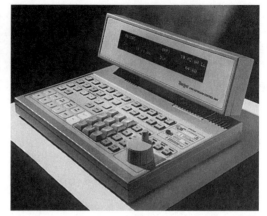

Fig. 8.24. The Cipher Digital Softouch (left) and Lynx (right) remote controllers.
(Photo Courtesy of Cipher Digital, Inc.)

The remote controllers pictured above are some of the most widely used. Note the differences among them. Often the appearance of the unit indicates the function of the system and the accessibility of the operating features.

Freewheel Lock Mode

In the event that time code on one or more tapes used in the interlock process is intermittent or faulty, the controller may be placed in **freewheel mode**. The controller will, if it receives a bad time code, estimate the speed and position of the transports and continue playing each. This mode will continue until the next valid time code address is received by the controller.

Event Triggers

The majority of synchronization controllers can trigger an external event at a given time-code number by sending out an **event trigger**. The trigger can be used to start equipment that would not normally read or respond to a time code. When the event trigger is issued, a relay closes or pulse is sent by the synchronizer.

The interface, or output, of this signal is commonly referred to as a **GPI**, or **general-purpose Interface**. The interface can, upon receiving a given time-code number, start an ATR pre-cued to a selection, play a compact disk or, according to Adam-Smith's Zeta 3 owner's manual, turn on a coffee pot.

MIDI Interfacing

Although MIDI is fully discussed in Chapter 11, it can be noted here that some controllers allow interfacing with a MIDI system. The controller will treat MIDI-connected equipment in much the same way as it would treat a transport system: stop, rewind and play commands can all be received and sent with properly equipped controller.

L. TYPES OF VIDEO DECKS

There are many different video decks in use, and those most widely used have been included here

224

as an example of how the various methods of timing code are used by different equipment. To complicate matters, some decks cannot handle certain types of time codes. It is imperative that both the engineer and the client understand the options and post-production limitations and procedures involved with each format. The various videotape formats are fully explained in Chapter 4. Their compatibility with certain types of time code are discussed in the following pages.

3/4-inch Decks

3/4-inch decks are commonly referred to as **U-Matic decks**, a format developed by Sony Corporation. The audio channels on these decks are labeled one and two, rather than left and right. The meter for channel one is on the left side of the machine and is sometimes considered the left channel. U-Matic is usually used for making reference copies of material recorded on a mastering format, for post-production work copies, for news recording and broadcast and so on. The maximum playing time of a U-Matic Cassette is one hour.

Sony VO-5800

The Sony VO-5800 is an industrial deck. That is, the circuitry is simpler and the mechanics less rugged than that of a broadcast deck. This deck is commonly referred to as a type 5 deck because it belongs to the Sony 5000 series.

Fig. 8.25. The Sony VO-5800 3/4-inch U-Matic Video Cassette Recorder
(Photo Courtesy of Sony Corporation)

This deck can be recognized by a shuttle knob used to play a tape in frame-by-frame or fast search modes, and by two meters for each audio channel. The VO-5800 will not record or play VITC or address track time codes. By using LTC, the unit is limited to recording a time code onto one audio channel. If the tape to be striped is a prerecorded, then only channel one can be used. This condition exists because the VO-5800 only has the provision for a "DUB/CH 1" control which allows for insert recording of an audio signal onto audio channel one without affecting the material on channel two or the on video portion of the tape. It should be noted that the audio inputs and outputs on the 5800 are unbalanced.

Sony VO-5850

The Sony VO-5850 is also an industrial deck, and is a more sophisticated version of the VO-5850. This deck is also a called a type 5 VTR.

Fig. 8.26. The Sony VO-5850 3/4 -inch U-Matic Video Cassette Recorder
(Photo Courtesy of Sony Corporation)

This deck also has a shuttle knob and three meters. Two meters are for audio channels one and two, and the third is to monitor videotape tracking. As with the VO-5800, the VO-5850 will not record or play VITC or address track time codes. Unlike the "DUB/CH 1" control, however, "insert" controls on the unit give the option of recording on either channel one or two. This feature makes it possible to record on either channel at any time without affecting the rest of the videotape's contents. Like the 5800, the audio inputs and outputs on the 5850 are unbalanced.

Sony VO-9800

Sony Corporation introduced a series of U-Matic decks designed to replace the type 5 (VO-5800 and VO-5850) decks. These are known as type 9 decks. Unlike the type 5s, the type 9 VTRs are compatible with both VITC and address track time codes. Therefore, they allow for both audio channels to be used exclusively for audio material. It should be mentioned that type 9 decks also have higher bandwidth (response to video signal) and thus higher signal quality than their type 5 predecessors. The VO-9800 is intended to replace the VO-5800, and as such lets the operator replace (i.e., insert) only audio onto audio channel one of an assembled videotape. This features is available as an optional plug in-circuit board that lets the 9800 read and record address track time codes, eliminating the need for an external time-code decoder. In addition, the audio on the 9800 is equipped with type C Dolby noise reduction. The audio inputs and outputs on the 9800 are balanced.

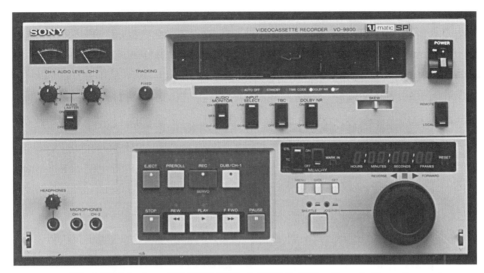

Fig. 8.27. The Sony VO-9800 3/4 Inch U-Matic Video Cassette Recorder
(Photo Courtesy of Sony Corporation)

Sony VO-9850

Like the VO-9800, the 9850 has higher video-signal bandwidth and is intended to replace the VO-5850. All type 9 VTR's are compatible with both VITC and address track time code, which again allows for both audio channels to be used exclusively for audio material. This model, like the 5850, allows for either or both audio channels to be insert recorded to replace or modify audio material. An optional board lets the 9850 both read and generate an LTC on the address track. The output of the generator is dedicated to the address track. As in the case of the 9800, the audio inputs and outputs on the 9850 are balanced and equipped with type C Dolby noise reduction.

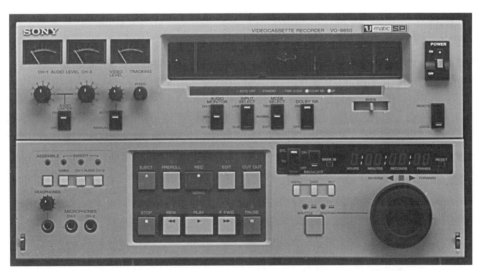

Fig. 8.28. The Sony VO-9850 3/4 Inch U-Matic Video Cassette Recorder
(Photo Courtesy of Sony Corporation)

Sony BVU-900

The Sony BVU series is a 3/4-inch U-Matic format intended for high-end editing and broadcast applications. The format, at the time of this writing, consists of what is known as "SP" (for supe-

227

rior performance) machines. In brief, the SP format has several advantages over the standard U-Matic machines, which include the VO-5800, VO-5850, VO-9800 and VO-9850. Briefly, the principle differences between this series and the type 5 and 9 decks include a 1-dB increase in video S/N, 10 additional lines of resolution, faster tape access and handling, Dolby type C noise reduction for the audio channels and a higher shuttle speed.

Fig. 8.29. The Sony BVU-900 3/4-inch U-Matic Video Cassette Recorder
(Photo Courtesy of Sony Corporation)

The recording and playback quality of this series VTR is higher than either type 5 or type 9 VTRs. Moreover, this type of deck costs more than twice that of a VO-5850. Still, this deck is a play-only deck and cannot record either video or audio. However, like the type 9 decks, the BVU-900 can read an LTC from an address or auxiliary track, allowing the two audio channels to be used exclusively for stereo audio material. The BVU series decks are also compatible with the VITC. The audio outputs on the BVU decks are balanced.

Sony BVU-950

The BVU-950 serves as a full-function record and play deck. All of the features found on the BVU-900 are on the 950. In addition, you can set the deck to both read and generate an LTC internally from and to the address track. As with the VO-5850 and VO-9850, either audio channel may be re-dubbed in the insert mode. Both the audio inputs and outputs on the BVU decks are balanced.

Fig. 8.30. The Sony BVU-950 3/4-inch U-Matic Video Cassette Recorder
(Photo Courtesy of Sony Corporation)

Betacam SP

Betacam is a format originally developed for ENG (electronic news gathering) and EFP (electronic field production) work. It has since evolved into the Betacam SP format. The audio and video signal quality of a Betacam SP Tape is considerably higher than that of the U-Matic formats.Besides the two conventional longitudinal audio tracks, two additional channels have been added. These are known as FM, or frequency modulated, tracks. These must be recorded simultaneously with the picture, and neither can be re-dubbed by inserting new audio material.

However, both longitudinal audio channels are equipped with Dolby type C noise reduction and each of these may be re-dubbed in the insert mode. All audio inputs and outputs on the BVW-75 are balanced.

Fig. 8.31. The Sony BVW-75 Betacam Video Cassette Recorder
(Photo Courtesy of Sony Corporation)

The time code functions of the BVW-75 are quite advanced and flexible, making it an ideal deck for post-production and mastering if one-inch or digital formats are not available. This deck can internally read and generate both the VITC and LTC, with the LTC being recorded to and read from a dedicated address track. Time-code user bits may be stored in memory and generated at any time. Additional functions, such as time-code preset numbers and internal character generation make it possible to create window dubs without an additional character inserter. The maximum recording and playing time available from a Betacam SP tape is 90 minutes.

One-Inch Type C

The one-inch type C video format is the only open reel format in use today. It has for years been considered by the video industry to yield the highest possible signal quality, and as such is frequently used for **mastering**. Mastering is the process of creating a final videotape, analogous to a mixed audio master. This includes the process of mastering on a "lesser" format, such as Betacam SP, and **bumping up**, or re-recording the final product, onto one-inch videotape.

Fig. 8.32. The Sony BVH 3000 One-inch VTR
(Photo Courtesy of Sony Corporation)

One-inch decks feature three longitudinal audio tracks, any one of which may be insert recorded. Dolby A and Dolby SR noise reduction is available for the BVH-3000 and all audio inputs and outputs are balanced. Furthermore, internal reading and generation of both LTC and VITC are possible with the BVH 3000. Maximum tape time on this deck is 126 minutes. Sony also offers a version of the one-inch VTR that incorporates analog-to-digital conversion of audio signals for recording digital audio directly onto the master tape. The actual track format is shown in Fig. 8.33:

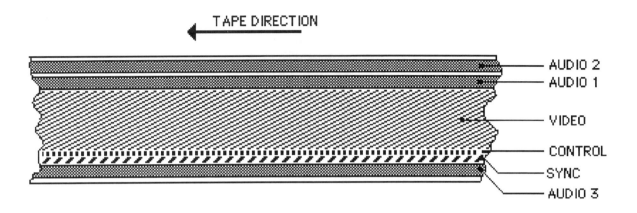

Fig. 8.33. The basic components of one inch type "C" videotape.

Digital

Sony also sells a series of fully digital video decks. These formats, D-1 and D-2, are not compatible with each other. In other words, a D-1 cassette cannot be played by a D-2 deck and vice-versa. Conversion between the two formats can be accomplished by a fully digital interface and the format converters made by Sony. Both units hold promise for becoming some of the most significant post-production tools, especially in the field of audio. Among the characteristics that make these formats extremely useful for post-production work is that audio or video in recorded in digital format offer significant improvements in signal-to-noise ratios and overall quality. Moreover, problems associated with signal quality degeneration because of generation loss are almost completely eliminated.

D-1 Format

Simply put, the D-1 format is the best quality video format available at the present time. The D-1 system uses component digital video to record and play back. Because it can obtain a digital video component signal directly from a Rank-Cintel URSA telecine, D-1 is used extensively in top level film-to-tape transfers, mastering and on-line editing.

At the present time, Sony's DVR-1000 is only one VTR using the D-1 format.

Fig. 8.34. The Sony DVR-1000 D-1 Format Video Cassette Recorder.
(Photo Courtesy of Sony Corporation)

The DVR-1000 utilizes two cassette sizes: Medium cassettes allow from 12 to 34 minutes of recording time; large sizes allows for 76 or 94 minutes.

Using a direct digital interface to a second deck, more than 20 generations can be copied without generation loss. The audio signal quality of the DVR-1000 is characterized by a 90-dB signal-to-noise ratio and a frequency response of 20 Hz to 20 KHz. The format includes four balanced and independently editable digital audio channels, each with digital and analog inputs and outputs, and an analog audio channel intended for use as a "scratch" track. The scratch track is useful in that digital tracks are less intelligible than analog audio signals at shuttle speeds, and the analog track helps locate specific audio material.

The DVR-1000 is compatible with the analog address track time code but not with the VITC. In the place of VITC, the D-1 employs a format time code called audio sector time code. Instead of being recorded into the vertical blanking interval of the video signal, the time code is written into the unused data portions of the audio tracks.

Internal generators and readers will handle both the address track time code and audio sector time code. An internal character inserter, similar to the BVW-75, allows for the creation of window dubs directly from the deck.

D-2 Format

The D-2 format is a cassette system intended to replace the one-inch type-C format. Unlike the D-1 system, the D-2 is a **composite video** deck. Composite video is the result of electronically combining the separate red, green, blue and sync video signals into a single signal.

Since the introduction of the D-2 format, many production and post-production facilities have seen an increase in clients bumping up their one-inch masters to D-2 and then generating multiple one-inch masters for distribution.

There are two decks currently available that support the D-2 format. These are the DVR-10 and the DVR-18. The principle difference between the two is that the DVR-18 will accept small, medium and large cassette sizes, while the DVR-10 will accept only the small and medium sizes. Small cassettes yield recording times of 6, 12, 22 and 32 minutes; medium cassettes give 6, 12, 22, 34, 64 and 94 minutes; and large cassettes allow 126, 156, 188 and 208 minutes. The advantages of these extended record and play times apply to the post-production of feature films.

Fig. 8.35. The Sony DVR-10 D-2 Format Video Cassette Recorder
(Photo Courtesy of Sony Corporation)

Fig. 8.36. The Sony DVR-18 D-2 Format Video Cassette Recorder
(Photo Courtesy of Sony Corporation)

As with the D-1 format, more than 20 generations can be made with either deck without generation loss. Both decks feature a 90-dB signal-to-noise ratio with a frequency response of 20 Hz to 20 KHz. To emulate of film-style recording, the format includes four balanced and independently editable digital audio channels, each with digital and analog inputs and outputs. An analog audio channel, intended for use as a "scratch" track is also included. As with multistripe 35-mm magnetic stock, music, narration, dialog, and effects can all be recorded on separate tracks and later updated.

This capability further indicates the merging of technologies and post-production practices of different media. Because direct digital copies can be made between decks without being subject to generation loss, feature films intended for broadcast may be mastered on the D-2 format. Subsequent dialog and narration dubs can then be made to masters intended for export to foreign speaking countries. Yet another use that could be made of all four channels is the reception of a stereo Dolby surround mix that requires that the audio be mixed not only in stereo, but in front to back as well.

Both the DVR-10 and the DVR-18 are compatible with analog address track time code and with VITC. Furthermore, internal generators and readers will handle both address track time code and VITC. An internal character inserter, similar to the BVW-75, permits window dubs directly from the deck.

SUMMARY OF VTR FORMATS AND TIME CODE COMPATIBILITY

GENERAL INFORMATION				AUDIO SECTION					TIME COMPATIBILITY	
Model	Format	Max. Tape Times	Common Usage	Number Audio Tracks	Audio Signal Type	Audio Insert Capability	Noise Reduction	Compatible W/VITC	Compatible W/Address Track Code
SONY VO-5800	U-Matic 3/4 Inch	60 Mins.	Reference Copies Rough edits Window Dubs Reference	2	Unbal	Ch.1 Only	None	No	No
SONY VO-5850	U-Matic 3/4 Inch	60 Mins.	Reference Copies Rough edits, Window Dubs	2	Unbal.	Ch, 1 and Ch. 2	None	No	No
SONY VO-9800	U-Matic 3/4 Inch SP	60 Mins.	Reference Copies Rough Edits, Window Dubs, EFP, ENG, Distribution	2	Bal.	Ch. 1 Only	Dolby C	Yes	Yes
SONY VO-9850	U-Matic 3/4 Inch SP	60 Mins.	Reference Copies, Rough Edits, Window Dubs, EFP, ENG, Distribution	2	Bal	Ch. 1 and Ch. 2	Dolby C	Yes	Yes
SONY BVU-900	U-Matic 3/4 Inch SP	60 Mins.	Play Only; Hi Quality 3/4 Inch Editing Computer Animation, Distribution	2	Bal	None	Dolby C	Yes	Yes
SONY BVU-950	U-Matic 3/4 Inch SP	60 Mins.	Hi Quality 3/4 Inch Editing, Computer Animation, Distribution.	2	Bal	Ch. 1 and Ch. 2	Dolby C	Yes	Yes
SONY BVW-75	Betacam SP	90 Mins.	Mastering ENG, EFP,	4 (2 Long-itudinal, 2 FM)	Bal	Ch. 1 and	Dolby C	Yes	Yes
SONY BVH-3000	One Inch Type "C" (Open Reel)	126 Mins.	Mastering, On-Line Editing, Film to Film Transfers.	3	Bal	Ch. 1 Ch. 2 Ch. 3	Dolby A Dolby SR	Yes	Not Used
SONY DVR-1000	D-1 Composite Digital	94 Mins.	Mastering, On-Line Editing, Film to Tape Transfers	5 (1 is Analog)	Bal Analog	All Channels	None	No: Uses Audio Sector Time Code	Yes
SONY DVR-10	D-1 Component Digital	94 Mins.	Mastering, On-Line Editing, Film to Tape Transfers.	5 (1 is Analog)	Bal Analog	All Channels	None	No. Uses Audio Sector Time Code	Yes
SONY DVR-18	D-1 Component Digital	208 Mins.	Mastering On-Line Editing, Film to Tape Transfers	5 (1 is Analog)	Bal Analog	All Channels	None	No: Uses Audio Sector Time Code	Yes

9
STAGES OF AUDIO POST-PRODUCTION

A. THE INTERLOCK SYSTEM AND POST-PRODUCTION STUDIO

Defining an audio and video interlock post-production system a little at a time makes it easily understandable (Fig. 9.1):

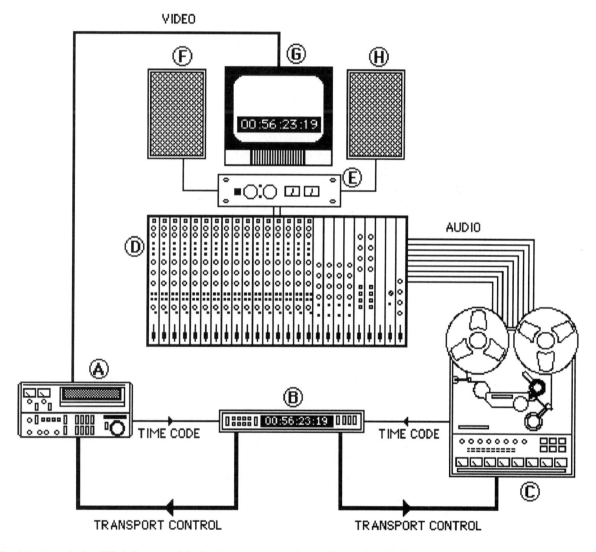

Fig. 9.1. A much simplified diagram of the basic components of an audio synchronization system.
(A) VTR with window dub, (B) Interlock controller, (C) Multitrack ATR, (D) Console, (E) Stereo Amplifier, (F) Left Audio Monitor, (G) Video Monitor (H) Right Audio Monitor

By necessity, the studios in which these audio-for-video post-production systems are located must be specialized. Compare the following diagram (Fig. 9.2) with those illustrating a Foley studio for film and a film mixing facility in Chapter 7. As we'll see in the next several chapters, this type of facility is replacing the conventional methods and studios associated with film post-production.

The use of an audio-for-video post-production facility lets the producer bypass traditional Foley work, film mixing studios, dialogue looping studios and, in some cases, even scoring stages. Because audio and video rely on electronic synchronization, these post-production systems shuttle much faster than film visual and sound media, which are mechanically and electrically synchronized. The higher speed reduces both the time and costs associated with established film post-production procedures. In addition, it is possible to post-produce a film by transferring it to video using the systems and techniques described in this text, yet still complete the final product in film. These and other techniques are discussed in detail in the remainder of this book.

The standard audio-for-video post-production studio varies in size according to its budget, the nature of the productions in which it is usually involved and the needs of its clients and staff.

Most studios are divided into at least two separate physical areas, each usually sound-isolated from the other and from surrounding areas. The area in which the console and other equipment are located is referred to as the **control room**. It is in the control room that all tape recording, monitoring, patching, processing and mixing activities take place. A separate area, known as an **isolation booth** or **iso booth** may be used to record any sounds, voice or music that are performed in the studio. As in a traditional Foley studio, these recordings can be synchronized to the picture by allowing the artist or artists to view the picture in real time. In some cases, sounds may be recorded non-synchronously and added to the multitrack ATR later.

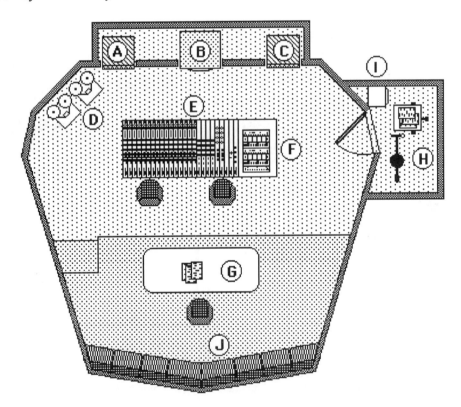

Fig. 9.2. Generalized layout of an audio post-production studio.
(A) Left Audio Monitor (B) Video Monitor (C) Right Audio Monitor (D) Multitrack and Two Track ATR's (E) Console (F) Effects, Patchbay and VTR enclosure (G) Producer's Desk (H) Isolation Booth (I) Isolation Booth Video Monitor (J) Additional Seating.

Fig. 9.3. Neve audio post-production console at Photomagnetic Studios, New York City. (Photo Courtesy of Neve Corporation)

B. TAPE PREPARATION

Most professional video productions are mastered in D-1, D-2, one-inch or Betacam format;. From these, work copies (usually 3/4-inch) are created to insure that the master will be played as little as possible, minimizing the chances of irreparably damaging it. Should the 3/4-inch copy of the master become lost or damaged, it is easy to create another from the original master.

Because there are several possible mastering variations, depending on the format of the video deck and of the type of time code to be used, the following explanations are limited to the use of work copies, namely, 3/4-inch SP format video decks and LTC. If a film is to be prepared for post-production in video, it must first be transferred to video. (For more details, refer to the relevant discussions at the end of this chapter.)

Before starting the audio post-production process, the finished piece should be completely edited in final form, and the titles and credits should be in place at both the start and end of the tape. If the visual material must subsequently be revised, the timings for the entire visual may be thrown off.

In addition, the audio on the videotape can consist of up to two tracks of dialogue if using address track longitudinal time code. In any case, the original audio material should be as simple as possible. The addition of sound effects, music, ambience, etc. should be avoided. Again, the tape should, if possible, consist of dialogue only.

C. STRIPING THE VIDEO MASTER

The inclusion of time code on the master tape is, again, dependent on the tape format that is used for the master videotape. However, assuming that time code does not exist on the master videotape, the first step in preparing a video master for post-production is to add time code. It's a good idea to begin striping as soon as the tape starts rolling. Some time code numbers — approximately 5 or 6 seconds— will be lost as the deck begins to run, but consequently all of the material will be striped (Fig. 9.4). The reason for striping the master is to have an originating time code reference that will be duplicated on subsequent tapes created during the audio post-production process. In the last stages of the process, some of the tapes will be re-synchronized to this original time code.

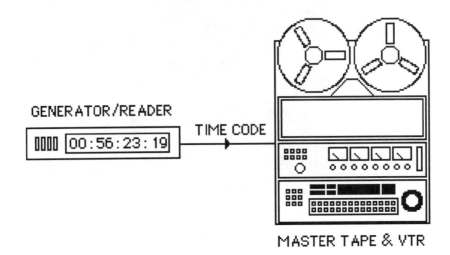

GENERATOR/READER

00 : 56 : 23 : 19

TIME CODE

MASTER TAPE & VTR

Fig. 9.4. Adding time code to a master video tape. (Note that the time code generator is genlocked, although this is not shown in this diagram.)

Recording Time Code on Multitrack Analog Audio Decks

Once the master videotape has been striped, the process must be repeated for the multitrack analog audio master tape to be used in the post sessions. There are several rules to follow when recording longitudinal time code on multitrack analog audio decks:

1. *It is vital that the multitrack ATR's speed control be set for "internal" control* (i.e., not controlled by ancillary equipment).

2. Time code is always recorded on the highest track number. For example, an eight-track deck would be striped on track number eight.

3. A **guard band** must be left between the time code track and the last track of audio signal. In the case of the eight track ATR, track six would be left blank. This is done to prevent crosstalk and subsequent interference with the time code signal.

4. Any noise reduction affecting the track to be striped must be bypassed. Noise reduction will alter the time code signal to the extent that it may become unreadable.

5. A minimum of thirty seconds of time code should be recorded before any program material starts. This allows time for the system to properly interlock. This practice is called **pre-roll**, and is standard procedure. If possible, try to stripe the tape with more than thirty seconds pre-roll.

6. Time code should be recorded between 0 and -5 VU.

For the remainder of this chapter assume that all references to the multitrack ATR indicate the use of pre-recorded time code on the multitrack tape.

Recording Time Code on Video Decks

1. The time code device and VTR should both be genlocked or otherwise synchronized to the video signal.

2. As in audio, time code is always recorded on the highest number audio track.

3. Any limiting or compression on the track to be striped must be bypassed.

4. A minimum of thirty seconds of time code pre roll should be striped before any program material starts. Again, if possible, try to provide for more than thirty seconds of pre roll.

5. Time code should be recorded between 0 and -5 VU.

D. THE WINDOW DUB

At this point the master tape will have its own code, whether it was generated before or after its completion. As previously discussed, it is absolutely necessary to make a copy of the master.

The master tape is played back through a window dubber which can read, generate, and character insert. The output of this device is fed to a second, usually 3/4-inch, VTR (Fig. 9.5). The time code and video signals are supplied to the window dubber, which is does three things at once:

• It reads the incoming code.

• It regenerates the code to be recorded onto the 3/4-inch VTR.

• It superimposes a matching display of the incoming time code numbers being read over the video image.

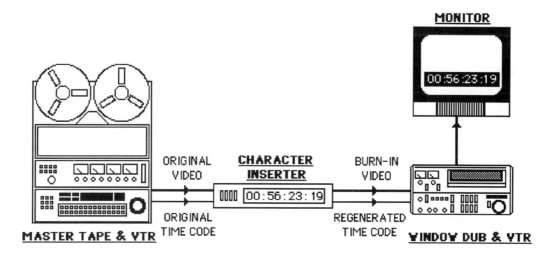

Fig. 9.5. Creating a window dub.

Again, the character inserter and both VTRs should be genlocked to ensure synchronization of time code to video. The subsequent recording, which is an exact copy of the master's time code and video, is called a **window dub**. Placing a time code display over a video image in this manner is also called a **burn-in display**. Because LTC cannot be read at high or low shuttle speeds or when the VTR is stopped or paused, the burn-in display gives the relationship of each time code number to each video frame, visually insuring frame accuracy. In this way, you can jog or shuttle the tape and pause at a specific frame and identify its corresponding time code number. Note that the audio material is not usually copied from the master videotape to the window dub copy.

When both the window dub and the multitrack master have been prepared and are ready for interlock, the five separate and distinct phases of post-production are performed. These are commonly referred to as **spotting**, **laydown**, **sweetening**, **mixdown**, and **layback**.

The steps of post-production are similar regardless of the media used. For example, someone working in film would have to establish comparable procedures. Because of differences in the technologies involved, however, these similarities end when the actual practices are observed. Specific conventions, such as the paperwork utilized, will differ between each type of post-production session.

E. SPOTTING AND CREATING A CUE SHEET

The first post-production phase requires that a written record of the visual material be compiled. This is done during what is known as **spotting**. On large productions, the **spotting session** may be attended by several sound editors, each of whom is assigned a specific aspect of the soundtrack with which to work, by the producers of the project, the composers, and by staff whose job it is to create or synthesize specialized effects. Spotting sessions for smaller projects may be attended by one sound editor or supervisor and by the producer.

The written record compiled during the spotting session will be used in planning the addition of specific sounds, such as dialog, narration, music and sound effects to the multitrack ATR. This log may take several different forms and will indicate specific edits, fades, scenes and actions that appear on the videotape. Each entry is identified by the time code numbers that appear in the window dub at that specific event.

Next, the window dub is placed in a video deck with jog and shuttle search capability, allowing the editor(s) to search by increments of single frames, freeze the picture, identify the time code number and to write down the frame information required. This is called creating a **breakdown** or a **cue sheet**. The cue sheet must be extremely detailed (Fig. 9.6):

```
┌─────────────────────────────────────────────────────────────────────┐
│  00:00:36:17      CUT   MS NIGHT INT. shadow of woman pulling down a soap box -│
│                         she looks around.                             │
│                                                                       │
│  00:00:36:26      CUT   Another door - Through curtain that covers window on door,│
│                         we see SOMETHING on other side of window pushing door │
│                         open.                                         │
│                                                                       │
│  00:00:37:11            Woman calls out, "HELLO?"                     │
│                                                                       │
│  00:00:38:02            She stops moving - looks off in distance.     │
│                                                                       │
│  00:00:39:07            Begins lowering soap box.                     │
│                                                                       │
│  00:00:40:05            Woman calls out, "WHO'S THERE?"               │
│                                                                       │
│  00:00:40:17            TITLE BEGINS FADING OUT.                      │
│                                                                       │
│  00:00:40:26            TITLE FULLY FADED OUT.                        │
│                                                                       │
│  00:00:42:00      CUT   ANOTHER SCENE - MS DAY INT. Woman with back to CAM │
│                         looking through dresser. CAM PUSHING IN to her.│
└─────────────────────────────────────────────────────────────────────┘
```

Fig. 9.6. Example of a breakdown or cue sheet used in locating specific events in a videotape.

The conventions of creating a cue sheet are specific and should be observed. These are as follows:

1. Dialogue is capitalized and put in quotes.

2. Camera actions and locations are capitalized.

3. Capitalize the descriptive word that occurs at a key timing point. (See entry 00:00:36:26 in Fig. 9.6.)

4. Scenes that cut from one to the next are indicated by the word CUT. (See entry 00:00:36:26 in Fig. 9.6.)

5. Descriptions are usually abbreviated to save space:

BG	Background
CAM	Camera
CU	Close Up
DIAL:	Dialogue
EL	End of Line (of dialogue)
EXT	Exterior
FG	Foreground
FS	Full Shot
INT	Interior

243

LS..Long Shot
MOS ....Without original (production) sound
MS..Medium Shot
NARR:...Narrator
O.C..Off Camera
O.S. ....Off Stage
POV ....Point Of View

There is no doubt that a computer can make the task of creating and constantly updating a cue sheet a bit less grueling. Software that is specially developed to handle this chore, and which integrate other tasks as well, is discussed in Chapter 12.

If preparing a cue sheet seems like a lot of work, you might take comfort in the fact that one generated for the post-production of a feature film is commonly referred to as a bible, the thickness and amount of information contained in each being somewhat similar.

Yet a second method of creating a cue sheet is to integrate the example shown in Fig. 9.7 with a conventional track sheet used in multitrack production situations (see Chapter 6). Such a sheet may look like the following:

Note that this type of cue sheet more closely resembles that of a film cue sheet in that it contains scene information, timing information, the specific location of audio material and on which tracks they appear. This will help to plan the placement of specific sounds during spotting and to serve as a conventional track sheet during the recording sessions.

The method used to log scene information and to create the cue sheet is entirely subjective; either or both may be used.

F. LAYDOWN

The process of **laydown** involves the *synchronized* transferring of original field or location recorded audio material to the multitrack master. This audio may originate from:

• Field- or location-recorded videotape tracks, or

• Separate synchronous field- or location-recorded audio.

Field- or location-recorded audio that is recorded on one or more audio tracks of the portable VTR will usually be edited with the video to form the final edited videotape master. This master will, of course, contain both audio and video incorporated into one physical reel or cassette This method is called **single system recording** (Fig. 9.8).

ILLUSTRATION NO.IX-1, FIG IX..8

Soundesign NY

	Client	Producer	Date
	Artist/Product	Engineer/Assistant	Reel __ of __ Page __ of __

30 ips ☐ 15 ips ☐ 7.5 ips ☐

dolby A ☐ dBx ☐ No NR ☐

Master ☐ Safety ☐ Transfer ☐

SMPTE ☐ 29.97 DF ☐ 29.97 NDF ☐

Heads Out ☐ Tails Out ☐ Spooling ☐

Lock: MAC ☐ Lock: VTR ☐ Lock: ATR ☐

Comments:

SMPTE/SECT	Track 1	Track 2	Track 3	Track 4	Track 5	Track 6	Track 7	Track 8
00:01:23:12 MS NIGHT INT. shadow on wall								
00:01:32:22 Another door thru curtain								
00:01:37:11 Woman calls out, "HELLO?"								
00:01:42:01 Begins RAIS-ING gun								
00:01:43:28 Door OPENS								

Fig. 9.7. A cue sheet integrated with a multitrack track sheet.

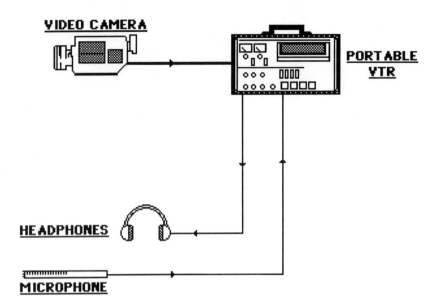

Fig. 9.8. The creation of a single system or single format videotape production master. Both audio and video are incorporated into one physical tape.

Separate synchronous field- or location-recorded audio can be obtained by having two separate decks for audio and video recording. This method of recording is analogous to the double system method of recording and shooting film commonly referred to as **split format recording** or **double system recording** (see Chapter 4). This method of recording will yield considerably audio higher results as both the signal-to-noise ratio and the frequency response of the deck are superior to that of its video counterpart. The split format system depends on both the VTR and ATR recieving an identical time code from a portable time-code generator during recording (Fig. 9.9).

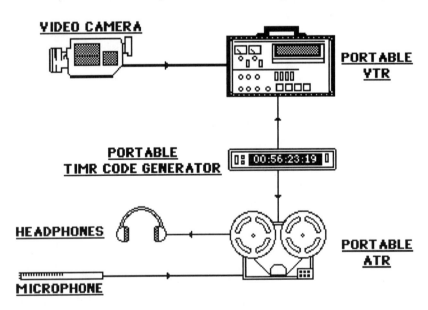

Fig. 9.9. The creation of a double system or split format videotape production master. Both audio and video are recorded seperately onto two physically seperate tapes.

246

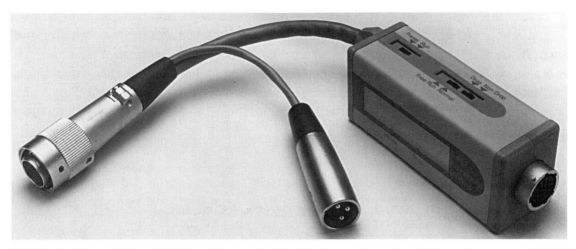

Fig. 9.10. The Fast Forward P1 portable time code generator. The 14-pin connector is placed between the camera and VTR, eliminating the need for additional cables and connectors normally required when a stand-alone generator is used. (Photo Courtesy of Fast Forward Video)

Note that, although once in fairly widespead use, the double system (or split format) video system is rapidly falling into disuse. The audio quality provided by contemporary formats, such as Betacam, one inch, and even 3/4 SP have rendered the use of this system practically obsolete. However, references to its use remain in this text since the author feels that it may help the reader to further understand the possibilities that exist in multi-media synchronization.

The split-format audio and video tapes may then be re-synchronized in the post-production studio to single video cassettes or tapes, but this defeats the original purpose of obtaining higher audio quality. Alternatively, the two may kept separate throughout the editing process. In that case, a specialized editing system is required. Such a system uses an editing controller, a minimum of two ATRs and at least two VTRs, all of which must be interlocked and synchronized (Fig. 9.11).

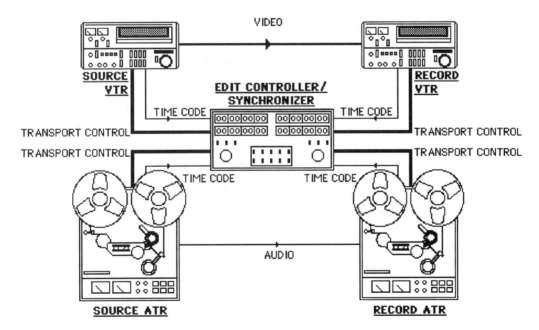

Fig. 9.11. An "off-line" split format video editing system, in which two seperate auio and two seperate video decks are controlled by a single editing controller.

247

In all cases, the relationship between the original time code and audio material remains unchanged. The transferring of the audio on the videotape to the audiotape is called **stripping** or **laydown**. *While this process takes place tit is absolutely vital that he multitrack ATR's speed control is set to external control so that its speed is regulated by the synchronizer.* In addition, we assume that the time code on the multitrack master was recorded prior to this point. Fig. 9.12 illustrates a single system master and a multirack ATR interlocked in the process of stripping or laydown.

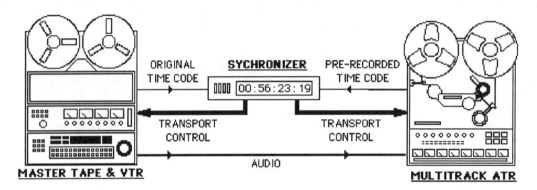

Fig. 9.12. Stripping, or layback, of a single system master videotape.

If the master tapes are in split format form, the audio material is again dubbed to the multitrack ATR. (Fig. 9.13).

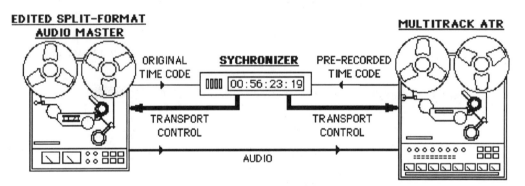

Fig. 9.13. Stripping, or layback, of a split format system master tape.

Again, the success of this process relies entirely upon the relationship between both audio and video time code numbers being precisely maintained. Once the layback is completed, the VTR playing the window dub copy and the ATR with the stripped (copied) audio are both interlocked. Depending on the type of system being used, the controller is set to either run both machines (control synchronization) or made to control the multitrack deck (chase synchronization). In either case, the multitrack ATRs speed control is again set to "external" to interlock the system, so that the original relationships that existed between audio, video, and time code on the master tape are maintained during duplication.

G. SWEETENING

Once the audio and video are now effectively divorced, we are now in a position to add audio onto the multitrack ATR. The synchronization of any material added must be visually compared to the image which is interlocked to the ATR. As in film post-production, sounds are divided into four categories of dialog, narration, music and sound effects. The process of dealing with each are varied, as are the techniques and technologies available to the engineer dealing them. As in any creative field, the choices made about how these techniques are executed are subjective and determined by cost, the equipment available, the engineer's expertise, and, most importantly, the client's vision.

Sound Effects

Sound effects recorded on the multitrack ATR may originate from any of five sources:

- Prerecorded effects originating from a commercially available library.

- Prerecorded effects originating from a personal library.

- Prerecorded effects obtained on the locations on which the production was shot.

- Live acoustic effects created in the studio, similar to Foley work, which are either recorded in sync to picture or asynchronously.

- Live electronic effects created in the studio which are also recorded either in sync to picture or asynchronously.

Sound Effects Libraries

Commercial sound-effects libraries were originally available only on LP (long-playing phonographic) records, but these have largely been replaced by libraries recorded on CDs (compact disks). CDs are less prone to scratching and breaking than LPs. In addition, in CDs the sound is stored digitally, which eliminates the hiss and scratches associated with LPs. Also, because no mechanical contact is made to read the CD, it is not subject to the wear and signal degeneration that accompanies the repeated playing of LPs.

Fig. 9.14. A sound effects library on CD. Libraries like this one are usually supplied with a catalog to allow the user to look up specific sounds easily. (Photo Courtesy of Network Production Music, Inc.)

By using CDs, the location of specific sounds is made easier as well. **Cueing**, or the setting up, and playing of specific sounds is performed by merely pushing a set of buttons (Fig. 9.15). This is because recordings on CDs are arranged in tracks arranged in ascending order. Individual tracks may be further subdivided into index numbers that identify exact sounds in the track (Fig. 9.15).

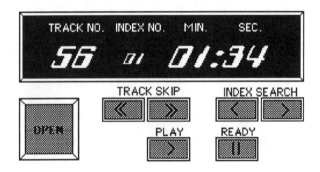

Fig. 9.15 A typical professional CD player's display and partial view of controls. "Track skip" causes the CD to skip silently from one track to another in either direction. "Index search" acts similarly to a shuttle control. The "ready" control will cause the CD to pause; "play" will set it in motion. In some cases, the time readout can be set to indicate remaining or elapsed time.

This arrangement permits almost instant access to any number of tracks and corresponds to catalogs supplied with CD sound effects libraries: Such catalogs list every sound contained in the library by CD number and by track and index number. The duration of each sound is also usually indicated (Fig. 9.16).

SOUND EFFECT	DESCRIPTION	VERSION	TIME	CD	TRACK	INDEX
Gravel	Shoveling Gravel		:41	3	2	
Grinder	Turn on...grind metal		1:03	12	3	
Hack Saw	Sawing steel pipe		:34	5	41	
Hammer	Nail pulled from wood	1	:12	13	34	
Hammer	Nail pulled from wood	2	:15	13	35	
Hammer	Hammering metal		:56	13	36	
Handsaw	Cutting wood, slowly		1:34	14	22	
Handsaw	Cutting wood, fast		1:45	14	23	
Jigsaw	Turn on...turn off		:44	14	25	

Fig. 9.16. Example of a listing for a CD based sound effects library.

Personal libraries are compiled in the course of production and post-production sessions by sound engineers, producers and clients. These may be stored in several different formats, such as reel-to-reel tape with the different effects being separated by leader for identification. Increasingly, these libraries are stored in digital formats, which are explained in Chapters 10 and 13.

Prerecorded effects obtained where the production was shot, i.e. on location, can be recorded either in synchronization or out of synchronization (asynchronously) and added later to picture by recording them onto the multitrack ATR.

In either case, sounds or sound effects stored on reel-to-reel may be placed on a two-track ATR (or other suitable deck), the material cued up to the leader (see Chapter 7), and the deck started by hand by pressing "play" at the correct time. If closer synchronization is necessary, the two-track may be striped, the offset between the two-track and multitrack calculated and the multitrack temporarily made to chase the two-track during that particular laydown. When the recording is finished, however, the synchronizing system may be returned to normal operation, i.e., control synchronization.

Equipment Connections

Because a variety of sounds and sound effects may submitted in a multitude of formats, a method of transferring sounds must first be determined. The two ways in which this may be done are:

• Connecting the playback equipment directly to the multitrack ATR, or

• Connecting the playback equipment to the multitrack ATR via the console.

If the first method is used, the outputs of all playback devices are connected through the patch bay directly to multitrack deck. This method provides for a "cleaner" sound because passing signal through additional electronics increases the amount of noise. This method of direct transfer is known as **E to E**, or **electronics to electronics** (Fig. 9.17). The multitrack is monitored through the console in the usual fashion. Assuming that the levels of prerecorded material are within acceptable range, the levels recorded on the multitrack will reflect and match these.

251

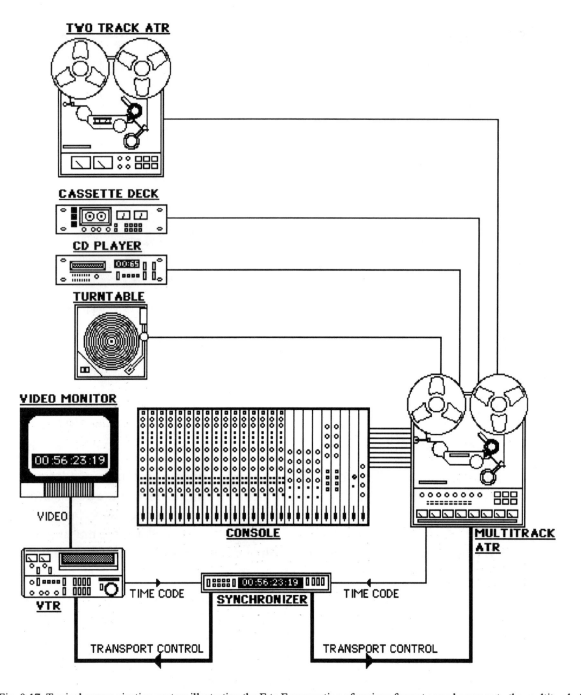

Fig. 9.17. Typical syncronization system illustrating the E to E connection of various format sound sources to the multitrack ATR.

The second method is used when signal manipulation such as level control, panning, EQ or other processing is necessary. Here, all playback devices are connected to the line inputs of the console and assigned to the ATR via the matrix (Fig. 9.18):

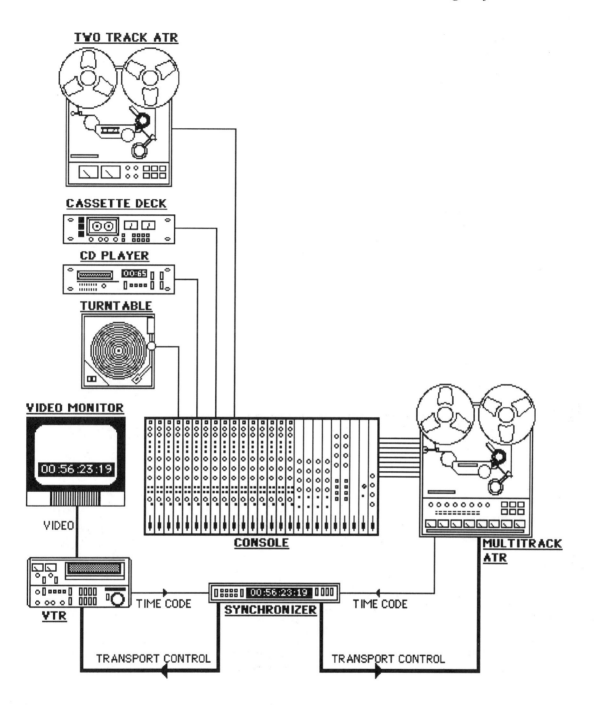

TWO TRACK ATR

CASSETTE DECK

CD PLAYER

TURNTABLE

VIDEO MONITOR

00:56:23:19

VIDEO

CONSOLE

MULTITRACK ATR

VTR

TIME CODE

00:56:23:19

SYNCHRONIZER

TIME CODE

TRANSPORT CONTROL

TRANSPORT CONTROL

Fig. 9.18. Typical syncronization system depecting the conventional signal routing of various format sound sources to the multi-track ATR via the console.

Live Sound Effects

In some cases, prerecorded sound-effects libraries may not contain the desired sound or the sound they do contain may be unsuitable. For example, the need to synchronize specific aural events, such as footsteps to picture, may preclude the use of a particular library sound. In such cases, effects can be created by:

- Performing that effects live and in synchronization with the picture.

- Using electronic playback systems, which allow precise control of the effect, including its start time and its duration.

The practice of creating effects live to a picture is similar to the methods used in a Foley studio. An isolation area is required so that the monitor playback and other unwanted sounds are not picked up by the studio microphones (Fig. 9.19). The advantage of Foley work in an audio-for-video post-production studio is that the shuttle and rewind speeds of the system are far superior to that of sprocketed media, allowing for additional takes or re-takes to occur at a much faster rate.

The items used for creating or replacing the synchronous sounds — such as doors, guns, etc. — are known as **props**. These are brought into the studio and recorded onto separate tracks of the ATR. Samplers and synthesizers may also be used to create or manipulate specialized effects. The looping and punch-in functions of the synchronizer may be used in the same manner that film loops are used in a traditional Foley studio (see Chapter 7).

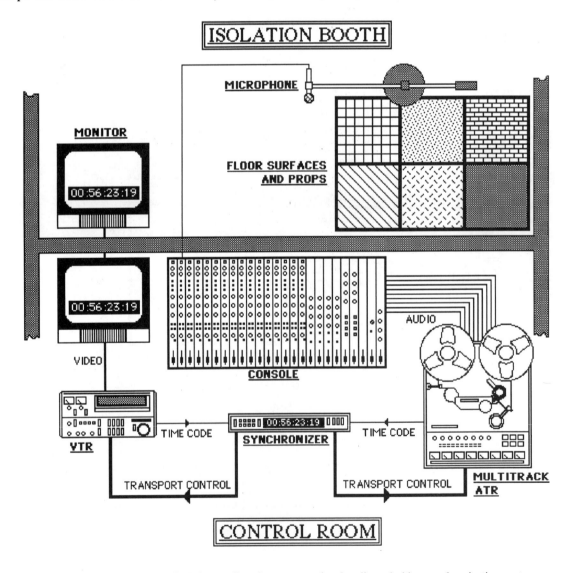

Fig. 9.19. Simplified view of a Foley studio using a conventional audio and video synchronization system.

Sound Effects, Sampling and MIDI

More sophisticated techniques of synchronous sound effects recording involve the use of MIDI and sampling. These subjects are explained in depth in Chapters 10, 11, and 12. For now, it is enough to say that a combination of MIDI and sampling can provide frame-accurate synchronous triggering of sound effects, such as footsteps and gunshots.

Dialog and Narration

By recording an announcer or actor as they view the picture, replacement and new dialogue or narration can be also recorded in synchronization to the picture. Again, by using the looping and punch-in functions of the synchronizer, an ADR set up can be created in the same way as in a looping stage without having to physically create the loops of film and fullcoat (see Chapter 7).

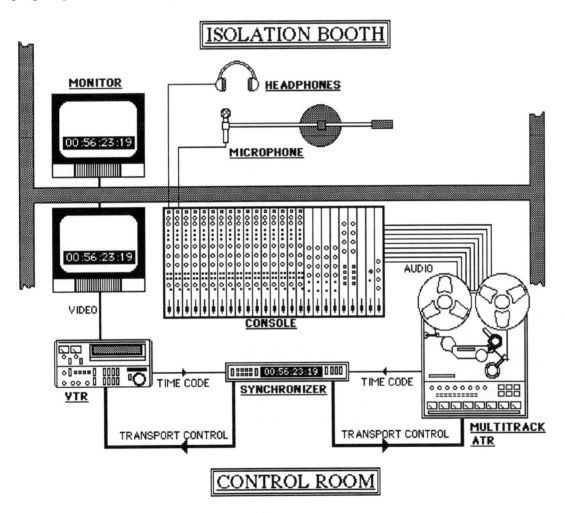

Fig. 9.20. Simplified view of an ADR studio using a conventional audio and video synchronization system.

Music

Music may originate from two sources:

• It can be written for the specific production.

• It can be obtained from prerecorded libraries.

The goal of composing for picture, known as **scoring**, is to create a direct interaction between visual and auditory perceptions. Therefore, original music brings the greatest degree of expression to a given visual. The process of scoring is explained in detail in Chapter 15. Music can be created in the studio by utilizing electronic methods, traditional approaches or both. MIDI systems can play an important role in this process. (Chapters 11 and 12 give full descriptions of the process.)

If the original music is recorded in the studio, then the session may take on the aspects of music production, with the exception that the added element of a synchronized visual is present. The traditional approach — having studio musicians directed by a composer — requires that the composer view the material while conducting. The music may either be live-mixed onto two tracks of the original multitrack master, or recorded onto a new multitrack tape which is striped, interlocke, and later mixed onto a two-track ATR. This mix is then re-recorded onto the original multitrack tape containing the dialogue, narration and effects.

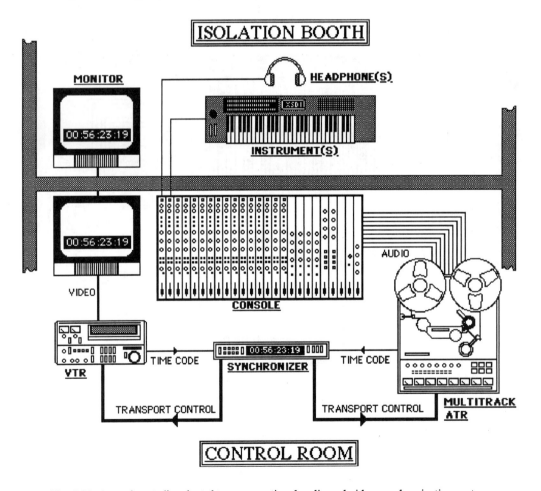

Fig. 9.21. A scoring studio adapted to a conventional audio and video synchronization system.

Production music libraries are most often used because they are cost effective. Like sound effects, these libraries are usually packaged on compact disk.

Fig. 9.22. A production music library on CD.
(Photo Courtesy of Network Production Music, Inc.)

As the previous examples show, the studio differs little when used for Foley, looping and scoring sessions. Unlike film studios, which have to be specialized because of the different types of equipment required for each task, the typical audio-for-video facility may be able to handle all of the post-production phases normally associated with film. The flexible nature of the facility, the reduction of operating costs (which are passed on to the client) and the increased speed at which it operates, makes it superior in many ways to its film counterparts.

CD Playback Systems

CD players have additional features that make them ideal for sound effects and music "laydown." Because they are digital and not subject to mechanical contact, some CD players allow for the looping of any portion of the CD, similar to the effect obtained by using a tape loop (see Chapter 5). This feature can be a great help when an ambient sound track or music selection is too short to meet the picture length requirements.

Fig. 9.23. The Tascam CD-501 CD Deck With remote control. This particular deck can be easily interfaced with a GPI. (Photo Courtesy of Tascam/Teac Professional Division)

By interfacing a CD player to a synchronizer controller's GPI (see Chapter 8), a CD can be set to play at a specific time by programming the controller's event trigger. All that is required is the proper equipment, selection of the CD and track and programming of the controller. When the time code number is reached by the controller, the CD player will start the selected track on the CD, which can be recorded onto the multitrack ATR (Fig. 9.24).

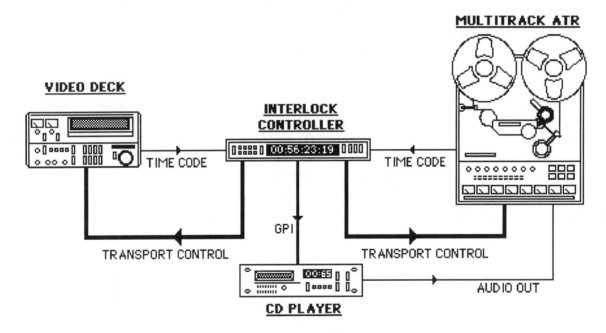

Fig. 9.24. Triggering a CD player with a synchronizer equipped with a GPI (general purpose interface).

One manufacturer, Gefen Systems, has devised an ingenious method of accessing CD sound libraries. This system use a computer, specialized CD player, interface and software. The player, a Sony CDK-006, holds removable racks which can contain up to 60 separate compact disks. The CDK-006 is connected to the computer via the interface. The computer, supplied with software, contains listings of the effects available according to the library's manufacturer. When the effect is selected on the computer's screen, the computer then instructs the player via the interface, to locate

selected on the computer's screen, the computer then instructs the player via the interface, to locate that particular disk and track number and to play it. Furthermore, this system will interface with a synchronizer's GPI, allowing controlled play of CD and track by time code number. This type of system is a tremendous time saver, as it avoids the necessity of both physically locating the effect in the catalog and its corresponding disk, and inserting and removing disks from the player (Fig. 9.25).

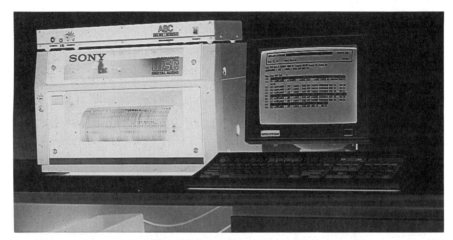

Fig. 9.25. The Gefen M&E organizer system. Although pictured here with an IBM-compatible computer, this system also works with an Apple Macintosh™ computer.
(Photo Courtesy of Gefen Systems)

H. MIXDOWN

When all the required material has been recorded on the multitrack master to the client's satisfaction, the multitrack tape must be mixed onto another ATR or VTR. During this phase, called **mixdown**, **mix** or **remix**, the control synchronization system may be set to loop consecutive segments of the visual while level, panning, EQ and processing adjustments are made on each channel. When the client approves the final sound mix, it is recorded onto an ATR or VTR.

Because sound levels vary and because there exist a multitude of changes to each signal, an automated mixer is a necessity during the remix. In audio post-production applications, the audio must, in most cases, closely follow the video. For example, a train approaching and passing to the left of the screen would be accompanied by an increase in level. In stereo, this would also indicate a change in panpot position. Trying to do this by hand and remembering every change made on the console is nearly impossible. As the number of tracks used increases, continuous manual mixing of the material is indeed impossible.

Also, most automated consoles have the advantage of having the ability to be able to recall a mix at a later date, making it possible to update the sound blend at a later time with minimal effort. Automated mixers are discussed in Chapter 12.

I. LAYBACK

The **layback** is the final phase of audio post-production. This is the stage in which separated audio and video are reunited to one physical media. The mixdown, as mentioned, can be recorded on either a mastering ATR or to a VTR. At this point, there exist several options:

usually possible to insert the audio directly onto the tracks of the master videotape This is particularly advantageous if one of the newer digital formats are used. (Fig. 9.26).

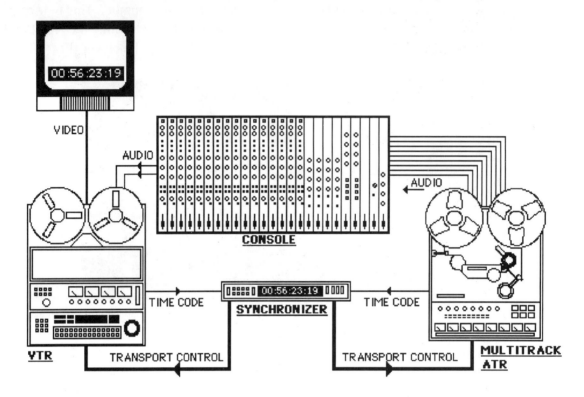

Fig. 9.26. Layback (mixing) of completed post-production audio onto a master videotape.

• Remixing onto either a center-stripe two-track or four-track ATR for re-synchronization to film. This option is discussed toward the end of this chapter. Note that the time code, in addition to the mixed audio, may be either be pre-recorded or regenerated and recorded simultaneously onto the mixdown ATR. If time code is regenerated and recorded simultaneously, the mixdown ATR does not necessarily have to be synchronized or controlled, because there is nothing on the tape that the audio has to be synchronized to. Recording time code with the mix insures maintains the original relationship of time code to picture and multitrack audio. The ATR may be an analog or digital two-track if the mix is mono, or a center-stripe two-track or four-track if the mix is to be in stereo. The decision for recording in mono or stereo depends on the film's final format. For example, a mix resolved to 16-mm optical would have to be in mono, as this format simply does not support stereo in (Fig. 9.27).

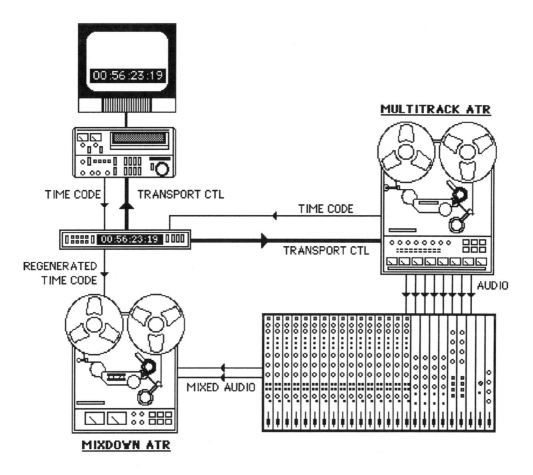

Fig. 9.27. Layback of completed post-production audio onto a master audiotape.

• Remixing directly onto a layback ATR. The **layback ATR** is a specialized deck with head configurations and specifications that exactly match that of a type-C, one-inch VTR. The layback deck accepts the one-inch master videotape directly onto its transport. At that time, the layback deck treats the one-inch master videotape simply as audio tape; it cannot reproduce picture information (Fig. 9.28).

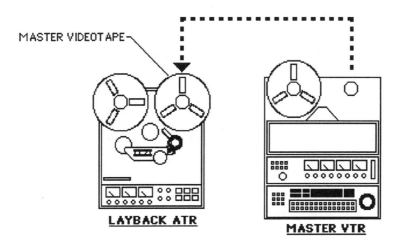

Fig. 9.28. Master videotape switched from a layback ATR to a VTR.

This approach has such production advantages such as optimized audio performance without tying up the much more expensive one-inch deck. In addition, the layback ATR will have both a greater frequency response and signal-to-noise ratio than a one-inch VTR. Because the video master tape containing the original image is on the layback deck, the concept here is to synchronize new audio to the original time code that was recorded on the tape at the beginning of the post-production process. To accomplish this, the layback VTR, the multitrack ATR and the VTR must all be controlled by a synchronizer. The VTR is used to generate picture information, as the layback ATR obviously cannot reproduce the video image (Fig. 9.29, the master videotape is shown in black).

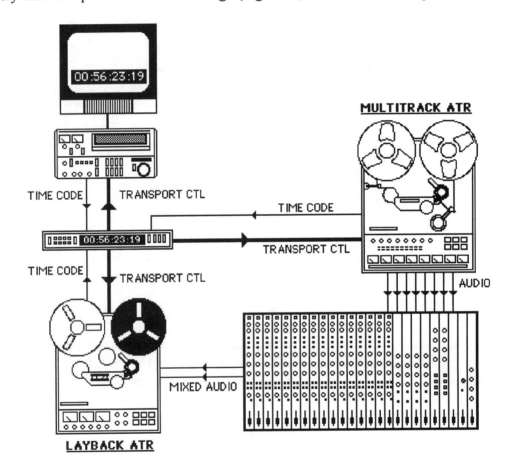

Fig. 9.29. Using a layback ATR for recording the mixed post-production audio onto a master videotape.

However, with the introduction of the D-2 format and hard disk recording systems (see Chapter 10), the layback ATR has rapidly become a rarity in the audio post-production facility. At the time of this printing, every manufacturer who had produced these decks at one time or another had stopped offering these for sale. Indeed, it's now very difficult, if not impossible, to find one. The reasons cited by various manufacturers for the demise of the layback ATRs are:

• Clients were wary of not having the video image originate from the video master, and loss of audio to video synchronization would not be detected until after the fact.

• Many engineers and their clients feel that the treatment of a video one-inch master by an audio transport is risky. Videotape is much thinner than audiotape, and the destruction of a video master by tearing or stretching could be disastrous.

- More second-hand one-inch decks will become available with the advent of the D-2 format, and the layback ATR is no longer considered cost-effective. In addition, because the video mastering standard has changed, the purchase of a layback ATR is no longer warranted.

- Hard disk recorders synchronize more easily, yield better sound quality and are more cost-effective. These are discussed later in the book.

J. FILM TO VIDEO TRANSFERS

Since this book mainly deals with audio post-production of visual material, regardless of its origin, various means of incorporating film into the current technological scope must be examined.

Since film production and post-production techniques have been firmly established for decades, one might well ask, "Why bother?"

Many producers feel that film has the superior image quality, although there are those who, with the advent of high definition video, would contest this. In addition, film is the only medium that is globally shown in projected form, although there exist video projectors of astounding quality.

However, the conventional technologies and methods of film post-production — as discussed in the beginning of Chapter 8 — are archaic, time consuming, costly and require extremely complex and costly facilities. Post-production of film using the techniques in this book will save the filmmaker time and money and generally result in equal or better quality sound. The synchronization systems used are faster and more reliable, and are quickly on their way to becoming an accepted part of filmmaking. Therefore, film-to-tape transfers are the cornerstone of the modern film post-production process.

When first introduced to these techniques, most film producers express concerns about having their product remain in video form. We'll soon discuss how film-to-tape transfers are used to create the audio portion of the film, and how the audio may be resolved back to the film. The video is used only as a visual reference in the post-production process. Nothing, however, requires that this be the case once audio post-production has been completed. Whether or not the material is to remain in video is purely up the client.

The second concern most often expressed is that of synchronization loss. Many film producers feel that leaving the realm of sprocketed media will result in almost certain disaster, leaving them with an out of sync, unusable soundtrack. This is simply not the case. Resolving synchronization between time code and magnetic film sound format is a relatively simple matter.

It is, of course, necessary to transfer film to video for broadcast and distribution purposes. At this point, the film is in completely finished form and the audio portion of the answer print is either in optical or magnetic form. However, because we are dealing with post-production, we must assume that the picture is completed and the sound, save for some dialog, is not. Therefore, any audio will usually be on magnetic stock if the picture has been edited, or on 1/4-inch tape if it has not.

To take advantage of the systems and techniques discussed in this text, it is necessary that film be first transferred to video, because interlock obviously requires the use of video tape. To fully understand how these systems work and are synchronized, we must explore the concepts under-lying the transfer process.

Frame Rates, Speed Shifts and 3/2 Pulldown

Film can be shot, depending on the camera's capabilities, at several different frame rates. The two most important to this issue are 24 fps, the most common frame rate, and 29.97 fps. As discussed, NTSC video also has a frame rate of 29.97. Therefore, shooting in 29.97 ensures a 1:1 relation-ship between the film and video. (Cameras, such as those made by Aaton, which indicate that the motor speed is set to 30 fps, actually have a motor speed that corresponds to a 29.97-fps rate.)

But if a film is shot at 24 frames, some compensation must be made for the shift to video's 29.97 frame rate. Depending on the type of device used to transfer the film to video, this is accomplished in one of two ways.

On older systems, the film is held in a gate by a claw. The video camera records one film frame into three fields, the film projector's shutter closes, and the next film frame is pulled through and recorded into two video fields. This process is repeated until the transfer is complete. Because of the alternation between three and two fields, this system is called **3/2 pulldown** (Fig. 9.30).

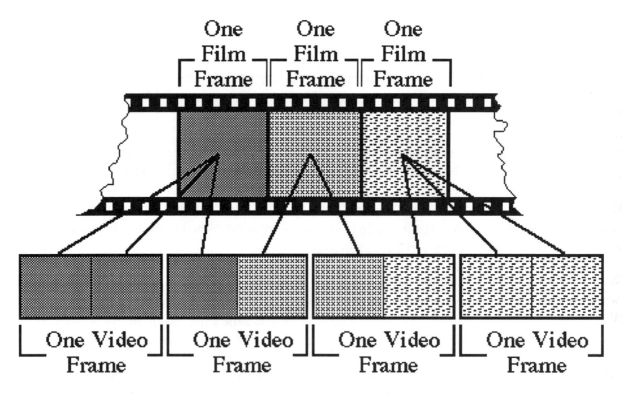

Fig. 9.30. Illustration of the relationship between film frames and video fields during the use of the 3/2 pulldown system. (One video field is half of one video frame.)

Our discussions, however, will be oriented towards the use of the Rank-Cintel system, as this has emerged as the industry's standard for transfer processes. The Rank-Cintel system runs the film at an actual frame rate of 23.97 frames, ensuring an even frame rate relationship between the two media. Mathematically, this results in a 0.1 percent (that is, 1/10 of 1 percent) reduction in film speed. This speed shift will result in a pitch reduction in the audio material. However, this pitch shift is not detectable by the human ear. Moreover, as we'll see later, this shift is compensated for at the end of the post-production process.

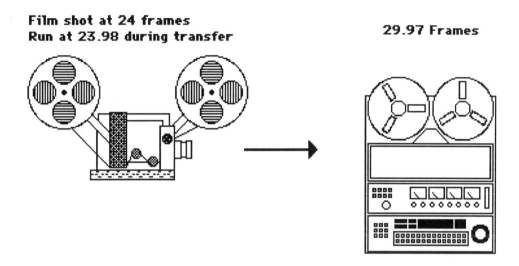

Fig. 9.31. Transfer rate of film when transferred to video.

Simultaneous Transfer of Audio

At this point, the audio is usually in the form of magnetic stock, usually consisting of edited and synchronized dialog only. It is possible to transfer unedited 1/4-inch reels and dailies to video by simultaneously striping each and interlocking them for post-production. It is also possible to edit film in video form and to then have the film negative edited by a negative cutter supplied with edit decision lists generated by the editing device. The possibilities are practically endless. For the sake of clarity, these discussions must be limited to the scope of audio only, as the film must always be in final edited form when it reaches the audio post-production phase.

If the original audio tapes are transferred when the film is in daily form, these should be time coded at a rate of 30 fps. This will result in a smooth reduction to 29.97 during the transfer process which almost all transfer and synchronization devices can read.

When the film is transferred to video, the mag dubber must be interlocked to the projector or may be interlocked to film within the transfer device itself. This insures the synchronous transfer of film and sound.

The audio may be recorded onto either the VTR (Fig. 9.32) or onto a separate ATR (Fig. 9.33). The best results are obtained when the audio is transferred directly onto the multitrack format that will be used for post-production or onto a digital ATR, saving generation loss. The next best solution is to transfer the audio onto a two-track, center stripe two-track or four-track ATR. In either case, both the VTR and the ATR must be striped simultaneously to maintain the sync relationship between sound and image.

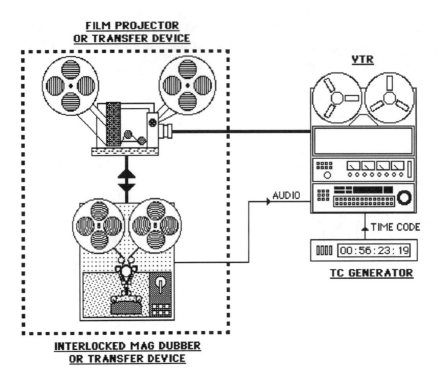

Fig. 9.32. Relationships between picture, audio, and time code during film to video transfer. Again, the time code generator is genlocked (but not shown as such).

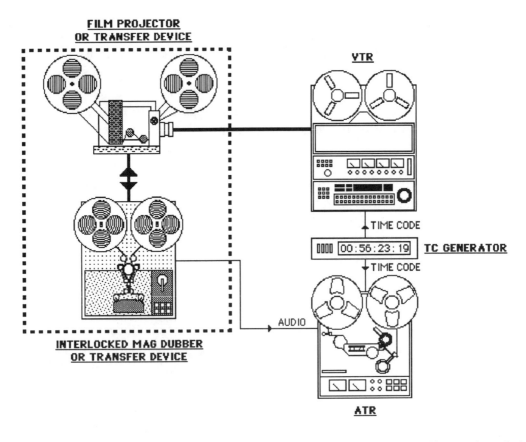

Fig. 9.33. Relationships between picture, audio, and time code during film to video transfer. In this case, the audio is transferred onto a seperate ATR. Again, the time code generator is genlocked.

As previously stated, if the audio is transferred to the VTR or to an ATR format other than the one used for multitrack post-production work, the audio and time code must be transferred to the multitrack ATR. This process takes place before and during laydown and was described earlier in this chapter.

The important concept to grasp is that the audio can originate in, and be transferred to, practically any format. Most professional film-to-tape transfer facilities are equipped to handle a variety of processes. It is the decision and responsibility of the client to understand these processes and to properly plan out each step.

Transfer of Negative or Print

The filmmaker has the option, depending on the type of device used, to transfer to video from either the print or negative of a film. The decision is largely subjective but must take into account the image quality, control over picture, and the costs and time involved. Transferring directly from a negative saves the producer the added time and cost of creating a print. Color correction can be handled by a Rank-Cintel system during the negative transfer process to video.When creating a print, however, color values must first be worked out. In addition, the shadow detail is lower on a print than on a negative. These and many other factors will influence a client's decision.

Types of Transfer Devices

There are basically three types of transfer systems in existence. These are known as optical, charge-coupled device and flying spot. Each is capable of specific functions and, because of the way each operates, yields a different signal quality.

When it was first done, transferring film to video presented a plethora of problems. These included flare, "trails" caused, for example, by headlights passing at night, "hot spots" caused by uneven light distribution, and so on. As the technology has developed, however, many of these problems were gradually overcome.

Optical

The simplest type of transfer systems rely on an optical system where the image is projected onto a lens or optical surface and is recorded by a video camera. These systems cannot transfer a negative image to videotape, nor do they allow the color correction of a film image during the transfer process. Optical transfer systems are used for noncritical applications, such as educational, industrial or some cable television projects. Optical systems yield the lowest video quality out of all three systems. Until about fifteen years ago, these were the only type of transfer systems available.

The Uniplexer

The basic, most inexpensive type of transfer device is known as a **uniplexer**. The optics and image reversal processes involved are much more complex than is indicated here, but for simplicity's sake, the basic layout for a uniplexer is as follows (Fig. 9.34):

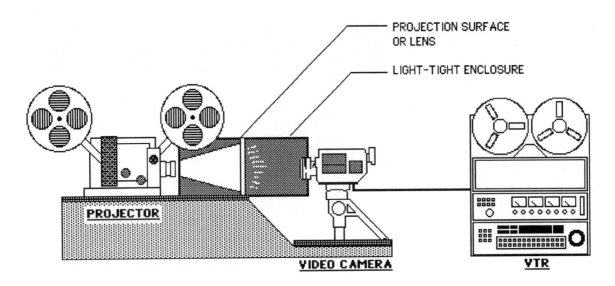

Fig. 9.34. A uniplexer film to tape transfer system.

The film projector projects the image onto what is either a rear-projection surface or lens, which in turn is enclosed in an housing that prevents any ambient light from entering. The image, in turn, is recorded by a video camera which feeds a deck. In this case the film projector is equipped with a special five bladed shutter to eliminate the flicker caused by the frame rate discrepancy between the two media.

The Multiplexer

The **multiplexer** or **film chain** is a device that works on a principle similar to that of the uniplexer, except that multiple formats, including 35-mm slide, super 8-mm, 8-mm, or 16-mm film can all be transferred to video. A multiplexer is basically an "island" of projection devices with mirror assemblies located in its center. These transpose the virtual image from various film media directly into the video camera. The image source is selected by rotating the mirror manually inside the island. Flipping the mirror then causes the image to be directed from any one of the projectors to the video camera at any given time.

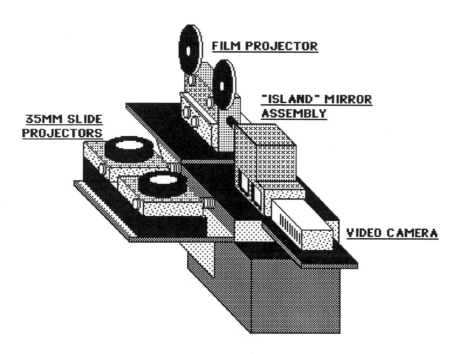

Fig. 9.35. A multiplexer.

CCD

The **charge coupled device**, or **CCD**, was developed to overcome many of the image problems caused by optical transfer systems. In much the same fashion as an optical system, a film projector is used to project the image onto a surface. However, in the case of the CCD approach, the image is projected into a prism fitted with dichroic filters. These filters then split the image into its **component** form consisting of separate red, green and blue (called RGB) signals.

Each of the three color segments of the image is then focused on its own CCD. Each signal picked up by the CCDs is then output in digital form and subsequently stored field by field into a **field store device**. When the field store has completed compiling a full field of video information, the signal is "released," converted to composite analog video and is recorded by a VTR. Thus, the equivalent of the 3/2 pulldown is accomplished in field store. No mechanical alteration of the projected image is required with this system (Figs. 9.36 and 9.37).

269

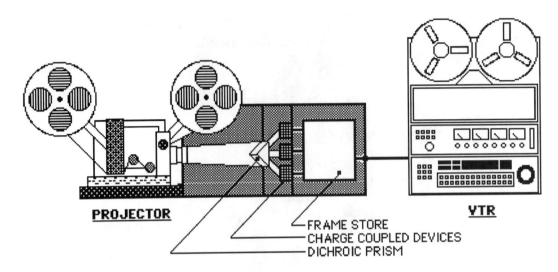

Fig. 9.36. Graphic representation of a CCD transfer system.

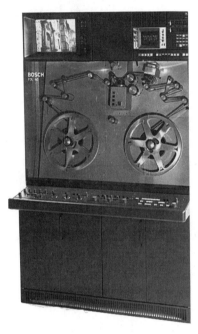

Fig. 9.37. A CCD telecine.
(Photo Courtesy of BTS Broadcast Television Systems, Inc.)

Flying Spot Telecine

The ultimate film to tape transfer system utilizes a system unlike the optical or CCD techniques. In both prior types of systems, the film is projected onto an imaging device, whether optical or electronic sensing. However, the third type of system uses an electron gun to scan each film frame. Hence the name of the system, flying spot.

The gun projects a beam through each frame in a side-to-side scanning motion as the film is run through the gate, or scanning assembly. The beam is then registered on photomultipliers, which sense changes in light level from the beam. You can think of this technique as passing a light ray back and forth through the film. When dark areas in the film frame are encountered, the light output of the beam drops accordingly. The output of the photomultipliers is then converted from analog to digital format and stored in much the same way that a CCD system will store separate fields of video information. (Figs. 9.38 and 9.39).

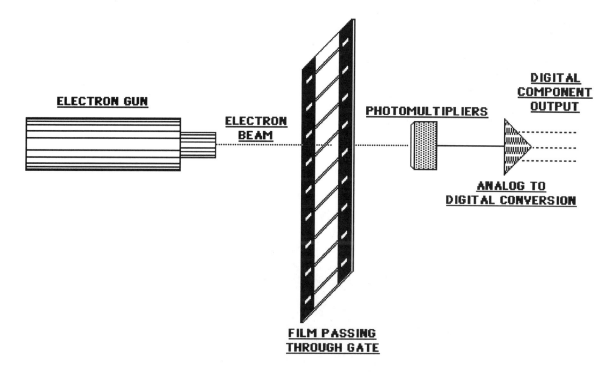

Fig. 9.38. Greatly simplified diagram of the flying spot system.

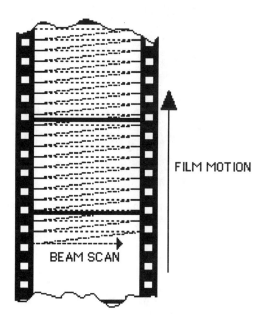

Fig. 9.39. Representation of electron beam motion.

The advantages of the flying spot system should be obvious: Because a dot of "light" in rapid motion is used to translate the image on the film, this method of transferring film to tape is not subject to light retention problems. Trails, hot spots and uneven imaging are all eliminated. A

271

photo multiplier will sense an increase or decrease in light, and instantly produce the equivalent change in electrical output. In addition, this approach allows the system to deal with extreme levels of light and dark, surpassing the abilities of either optical or CCD systems to reproduce ranges in picture contrast.

The output of the Rank-Cintel system is in RGB component signals. These can be supplied to a properly equipped video deck as separate red, green and blue analog signals to form a composite image. Providing the colors as separate signals allows for color correction and image manipulation as the film is being transferred and eliminates problems associated with purely composite video.

A recent significant advance in flying spot technology was introduced by way of the Rank-Cintel URSA system. When the Society of Motion Picture and Television Engineers (SMPTE) developed what was known as the CCIR 601 standard, which set specific operating standards for digital video called 4:2:2, this standard was quickly adopted by many manufacturers. As a result, Rank-Cintel produced the URSA which employs this standard (Fig. 9.40).

Fig. 9.40. The Rank-Cintel URSA flying spot telecine. As previously mentioned, Rank-Cintel is the leading manufacturer of flying spot telecines. This model is considered to be the best device currently available for film to videotape transfers. The rectangular assembly in the center just above the control panel is the gate through which the film passes.
(Photo Courtesy of Rank-Cintel, Inc.)

As a result, the scanned image can be transferred directly in digital component form to a digital VTR such as the Sony DVR-1000.. This system allows for the transferring of film to video without entering the analog domain (Fig. 9.41). The specific aspects of this format are discussed in Chapter 9.

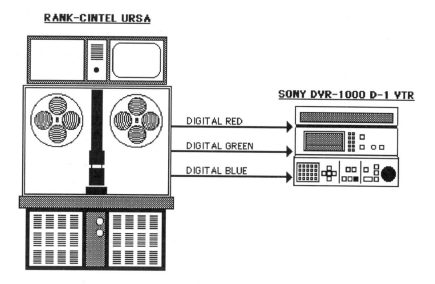

Fig. 9.41. Representation of a Rank-Cintel URSA system, producting component digital video output.

In this way a film may be transferred, the audio post-production completed in digital form, and the finished mix resolved back to film and simultaneously allowed to remain in digital video.

The Rank-Cintel systems use a capstan drive to run the film through during transfer. Because the sprockets have been all but eliminated, the film negative can be properly driven through at various speed without risk of damage to the media. If the Rank-Cintel system and VTR are properly synchronized and controlled (Fig. 9.42), a film can be assemble edited onto a videotape directly. Negative dailies can be shot and transferred in this manner.

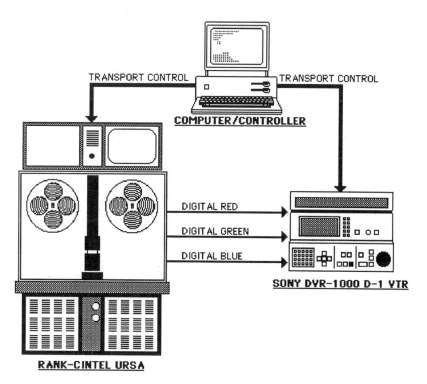

Fig. 9.42. Representation of a Rank-Cintel URSA system and a transport control synchronizer.

The URSA system is also capable of creating optical effects: An image may be slanted, rotated or twisted optically.

In short, the evolution of film-to tape-transfer systems has followed the trend of merging technologies. This is yet another step in the comingling between the different media.

K. SUMMARY-USING VIDEO FOR FILM AUDIO POST-PRODUCTION

In review, it is necessary to transfer a film to videotape for audio post-production work. The advantages to utilizing this system as opposed to the conventional film post-production processes are:

- Film has the superior image quality and is the only medium that is currently shown in projected form. Video is used only as a visual reference in the audio post-production process.

- Resolving synchronization between time code and magnetic film sound format is a relatively simple matter.

- Time code is a faster and more accurate method of synchronization than traditional biphase and sprocketed. Audio and video post-production systems shuttle much faster than film visual and sound media, which are mechanically and electrically synchronized. In this way, they reduce both the time and costs associated with established film post-production procedure.

- Unlike film studios, which have to be specialized because of the different types of equipment required for each task, the typical audio-for-video facility may be able to handle all of the audio post-production phases normally associated with film. Traditional Foley, ADR, mixing and scoring facilities can all be circumvented. In addition, the sound transfers and flatbed editing of music, dialog and sound effects can also be avoided.

- It becomes possible to use even more technologies — these are discussed in the remaining chapters of this book — that facilitate the audio post-production process to an even greater extent. This allows for more spontaneous creative, expression and further savings in both time and associated costs.

At this point, all that remains is to grasp the concept of audio post-production for film using the techniques so far. Subsequent discussions in the chapters that follow will, of course, have a bearing on the film audio post-production process, such as how the finished audio can be re-synchronized to film. This enables all of the techniques mentioned to be employed to the filmmaker's benefit.

Step One: Film to Video Transfer

The first step is to transfer the film to videotape. However, the film must first be in the final stages of editing and should conform to the following guidelines:

•The film should be in final form. All credits and titles should be in place, and Academy Leader should be placed at the head of the film. One may also place the leader at the tail of the film to double check sync, but this is generally redundant.

- Any audio should consist of edited and synchronized dialog on magnetic stock. The beep opposite the Academy Leader "2" frame should be in place.

The film is then transferred to video. Again, the film will run at 23.97 frames, or 0.1% slower. The audio and videotapes should be striped simultaneously and the tapes prepared as discussed.

Step Two: Post-production

Any post-production work done will follow the descriptions already given. The multitrack audio and videotapes are interlocked, and the stages of laydown, sweetening and mixing will follow. During the sweetening process, any ADR, scoring, Foley and other sound effects work will be completed to the producer's satisfaction.

Step Three: Resolution of Mixed Audio to Film

The final audio is mixed onto audiotape and the original time code is simultaneously regenerated onto a separate track of the mix. Again, whether this is stereo or mono depends on the film's format. Either a two-track, two-track with center stripe time code, or four-track ATR can be used. The ATR and a mag dubber are then synchronized, and their speeds carefully controlled by an interlock device capable of resolving both time code (from the ATR) and biphase (from the dubber). Both machines are put into control synchronization, and the mag dubber is made to run at 23.97 frames per second by the interlock controller as the audio is dubbed over to mag stock (Fig. 9.43).

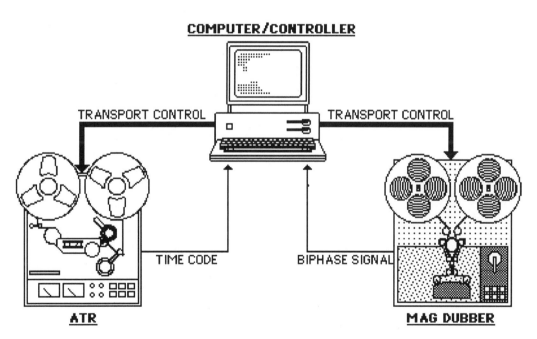

Fig. 9.43. Synchronization of an ATR and mag dubber.

When the dub has been completed, the dubber and negative are sent to a lab, which creates an answer print. Because the equipment running both film and mag stock is now running at exactly 24 frames per second, the 0.1% speed shift has been resolved back up to the actual frame rate of 24.

L. POST-PRODUCTION SUMMARY

The following is an overview and summary of the post-production routines discussed in this book. Note that some of the processes shown are not exactly as described in the text. There is no point in trying to describe the almost endless variations and combinations that can be achieved by transferring between different media. It is up to the client and/or the post-production supervisor to determine which course of action suits a particular project best. It is, however, paramount that all the aspects of this process be understood so as to gain a clear understanding of the options possible. In brief, always genlocking time code, observing correct time code recording procedures, and transfers to and from film media at proper frame rates will *always* insure a synchronous relationship between sound and picture, regardless of which variations of these practices are employed.

1. Prior to starting: The finished piece, whether film or video, must be completely edited in final form.

Editing:

2. If starting in film, footage from the dailies is screened and takes are selected.

DAILIES

3. Selected takes from the production audio are synchronously transferred to magnetic stock.

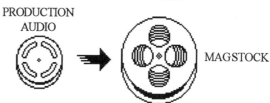

PRODUCTION AUDIO

MAGSTOCK

4. The selected takes are edited out from the dailies and from the mag stock in "clips", synchronized, labled, and stored.

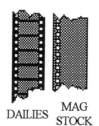

DAILIES   MAG STOCK

5. The footage and production dialogue are edited, creating the workprint and main dialogue track. Academy leader and the beep are added.

Transfer:

6. A workprint or the negative and the audio must be transferred to time coded video. The film media are run at 23.98 frames per second. If the product is not required in video form, the transfer may be made directly to a time-coded window dub; there is no need to create a master videotape.

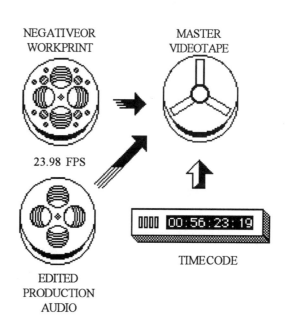

NEGATIVEOR WORKPRINT

MASTER VIDEOTAPE

23.98 FPS

EDITED PRODUCTION AUDIO

00:56:23:19

TIMECODE

277

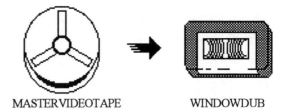

MASTER VIDEOTAPE   WINDOW DUB

7. If the product originates in video, a window dub is made from the master edited videotape.

Laydown:

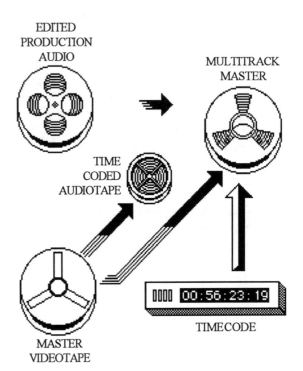

EDITED PRODUCTION AUDIO

MULTITRACK MASTER

TIME CODED AUDIO TAPE

MASTER VIDEOTAPE

TIME CODE

8. The production audio is copied to the master multitrack ATR from the original mag stock, the master videotape, or a time coded audio tape dubbed from the original source. In extreme cases it may be copied from the window dub. However, dubbing the production audio to a digital time coded audio tape format and then to the multitrack ATR will degrade the signal least of all. The time code on the multitrack master may be pre-recorded, and the multitrack master then synchronized to the original audio source, or can be regenerated as the audio is dubbed. Either method will work.

Spotting:

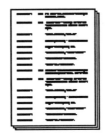

9. A cue sheet is created from a window dub copy of the master tape.

Sweetning:

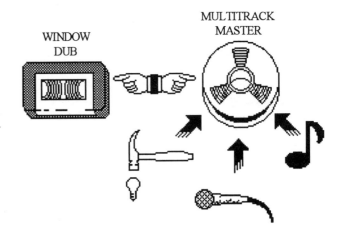

WINDOW DUB

MULTITRACK MASTER

10. The multitrack ATR is synchronized to the window dub and music, sound effects, and/or replacement and/or additional dialogue are added to the multitrack ATR.

Mixdown:

11. The completed multitrack ATR, still synchronized to the window dub, is played back and its tracks mixed down, usually through an automated recorder. The completed mix is recorded onto another time-coded audio tape, preferably digital.

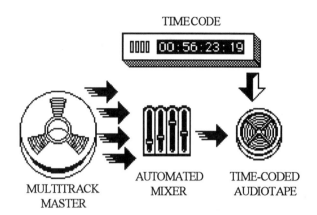

TIMECODE

00:56:23:19

MULTITRACK MASTER

AUTOMATED MIXER

TIME-CODED AUDIOTAPE

Layback:

12. The completed time coded mix may be synchronized to the original master videotape and the audio dubbed. If the final product is to be projected in film, the mix can be transferred directly to multistripe magnetic stock, or, in the case of 16mm film, directly to optical. In either case, the speed shift created during the original film to tape transfer must be compensated for. In the case of 16mm optical, the optical must be run at 23.98 frames; when married to the negative to create an answer print, it is run at its normal rate at 24 frames. Conversely, the audio mix may be brought up to 30.00 frames as the optical is run at its normal rate of 24 frames. Either method will yield frame accurate results.

If the film was transferred from a negative to a master videotape, then the same mix may be re-dubbed to the video master as well as to the multistripe magnetic stock (or to optical), eliminating the need for a final film to tape transfer for ditribution.

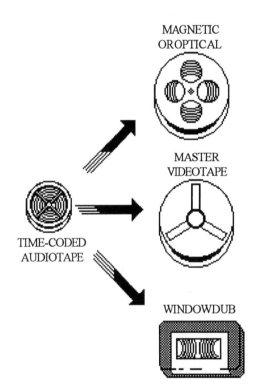

MAGNETIC OR OPTICAL

MASTER VIDEOTAPE

TIME-CODED AUDIOTAPE

WINDOWDUB

10
SAMPLING AND DIGITAL AUDIO

A. DIGITAL VS. ANALOG AUDIO

Digital audio was first developed in the early 1970s as a solution to the problems encountered with analog systems. These problems include distortion, crosstalk, flutter, hiss, print-through, limits in dynamic range, limited shelf life and generation loss. Moreover, once in digital form, audio can be easily manipulated, processed and edited, and this makes it a very useful tool for audio post-production.

Because analog audio systems record a series of magnetic fluctuations on tape, the quality of analog's signal reproduction, that is, its playback, depends on the quality of these fluctuations. Hence, any loss of tape magnetism will cause a loss of signal quality.

Digital audio, in contrast, uses tape as a data storage medium in a manner similar to the way a computer uses a floppy disk. Because what is recorded does not depend as critically on the tape's condition for proper signal playback, many of the problems associated with analog audio systems are eliminated. All that is required is for the storage media to be in good enough condition to allow the reading of the information stored on it.

Consequently, digital recording has a maximum dynamic range of 110 dB; analog reaches an average range of about 70 dB. Digital is almost free of noise, flutter and signal degeneration caused by generation loss. And, digitally recorded tapes have a longer shelf life than their analog counterparts.

However, digital is not without its own set of problems. The overall quality of the digital sound is so clean and transparent that some people interpret this as cold and harsh, preferring for the "warmth" of analog systems. However, what some regard as the "warmth" of analog systems is merely harmonic distortion.

Furthermore, digital systems have difficulty with the reproduction of frequencies above 20 kHz. The response drops dramatically after this point. Analog systems have a more gradual roll off after 20 kHz. Because 20 kHz is the high-frequency limit of human hearing, however, a sharp drop off is not a much of a problem.

Moreover, the cost of digital tape machines is still high compared to analog machines. Some engineers feel that the differences between digital and the proper analog equipment and formats are not easily perceived, and that the high cost of digital equipment is not justifiable. However, as the market becomes saturated with digital equipment, the prices of these systems are bound to drop. (Some of us remember, for example, when pocket calculators sold for $500.) Ultimately, digital recording promises to be an increasingly integral part of audio post-production in the years to come.

B. THE DIGITAL RECORDING PROCESS

Digital audio systems operate by "reading" an incoming analog waveform, "slicing" the waveform into thousands of **bits** (*binary digits*) and converting (encoding) these "slices" into a series of pulses. For now, we'll assume that these pulses are to be recorded on tape. This system of recording is called **pulse code modulation** or **PCM**. These pulses do not directly represent the original waveform as analog signals do; instead, they are data — numbers — that allow the equipment to read and re-create the original audio signals.

To fully understand the process, one must first gain an overview for the entire digital recording process. As is explained later in this chapter, parts of digital recording technology are sometimes used in different ways, depending on the application. Recording takes place within the digital device in four basic stages. These are **anti-aliasing**, **sampling**, **quantizing** and **coding** (Fig. 10.1).

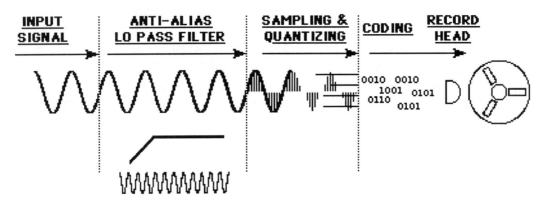

Fig. 10.1. The basic stages of analog-to-digital conversion.

Anti-aliasing

The first step in the digital process is to eliminate any frequencies beyond the digital recording system's range. These frequencies are not audible to the human ear, and if included in the digital recording will be transposed down during playback and create erroneous audible signals. To avoid this problem these frequencies are prevented from passing on by means of a low-pass filter. In this case, "low pass" means all frequencies below the range of human hearing, and these are the ones allowed to pass along into the recording system. This filter is also called an **anti-aliasing filter**.

Sampling

The next step in the conversion process entails the translation of an analog voltage into digital information. As a waveform enters the digital device, voltages at fixed intervals are converted to pulses in a process called **sampling**. Each individual sample is like a snapshot of one instance of the audio waveform. By itself, each sample means very little. But when all the snapshots are put together in sequence, the original waveform becomes recognizable (Fig. 10.2).

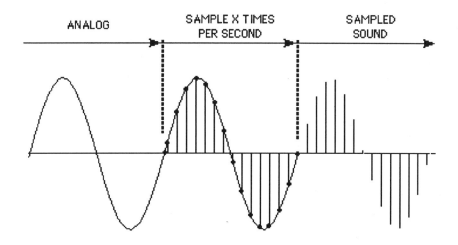

Fig. 10.2. Digital sampling of analog audio

The number of times per second that the waveform is sampled is called the **sampling rate** or **sampling frequency**. If, for example, a waveform is sampled at 28 kHz, then 28,000 samples of the signal have been taken in one second. These samples are the signal "slices" mentioned earlier. For signals to be properly converted into digital information, or digitized, the sampling rate must be at least twice the highest audio frequency to be reproduced. Otherwise the the higher frequencies will not be sampled frequently enough to provide information for proper digital recording and playback. In short, the more "snapshots" or "slices" you take, the more accurate the playback signal (Fig. 10.3).

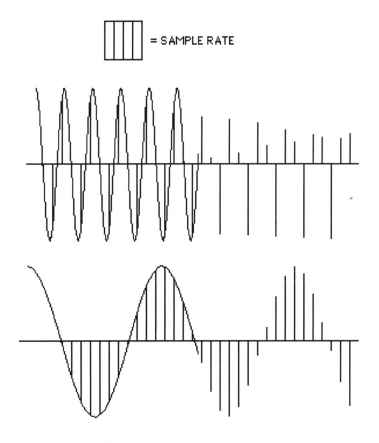

Fig. 10.3. Comparative illustration between short (high-frequency) and long (low-frequency) wavelengths. At the same sample rate, enough information is provided for the recording and decoding of all but higher frequencies.

Increasing the sampling rate will increase the "resolution" of the digital signal. For example, if we were to record a signal whose maximum frequency reached 10 kHz, then we would have to use a sampling rate no lower that 20 kHz. Sampling a given signal more frequently will result in progressively more accurate reproduction of original signals, especially at progressively higher frequencies (Fig. 10.4).

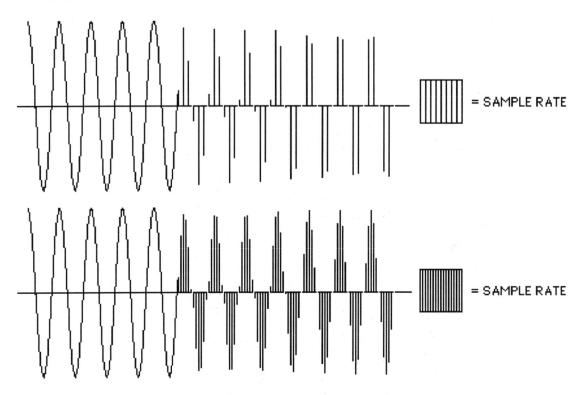

Fig. 10.4. Comparative illustration between two sample rates for the same high frequency. The upper half of the illustration depicts a sampling rate twice that of the rate shown in Fig. 10.3. In the lower half, the rate has again been doubled. Note the increased similarity to the original waveform.

Because frequencies above 20 kHz are generally not preceived, any differences in sound quality at sampling rates above 40 to 45 kHz is irrelevant. In reality, however, a 40-kHz sampling rate is considered too low. Consequently, digital equipment uses standardized sampling rates of 44.1 kHz, 48 kHz or 50 kHz. Compact disks, for example, usually use a sampling rate of 44.1 kHz.

Quantizing

During the sampling process the analog signal is broken down into discrete steps or values. These values are called **quantizing levels**, and the process itself is called **quantizing**. The more quantizing that occurs, the higher the "resolution" of the sound. Engineers refer to the number of bits to describe a particular quantizing level. For example, a one-bit system would indicate simply if a voltage were present or not, but give no information about its value. This would hardly be sufficient for recreating an analog signal. Where one-bit systems have two quantizing levels, two-bit systems have four levels, three-bit systems have eight levels, four-bit systems 16 levels and so on. The standard bit rate for today's professional sampling systems is 16 bits, which yields a total of 256 levels. (Fig. 10.5).

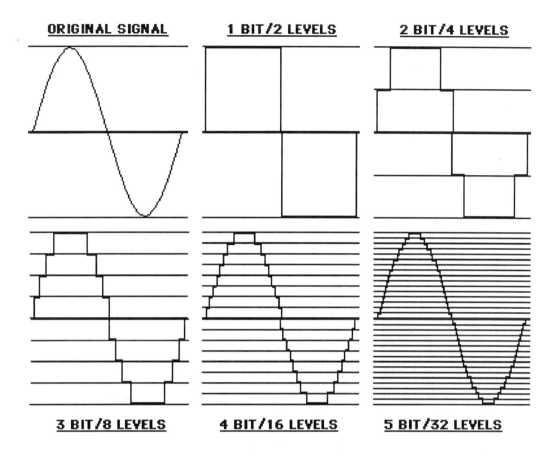

Fig. 10.5. Differences in quantizing levels. As the number of levels increases, the reconstruction of the original analog signal becomes more accurate.

Coding

During the quantizing process bits are generated as the analog signal reaches or falls below a given quantizing level. Pulses are coded as a binary "1" for on, and and a binary "0" for off. Specific combinations of these binary digits, called a **binary code**, represent the voltage level of an analog signal at a particular point in time.

If a voltage exceeds, say, the sixth quantizing level but not the seventh, then a particular code will be sent out.that corresponds to that level. In this way, binary codes are preassigned and correspond to specific, minute voltage fluctuations. Again, the greater the number of quantizing levels, the smaller the voltage variations that are detected and converted into binary information (Fig. 10.6).

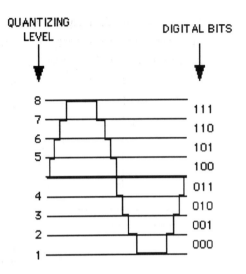

Fig. 10.6. Representation of coding created by exceeding various quantizing levels.

If you also consider that the signal-to-noise (S/N) ratio increases with the number of bits used in the sampling process, it is easy to understand why equipment having a higher resolution is more desirable. The formula for the calculation of a digital signal-to-noise ratio is (Fig. 10.7):

$$S/N = 6 \text{ x (no. of bits)} + 1.8 \text{ dB}$$

Fig. 10.7. Formula for the calculation of a digital signal-to-noise ratio.

For a 16-bit system, this yields a S/N ratio of 97.8 dB, about 15 to 40 dB higher than that of a comparable analog ATR.

Conversion Back to Analog

When a digital signal is converted back to analog, the sequence of events are more or less the reverse of that for recording (Fig. 10.8).

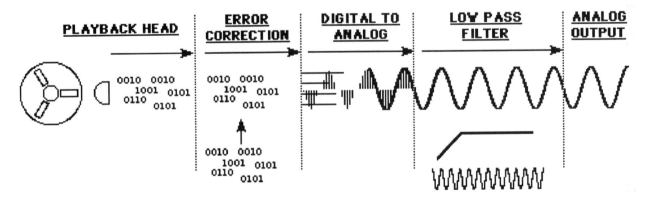

Fig. 10.8. Conversion of signal from digital back to analog form.

However, there are two notable differences in the conversion back to analog. For one, filters are introduced after the actual conversion process. These filters block unwanted high frequencies that are produced during sampling, act to smooth out the discrete step voltages and help restore the signal to its original analog form (Fig. 10.9). Second, so-called error-correction codes are introduced to the signal upon decoding to prevent reading errors generated by foreign matter or dust on the tape or tape path.

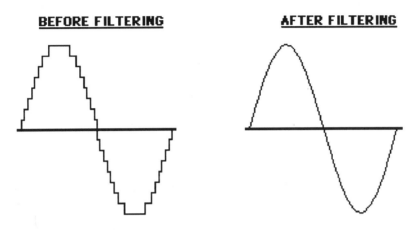

Fig. 10.9. Filtering a signal during conversion to analog.

Error Correction Codes

Because the density of digital information can run as high as 20,000 bits per square inch on 15-ips tape, the error correction codes are introduced to both detect and mask any anomalities in the tape. The three error correction codes in common use are the cyclic redundancy code, the Reed-Soloman code and the cross-interleave code (CIC). The cyclic redundancy and Reed-Soloman codes detect errors along the width of each track; the CIC code reduces errors caused by dropout.

C. DIGITAL AUDIOTAPE FORMATS

Because digital tape stores pulses containing the signal information, and not the signals themselves, digital audiotape is slightly different than analog tape. In addition, the formats differ significantly from each other, like their analog counterparts.

Digital Audiotape Specifications

Tape used for digital recording is thinner than standard analog tape. Because only data is being stored, the thickness and width of a digital track need not be as great as with analog tape. And because the high bit-density per inch can cause playback problems, — problems that may not be solved by correction codes — the use of higher tape speed is generally preferred.

The width of digital tape, as mentioned, is much less than is required for analog recording. Quarter-inch tape may be used with 12 tracks, 1/2-inch tape with 28 tracks, and 1-inch tape with 40 tracks. It is also crucial that digital tape be handled carefully because it is much more sensitive to dirt, dust, oil deposits from fingers, and so on. With careful handling, however, digitally recorded tapes can be expected to have a much longer storage life than their analog equivalents.

287

Unlike analog formats, which have standard running speeds of 7.5, 15 and 30 ips, the tape speed on digital ATRs varies with different machines. Some models operate at 7.5, 15, 22.5, 25, 30, 35 and 45 ips. In addition, tapes recorded on one type of ATR are not always compatible with machines of a different manufacturer. These variations and incompatibilities result from a lack of uniform standards in the industry as well as manufacturers rushing to get their products to market. Nevertheless, the operation of digital ATRs is similar to analog decks. All transport and record functions, such as rewind, fast forward, stop, play, edit, record and cue are analogous.

Digital recorders use one of two main PCM formats. Recorders are also catagorized as stationary and rotating head types.For these, stationary head recorders include multitrack ATRs and mixdown ATRs; rotating head recorders are specialized audio recorders and videotape recorders

DASH

To standardize the digital format, several manufacturers have agreed to develop products that conform to what is called the Digital Audio Stationary Head, or DASH, format. The specifications of this format extend to both multitrack and mastering ATR's, and are as follows (Figs. 10.10 and 10.11):

DASH Format Specifications

SAMPLE RATE	TAPE SPEED		
	SLOW	MEDIUM	FAST
44.1 KHz	6.89 IPS	13.78 IPS	27.56 IPS
48 KHz	7.5 IPS	15 IPS	30 IPS

Fig. 10.10. DASH format specifications.

Note that there are two possible sampling rates. The 48-kHz rate is preferred by many in the industry and is recommended by the Audio Engineers Society. The 44.1-kHz sampling rate is used mostly for the mastering of compact disks. Note also that the tape speed at the 44.1 kHz rate is reduced. This is done to maintain the same density of data on the tape, regardless of the tape speed.

TRACK DENSITY	1/4 INCH TAPE		1/2 INCH TAPE	
	NORMAL	DOUBLE	NORMAL	DOUBLE
NO. OF TRACKS	8	16	24	48
DIGITAL CHANNELS AT FAST SPEED	8	16	24	48
DIGITAL CHANNELS AT MEDIUM SPEED		8		24
DIGITAL CHANNELS AT SLOW SPEED	2	4		

Fig. 10.11. DASH track densities.

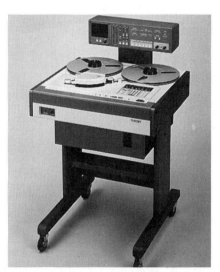

Fig. 10.12. The PCM 3402. This is a DASH format two-track recorder produced by Sony Corporation. It is a two-speed recorder and will run at the low and medium speeds for both sample rates indicated in Fig. 10.10.
(Photo Courtesy of Sony Corporation)

It is worth noting, when preparing their stereo masters, an increasing number of engineers are opting to mix down on two tracks of the same DASH multitrack ATRs that is used to record basic tracks. This is analogous to "bouncing" in stereo analog, except that the original tracks are not erased. This type of approach to audio production and post-production results directly from the excellent signal qualities that digital technology offers.

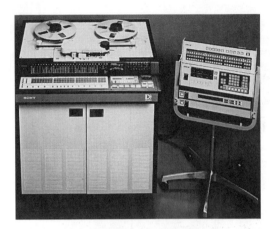

Fig. 10.13. DASH Format 24- and 48-track recorders, respectively. Each is pictured with an autolocator. (Photo Courtesy of Sony Corporation)

The DASH format lends itself to both electronic and traditional cut-and-splice editing. An electronic editing configuration is similar in concept to that used for videotape editing: One or more digital ATRs may be used as the source decks, while a master recorder is used to record the compiled sequences of audio material. Obviously, all the ATRs used in such a system must be synchronized.

Fig. 10.14. The A-DAM digital ATR. This model departs from the conventional format. It is of modular design and construction, and expandable by eight channels at a time, allowing for eight-, 16- and 24-track configurations. The entire program material is recorded on an 8-mm video cassette. (Photo Courtesy of Akai, Inc.)

Rotary Head PCM Recorders

As mentioned earlier, rotary head recorders can take one of two forms:

• Specialized Audio Recorders: These are stand-alone units that use the same principles of VTR heads. A tape moves across a rotating drum containing the various audio heads.

• Video Recorders: These are used to record PCM audio in one of two ways. Either the analog-to-digital converter (described below) is built-in, as with the D-1 and D-2 formats, newer type C VTR's, and some video 8mm units, or an analog VTR is used in conjunction with a separate stand-alone unit.

Specialized rotating head audiotape recorders are called DATs, short for Digital Audio Tape recorders. These use a cassette that resembles a standard analog audio cassette.

Fig. 10.15. The Sony PCM-2500 professional DAT recorder. This particular model is intended for studio use. (Photo Courtesy of Sony Corporation)

Fig. 10.16. The Sony PCM-TCD-D10 DAT recorder. This particular model is portable and extremely useful for capturing production sound, sound effects and dialogue. In many instances production sound engineers will use this or a similar device to record on location in place of, or in conjunction with, a conventional analog recorder used with reel-to-reel film. (Photo Courtesy of Sony Corporation)

If a VTR is properly equipped with a digital converter, analog audio may be sent directly into the deck. The analog signal is then converted internally and recorded directly onto the videotape in digital form. On playback, the deck will reconvert the digital signals back to analog form. If no provisions exists for built-in analog-to-digital conversion, then a separate device must be used for this purpose. This type of device is called a digital-to-analog converter, or **D/A converter**. A device used for the reverse tranlation, that is, analog-to-digital conversion, is called an **A/D converter**. In many cases, the same device contains both converters and, therefore, has the capacity to translate signals between the two formats in either direction (Fig. 10.17).

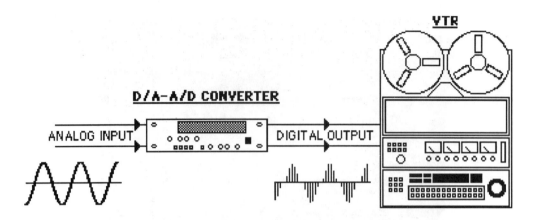

Fig. 10.17. VTR with and A/D conversion device.

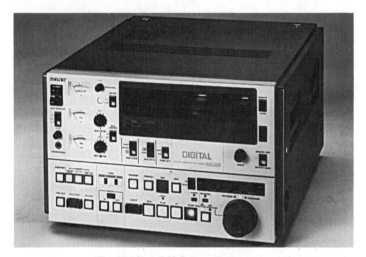

Fig. 10.18. A PCM converter.
(Photo Courtesy of Sony Corporation)

Portable DATs and VTRs equipped with PCM audio have the advantage of being relatively low cost while providing superior signal quality. Today, there is simply no better way to effectively record high-quality audio in the field. If additional dialog, ambiance or sound effects are required for a particular project or application, then a PCM rotary head recording device is presently the best possible choice. However, the basic disadvantage to using a DAT recorder is its low tolerance for abuse — dropping one will almost invariably damage or destroy it. Synchronization to film is maintained because a rotary head digital recorder must, like a film camera, operate at an exact and constant speed during both playback and recording. For added security, a signal from an additional time code or pilot tone generator can be added onto a spare track.

Fig. 10.19. The Sony DMR-400 Digital Recorder. This unit is based on the U-Matic format and is produced for recording and mastering PCM audio. It is used with the PCM-1630, pictured in Fig. 10.18.
(Photo Courtesy of Sony Corporation)

Mastering videotapes with PCM is an optimum way to prolong audio quality without sacrificing signal quality to generation loss. However, the final tapes intended for distribution must not be encoded with analog PCM. Most private viewing facilities lack the converter required to decode the audio tracks.

D. DIGITAL INTERFACES AND COMPATIBILITY

Currently, several major obstacles preclude having a completely digital post-production studios. Because this technology is rapidly and constantly developing and changing, some manufacturers tend to rush their products market. Therefore, no one standard has been established for inter-equipment communication. With a widely used standard, equipment from different manufacturers would work together.

Instead, audio post-production systems and studios tend to have a combination of both digital and analog equipment. Much of the transmission of signal between pieces of equipment is done in standard analog form, and converters inside a particular piece of equipment will then convert the signal to digital, process it and send it back out as analog.

It is highly unlikely if not impossible that one could go out and buy a mixer, several ATRs, outboard equipment and all the items needed to make a studio work, and hope to work with all-digital data. The problem, that one manufacturer's interface might not work with another's, is significant. It is beyond the scope of this book to attempt to list the different types of data languages used. Moreover, because of the pace of change, by the time this book published, new interfaces and languages will have been developed.

However, some components will work together. Two DATs can be linked together via a common interface and data exchanged in that fashion. As we will see in the next several chapters, some samplers and computers share a common interface. This is extremely useful and powerful in the context of audio post-production.

E. TAPELESS DIGITAL RECORDERS

Perhaps one of the most exciting recent developments in audio is the evolution of *tapeless* recording systems. Because digital audiotape acts as a storage medium for data, alternative data storage methods borrowed from the computer industry can come into play. Such tapeless systems fall under two categories: hard-disk based systems and samplers.

Hard Disk Systems

Computers use hard disk-drive systems for data storage encoded in binary form. This data can take the form of written correspondance, a checkbook register, a manuscript for an audio post-production book or anything else you can process with a computer.

Because a hard disk stores binary data, getting it to act as a tape recorder is relatively easy if the data being stored is digital audio information. What is also needed is **random access memory**, or **RAM**, which gives instant access to any sound stored within the hard drive. Say you were working with a hard drive, and you wanted to hear something recorded at 12 minutes, 13 seconds into the piece. By the time you've finished reading this sentence, you would have already accessed and heard that sound. The time saved by using a hard drive based system is astounding. One need never wait for the tape to rewind or fast forward before playing. This feature alone can save countless hours in the post-production process.

All hard drive systems use time code as a reference and most systems can accept longitudinal time code and VITC directly. Upon receiving the first valid time code address, the hard disk will "interlock" instantly. This also saves time because it precludes the need to wait for the audio to chase, park, interlock and then lock to the code, a process that can take from five to fifteen seconds.

Memory

The amount of time available for recording on a hard disk drive depends on its design and is determined by:

- The sample rate used in the analog-to-digital conversion, and

- The amount of memory storage available in the drive itself.

Digital data is commonly is measured in **bytes**, which consist of eight bits each. Memory storage is usually specified in 1,024-byte increments called **kilobytes (Kbytes)**, million-byte increments called **megabytes (Mbytes)** or billion-byte increments called **gigabytes (Gbytes)**. For example, a disk drive with a storage capacity of two megabytes will contain more sound information than one having 40 kilobytes. As the sample rate increases, more bits are generated, requiring more storage space. Obviously, recording three minutes of audio generates more bits than two minutes worth of audio. For this reason hard disk systems used for audio are specified in **track minutes**.

If a particular drive has 60 track minutes in mono, that same device will have 30 if stereo is used because twice as much information is being recorded. Recording four tracks will give 15 minutes of recording time, eight will allow 7.5 minutes, and so on.

On any hard drive system, then, the amount of recording time is limited by:

• The sample rate,

• The storage capacity of the system, and

• The length and format of the material to be recorded.

The design of almost all hard drive systems is modular. To add more memory for greater recording time, many manufacturers offer memory options to increase the storage capacity of their product.

Multitrack Drives

Hard drives are configured in similar ways to ATRs: You can find systems intended for use as either multitrack recorders or mastering recorders. And as with digital ATRs, you can mix directly onto two unused "tracks" of the drive. Again, because the information is digitally encoded, no noise is added and no generation loss occurs.

One such system is the AudioFrame system by Waveframe Corporation. Like similar systems, the AudioFrame uses a computer to control its functions. This system uses 24-bit sampling, allows sampled sounds to be mixed and processed digitally, and is available in configurations of two, six, 14 and 28 Megabytes. In addition, the AudioFrame will convert to and from all popular digital formats. Sounds and groups of sounds can be named and instantly accessed through a database visible on the computer's screen. Also, random access editing can be carried out by directly copying, pasting and cutting particular pieces of sounds .

Fig. 10.20. The AudioFrame System
(Photo Courtesy of WaveFrame Corporation)

One of the most important features in the context of audio post-production is a particular device's ability to read time code and to trigger a sonic event. For example, you could feed time code to a properly equipped device, give it the proper instructions, and produce a synchronous sound effect with frame accuracy. AudioFrame does precisely this, accepting LTC and VITC directly.

Furthermore, it can perform mixing directly using a build-in audio processor that display the image of a console control panel on-screen, complete with EQ section, faders, panpots and so on.

Two-track Drives

A hard disk system that emulates the workings of a two track ATR is the Alpha Audio DR-2.

Fig. 10.21. The DR-2 Digital Hard Disk Recorder.
(Photo Courtesy of Alpha Audio Automation Systems)

The DR-2 acts as a center stripe two-track recorder, allowing access to any point within 1/10 of a second. The DR-2 allows fixed 16-bit sampling rates of 44.1 and 48 kHz, and a variable sampling rate of 2 to 50 kHz. Data capacity is 380 Megabytes, which provides 60 minutes of mono signal (30 minutes of stereo) at 44.1 kHz.

This unit also accepts what is known as the Sony P2 protocol, the most widely used for editing. This allows the DR-2 to interface with video editing systems and act as a standard ATR or on-line sound effects library. Multiple DR-2s can be linked to form a digital multitrack recorder.

Editing

Editing in the hard disk-based domain is the easiest and fastest method available because all that's required is the rearrangement of data. This type of editing is frequently referred to as **nondestructive editing** because the original data is first copied in the segments that will be used to make the edit. In this way the original data remains undisturbed.

Affordable hard disk editing systems are just becoming available. One particularly appealing system is the Dyaxis System, first introduced in 1987. This device can record two or four channels of audio simultaneously.

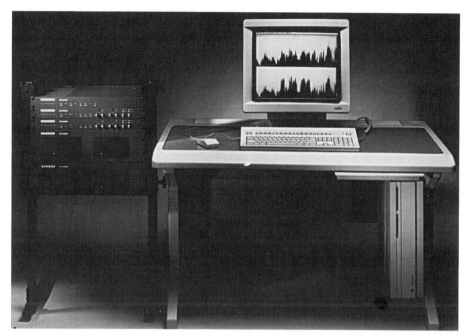

Fig. 10.22. The Dyaxis hard disk recorder, shown with an Apple Macintosh Computer. The screen is displaying a stereo waveform.
(Photo Courtesy of Studer Revox America, Inc.)

The Dyaxis uses an Apple Macintosh computer to control its various playback, recording and editing tasks. The Dyaxis hands time code in several different ways. Primarily, it can read and write both LTC and VITC at any frame rate, as well as read biphase signal generated by film equipment (such as mag dubbers). Furthermore, the Macintosh screen can display time code, film feet and frames, real time (in hours, minutes, seconds) or number of digital samples.

As all signals are digital, the system can provide mixing capabilities, signal processing, equalization and sampling rate conversion. In addition, it can perform **time scaling**. Time scaling lengthens or shortens a sound segment in time without affecting the pitch. This is done by removing or adding random inaudible samples so that the segment fits a particular time slot. One of the uses of time scaling might be to fit a 30-second commercial into a 29-second slot.

The Dyaxis system can also be controlled from an integrated into an external video editing system, making it an ideal tool for video post-production. However, its capabilities also extend far into the realm of audio post-production where, say for dialog replacement, it can replace the conventional methods of looping (film) and cycling (video). Instead of an actor speaking lines repeatedly while viewing the picture, portions of dialog can be adjusted to the picture after the recording has been made. This function is called **track slipping** and is analogous to time code offset, where a sound can be "slid" in either direction until the sound matches the picture. These procedures can save hours of studio time.

The designers of Dyaxis foresaw the need for start-to-finish, all-digital audio processing. Thus, production sound can be transferred from a DAT directly into the hard disk via a digital interface and the finished product can then be mastered, again with the use of digital interfaces, onto a Sony D-1 or D-2 format deck. This is significant because between the initial sound entering the microphone and the final product, all audio remains in digital form.

297

Dyaxis handles a wide variety of digital formats, and subsequently can work with many different makes of digital equipment. Its sampling rates are all 16 bit, and set to 32, 44.056, 44.1 or 48 kHz. In addition, any one of 100 other rates may be selected.

Track time obviously depends on storage capacity. The configurations for the Dyaxis system are as follows:

Storage	Available Time
105 Mbytes	10 minutes
320 Mbytes	32 minutes
640 Mbytes	1 hour
960 Mbytes	1.5 hours
1,200 Mbytes	2 hours
1,600 Mbytes	2.5 hours

Samplers

Samplers act in much the same way that digital hard disk recorders do, with two notable exceptions: They take the physical form of keyboards or standard rack-mounted equipment and the amount of digital information that they can process is much less. You cannot, for example, substitute a sampler for an ATR as you can with a hard disk recording system. However, samplers are some of the most cost-effective and practical tools for digital sound manipulation.

Fig. 10.23. The Emax II sampler. This particular model comes as eithera keyboard or rack mounted unit. (Photo Courtesy of E-Mu Systems, Inc.)

Fig. 10.24. The Akai S-1000 sampler.
(Photo Courtesy of Akai, Inc.)

A common mistake is to confuse synthesizers with samplers. A synthesizer generates its own signals using oscillators; a sampler requires that a signal be introduced into it. However, both can process signals in various ways.

Sampling is rapidly having an increasing influence on audio post-production for film and video, and has a variety of uses: You can fix an error on a multitrack or master tape, store short musical or spoken phrases, re-create instrumental timbres and voices, and reproduce or alter sounds for sound effects. More importantly, sampling can create sounds that are not otherwise available.

For example, *Star Wars* was certainly a popular and innovative film. Less well-known but just as cleverly created were the sound effects supporting the visuals, including sounds that were sampled and processed to yield previously nonexistant effects . Examples include:

- Darth Vader's fleet of ships featured an ingenious propulsion system: The sampled sound of an elephant bellowing digitally combined with a table saw. The two sounds were mixed in digital form, digitally processed and, as ships passed the screen, the pitch of the mixed sound was manipulated to simulate the **Doppler effect**. (The Doppler effect produces the sudden change in pitch of heard in a passing train's horn.When the train approaches a listener, the horn rises in pitch; once it passes, the sound's pitch suddenly drops. The shifts in pitch are caused by the compression of air waves ahead of a moving object and their expansion behind it.)

- Laser blasts are not everyday occurrences. To obtain them, the support cables (guy wires) on a large radio antenna were struck with a hammer and the sound digitally processed by a sampler.

- As land speeders zipped through primeval forests on distant planets, audiences unknowingly listened to digitally processed samples of a Los Angeles freeway recorded through a vacuum cleaner hose.

When used in conjunction with MIDI (discussed in the next three chapters) and time code, samplers can be extremely powerful and creative devices in the context of post-production.

F. USING SAMPLERS

Most samplers have the following controls:

- Input gain (adjusts the incoming signal level)

299

- Sample rate

- Sample time

- Sample placement (on the instrument's keyboard)

Sampling is a two-step process, where a sample is first recorded and then processed. The first step requires the following:

1. A signal is applied to the input of the sampler. Most samplers are extremely tolerant of signal values and will accept microphone to line-level signals.

2. The input threshold must be set. As with analog recording, too low a setting will result in excessive noise; too high a setting will result in distortion. The gain setting should initially be set to 0 dB and decreased or increased as required. Unlike analog recording, however, digital distortion does not increase gradually as the threshold is surpassed, but climbs very fast. Digital distortion sounds truly awful.

3. The sampling rate must be set. Again, lower sampling rates produce lower quality samples, but also allow for longer sampling times. In addition, the number of notes (semitones) up that the sample can be played also depends on the sampling rate. Generally, you set the sample rate to twice the highest frequency produced by the sound source.

4. The sampling time must be set. If a particular sound has a repetitive nature, such as a motor, tone, etc., the sampling can be used to stop at a pre-determined time. This function is useful for conserving sample memory. In addition, a single event such as a cough, door slam or dog bark will occur within a given time. Thus, the duration of the sound can be estimated and the sample time preset.

The best way to understand samplers is to examine two different models and explore the operations available. Although far more sophisticated sampling systems exist, these two models are both affordable and easy to use. And because the basic principles underlying sampler operation are universal, the operation of these less sophisticated models can be applied to similar devices.

The EMAX Sampler

The EMAX sampler is a basic, easily understandable sampler. Like many models, it is available in both keyboard and rack-mount packages (Fig. 10.25). Yet, although the sampler has a keyboard, it is less like a piano and more like a microcomputer that is controlled by switches that resemble piano keys.

Fig. 10.25. EMAX sampler in rack-mount and keyboard form. Both serve the same functions.
(Photo Courtesy of E-Mu Systems, Inc.)

Both the sample rate and sample length are adjustable in several different increments. Again, the sample rate will determine the available recording time. The rate/time ratios for the E-mu systems Emax (with sample memory completely clear) are as follows (Fig 10.26):

SAMPLE RATE	TIME (SECONDS)	MAX TRANSPOSITION UP (SEMITONES)
10kHz	52.0	25
16kHz	33.5	18
20kHz	26.0	13
28kHz	18.8	8
31kHz	16.6	6
42kHz	12.4	1

Fig. 10.26. Sample rates, times and transposition capabilities for the E-mu systems Emax sampler.

The EMAX can truncate, loop, autoloop, splice, combine, and reverse sounds. It can also perform both digital and analog signal processing. (These functions are fully described in the next several pages). Like almost all other samplers, it is compatible with MIDI, making it an invaluable tool for working with sound effects and music.

The EMAX has eight individual outputs and a stereo pair for a total of ten. The eight outputs can be assigned to any particular sound or groups of sounds, which in turn can be placed anywhere on the keyboard. This flexibility permits signal processing of individually sampled sounds by an external device, such as a mixer (Fig. 10.27).

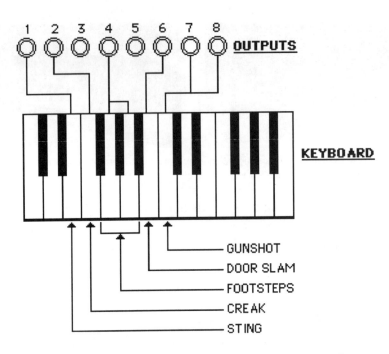

Fig. 10.27. Assignable output configurations of an eight-output sampler.

As seen in Fig. 10.27, individual sounds have been assigned to certain keys within the sampler. Assigning one sound effect to a key permits that solitary effect to be produced at any time. In this example, output 1 will produce the sound of a musical accent called a sting (see Chapter 15), output 2 will give the effects of a creak, output 6 will feed the sound of a door slam, and outputs 7 and 8 will give the sound of a gunshot. Moreover, by assigning the gunshot to two outputs, you can put a short delay on one of the outputs, creating a sweeping, fuller effect. Note, also, that the footsteps are assigned to two keys, both assigned to output 4. This arrangement allows the creation of two footsteps slightly different in pitch. Pressing the left-hand key produces a lower pitch effect, pressing the right-hand key gives the higher pitched effect. The manipulation of a sampled sound by altering its pitch is known as **transposition**, and can yield a wide range of effects. Outputs 3 and 5 are not assigned in this example.

The Emulator III Sampler

The Emulator III is a more powerful version of the EMAX, although both are very similar in operation and appearance. It is a stand-alone post-production tool that can synchronize directly with almost any format of time code, and can generate its own LTC. Like the EMAX, it is MIDI compatible. It can also translate SMPTE code to MIDI and vice-versa. In addition, the Emulator III has a Cue List mode, where specific sounds can be entered and triggered by SMPTE or MIDI commands.

Fig. 10.28. The Emulator III sampler in rack-mount and keyboard form. Both are identical in function. (Photo Courtesy of E-Mu Systems, Inc.)

The Emulator III can sample in stereo and has a mono, stereo and 16 individual channel outputs. Its internal RAM is 4 Mbytes, upgradable to 8 Mbytes. Four Mbytes gives 62 seconds of sampling at a 33.1-kHz sample rate. Noteworthy is the fact that the Emulator III will interface directly with the Dyaxis system, maintaining digital integrity throughout the system.

Digital Audio Processing

As mentioned, sampling is a two-step process, the second being the digital alteration of the sample. Many functions resemble effects produced by audio tape editing, including looping, splicing and crossfades. The following terms are commonly used to describe the digital manipulation of sound by most samplers:

- **Truncate**: This indicates the chopping off of the beginning or end (or both) of a sample. For example, if a sampled sound inadvertantly ended with a dog's barking, the bark could be removed by chopping off the end of the sample. This is analogous to editing with conventional audio tape (Fig. 10.29).

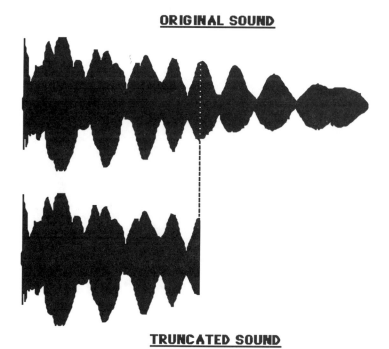

Fig. 10.29. Example of digital truncation of a sound sample.

• **Loop**: When a sample is recorded, it has a fixed duration. However, a loop can be created so that the sample repeats as long as the key is held down. This feature makes use of small samples and, therefore, conserves memory. In addition, looping can produce interesting effects when sounds that are not normally repetitive are made so. A looped gun shot sample, for instance, becomes a machine gun. This is analogous to creating an audio tape loop in analog editing (Fig. 10.30).

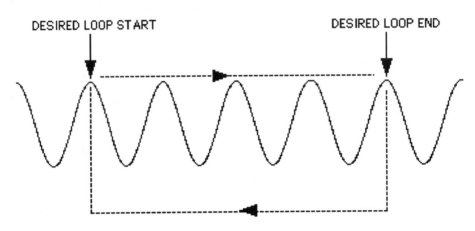

Fig. 10.30. Example of digital looping of a sound sample.

Creating a loop involves designating its start and end points, similar to the "in" and "out" points used in video editing. When the sound playing reaches the loop end, it will instantly return to the loop start. This cycle continues for as long as the key is pressed.

• **Autoloop**: When a sound is looped, a sudden change in amplitude at the loop point may cause an audible "glitch," or a click. Autoloop commands the microcomputer within the sampler to close the loop at the two most closely matched amplitudes (Fig. 10.31):

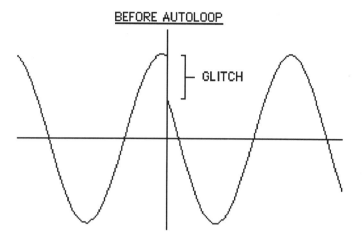

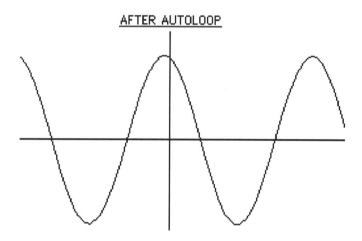

Fig. 10.31. Example of digital autolooping of a sound sample.

- **Splice**: This function splices two samples to create a sound with the attack of one sample and the decay of another. This would, for example, turn a door creak into a scream; a sigh into the sound of wind. Fig. 10.32 shows the placement of two original sounds into a splice. Sections "A" and "B" have been spliced together as shown.

ORIGINAL SOUNDS

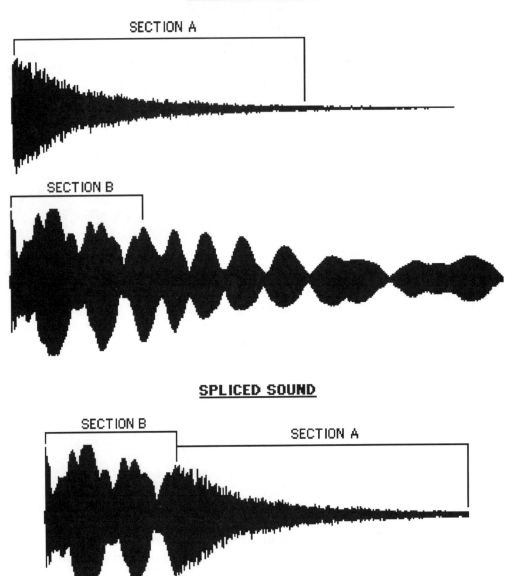

Fig. 10.32. Example of digital splicing of a sound sample.

- **Combine**: This two samples together to create a new sound, as described in the explanation of the sound effects for *Star Wars*.

- **Reverse**: An entire sound can be reversed, in which the attack becomes the end, and vice-versa. A similar effect can be created by physically reversing a tape on a deck (Fig. 10.33).

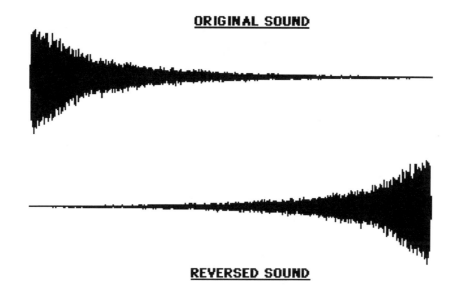

Fig. 10.33. Example of digital reversing of a sound sample.

- **Processing**: Like most synthesizers, samplers have a section that manipulates signals electronically. However, further discussion requires a working knowledge of analog and digital synthesizer programming, which is beyond the scope of this text.

Keyboard Nomenclature

For those with little musical experience, a brief description of keyboard layout is recommended because the names of individual keys will relate directly to sound placement and manipulation.

Keyboards are divided into octaves. A single octave can be easily identified by the repetitive arrangement of black and white keys (Fig. 10.34):

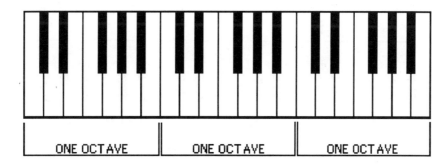

Fig. 10.34. Keyboard nomenclature, showing divisions of octaves.

Each white key within an octave is designated with letter, starting with C and continuing to D, E, F, G, A and B (Fig. 10.35).

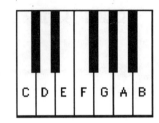

Fig. 10.35. Keyboard nomenclature, showing the various placement of notes on a keyboard.

Each black key within an octave is also designated with a letter. However, these letters refer to "sharps" (shown with a #) if it is above a key in pitch or flats (shown with a b) if below. Moreover, G sharp (G#) is another name for A flat (Ab), because only one black key sits between G and A (Fig. 10.36).

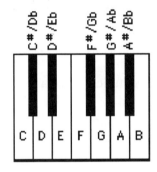

Fig. 10.36. Keyboard nomenclature, showing sharp and flat notes on a keyboard..

Individual key locations within an octave are designated by a number, and each octave climbs sequentially. Thus C1 and C2 are one octave apart, G2 is higher, and so on (Fig. 10.37).

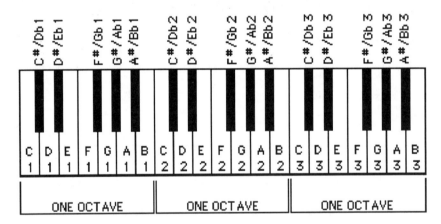

Fig. 10.37. Keyboard nomenclature, showing individual key locations are designated by name and number.

Fig. 10.37 illustrates the nomenclature of the keyboard across three keys. However, a larger keyboard would add a fourth set of octave keys — C4, D4 — and so on.

11
MIDI

A. INTRODUCTION

MIDI, the Musical Instrument Digital Interface, is playing an increasingly important role in post-production work. The MIDI system is used in many different applications. A film or videotape producer or post-production supervisor can effectively reduce costs associated with scoring and sound effects work. Used in conjunction with the other technologies described in this book, MIDI works extremely well as an event trigger for sound effects. Before the advent of this system, such techniques required composers, arrangers, a band or orchestra, sound effects libraries, tape editors, rerecording engineers, Foley studios and scoring studios. With MIDI, it is possible to greatly reduce the staff and facilities needed to accomplish the same tasks.

A working knowledge of music is not necessary to use a MIDI system for generating sound effects for film and video. However, to take advantage of MIDI's capabilities, a knowledge of the workings and capabilities of that system is essential. Entire books are written on the MIDI system, so by necessity this chapter is limited to the fundamental operations of MIDI.

B. MIDI BASICS

MIDI was developed in response to the need for a standardized communication protocol between different makes and models of electronic musical instruments. Several methods of interconnecting electronic instruments did exist prior to MIDI, however all preceding systems contained flaws that severely limited the user.

MIDI is a serial **bus system** capable of transmitting information on 16 separate channels. A MIDI bus system is connected in the manner shown in Figure 11.1.

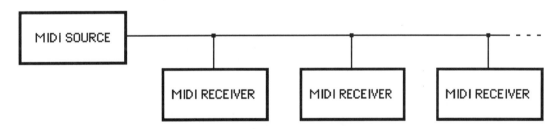

Fig. 11.1. Representation of a MIDI bus.

The term "bus system" indicates that all the devices in the system are electronically connected to one central transmitter or data source. At this point, we are not concerned with what the source or receivers are nor with what is being received or transmitted. Our goal at this point is simply to grasp the concept of the system.

As you can see in Fig. 11.1, anything transmitted by the source goes to all the receivers. Moreover, each of the receivers can be tuned to a specific channel, and if the source transmits information on several channels independently, each receiver will respond only to the information on its channel.

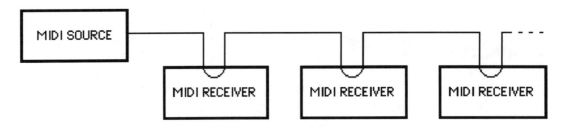

Fig. 11.2. Representation of a MIDI bus showing the looping through of the signal.

Notice that Fig. 11.2 differs from Fig. 11.1 in that the MIDI cable is connected *through* each receiving device, rather than connected onto the cable as in Fig. 11.1. In this way each device retransmits the information that it receives; the signal loops through and passes on to the next device in the MIDI signal path. This is what makes MIDI a bus system.

A key point to understand about MIDI is that *no audio signals* are transmitted through the MIDI cables. For that reason, it is best to think of a MIDI device as a microcomputer that sends and receives *data*.

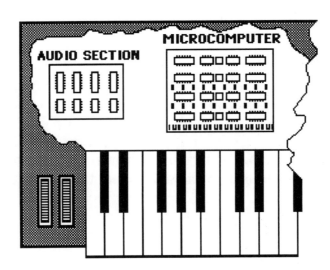

Fig. 11.3. The microcomputer and audio sections of a keyboard.

Fig. 11.3 illustrates a keyboard with its top cover cut open, exposing the various components. (In an actual MIDI device, you would see stacks of circuit boards and silicon chips.) Fig. 11.4 shows what happens when MIDI transmits data.

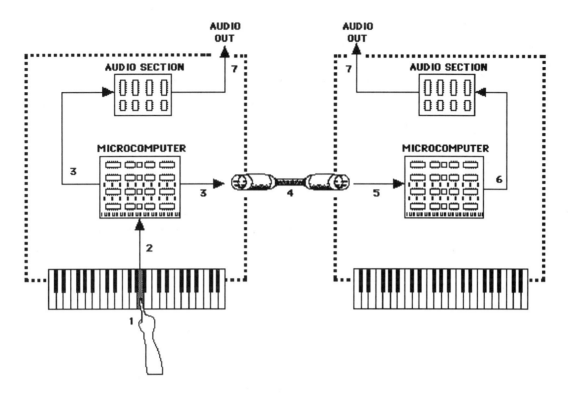

Fig. 11.4. The simultaneous MIDI transmission, reception and audio signal generation in two keyboards.

The events shown in Fig. 11.4, which happen in *millionths* of seconds, occur in the following sequence. A key (1) on the device originating the MIDI signal is pressed, which is picked up (2) by the microcomputer. The microcomputer then instructs (3) the audio section in the source device to produce a given sound. (Again, the microcomputer itself produces no audio signal.) At the same time the microcomputer transmits a MIDI signal over the MIDI cable (4) interconnecting the two devices. This message is received (5) by the microcomputer in the MIDI receiving device, which then instructs its (6) audio section to produce a given sound. Each audio section then produces an audio output (7).

As you can see, the MIDI signal acts between two microcomputers and the audio signals themselves are produced by the devices in the system. The contents of these MIDI signals and how they are used are explained in the rest of this chapter.

C. MIDI CONNECTIONS

MIDI devices are connected by a cable that terminates at each end with a five-pin "DIN" connector. The connector's gender is male at each end. The maximum length for a MIDI cable is 15 meters (about 45 feet), although it is possible to use a cable twice as long before encountering transmission problems (Fig. 11.5):

Fig. 11.5. A five-pin MIDI connector.

MIDI is a *serial* bus system, which means that all information and data is transmitted on a single cable that runs between any two pieces of equipment. The cable plugs into jacks located on each piece of MIDI equipment. MIDI equipment can have one or more of the following jacks (Fig. 11.6):

- MIDI In

- MIDI Thru

- MIDI Out

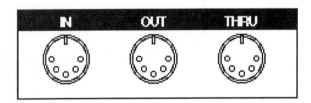

Fig. 11.6. A typical set of MIDI connections.

The MIDI "in" is the jack used for all incoming MIDI information. Any cables originating from an "out" or "thru" jack will be placed into the "in" jack of the next device in the chain. The MIDI "thru" jack performs the loop-through shown in Fig. 11.2, and it is here that the incoming data is duplicated and retransmitted. The "thru" jack connects two or more MIDI units in a system. Unless a MIDI device is located at the beginning or end of a MIDI bus, the "thru" jack is almost always the one used. MIDI "out" sends information originating from a MIDI device.

In some cases a MIDI device may only have two jacks, one of which is designated for both "thru" and "out." How this jack functions is usually determined by the user and controlled from the MIDI device.

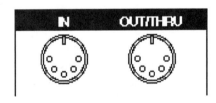

Fig. 11.7. Another set of MIDI connections, showing one jack used for both "out" and "thru."

D. BASIC SYSTEM CONFIGURATIONS

There are two basic methods of interconnecting instruments and other devices using MIDI: **daisy chaining** and **star networking**.

Fig. 11.8. MIDI instruments connected in a daisy chain configuration.

312

Fig. 11.8 shows four keyboards connected in a daisy chain configuration. Four is about the maximum number of devices that should be connected in a daisy chain. Beyond that, data transmission delays called, MIDI delays, will occur. The dark keyboard on the left of the figure is originating all MIDI data. Because the data is replicated at all the "thru" jacks, the originating keyboard can send information to any of the instruments in the chain. What the other devices receive depends on how they are tuned.

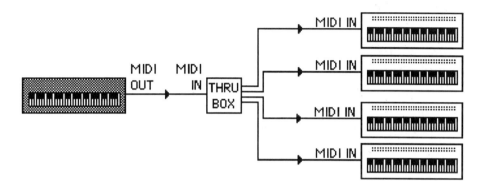

Fig. 11.9. MIDI instruments connected in a star network configuration.

Fig. 11.9 shows four keyboards connected in a star network configuration. A device called a **MIDI thru box** replicates the original MIDI signal into four equally strong separate outputs that feed the receiving keyboards. This type of system is used when an arrangement calls for more than four devices.

A combination of both types of interconnections can also be used, but to prevent MIDI delays no more than four keyboards or devices should be daisy chained.

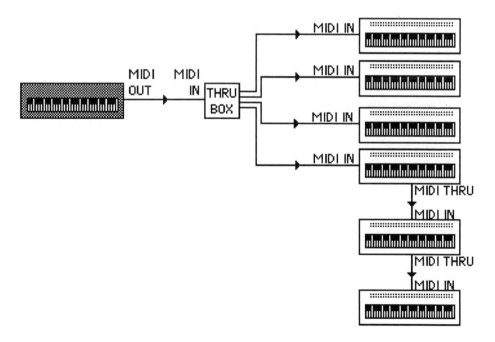

Fig. 11.10. MIDI instruments connected in a combination of both a daisy chain and star network configuration.

The combination of both connection types, shown in Fig. 11.10, is used for two reasons: to reduce the MIDI cable length and because the thru box shown has only four outputs.

E. BASIC MIDI FUNCTIONS

Before attempting to use any MIDI system, you must understand how to use every MIDI device in that system. For example, if a system connects several samplers of different manufacture, each will have a different way of accessing its internal configuration. Setting sampler "A" to receive information on a certain MIDI channel might be accomplished in an entirely different manner than in sampler "B." For simplicity, we will not discuss these control details, but rather refer you to any operating manuals for that MIDI device.

Although our examples have shown how several MIDI keyboards are connected, we have yet to discuss exactly why these connections are made.

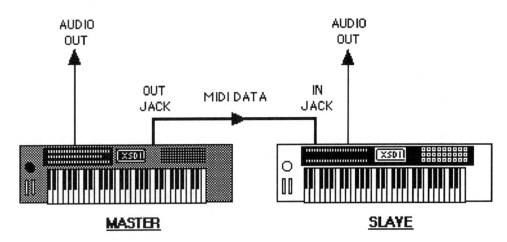

Fig. 11.11. MIDI connections between master and slave devices.

The setup shown in Fig. 11.11 is the simplest type of MIDI configuration: Two MIDI devices, shown as keyboards, are connected in a daisy chain configuration. As with the ATRs and VTRs used in interlock systems, the device originating the signal is called the master and the device receiving the signal is called the slave. Any notes played on the master will also play on the slave.

For example, if a particular sound is selected on the master device and another is selected on the slave, the two sounds will be layered together. Both sounds can be mixed through an audio console to form an entirely new sound. Moreover, several slaves can be added to the system.

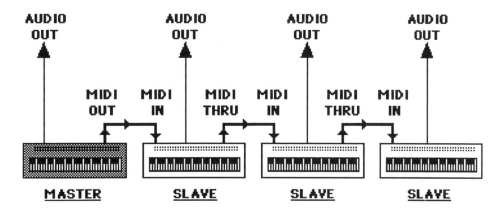

Fig. 11.12. MIDI connections between a master and multiple slave devices.

Fig 11.12 is similar to Fig. 11.2 in that both configurations use loops or MIDI "thru" jacks. This arrangement is an extension of the simple two keyboard setup shown in the Fig 11.11. Although anything played on the master will play on every slave, each slave can be set to an play entirely different sound.

Where more control was required, each MIDI device can be assigned to one of 16 different channels. In that way, notes played on the master keyboard will cause the different devices to sound, depending on which channel the master is transmitting on.

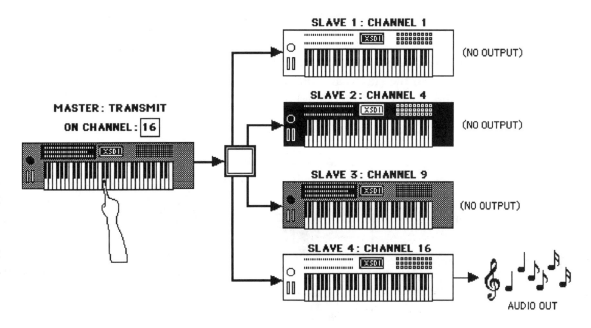

Fig. 11.13. Channel assignments for a master device and multiple slaves. Only the slave that is tuned to the same channel that the data is being transmitted on will respond.

For example, Fig. 11.13 shows four slave devices connected in a star network configuration. Each is set to a particular channel. Because the master device in this example is set to transmit on channel 16, only slave number four, which is set to channel 16, will produce an audio output.

In this way, by controlling the channel transmission characteristics of the master device, multiple sounds can be obtained simultaneously. In Fig. 11.14, the master is shown transmitting on channels four and 16; again, only the devices set to those channels will play. In this example, these are slaves two and four.

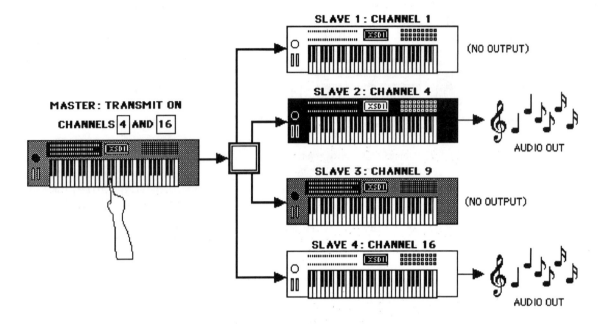

Fig. 11.14. Channel assignments for a master device and multiple slave. In this case, only the slaves tuned to channels four and 16 will respond.

Conversely, by changing the channels on which the slaves receive information, any or all can be made to play. In Fig. 11.15, all the slaves and the master are set to the same channel. Therefore, anything transmitted on the master will be played by all the slaves.

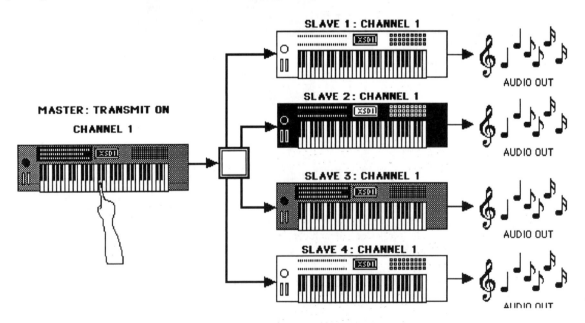

Fig. 11.15. All devices are set to the same channel and play when the master plays.

In short, the process of controlling all of the MIDI devices through the use of channels is the basis for controlling an entire MIDI system.

F. PARAMETERS AND MESSAGES

Much information is transmitted through a MIDI system. How this information is transmitted and received depends on how each device in the system is "tuned." Again, because each device will have a different method for accessing its controls, you must understand how to use every MIDI device in a system.

The following list gives the most basic types of MIDI messages, parameters and functions. Some devices will allow the user to access all of these functions; others will not:

Note On

This message is transmitted when the key of a MIDI synthesizer or other MIDI device is pressed. It instructs all devices in the MIDI system to turn on a specific note. At the same time, it transmits the following information:

- The channel number (one to16) for which the note should be turned on.

- Which note to turn on.

- The "on velocity" of the note.

Note Off

This message transmits an instruction to turn off a specific note. The data sent consists of:

- The channel number (one to 16) for which the note should be turned off.

- Which note to turn off.

- The "off velocity" of the note.

Velocity

Velocity is the measure of how long a keyboard key takes to go from its normal (up) position to its down position. If a key takes a longer time to depress, the instrument is played less forcefully and, therefore, more softly. Technically, the instrument is reacting to the speed of the key's motion, not the force with which it is struck.

Velocity is represented by values ranging from zero to 127, with 127 being the most forceful. To transmit velocity data, an instrument must have a velocity-sensitive keyboard. If an instrument has a keyboard that is not velocity sensitive, its default velocity is 64.

Program Change

Most keyboards and other devices have what are called **preset numbers**, **patch numbers** or **pro-**

gram numbers. These are ways to access different sounds. For example, if synthesizer A's program or preset number 15 contains a horn sound, the user could select that number. Preset 16 may contain a string or flute sound. By sending a patch change instruction through a MIDI system, one or more devices may be remotely controlled to switch presets, producing different sounds at different times. Patch numbers are represented by values ranging from zero to 128. However, some manufacturers produce instruments that display patch numbers differently than their corresponding MIDI number, so it is important to refer to any owner's manuals for details. Nevertheless, the data sent consists of:

- The channel number (1 to 16) over which the program change should occur.

- The selected preset (0 to 128).

Pitch Bend

The subject of pitch bend and its effects on MIDI data is a complicated one. Put simply, pitch bend is similar to what happens when you pluck a rubber band while stretching it. When this happens, the rubber band produces different notes that increase in pitch as it is stretched. Different keyboards have different types of pitch-bend controllers such as joy sticks, wheels and so on. Regardless, however, if a particular sound is played, changing the position of the pitch-bend controller changes the pitch of the sound.

Local Control

Local control allows the user to disconnect the keyboard and any controlling devices from the internal electronics of the instrument. When local control is turned off, the device responds only to the incoming MIDI data and will not respond to "local" commands, such as pressing one of its keys.

Omni Mode

When the omni mode of a particular device is turned on, the device responds to all incoming data regardless of its channel assignment.

Poly Mode

When an instrument is put into poly mode, it responds polyphonically. That is, it plays as many notes at one time as it can.

Mono Mode

When a particular instrument is put into mono mode, it responds monophonically, playing only note at a time.

Tune Request

Many keyboards have an auto-tune button. When pushed, the button calibrates the internal sound generators to a specific note, usually A-440. Sending a tune request message over the MIDI bus is the same as pushing every auto-tune button on every device at once.

All Notes Off

Sometimes, an instrument gets stuck and plays a note or notes continuously, refusing to respond to any attempts to stop it. This control tells every device to go silent.

Controller Numbers

Controller numbers are used by different manufacturers for different purposes. Controller number 23 on one type of device, for example, probably controls something quite differently on another device. Therefore, it is necessary to understand the purpose of each devices' controller numbers; information that can be found in the owner's manual.

G. SEQUENCING

Sequencing is the practice of electronically recording and playing back events. In the MIDI world, this function lets a user record a series of notes and other information transmitted over the MIDI bus. This means, among other things, that:

- Electronically recorded events do not rely on the storage media for the quality of sound. Because what is recorded and played back is data — not audio — the reproduction of the audio signal depends on factors other than the device's storage media.

- Sequenced material allows the event sequence to be changed at any time. Unlike auditory events stored on magnetic tape, which must be edited to be altered, an electronically stored sequence depends only on rearranging data.

Sequencers are the devices used to record songs, entire scores, musical passages, etc. However, some systems also allow you to sequence sound effects as well.

Sequencers record in two ways: The first is called **real-time entry** and is analogous to playing an instrument and recording it on tape: Stored events are played back exactly as they were recorded. The second method, **step-time entry**, lets an operator record a series of notes while separately and individually determining their time values. Using this function, for example, an "A" key is held down while a quarter-note key is pressed, resulting in an "A" quarter note. This function is used mostly in musical applications and, as such, is not covered in depth in this book.

There are three basic types of sequencers:

Built-in

Some electronic instruments and devices feature simple built-in sequencers that, for the most part, only recall note sequences in pre-fixed time intervals. This type of sequencer has limited memory and is difficult to use in post-production applications.

Stand-alone

Stand-alone sequencers are separate, dedicated devices. In many cases, these handle more advanced types of MIDI messages. Data is usually stored onto or recalled from another medium, like a floppy disk. The memory capacity depends on the design of the individual sequencer.

Fig. 11.16. The Akai ASQ-10 sequencer. Note the floppy disk drive on the upper left corner.
(Photo Courtesy of Akai, Inc.)

Computer-based

Sequencers using personal computers are by far the most versatile and the most expensive.

Fig. 11.17. A Macintosh SE computer set up for MIDI sequencing. The screen shows a sequencing software program. The white box underneath the computer is a MIDI interface required for computer sequencing.
(Photo Courtesy of Opcode Electronics)

There are many advantages to using a computer as a sequencer. Among these are:

• A computer provides two MIDI message output locations. Most computers are equipped with a **modem port** and a **printer port**, which are normally used for peripheral equipment. In the context of MIDI, most software manufacturers allow for different MIDI messages to be transmitted independently over each port, allowing the same channel number to be used for two separate devices. Using both the printer and modem ports effectively doubles — to 32 — the amount of usable MIDI channels at any given time.

- Using a computer gives you creative freedom. One computer can perform different tasks, as we will show further on.

- A computer allows many different system configurations and a variety of systems to be controlled at a given time.

- A computer gives wide control over all MIDI parameters. Most stand-alone and built-in sequencers let the user control only the notes being played at the time. In contrast, most computer-based sequencing systems give access to some or all MIDI parameters. In addition, some computer-based sequencing programs will let the user view actual note information, which is an invaluable post-production tool. This facility is discussed in greater detail in Chapter 12.

- A computer's memory is expandable. Unlike other types of sequencers, most computers can be upgraded to have more internal memory and disk drive storage.

Depending on the brand of computer used, several items will have to be purchased for it to work properly as a sequencer:

- The computer: Computers vary greatly in appearance, price, performance, speed, configuration, memory, expansion options, display types and ease of use. The one computer that has evolved as the most popular for post-production work is the Apple Macintosh, although others, such as the IBM, IBM clones and the Amiga, are also capable of similar functions.

- A MIDI-computer interface: This device translates the data coming out of the computer port to MIDI. Some computers have a built-in port, which is fine for a small system. The interface is made for a specific brand of computer. Some units have multiple MIDI ports, saving you the trouble of buying a thru box.

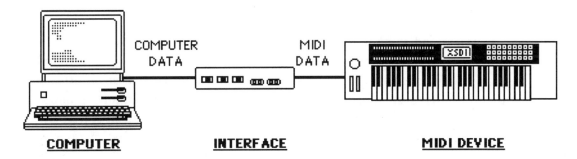

Fig. 11.18. Typical connection of a personal computer to a MIDI device through an interface.

Fig. 11.19. Two types of computer-to-MIDI interfaces. The unit on the left has one MIDI input and three MIDI outputs. The unit on the right has six outputs and can be rack mounted.
(Photos Courtesy of Opcode Electronics)

- Software: Without a set of operating instructions, a computer is a mindless, useless collection of chips, metal, and plastic. Software is the set of instructions that tells the computer what to do and how to do it. When buying MIDI software, make sure it gives you control over all MIDI parameters. Conversely, be aware of its limitations. There is a staggering variety of different types of software currently on the market, some of which is discussed in chapters that follow.

A Note About Compatibility:

If you plan to set up a computer-based sequencing system, make sure that each device and software program is compatible; that is, able to operate with each other. To ensure that the different elements of your system are compatible, spend as much time as you can to properly select those elements. The manufacturers mentioned in this chapter are known to be particularly helpful in this regard.

H. MIDI EQUIPMENT

There is a wide variety of MIDI equipment and much of it can work in audio post-production. By way of introduction, most of the basic types of equipment are covered in the remainder of this chapter.

Controllers

With so many samplers and synthesizers available, and with some of these accessible in rack mount form, larger MIDI systems tend to make use of a **MIDI controller**. A controller is basically a master data originator that supplies information throughout the system. It greatly simplifies the operation of a MIDI system because you are no longer required to run from one keyboard to the next to generate the messages needed for operation. By letting you select MIDI transmission channels and other parameters directly from the front panel, a controller operates any number of devices from a central location. A controller is also necessary to operate a sampler or synthesizer that is rack mounted.

Controllers are available in keyboard and guitar packages. Keyboard controllers emulate piano keyboards in that they have a full set of 88 weighted keys, giving a more natural playing feel.

Fig. 11.20. A keyboard style of MIDI controller.
(Photo Courtesy of Kurzweil Music Systems, Inc.)

Guitar controllers are primarily intended for guitar players who are unable or unwilling to use a keyboard. These evolved from much research and development to address MIDI delays caused by the time required for a string to start vibrating. However, many of the problems associated with early MIDI guitar controllers have since been overcome or compensated for.

Fig. 11.21. A MIDI guitar controller. This device, unlike a standard electric guitar, produces no analog signal. (Photo Courtesy of Yamaha Music Corporation)

Any MIDI keyboard can serve as a controller by simply designating it as such. In that case, the system must be configured to allow it (see Fig. 11.15).

SMPTE Interface Devices

In Chapter 8 we examined the interlocking of various ATRs and VTRs though the use of time code. Time code is also used to connect a MIDI system with these interlocking systems. The device that is interlocked in the post-production system is the sequencer. Interlocking a MIDI keyboard alone is of no use because it is the sequenced data that must be slaved to the master code. The data will then instruct the MIDI devices within the system to play by sending out MIDI messages. Because the sequencer is slaved to code, the messages are produced relative to time code.

MIDI uses its own timing system called **beats**, which are pulses that are sent out every quarter note. When the sequencer receives enough pulses, it assumes that the next series of pulses determines the next quarter note and so on. If the sequencer being used is a computer, having the sequencer substitute time code instead of pulses is a simple matter. Time code, after conversion to MIDI, is commonly called **MIDI time code**.

The ability to interlock a computer that sequences MIDI information to time code requires the following:

- A software package that allows the computer to act as a sequencer and which provides for an external sync source (this is covered in detail in Chapter 12).

- An interface that converts SMPTE time code to MIDI time code.

With these two elements, the system is connected in the manner shown in Fig. 11.22.

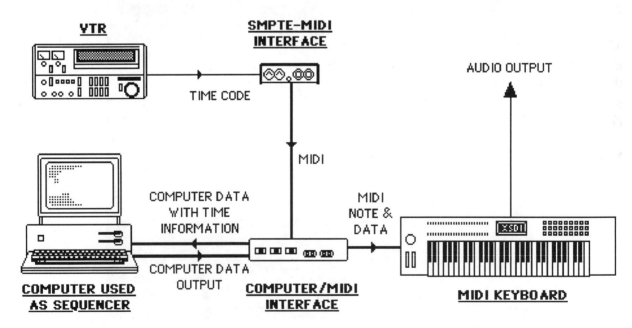

Fig. 11.22. Typical connection of a computer and MIDI device to a VTR that is reproducing time code. The computer, by means of the various interfaces, is able to read the SMPTE code and "chase" the VTR.

The interface converts SMPTE time code to MIDI time code, which is then fed into the computer through the computer-to-MIDI interface. The computer-MIDI interface converts the incoming code to computer data, which in turn can be interpreted by the software being run by the computer.

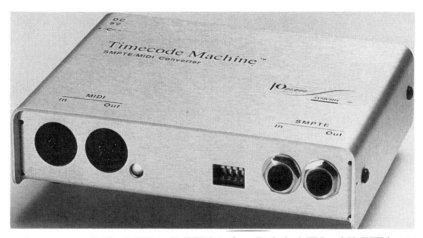

Fig. 11.23. An inexpensive yet very effective MIDI-to-SMPTE interface. Both the MIDI and SMPTE inputs and outputs are clearly visible on the front panel.
(Photo Courtesy of Opcode Electronics)

Patch bays

MIDI patch bays are used for the same reasons as are audio and video patch bays: to avoid having to crawl behind equipment to change the signal routing. In addition, they allow for a wide variety of signal configurations.

However, MIDI is a stream of digital data, not an audio signal, and therefore the patch bay works differently. MIDI patch bays serve to rearrange the configuration of an entire MIDI system.

MIDI patch bays are not really patch bays, but **routing switchers**. Usually, a routing switcher has an equal number of inputs and outputs and works electronically without jacks or patch cords. With the push of a button, it connects any output to any input. The capacity of a particular routing switcher is designated in the same way as is a console's: An 8x8 switcher describes a unit with eight inputs and eight outputs.

Most MIDI patch bays have both a display and buttons located on the front panel (Fig. 11.24).

Fig. 11.24. An 8x8 MIDI patch bay.
(Photo Courtesy of J.L. Cooper Electronics)

The numerical display in Figs. 11.24 and 11.25 indicates which input the MIDI data is originating from. The corresponding number below each digit indicates the output the input is routed to.

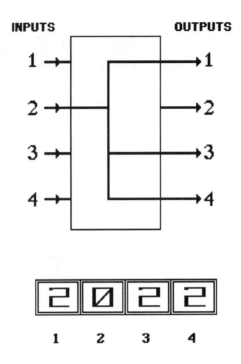

Fig. 11.27. Another graphical representation of the front panel display of a 4x4 MIDI patch bay. In this case, one source has been routed to three outputs.

A more realistic system using a MIDI patch bay would resemble the following (Fig. 11.28):

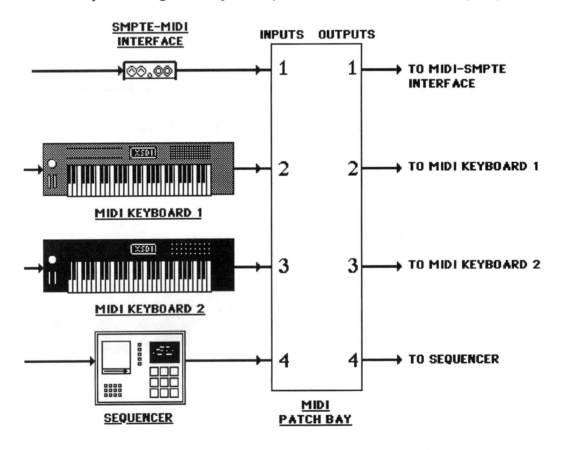

Fig. 11.28. Typical connection of a 4x4 MIDI patch bay to various devices.

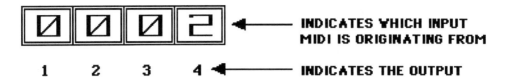

Fig. 11.25. Graphical representation of the front panel display of a 4x4 MIDI patch bay.

For example, in a 4x4 patch bay, if input two is routed to output one and input three is routed to output four, the result would be as shown in Fig. 11.26.

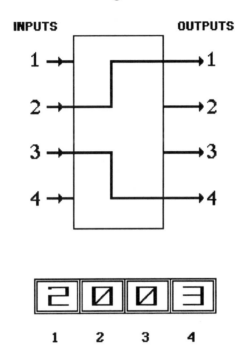

Fig. 11.26. Graphical representation of the front panel display of a 4x4 MIDI patch bay and the same routing plan as it occurs in the patch bay.

In another example, if input two is routed to outputs one, three and four, the connections and corresponding display would be as follows (Fig. 11.27):

At the press of a few buttons to assign inputs and outputs, we can designate either keyboard as the controller, assign either keyboard or the SMPTE-to-MIDI interface to the sequencer's input and, so on. Note that the same input and output number is assigned to a given type of MIDI device. This is a much more straightforward and simple manner of keeping track of what is being routed. At the same time, no output should ever be routed a device that is assigned to an input of the same number. This can result in absolute havoc, as it similar to the analog feedback loop that causes audio systems to howl.

System configurations are arranged and stored in "patches" as are sounds on a synthesizer or sampler. An entire system can be reconfigured by pressing a few buttons, or in the case of the patch bay shown in Fig. 11.24, by remotely sending MIDI patch change information.

Automated Mixers

One of the most useful and exciting recent developments in MIDI-based hardware is the development of automated mixing. Automated mixing has been around for a number of years, but until recently has been available only in consoles dedicated to this task. Furthermore, the cost of these were prohibitive, ranging between $50,000 to $100,000. The price alone kept automated mixing out of the hands of all but top-level professional facilities. Today, however, automated mixing is considered by many to be a competitive necessity.

The principle behind automated mixing is fairly simple: A computer, referenced to time code originating from the multitrack ATR, is used to "record" the movements of controls (i.e., fader, pan pot, eq, etc.) made in the normal course of mixing (Fig. 11.29).

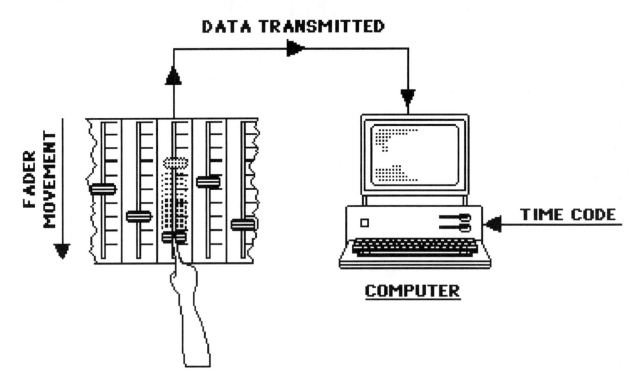

Fig. 11.29. MIDI data (generated by a fader move) sent to a computer with a time code reference.

328

When the tape is played pack, time code is once again supplied to the computer, which then regenerates the same signals back to the originating controls, and the mix is "re-performed" (Fig. 11.30).

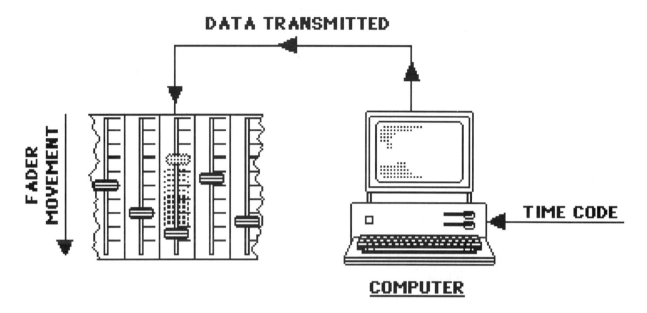

Fig. 11.30. MIDI data sent by a computer with a time code reference to a MIDI-based mixer.

On the expensive, full-function automated consoles mentioned earlier, the computer required to store and recall control changes is built directly into the console. Fortunately, the advent of MIDI has made such technology accessible to smaller studios by using MIDI messages to automate many of the functions found on a conventional mixer, as we will see in the rest of this chapter.

Automated mixers are available in several different types: Some are full-function, stand-alone mixers, while others are designed to be integrated into existing systems and consoles. Still others are available as full-function consoles greatly reduced in size; instead of 48 or more automated inputs, a mixer might be supplied with eight inputs.

In addition, the levels of automation available depend on the device's design. For example, the last several years have seen the introduction of several customary format consoles. These look and perform just as any other medium- to large-format console might except that the channel mutes are controlled by externally generated MIDI messages. This degree of control, although a step in the right direction, has little bearing on audio post-production work, where a high degree of automation is required for speed and efficiency. Automation, to be effective, must include control of at least mutes and fader level.

Types of Automation

How control movements are recreated depends on the type of automation system being used. There are three techniques for automating a mixer's control functions:

- Voltage-controlled amplifier (VCA)

- Motorized

- Digital

VCA mixers operate by controlling the amplifier's gain with a DC (direct current) signal. For example, a one-volt change in the DC control signal will cause a 10-dB gain change. In operation, the changes made to a fader's position alters the DC voltage, which is then converted into digital data and stored by a computer. Upon playback, the sequence is reversed.

Motorized control is presently limited to fader operations and works by driving the fader with a small motor. This system works much like VCA-controlled mixers with the exception that upon playback the faders actually move, recreating the mix as it was last stored.

Digital control requires that the mixer be fully digital. That is, all audio information flowing within it must be in digital form. This can be accomplished by either converting analog information to digital form as it enters the mixer or by having the mixer accept audio in digital form directly. In either case, the audio, being in digital form, can be easily controlled. Digital control is one of the most effective methods of automation because every console function can be accessed by digitally altering the audio data.

Examples of Integrated and Add-on Mixers

As mentioned, integrated and add-on mixers are used in conjunction with existing consoles, and their capabilities are determined by their design. Most automated mixers intended for integration with conventional consoles usually control level only. This is because these mixers are normally placed between the output of the multitrack and the input of the console (Fig. 11.31).

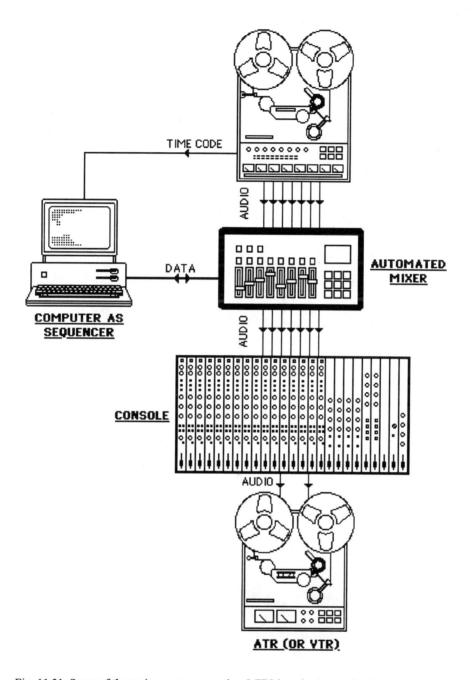

Fig. 11.31. Some of the various components in a MIDI-based automated mixing system

One such device is the Magi II console automation system from J.L. Cooper Electronics. The Magi II system consists of faders and mutes in 16-, 32-, 48- and 64-channel configurations and, unlike the other mixing systems discussed in this chapter, requires an SMPTE time-code input. The advantage of this system is that, unlike many other integrated mixers, it works without MIDI. Instead, time code is supplied directly into the unit, eliminating the need for an SMPTE-to-MIDI converter and MIDI sequencer. Faders and mutes are programmed and recalled in real time. The Magi II is available in groups having up to 16 inputs.

Fig. 11.32. A VCA automation system intended for use with a standard studio console.r.
(Photo Courtesy of J.L. Cooper Electronics, Inc.)

Examples of Stand-alone MIDI Mixers

Another type of mixer that has gained tremendous popularity is the Yamaha DMP-7. The DMP-7 is a fully digital mixer available with either analog or digital inputs. If the analog version is used, all audio is converted into digital form upon entering the mixer and then back to analog upon leaving.

Fig. 11.33. The Yamaha DMP-7 fully automated 8x2 mixer operates on MIDI.
(Photo Courtesy of Yamaha Corporation)

The DMP-7 is a full-function, stand-alone mixer that operates entirely on MIDI. It has eight inputs and two outputs and connects to other DMP-7s to provide even more inputs. Unlike integrated mixers, the DMP-7 does not require the use of an additional conventional mixer. Instead, it goes directly between the multitrack ATR and the mixdown deck, which may be either a VTR or ATR (Fig. 11.34).

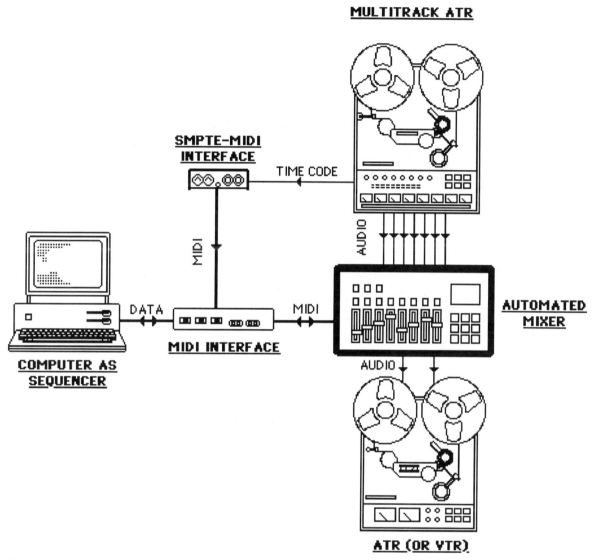

Fig. 11.34. Some of the various components in a MIDI-based automated mixing system illustrating the time code system.

Because the DMP-7 operates entirely on MIDI, it requires both an SMPTE-to-MIDI interface and a sequencer. Note that the time code originating from the multitrack ATR is converted to MIDI and "recorded" in real time by the sequencer or, in the case of Fig. 11.34, the computer. The time code serves as the time base reference for the mixer. Also, all data originating from, and returning to, the DMP-7 is MIDI data. Fader moves, mutes, pans, effect sends and returns — every conceivable mixer function — will generate MIDI messages. These messages can be stored in real time by the computer or sequencer and, when recalled, sent back to the mixer. This procedure is identical to standard sequencing practice using a keyboard or other musical device, with the exception that a MIDI mixer is being used in place of a musical instrument.

Because many sequencers recognize only 127 notes of MIDI note information, they also use so-called controller numbers. For example, the DMP-7 may use note number 64 to indicate a fader move for channel seven. Similarly, the channel on-off may be operated by controller number six. These controller and note parameters can be changed easily by the user.

The MIDI information is retrieved and resupplied to the mixer, where it is reinterpreted into fader moves. Where faders are motor-driven, all other functions are digitally controlled. A large variety of effects, including flanging, chorus, delay and stereo reverb are included and can be accessed internally.

The DMP-7 works on "scene changes" that are analogous to program or patch changes on a sampler or synthesizer. Mix setups can be stored in various scenes and changed from one to the next by remotely sending MIDI patch change information. One scene, for example, might be used for the start of a piece, where all faders are off. The next might be where the music starts, and the faders set accordingly and so on. In addition to these changes, real-time control of the faders and other controls may be accomplished simply by putting the sequencer or computer into "record" mode while slaved to external code.

Because the fader and control moves are stored by the computer as MIDI data, the entire real-time mix can be recalled at any time. The actual scenes and their setups, however, can be stored in a RAM (random access memory) cartridge, which plugs directly into the mixer. In addition, scenes can be stored within the sequencer or computer through what is called a MIDI bulk dump.

This option of having both scene changes and real-time control offers tremendous creative freedom. Coupled with the software discussed in the next chapter, this arrangement is the next best thing to having a $100,000 automated mixer.

12
MIDI POST-PRODUCTION SOFTWARE

A. INTRODUCTION

There are many software packages for working with MIDI-based systems. Understanding what the different types of software can do is a relatively simple matter. However, upgrades are frequent. Therefore, by the time you read this, much of the software discussed in this chapter will have already been updated to newer versions. Still, explanations of the basic operation of each type of software will help you become familiar with the basic principles and underlying concepts.

Each of the software categories discussed in this chapter performs a different set of tasks, and each task is becoming more specialized. The discussions in this book are for software intended for the Apple Macintosh, probably the most popular computer for audio post-production work. As a result, some knowledge of Macintosh computer operation is assumed. At the same time, discussions regarding specific software packages are not meant to duplicate that package's instruction manual. As a result, many of the finer operational aspects every software package have been omitted.

File Formats

The end product of a computer program, or **application**, is often called a **file**. A file can consist of a sequence, sound effect and so on. In the case of a word processing application, a file might consist of a letter to a publisher, a book or a Christmas shopping list. In any event, files are stored in the computer in one of several formats. In the past, it was impossible to exchange MIDI information created by different applications. However, the primary manufacturers of MIDI software have agreed on an interchangeable format called a MIDI file. Most MIDI applications will store files in either their own format or in the MIDI file format.

B. EDITOR-LIBRARIAN

An editor-librarian application is used exclusively with sampling keyboards. It transfers digital sound samples back and forth between the sampling device and the computer. Sample data is not transmitted via MIDI. Instead, a special cable interconnects the sampler and computer. When a sample is transferred to a computer, it is automatically converted to a format that the computer can work with. The process works in reverse as well: Once in the computer, a sample can be stored in computer format, as on floppy disks (Fig. 12.1).

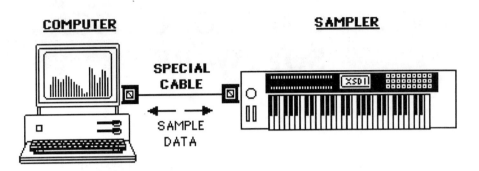

Fig. 12.1. Transferring sample data between a sampler and a personal computer.

Once stored, sounds can be recalled and transferred to the sampling keyboard. This operation is especially useful for creating and storing sound effects. Most programs in this category will also let you manipulate samples in several ways while displaying the waveform on the screen. Manipulative techniques of digitally stored sound include physically redrawing a waveform, creating a new sound by mixing two or more samples, digital EQ of the samples and using other techniques similar to those discussed in Chapter 10. The storage and manipulation of sounds and sound effects is an indispensable tool for audio post-production.

- A word of caution: Samples require a tremendous amount of memory. A computer with less than one megabyte of memory may be inadequate for the job. In addition, most manufacturers recommend that you use a hard disk to store the samples. The alternative — storing sounds on floppy disks — is slow, inconvenient and can eventually cost as much as a hard disk drive.

Digidesign's Sound Designer

Sound Designer is an editor-librarian application published by Digidesign, Inc. As with all applications of this type, *Sound Designer* works in conjunction with a sampling keyboard like the *EMAX* by E-Mu systems (Fig. 10-25). Again, bear in mind that at no point does MIDI come into play here. Rather, a special cable supplied with the software links the computer to the keyboard.

With *Sound Designer* , sampled data can be transferred in digital form between the computer and the sampling keyboard. Once stored in the computer, a sound is displayed as a waveform (Fig. 12.2).

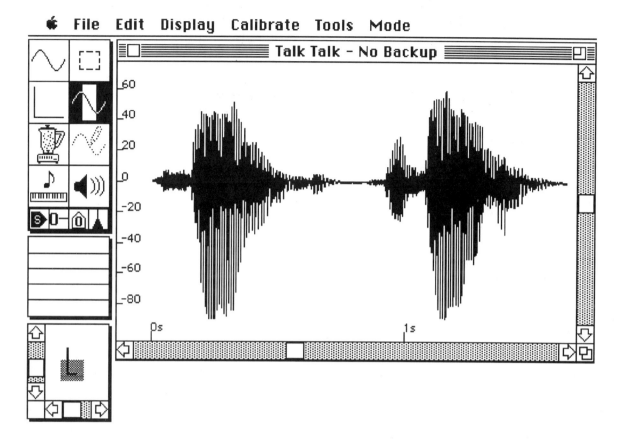

Fig. 12.2. The waveform shows sound of a man saying the words "talk, talk"

The full picture that appears on the Macintosh screen, as shown in Figure 12.2, is called a window. The upper left box of symbols is the *tool palette* and lets the user perform the various functions, discussed further on. At the top of the window is the *menu bar* from which many primary application functions are accessible.

The user can "zoom in" on any portion of the wave and alter it. This process is represented in the sequence of illustrations from figures 12.2 to 12.5. The portion of the wave selected is indicated by a dotted rectangle. Each successive window in figures 12.2 to 12.5 is an enlarged view of the dotted rectangle in the prior window.

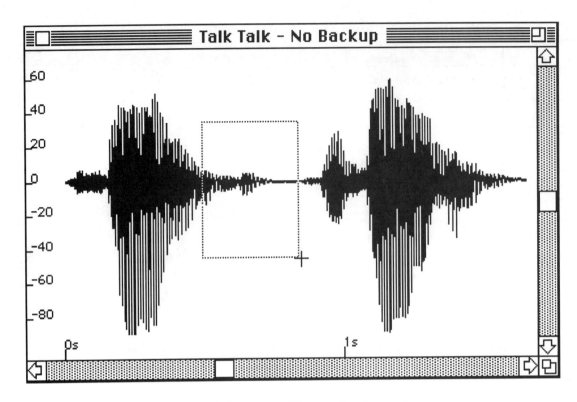

Fig. 12.3. Selecting an area of the waveform to zoom in on.

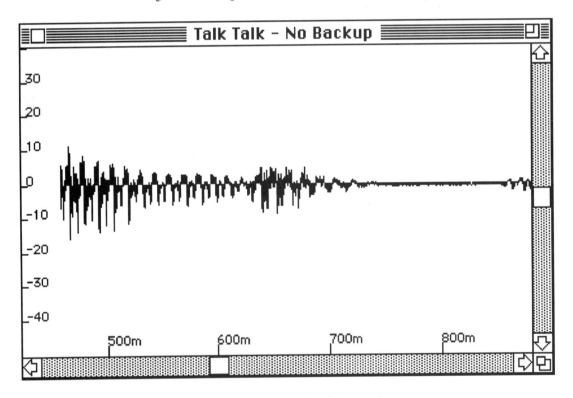

Fig. 12.4. The enlarged section of the waveform.

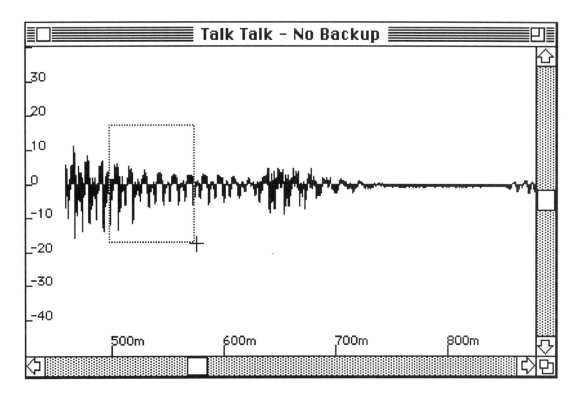

Fig. 12.5. Zooming in on the enlarged section.

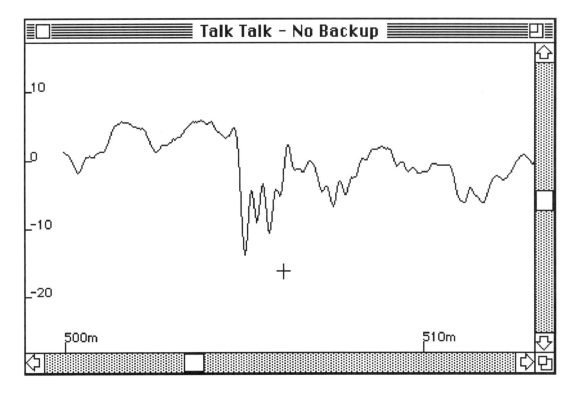

Fig. 12.6. Detail of waveform.

Among its many features, *Sound Designer* lets a user view the graphic representation of a waveform's frequency content, called its *frequency plot.*. This plot allows for the precise analyses and manipulation of sounds frequencies and timbre (Fig. 12.6).

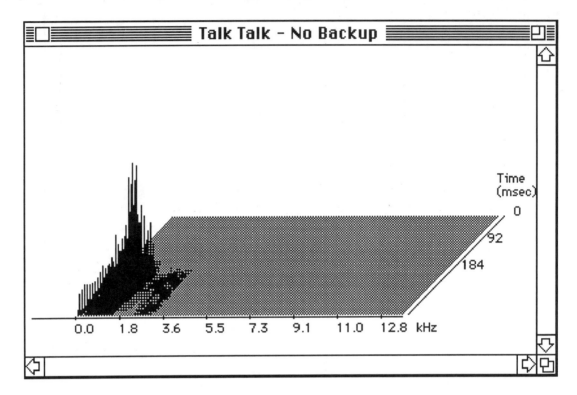

Fig. 12.7. Frequency plot of a sample.

Once the frequency content of a sound is determined, the equalization can be changed digitally by a built-in equalizer. These functions are analogous to the types of equalization discussed in Chapter 5 and include shelving, cutoff, bandpass, peak and notch filtering. All aspects of these filters are completely controlled by simply typing in the appropriate numbers (Fig. 12.7):

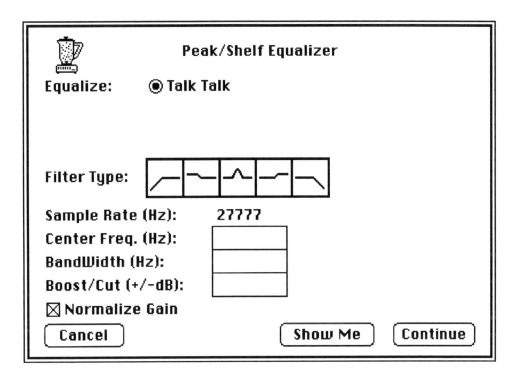

Fig. 12.7. Equalization window.

Other functions include mixing of two samples: merging, gain change and crossfading of a loop point in the sound (Fig. 12.8):

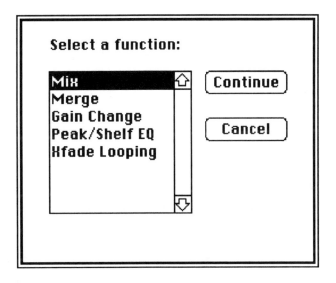

Fig. 12.8. Sample modification options.

Sound Designer also performs a number of other functions. These include placing loop points in a waveform and allowing the user to configure and control the sampling keyboard from the computer. Furthermore, when samples are transferred back to the sampler from the computer, the software can determine their actual placement on the sampler's keyboard. Again, the amount of sound that can be stored is determined by the sampler's memory capacity, an important resource for audio post-production work.

C. SEQUENCING SOFTWARE

Sequencing software instructs a computer to act as a sequencer and function in a manner similar to a multitrack ATR. Controls emulating transport functions might be displayed on the screen and "tracks" made available. In most cases, each track will:

• Have the ability to be turned on, off or be put into solo

• Display note, timing, velocity and other related information

• Be available in unlimited quantity

• Be assignable to any combination of MIDI channels

Try to avoid using software that limits the amount of available tracks at any given time. In addition, some sequencing software is specifically designed for post-production applications, as we will soon discuss.

Mark of the Unicorn's Performer 3.3

One particularly popular sequencing application available is *Performer* Version 3.3 by Mark of the Unicorn, Inc.

Introduction

What appears on the computer display are multiple windows, each of which has a specific function, and each of which can be "opened" (displayed) and "closed" (removed from the display) independently. *Performer*'s designers have included a displayed control panel that provides functions such as start, stop, rewind and record (Fig. 12.9).

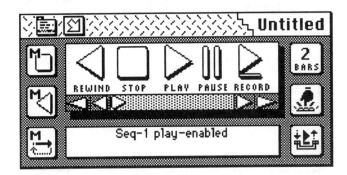

Fig. 12.9. The transport controls.

The metronome window lets you vary the tempo and meter as required. Tempo is described in **beats per minute** or **BPMs** (Fig. 12.10).

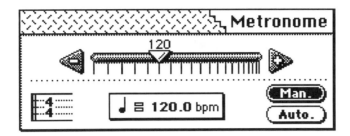

Fig. 12.10. The tempo controls.

A counter similar to that found on an ATR shows the precise location of the sequence at any time. In Figure 12.11, the display of 1|1|000 indicates that the sequence is on the first bar, first beat, note 000.

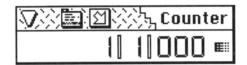

Fig. 12.11. The counter.

This is feature tells you precisely where something is in relation to the tempo. And although the feature is unrelated to audio post-production, the display can easily be changed to show beats and measures, real time or a combination of these. In this way, a given sequence can be matched exactly with picture. Fig. 12.12 shows the counter set for (top to bottom) SMPTE, bars and beats, and real time.

Fig. 12.12. The counter displaying SMPTE, musical, and real-time information.

Accurate use of time code indicates that the frame rate is established, and this is precisely what *Performer* allows. (Fig. 12.13).

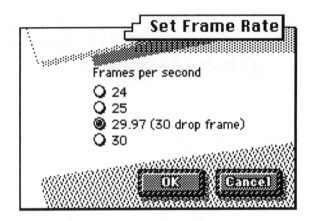

Fig. 12.13. Frame rate selection.

Performer also displays a MIDI window that shows exactly which channels are being received over which port. This is particularly useful for troubleshooting (Fig. 12.14).

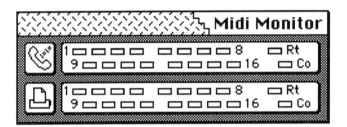

Fig. 12.14. MIDI data transmission and reception monitor.

Synchronization

Synchronization, as we have said, is essential for audio post-production and this is equally true for computers that serve as ATRs. *Performer* allows the computer to be "slaved" to various sources including SMPTE time code received in the form of MIDI. Fig. 12.15 shows how the various synchronization sources are selected.

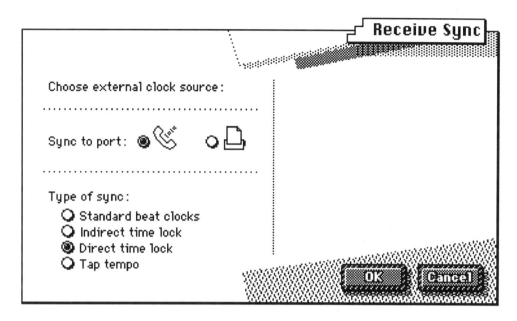

Fig. 12.15. Selecting the port and type of synchronization signal.

For added accuracy, individual sequences called chunks can be given various start times. Again, as is characteristic of *Performer*, these are displayed in measures, real time and frames. When slaved to an external synchronization source, a particular sequence will start only when the designated time-code address is received.

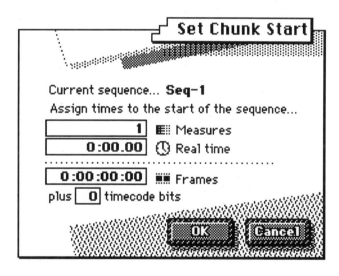

Fig. 12.16. The sequence start window.

Sequences and MIDI Information

Note and other MIDI information is stored in what can be thought of as a layered system. Sequences (chunks) are the primary method of arranging information (Fig. 12.17).

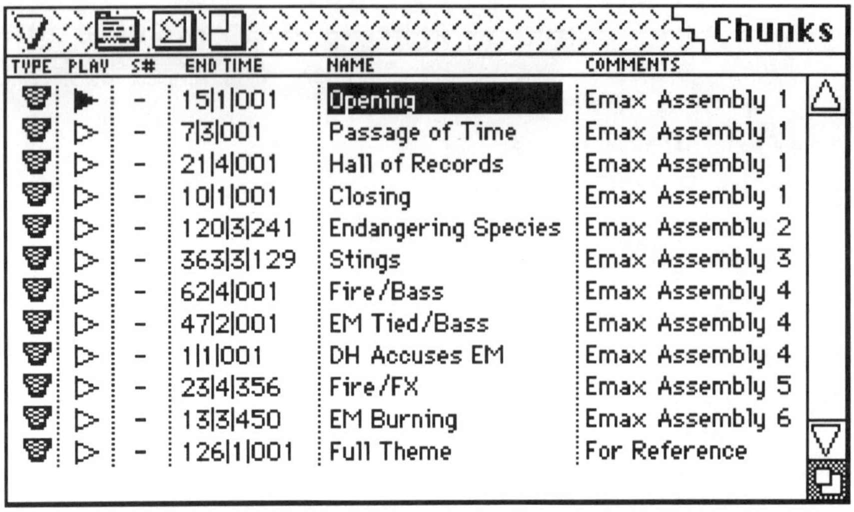

Fig. 12.17. A sequences list.

Within each chunk are stored various tracks analogous to tracks on a conventional multitrack ATR. The number of tracks is determined by the user. Each can be muted, heard in solo, recorded, erased, deleted and edited. In Fig. 12.17 the chunk titled "opening" is highlighted and the tracks contained within it are shown in Fig. 12.18:

Fig. 12.18. Tracks within a sequence.

The symbol under the column marked "REC" is comparable to a "record ready" function on an ATR. The dark triangles under the "PLAY/CH." column indicate that those particular tracks will be heard when the sequence is played. The "M1," "M2" and "M3" symbols indicate the MIDI channels and ports on which each track will transmit data.

Note that any combination of transmissions among the 16 channels and two ports ("M" for modem and "P" for printer) is possible. Again, only the devices tuned to those channels in the poly **((MN: DO YOU MEAN ""PLAY?" IF SO, PLEASE FIX AND DELETE THIS QUERY— GB))** mode will respond to that data. The track titled "1/8" notes is highlighted and opening the track will reveal the MIDI information contained within it (Fig. 12.19).

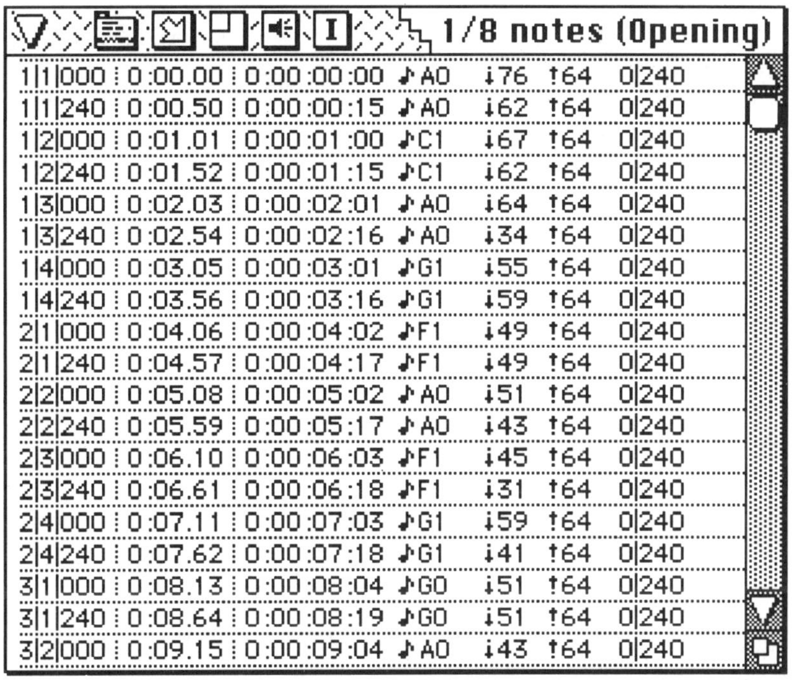

1|1|000	0:00.00	0:00:00:00	♪A0	↓76	↑64	0|240
1|1|240	0:00.50	0:00:00:15	♪A0	↓62	↑64	0|240
1|2|000	0:01.01	0:00:01:00	♪C1	↓67	↑64	0|240
1|2|240	0:01.52	0:00:01:15	♪C1	↓62	↑64	0|240
1|3|000	0:02.03	0:00:02:01	♪A0	↓64	↑64	0|240
1|3|240	0:02.54	0:00:02:16	♪A0	↓34	↑64	0|240
1|4|000	0:03.05	0:00:03:01	♪G1	↓55	↑64	0|240
1|4|240	0:03.56	0:00:03:16	♪G1	↓59	↑64	0|240
2|1|000	0:04.06	0:00:04:02	♪F1	↓49	↑64	0|240
2|1|240	0:04.57	0:00:04:17	♪F1	↓49	↑64	0|240
2|2|000	0:05.08	0:00:05:02	♪A0	↓51	↑64	0|240
2|2|240	0:05.59	0:00:05:17	♪A0	↓43	↑64	0|240
2|3|000	0:06.10	0:00:06:03	♪F1	↓45	↑64	0|240
2|3|240	0:06.61	0:00:06:18	♪F1	↓31	↑64	0|240
2|4|000	0:07.11	0:00:07:03	♪G1	↓59	↑64	0|240
2|4|240	0:07.62	0:00:07:18	♪G1	↓41	↑64	0|240
3|1|000	0:08.13	0:00:08:04	♪G0	↓51	↑64	0|240
3|1|240	0:08.64	0:00:08:19	♪G0	↓51	↑64	0|240
3|2|000	0:09.15	0:00:09:04	♪A0	↓43	↑64	0|240

Fig. 12.19. Data contained within a track.

As shown, each note is indicated by (from left to right) bar and beat, real-time and time code frames. Any combination of these can be displayed by the user. It is possible, for example, to display all information in only time code frames or both frames and beats or some other units.

Following the small eighth-note sign is the name of that particular note — G1, AO, F1 (refer to the end of Chapter 10 for keyboard nomenclature) — followed by its on velocity, off velocity and duration.

Any aspect of this information can be changed on screen, including the placement of the note itself in relation to time. Furthermore, notes and other MIDI data can be entered directly through the computer keyboard. Notes and data can also be cut, deleted and reinserted at various point. In addition, the note information can be displayed graphically (Fig. 12.20).

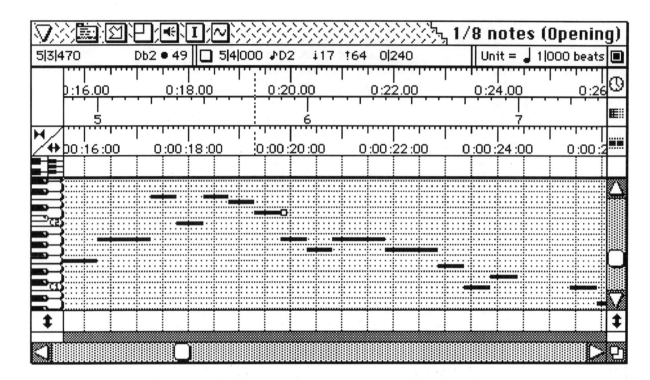

Fig. 12.20. Graphical display of the data shown in Fig. 12.19.

The graduated scales— the rulers — at the top of the window indicate the locations of notes and data by (top to bottom) real time, bar and beat and frames. Any display combination of the three is possible. The keyboard on the left represents the MIDI keyboard that will receive the information and is designated at each octave with C1, C2, etc. The thick black lines in the grid represent the notes, with their location in time indicated by the rulers and their nomenclature indicated by the keyboard. The length of each line represents the note's duration.

Any aspect of any note can be changed graphically directly on screen, making the software a perfect tool for triggering sound effects, as will be discussed in the next chapter.

Other Features

Additional features of *Performer* include looping, which is the continuous playing of a selection; quantizing, which is automatically correcting the timing of notes; and playing backwards. Furthermore, because individual tracks can be used to record *any* type of MIDI data, and because the content of each track can be edited, *Performer* can be used to record nonmusical data, like that transmitted by an automated MIDI mixer. To indicate the possible data content of any track, the software has a legend that can be viewed at any time. The symbols for each type of data are displayed in the tracks and appear in Fig. 12.21.

```
┌─────────────────────────────────┐
│ ▽ ⊠        Legend               │
├─────────────────────────────────┤
│ Location Pitch  On   Off  Duration│
│ 1|1|000  ♪C3   ↓64  ↑64  1|000   │
├─────────────────────────────────┤
│    ♪          Note              │
│    ∿          Pitch Bend        │
│    ▪          Patch Change      │
│    ▲          Controller        │
│    ↓          Mono Key Pressure │
│    ↓↓         Poly Key Pressure │
│    ▣          System Exclusive  │
│    ↺          Loops             │
│    ▯          Markers           │
│   4/4         Meter Change      │
│  Eb Major     Key Change        │
│  ♩ = 120.0    Tempo Change      │
└─────────────────────────────────┘
```

Fig. 12.21. MIDI data legend.

If used for the scoring of film or video, the software can trigger tempo changes at a given sequence to achieve the correct timing relationship of music to picture (Fig. 12.22).

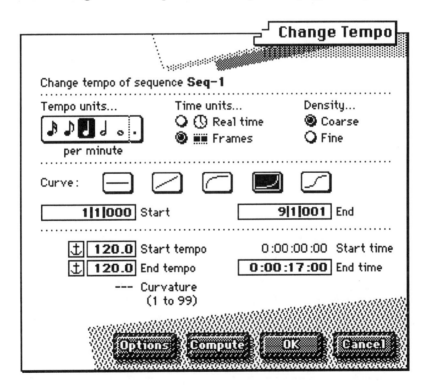

Fig. 12.22. Sequence-tempo alteration window.

However, because the use of this feature has more musical than post-production value, detailed discussions of tempo change and scoring are reserved for the last chapter.

Remote control of the computer as sequencer is essential in large facilities because the computer can be located away from the console or musician using it. In this way, any function can be initiated by the computer keyboard, MIDI data or both. (Fig. 12.23).

349

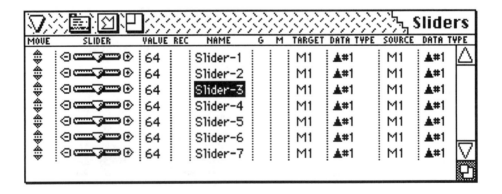

Fig. 12.23. MIDI remote controls window.

Automation

Automated mixing, as previously discussed, is a vital part of modern audio post-production. For this very reason, *Performer* includes what are known as "sliders" (Fig. 12.24).

Fig. 12.24. Sliders window.

Sliders are a useful method of controlling and monitoring MIDI data. As many sliders as desired can be created and each can be assigned to any MIDI channel or port to control or monitor a function.

Sliders serve two functions. First, they can continuously monitor the MIDI data being played from a target track or MIDI channel, moving in real time to reflect the data's current value. Second,

350

when the user takes control of them, sliders generate continuous MIDI controller data in real time and send the data to either a *Performer* track or a MIDI channel. When the user takes manual control of a slider, it temporarily overrides the data already in the track. Sliders can also be combined to create entire consoles (Fig. 12.25).

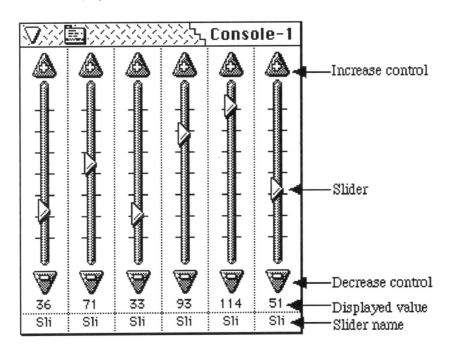

Fig. 12.25. Console display.

Because sliders can be used to generate or monitor MIDI data, they can be serve as the controls of an automated mixer, such as the DMP-7. By using enough sliders, and by assigning the proper target controller numbers, they let the operator mix audio directly from the screen of the computer by controlling the mixer directly.

Summary

As we have seen, MIDI software must be diverse and flexible, and *Performer* is no exception. Although the software might seem involved and complicated, with time and practice, its use and operation will become clear.

In summary, *Performer* can, given the proper MIDI setup and at least one sampler, be used to:

• Score a film or video

• Trigger sound effects

• Create automated mixing

These functions will be explored in greater detail in Chapter 13. Finally, *Performer* files can be saved in either their own or a MIDI file format for integration with other applications.

D. POST-PRODUCTION SOFTWARE

Opcode's Cue : The Film Music System

Cue is an impressive application intended for scoring films, creating sound effects triggers and generating cue sheets. However, it does much more. For example, it can also:

- Lay out a title page

- Allow the programming of MIDI tempo and meter changes

- Create custom score paper

- Display a click book

- Generate a performing rights cue sheet

- Lock to MIDI time code

- Generate MIDI event triggers for sound effects

- Display streamers and punches

- Read and create MIDI files

- Generate SMPTE time code

These are just some of the functions this product can handle. Those post-producing films in video post-production can benefit as well because several columns of timing information can be displayed. The formats available include 16- and 35-mm film and 24-, 25- and 30-frame SMPTE. Fig. 12.26 shows a typical cue sheet created with Opcode's *Cue*.

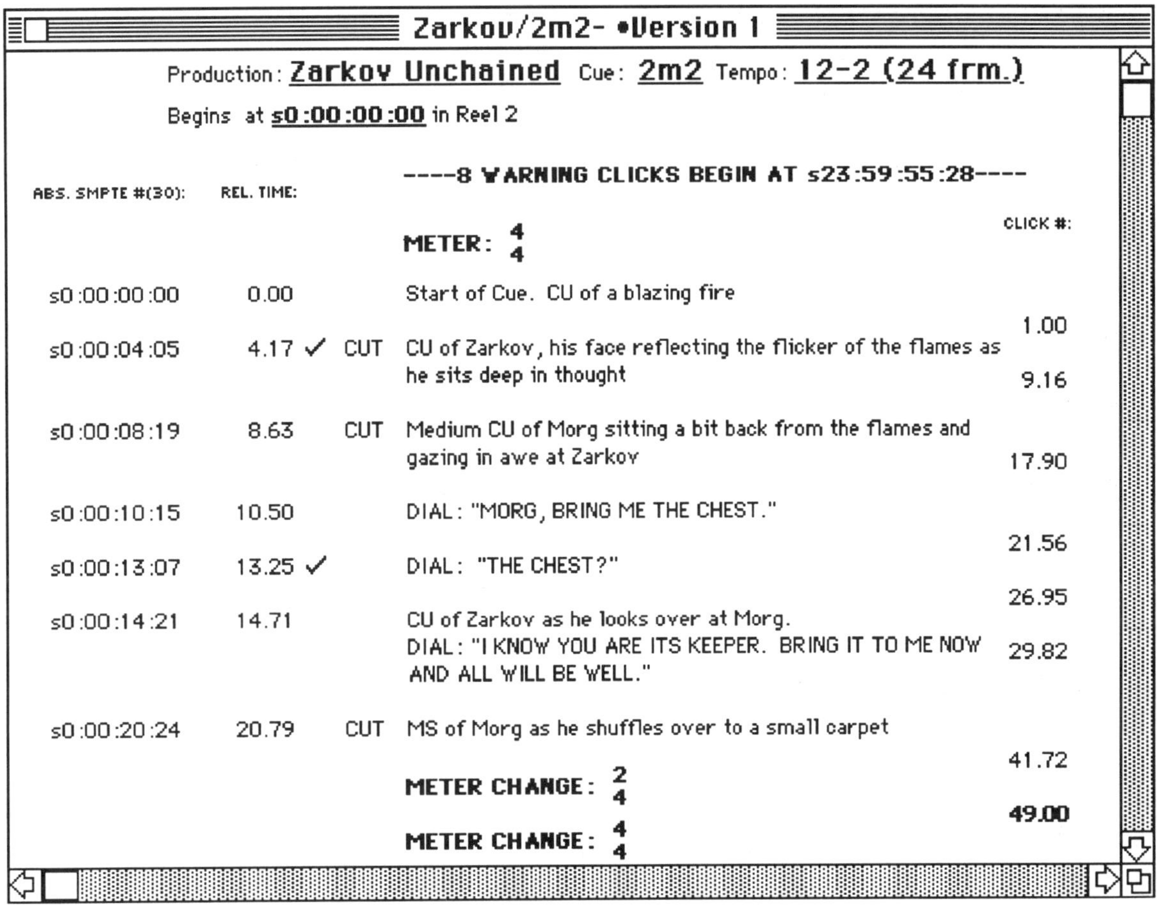

```
┌─────────────────────────────────────────────────────────────────────┐
│ ≡≡≡≡≡≡≡≡≡≡≡≡≡≡≡ Zarkov/2m2- •Version 1 ≡≡≡≡≡≡≡≡≡≡≡≡≡≡≡       ⇧ │
│       Production: Zarkov Unchained  Cue: 2m2 Tempo: 12-2 (24 frm.)  │
│       Begins at s0:00:00:00 in Reel 2                              │
│                                                                     │
│                        ----8 WARNING CLICKS BEGIN AT s23:59:55:28---- │
│  ABS. SMPTE #(30):   REL. TIME:                              CLICK #: │
│                                   METER:  4                         │
│                                           4                         │
│  s0:00:00:00    0.00          Start of Cue. CU of a blazing fire    │
│                                                              1.00   │
│  s0:00:04:05    4.17 ✓  CUT   CU of Zarkov, his face reflecting the flicker of the flames as │
│                               he sits deep in thought        9.16   │
│                                                                     │
│  s0:00:08:19    8.63    CUT   Medium CU of Morg sitting a bit back from the flames and │
│                               gazing in awe at Zarkov        17.90  │
│                                                                     │
│  s0:00:10:15    10.50         DIAL: "MORG, BRING ME THE CHEST."     │
│                                                              21.56  │
│  s0:00:13:07    13.25 ✓       DIAL: "THE CHEST?"                    │
│                                                              26.95  │
│  s0:00:14:21    14.71         CU of Zarkov as he looks over at Morg. │
│                               DIAL: "I KNOW YOU ARE ITS KEEPER. BRING IT TO ME NOW  29.82 │
│                               AND ALL WILL BE WELL."                │
│                                                                     │
│  s0:00:20:24    20.79   CUT   MS of Morg as he shuffles over to a small carpet │
│                                                              41.72  │
│                               METER CHANGE:  2                      │
│                                              4                      │
│                                                              49.00  │
│                               METER CHANGE:  4                      │
│                                              4                      │
│                                                                     │
└─────────────────────────────────────────────────────────────────────┘
```

Fig. 12.26. The cue sheet window.

A click book is a tool used by composers for setting timing and tempo information in a musical passage intended for use with a visual image. *Cue* also provides a display of this information, as shown in Fig. 12.27:

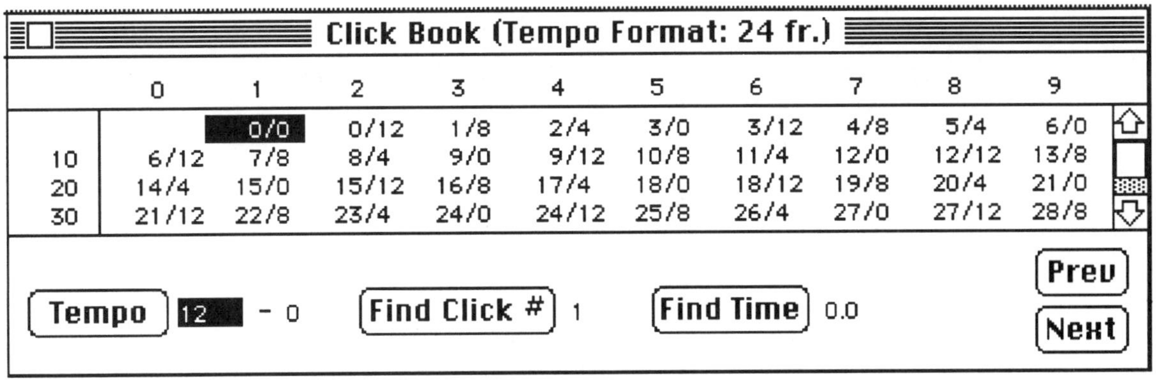

```
┌─────────────────────────────────────────────────────────────────────┐
│ ≡≡≡≡≡≡≡≡≡≡≡≡≡ Click Book (Tempo Format: 24 fr.) ≡≡≡≡≡≡≡≡≡≡≡         │
│         0      1      2      3      4      5      6      7      8      9 │
│ ─────────────────────────────────────────────────────────────────── │
│                [0/0]  0/12   1/8    2/4    3/0    3/12   4/8    5/4    6/0  ⇧ │
│    10   6/12   7/8    8/4    9/0    9/12   10/8   11/4   12/0   12/12  13/8 │
│    20   14/4   15/0   15/12  16/8   17/4   18/0   18/12  19/8   20/4   21/0 │
│    30   21/12  22/8   23/4   24/0   24/12  25/8   26/4   27/0   27/12  28/8  ⇩ │
│ ─────────────────────────────────────────────────────────────────── │
│                                                            ┌──────┐ │
│                                                            │ Prev │ │
│  ┌────────┐              ┌──────────────┐  ┌───────────┐  └──────┘ │
│  │ Tempo  │ 12  - 0      │ Find Click # │1 │ Find Time │0.0 ┌──────┐ │
│  └────────┘              └──────────────┘  └───────────┘  │ Next │ │
│                                                            └──────┘ │
└─────────────────────────────────────────────────────────────────────┘
```

Fig. 12.27. Click book window.

Performing rights and credits can vary from one cue to another. Yet another *Cue* window simplifies the job of entering and keeping track of this information (Fig. 12.28).

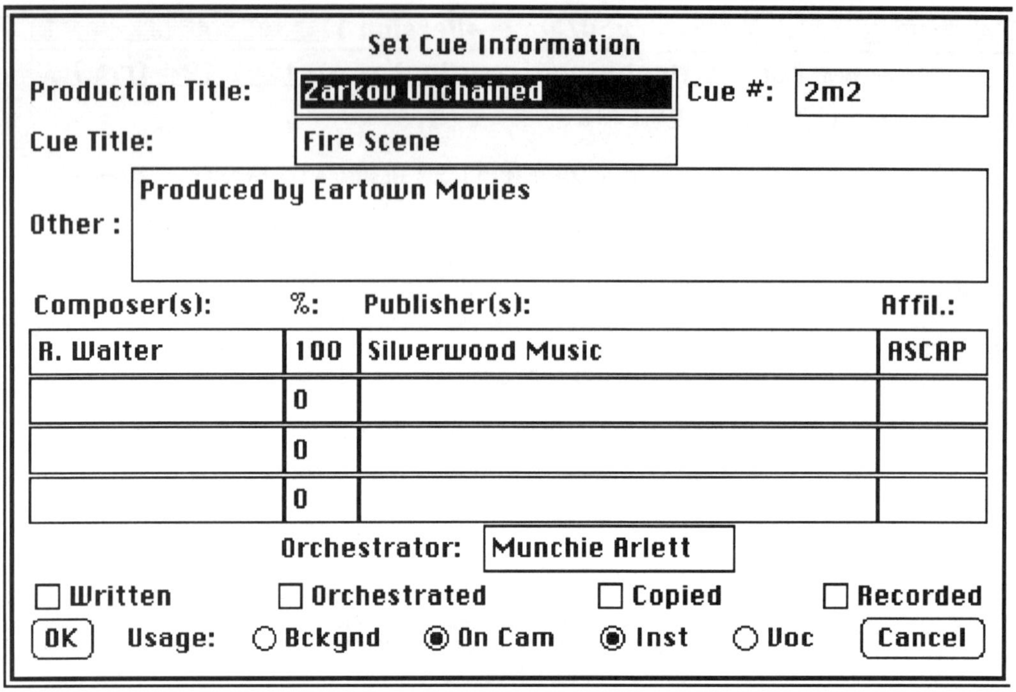

Fig. 12.28. Cue information window.

Cue can also trigger sound effects prepared on a sampler via MIDI. If, for example, a cue sheet is prepared, the actual sound effects can be triggered directly from the cue sheet. The computer can then be locked to time code from the VTR or ATR and the effects triggered by a sampling keyboard. The duration, velocity, channel, note and duration of each effect can be entered either by MIDI or from the computer's keyboard (Fig. 12.29).

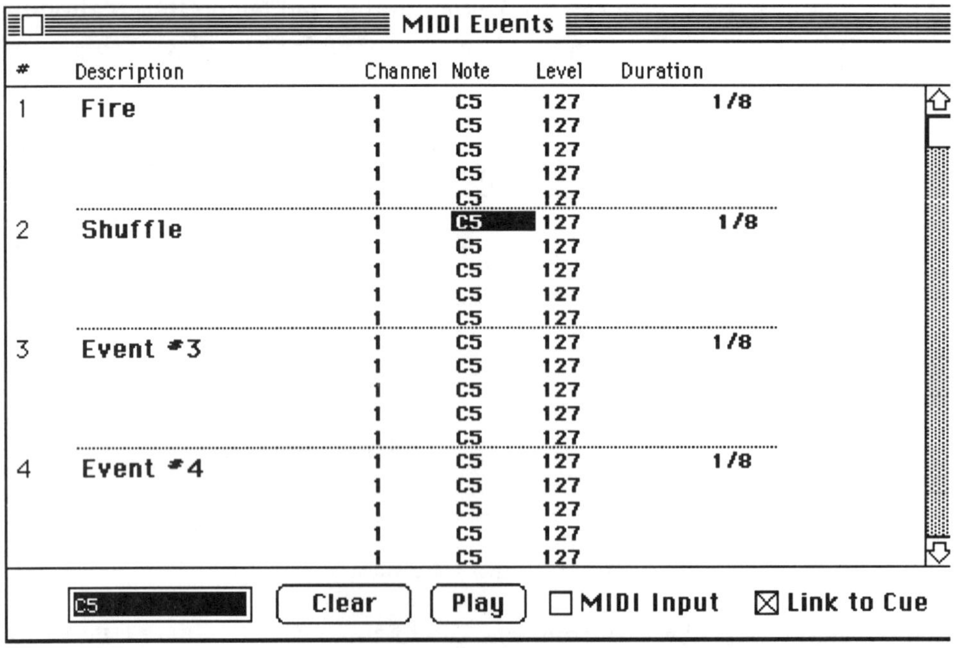

Fig. 12.29. MIDI note triggers window.

The event triggers now appear in the cue sheet and can be played back in real time. Compare this cue sheet with the example shown in Fig. 12.30.

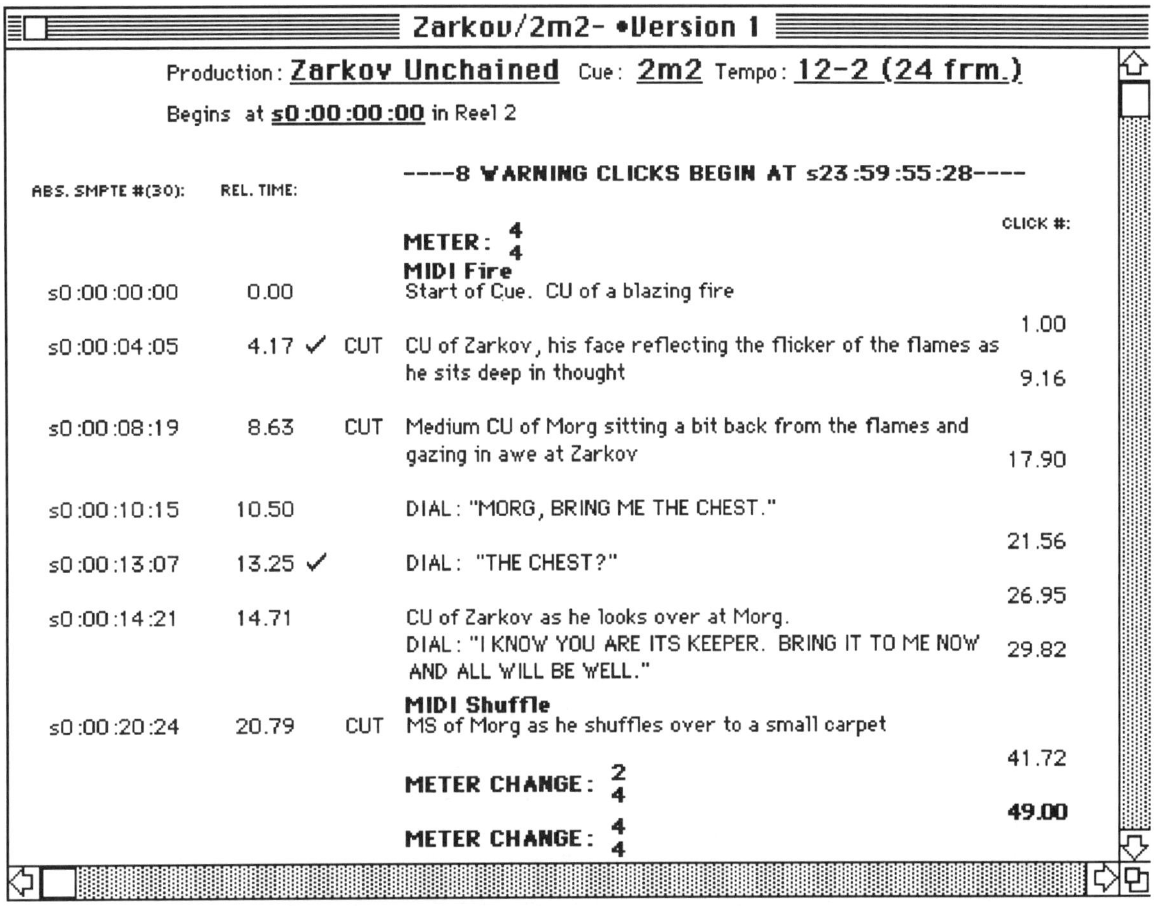

```
┌─────────────────────────────────────────────────────────────────┐
│ ≡≡≡≡≡≡≡≡≡≡ Zarkov/2m2- •Version 1 ≡≡≡≡≡≡≡≡≡≡                       │
│      Production: Zarkov Unchained  Cue: 2m2 Tempo: 12-2 (24 frm.) │
│      Begins at s0:00:00:00 in Reel 2                              │
│                                                                   │
│                        ----8 WARNING CLICKS BEGIN AT s23:59:55:28----│
│  ABS. SMPTE #(30):   REL. TIME:                                   │
│                                                      CLICK #:     │
│                           METER: 4/4                              │
│                           MIDI Fire                               │
│  s0:00:00:00   0.00       Start of Cue. CU of a blazing fire      │
│                                                         1.00      │
│  s0:00:04:05   4.17 ✓ CUT CU of Zarkov, his face reflecting the flicker of the flames as│
│                           he sits deep in thought       9.16      │
│  s0:00:08:19   8.63   CUT Medium CU of Morg sitting a bit back from the flames and│
│                           gazing in awe at Zarkov       17.90     │
│  s0:00:10:15   10.50      DIAL: "MORG, BRING ME THE CHEST."        │
│                                                         21.56     │
│  s0:00:13:07   13.25 ✓    DIAL: "THE CHEST?"                       │
│                                                         26.95     │
│  s0:00:14:21   14.71      CU of Zarkov as he looks over at Morg.   │
│                           DIAL: "I KNOW YOU ARE ITS KEEPER. BRING IT TO ME NOW  29.82│
│                           AND ALL WILL BE WELL."                  │
│                           MIDI Shuffle                            │
│  s0:00:20:24   20.79  CUT MS of Morg as he shuffles over to a small carpet│
│                                                         41.72     │
│                           METER CHANGE: 2/4                        │
│                                                         49.00     │
│                           METER CHANGE: 4/4                        │
└─────────────────────────────────────────────────────────────────┘
```

Fig. 12.30. Cue sheet showing location of MIDI triggers.

This method of generating frame-accurate sound effects not only saves you from having to juggle up to four different programs, it also allows for the instant changing of all information given in the cue sheet. For instance, consider the following scenario: You are nearing the end of completing the effects for a film when suddenly you receive a frantic call from the post-production supervisor. Three seconds have been added to the beginning of the film and you are asked if you can replace the effects in sequence. The answer, if you're working with *Cue*, is "yes." It is a simple matter to make a single entry and have *all* the cues and effects automatically readjusted. The advantages of this compared to using a conventional typewritten cue sheet are enormous.

Cue also generates SMPTE time code, provided you have the proper hardware. The window provided for this function is seen in Fig. 12.31.

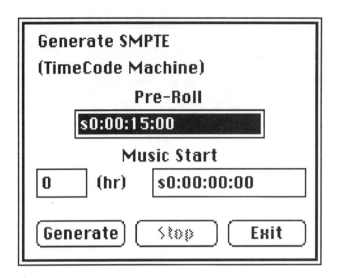

Fig. 12.31. SMPTE time code generator window.

Cue will generate streamers and punches when playing back the cue. (Streamers and punches and their use in film scoring are fully explained in Chapter 15.) The playback window is seen as in Fig. 12.32.

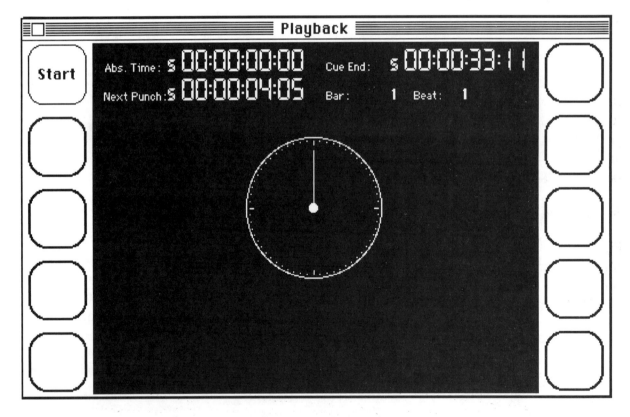

Fig. 12.32. The punch window.

Cue is an indispensable tool for any audio post-production facility specializing in MIDI applications for the film or video maker. Moreover, the documentation that accompanies the software is friendly, well-written and concise.

Summary

As with *Performer* , MIDI files can be "exported" and "imported" for use with other programs. In summary, *Cue* can, given the proper MIDI setup and at least one sampler, be used for:

- Scoring a film or video

- Sound effects triggers

- Creating cue sheets

- Resolving film and time-code counts

Digidesign's Q-Sheet A/V 1.01

Up to this point we have explored how two sequencing and cue sheet applications operate. Full explanations of their specific uses will be given in the next chapter. Still, you can begin to see similarities between the two: Both lock to time code, both can be used to trigger MIDI events from time code and both can resolve to various frame rates. All of these aspects also apply to the next type of software, which, in many ways, contains features similar to the two previous applications. However, Digidesign's *Q-Sheet A/V* also contains a unique set of features ideal for audio post-production.

Q-Sheet A/V (version 1.01) is intended for use as both a MIDI event trigger and automated mixer sequencer. Unlike *Performer* , *Q-Sheet A/V* is not designed to handle multiple tasks such as musical and sound effects MIDI sequencing. Still, it is a straightforward sequencing application, presumably intended for users with little or no musical background. In this regard it is an excellent program that is relatively simple to learn and operate. All the user is required to have is a basic understanding of the Macintosh computer, interlock, time code, MIDI and sampling. All of these skills are best developed with constant practice on a system.

Introduction

Fig. 12.33 illustrates one of *Q-Sheet A/V*'s main windows, which contain the specific tracks of MIDI information. Individual tracks can be edited or deleted entirely. Additional tracks can be added by the user. This kind of flexibility is what makes MIDI software of this type so powerful.

The window in Fig. 12.33 is a demonstration created the software's publisher and will be used to explain this application. From left to right, various symbols are given in the window. These have been labeled by the author.

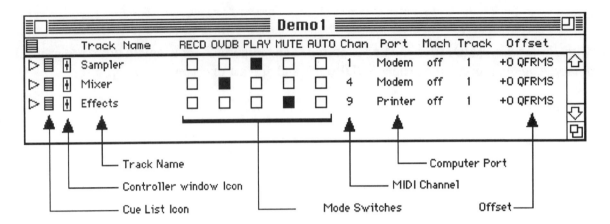

Fig. 12.33. MIDI configuration window.

The Cue List Icon and Controller Window Icon each display additional windows when selected by the user. These will be explained further in the next several pages. The track name indicates that track's individual function. Thus, in Fig. 12.33, one track controls a sampler, an automated mixer and various MIDI-controlled effects units. The name of each track can be edited by the user. The mode switches determine the status of each track, much like the track function switches of a multitrack ATR. The MIDI channel and computer port are both selectable, and determine each track's source and destination. Finally, the offset for each individual track is given in quarter frames. Typing in "4" to any track would offset the track by one time code frame. This is called **subframe accuracy** and is an invaluable feature when working with MIDI controlled events for sound effects and mixing.

Synchronization

This application, like the two previous examples in this chapter, can be set to run independently or slaved to time code. Time code frame rates are selectable and synchronization is achieved with MIDI time code, which requires the conversion of SMPTE to MIDI. Control of the sequence, when set to run independently, is carried out with the following window (Fig. 12.34).

Fig. 12.34. The sequence control window.

When slaved to time code, the window appears as the following (Fig. 12.35).

358

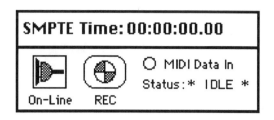

Fig. 12.35. The sequence control window shown when slaved to external code.

As with other programs, the windows resemble the tape transport controls of a conventional ATR.

Sequences and MIDI Information

When selecting the cue list icon (Fig. 12.33) of a given track, the information contained within that track is displayed and specific events and data can be edited, copied, cut, pasted or deleted. In Fig. 12.36, the track titled "Sampler" has been selected and the information contained within it is displayed.

	Time	Event Name	Event Data			
	00:00:00.00	Setup Sampler	⊡ 13			
	00:00:01.17	Door Opens	♪ A1	↓97	↑0	→00:00:02.20
	00:00:02.04	Switch on light	♪ C4	↓116	↑0	→00:00:02.25
	00:00:03.17	Adjust filter	⊘ 31	1 event		
	00:00:04.25	Footstep 1	♪ C3	↓96	↑0	→00:00:05.25
	00:00:05.09	Footstep 2	♪ C#3	↓83	↑0	→00:00:06.09
	00:00:07.06	Gunshot	♪ D4	↓97	↑0	→00:00:08.28

Demo1: Sampler Cue List

Fig. 12.36. Data window illustrating event triggers.

From left to right we see: The time the event starts displayed in SMPTE time code. The name of the specific event, the type of data being transmitted at each event, the down velocity, the up velocity and the time each event stops. From time 00:00:00:00 down, the track contains: A patch change, note A1, note C4, controller number 31, note C3, note C#3 and note D4. In each case, a specific sound is stored within the sampler at these locations. When the software receives each time code address shown, a MIDI message is sent to the sampler and the sound stored on that key will be played. This is the basis for using a MIDI event trigger.

To facilitate the relationship of note-to-sample information, Digidesign provides a keyboard "map." The map is a graphic representation of the keyboard and "pops up" when selected (not shown). In this way you can graphically select which note will be played at a given time code address (Fig. 12.37).

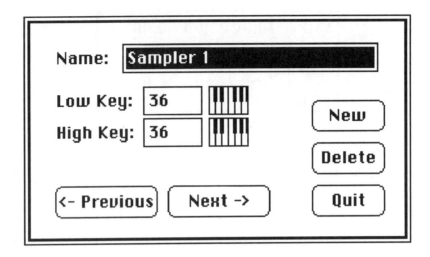

Fig. 12.37. The event control window in graphic form.

Because each aspect of the data displayed can be edited, it is only logical to assume that the start and stop times of each event can be edited. When either are selected, the next window appears and the times changed as desired. Note again that quarter frame timing is provided (Fig. 12.38).

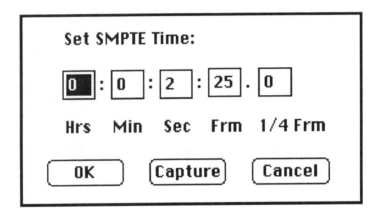

Fig. 12.38. Event trigger modification window.

Automation

In much the same way that *Performer* provides sliders, *Q Sheet A/V* lets a user create graphics controls on-screen. In selecting the Controller Window Icon shown in Fig. 12.33, a new window appears. Controllers take four different forms, all of which can be drawn by the user and put into the automation window. These graphical representations of counters, buttons, knobs and counters can be drawn in different sizes. The examples shown in Fig. 12.39 were drawn by the author.

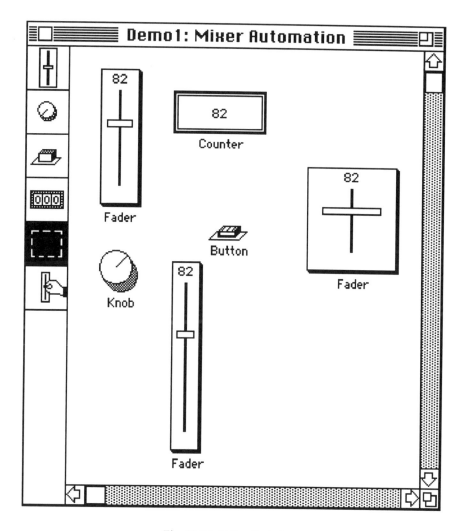

Fig. 12.39. "Mixer" window.

Each type of controller can be assigned to any MIDI controller numbers and the name of each can be edited by the user. In this way an entire console controlling a properly equipped mixer like the DMP-7 can be created and used to mix a given audio segment. The value of each controller — 0 to 127 — is also displayed.

Timing Displays

As illustrated in Fig. 12.33, the start and stop times of each event are illustrated in SMPTE code. This display, however, can be easily changed to reflect frame counts in 16- mm (Fig. 12.40) and 35-mm film (Fig. 12.41). This is a useful feature that is becoming more common to MIDI post-production software and can greatly help the post-production engineer resolve back to film. In addition, a cue sheet supplied by a sound or music editor, if given in feet and frames, can be instantly correlated to the cue sheet generated by the application.

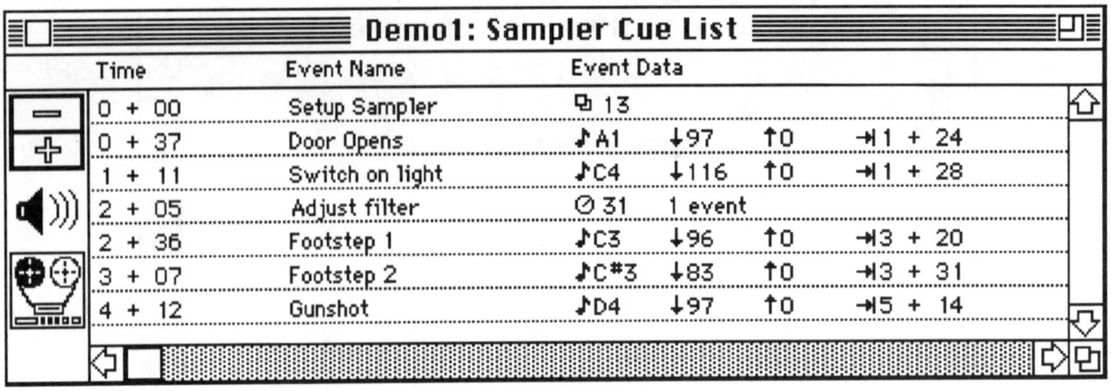

Demo1: Sampler Cue List		
Time	Event Name	Event Data
0 + 00	Setup Sampler	🗗 13
0 + 37	Door Opens	♪A1 ↓97 ↑0 →I1 + 24
1 + 11	Switch on light	♪C4 ↓116 ↑0 →I1 + 28
2 + 05	Adjust filter	⊘ 31 1 event
2 + 36	Footstep 1	♪C3 ↓96 ↑0 →I3 + 20
3 + 07	Footstep 2	♪C#3 ↓83 ↑0 →I3 + 31
4 + 12	Gunshot	♪D4 ↓97 ↑0 →I5 + 14

Fig. 12.40. Event window with data in 16-mm feet and frames.

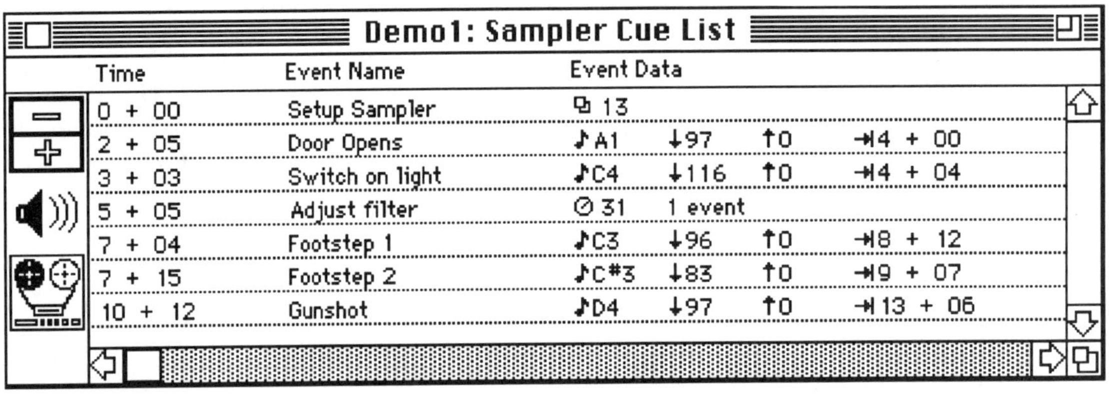

Demo1: Sampler Cue List		
Time	Event Name	Event Data
0 + 00	Setup Sampler	🗗 13
2 + 05	Door Opens	♪A1 ↓97 ↑0 →I4 + 00
3 + 03	Switch on light	♪C4 ↓116 ↑0 →I4 + 04
5 + 05	Adjust filter	⊘ 31 1 event
7 + 04	Footstep 1	♪C3 ↓96 ↑0 →I8 + 12
7 + 15	Footstep 2	♪C#3 ↓83 ↑0 →I9 + 07
10 + 12	Gunshot	♪D4 ↓97 ↑0 →I13 + 06

Fig. 12.41. Event window with data in 35-mm feet and frames.

All events can be advanced or retarded by a given amount if last minute edit changes are made to the visual.

Finally, all information stored in the file can be easily compiled and printing, providing a type of edit decision list or rerecording log. As with *Performer* and *Cue* , *Q-Sheet A/V* MIDI files can be "exported" and "imported" for use with other applications. In summary, *Q-Sheet A/V* can, given the proper MIDI setup and at least one sampler, be used for:

• Sound effects triggers

• Automated mixing

• The creation of EDLs and logs

• Resolving film and time code counts

362

13
TOTAL AUDIO
POST-PRODUCTION

A. INTRODUCTION

To help clarify the concepts presented so far, we will follow an imaginary post-production session. The topics, problems and solutions presented are based on the author's practical experience and are necessarily subjective. Many other engineers would undoubtedly arrive at different but no less satisfactory solutions to the same problems. Again, the goal of this session is only to exemplify the use of the equipment and techniques outlined thus far, and not to present an absolute and final approach to audio post-production.

The equipment used in this session are as follows (see Fig. 9.2 for a diagram of the actual studio):

- One synchronizer

- Two 3/4-inch VTRs

- One multitrack ATR

- One two-track ATR

- Two Apple Macintosh computers

- Assorted software for the Apple Macintosh computers

- One MIDI-to-computer interface

- One MIDI-to-SMPTE interface

- One audio console with audio and video patch bays

- Assorted outboard audio effects and processors

- Assorted synthesizers and a sampling device

- One Yamaha DMP-7 automated mixer

- One video monitor

- An audio monitoring system

- Microphones

B. THE CONSULTATION

It is common practice for a prospective client to set up a preliminary meeting with the post-production facility to discuss the nature of the project, its requirements, the studio's capabilities, the engineer's competence, the underlying principles of the post-production techniques and processes, and any financial matters. This meeting is usually heldwithout charge to the client.

In our hypothetical case the client is a young filmmaker who read an ad for the facility, which indicated that its capabilities included all sound recording, mixing and processing. The facility engineer, being familiar with traditional film post-production processes, is able to discuss various aspects of the studio and the project in detail and compare both the traditional and modern approaches with the client. The main points raised and discussed during the consultation are as follows:

- The client has had no previous knowledge of, or experience with, an audio/video-based post-production system. Furthermore, he has, up to this point, thought that MIDI indicated a skirt length and that sampling was something you did in a gourmet deli.

- Because the client's background extends only to traditional film post-production techniques, he is surprised that the facility can not only mix, but also record and compile all of the tracks. Up to this point, the client has relied on the separate recording of all voice, music and sound effects; the transfers of sounds to spools of magnetic film stock; and the arrangement of these spools into tracks for mixing. He wisely recognizes the time and expenses saved and agrees to proceed.

- The client had planned to compile a 16-mm answer print and then have a video transfer of the film made for distribution to various film festivals. Because the use of this system depends on the film being transferred to video, the client decides to transfer the cut negative — as opposed to the positive — because the final mix will be resolved to both film and video. Transferring the negative will give the best possible image quality.

- The client has completed one synchronous track of dialog on the flatbed editor and started compiling an asynchronous sound effects track. The form of all audio must be taken into account prior to the transfer. Because the mix is to be resolved to both film and video, and because the video will be used for distribution, the client and engineer both agree to have the film transferred in the following manner:

- On a Rank-Cintel, from a negative at 23.98 frames per second, a 29.97-frame per second non-drop frame time code genlocked to the video signal is generated onto channel two of the videotape by the transfer facility...

- To 3/4-inch U-Matic video.

- The audio is to be dubbed simultaneously onto channel one of the VTR.

- The unfinished sound effects track is to be discarded and recreated in the studio.

- The film is to be configured with Academy leader and "beeps" as described in Chapter 9.

At this point, let's explore some of the possibilities that can present themselves. If, for example, the client had two synchronous tracks of dialog, then their transfer would depend on, first, the track capacity of the video format being used for post-production, and, second, the audio formats available at the transfer facility. Some of the options that might be considered are:

VTR has only two tracks: Because one audio channel must be used for time code, the client can transfer the audio to two tracks of a four-track deck; two separate reels of half track; or two tracks of a half track, center-stripe ATR. In each case the audio is transferred simultaneously with picture while the audio and video tapes are striped with time code. The end result is that all video and audio materials are referenced to exactly the same time code numbers. Any separate reels of audio are rerecorded during layback to the multitrack ATR in synchronization, described further on.

VTR has three or more tracks: Including the use of address track, the video formats that can handle three or more channels of audio and time code. This is especially useful because it avoids the use of separate audio reels. At the same time, separate reels can result in higher audio quality. If address track time code is used, then the transfer facility must record SMPTE code into it as the film is recorded onto video.

C. WORKSHEET

What follows is a guideline for some of the options available during film to videotape transfers. It also illustrates the limitations imposed by one facility or another, the type of equipment used, and so on. The reader should keep in mind that the successful treatment of any post-production application usually depends on the creative applications of solutions. In other words, no process is engraved in stone. The only rule is that the end result must work.

If the filmmaker wants to:

☐ Strike an answer print with no video master for distribution (film-video-film):
  The transfer can be made from a work print or slop print.

☐ Strike an answer print with a video master for distribution (film-video-film):
  The transfer should be made from the cut negative.

☐ Finish in video only, without returning to film (film-video):
  The transfer should be made from the cut negative.

If the audio consists of:

☐ One synchronous dialogue track only:
  The track can be dubbed to one channel of the VTR and time code recorded later.

☐ Two or more synchronous tracks:
  The tracks can be dubbed to two channels of the VTR if the video format has a minimum of three channels. If the format has address track code, the code must be recorded simultaneously. If the format has three or more independently editable tracks, than time code can be added later. If the video format has only two tracks, then the audio must be dubbed onto a separate

reel of audiotape during the transfer. Time code is recorded simultaneously onto all video and audio tapes.

The transfer must be made at:

❑ 23.98 frames per second

The transfer must be made onto:

❑ NTSC 3/4 U-Matic

❑ NTSC 3/4 U-Matic SP

❑ NTSC Betacam SP

❑ NTSC one-inch Type "C"

❑ NTSC D-1

❑ NTSC D-2

Video Time Code must consist of:

❑ Non-drop frame 29.97 longitudinal time code on channel one

❑ Non-drop frame 29.97 longitudinal time code on channel two

❑ Non-drop frame 29.97 longitudinal time code on channel three

❑ Non-drop frame 29.97 longitudinal time code on channel four

❑ Non-drop frame 29.97 longitudinal time code on address track

❑ Non-drop frame 29.97 vertical interval time code

❑ No time code on any part of the videotape

D. TAPE PREPARATION

From the above choices, it is clear that the preparation of the tape depends on how the film was transferred. Instead of listing each and every possible method, we assume that the client chose to transfer his film to 3/4-inch non-SP U-Matic video. The audio was transferred to channel one of the videotape and the transfer facility dutifully added time code onto channel two. To check the code's content and accuracy, we patch the output of VTR channel two (time code) into the synchronizer's master time code input. To everyone's horror, we find that the transfer facility used drop frame time code.

Drop frame time code is used almost exclusively in broadcast applications when the accurate timing of program length is required. The particular model synchronizer we are using cannot accurately read the code and goes beserk when it tries to read the missing frames. Quickly we patch the synchronizer's time code output to the input of VTR channel two, genlock the video to the generator, place the deck in edit/channel two mode and rerecord new non-drop frame time code on the video tape. To save time, we take the output of the VTR and patch it into the highest channel number of the multitrack ATR, being careful to keep the ATR in fixed-speed mode and bypass the noise reduction on the channel being striped.

When both tapes are striped, the time code from each deck is patched into the synchronizer and the synchronizer is set to interlock both decks. The multitrack ATR is set to external-speed mode and the original audio is dubbed onto the ATR.

With that done, two widow dubs are made from the master: One with time code and without audio and one with audio but without time code. We now have the following:

• A master 3/4-inch videotape with time code and audio,

• A multitrack audiotape with with time code and original audio,

• A window dub videotape with time code and without audio, and

• A window dub videotape without time code and with original audio.

E. CREATING A CUE SHEET

The next step is to create a cue sheet using the widow dub copy with audio and without time code. Invariably, clients become restless during this process, as it is slow, tedious and boring. In their eyes, nothing is happening, and the studio clock is ticking, counted in dollars per hour.

The cue sheet can be compiled in any number of ways, but the fastest way is to use a computer. In our example, *Opcode's Cue 3.0: The Film Music System* is ideal, as it resolves both the SMPTE times and the footage counts used in film.

To speed the process, the computer is left on during the session. At any time, the engineer can lean over and type in or delete cue points as needed. In the interest of speeding things up, only the start number of each significant scene or edit is typed in. Other cues will be added as the session progresses.

Because the synchronizer we are using can store up to 99 memory locations, the SMPTE time code numbers that occur at the start of every scene have been entered to synchronizer memory, as well as into the cue sheet. In this way we can send the VTR and ATR to any scene at a moment's notice. To make things simpler, we've done this so that scene one is stored in memory 01, scene two in memory 02 and so on. Having the memory numbers and correspond to scene locations saves time during the session. It avoids the need to look up the corresponding time code numbers logged in the cue sheet before entering the memory locations in the synchronizer.

F. SWEETENING

The order in which the three categories of sound (dialog, music and effects) are added depends almost exclusively on the client's preference. In most cases the client will choose to first work with dialog, considered by many to be the most crucial sonic aspect of a film.

Dialog and Narration

The ADR Session

Our client has decided that the location ambience in scenes three and seven is overpowering the dialog recorded during production and that the dialog in scene one was recorded at too low a level to be usable. The replacement of production dialog requires the client to have the actors who originally took part in the film return to the studio for a dialog replacement session. Each scene requires the recording of a different combination of actors appearing on screen as follows:

- **Scene 1** Ext Day
  Mary
  John

- **Scene 3** Int Day
  Mary
  John
  Matt

- **Scene 7** Int Night
  Jane
  Matt
  Gary

The lines to be replaced are reviewed and the start and stop SMPTE numbers of each dialog within the scene are logged into the cue sheet. At this point, either a separate track sheet or a cue sheet that doubles as a track sheet should be used to log both the contents of each track and its time code numbers. If, for example, Mary's dialog is recorded on track two beginning at 00:03:45:12 and ending at 00:04:14:21, the track sheet should reflect this information.

Once this information is logged, the actors are placed into the isolation booth and given headphones and a small video monitor. At this point, the synchronizer is set to do four things:

- Play the VTR and ATR for about five seconds before the dialog begins

- Have the ATR record (punch in) about one second before the dialog begins

- Have the ATR stop recording (punch out) about one second after the dialog ends

- Have the VTR and ATR stop and rewind to the original play position and repeat the cycle

In this way the synchronizer — in a process called **cycling** — "loops" the ATR and VTR and directs the ATR to punch in and out at the specified times. The process continues until we stop it. One track per actor is used and the track record function for the corresponding track is engaged so that, when the synchronizer sends its punch-in and punch-out commands, the ATR will record only on that track.

The microphone used to record the actor is positioned, set to the proper pickup and filter settings, and the overall console assignments and recording levels are set. It is essential that the tonal quality between the production dialog and the replaced dialog be matched as closely as possible using EQ. This matching will help give the effect that all of the dialog originated during the production. If the replacement dialog is noticeably different, then the point of replacing the dialog is lost.

The synchronizer is set to start cycling while the actor performs repeated takes to lip sync his or her lines. When the producer decides to review a particular take, we defeat the track function select (or the synchronizer-record enable) and monitor the recorded track while viewing picture. For an exact comparison, we can simultaneously monitor both the original and the replaced dialog to check the relative timing of the new track. The actual setup used for this session can be seen in Fig. 9.2.

Because some of the actors in our session have more than one scene, and because each has a dedicated track, we leave the set up in place so that one actor can do all of his or her lines in one sitting. For example, Mary's lines are recorded on track two. She first records scene one and then scene three. She is followed by John who records for the same scenes on track three. Matt records on track four, doing scenes three and seven. Finally, Jane and Gary record for scene seven on tracks five and six, respectively (Fig. 13.1).

			Track 1	Track 2	Track 3	Track 4	Track 5	Track 6	Track 7	Track 8	Track 24
SMPTE	SECT										
01:00:03:06	Scene 1	EXT DAY	Source Audio	MARY	JOHN						SMPTE
01:01:33:16	Scene 2	EXT DAY									
01:01:58:22	Scene 3	INT DAY		MARY	JOHN	MATT					
01:02:19:27	Scene 4	INT DAY									
01:03:02:19	Scene 5	INT DAY	Source Audio								
01:03:03:21	Scene 6	EXT NITE									
01:03:59:01	Scene 7	INT NITE				MATT	JANE	GARY			

Header fields: Soundesign NY — Client KIPI — Producer — Date — Artist/Product Demo Session — Engineer/Assistant — Page: 1 of 5 — Reel: _ of _

30 IPS ☒ DOLBY ☐ MASTER ☒ SMPTE ☒ HEADS ☐ COMMENTS/NOTES
15 IPS ☐ DBX ☒ SAFETY ☐ RATE 29.97 TAILS ☒
7.5 IPS ☐ NO NR ☐ TRANSFER ☐ DF/NDF NDF ☐

Fig. 13.1. The track sheet for a hypothetical post-production session showing track and time placement of ADR dialogue.

The track planning of this session brings us to an important concept in modern audio post-production: Because each scene occurs at different times within the film — that is, scenes do not overlap — we need not adhere to the conventional ways of categorizing different types of sound on each track. In other words, track six does not have to contain sound effects only, and track four need not consist of dialog only. Thus, the contents of each track can vary from scene to scene because we will be using automated mixing to separate each track into different EQ, panning, effects and playback levels (Fig. 13.2). However, it is advisable to retain some semblance of track organization, if for nothing else than to speed up the mixing process.

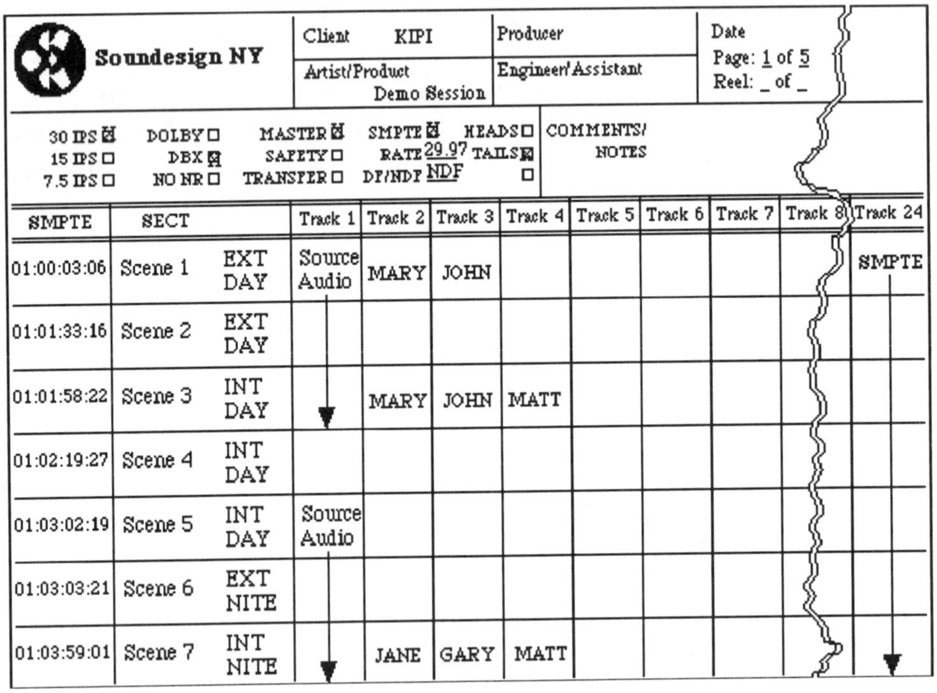

Sounddesign NY			Client KIPI		Producer			Date	
			Artist/Product Demo Session		Engineer/Assistant			Page: 1 of 5 Reel: _ of _	

| 30 IPS ☒ DOLBY ☐ MASTER ☒ SMPTE ☒ HEADS ☐ COMMENTS/ |
| 15 IPS ☐ DBX ☒ SAFETY ☐ RATE 29.97 TAILS ☒ NOTES |
| 7.5 IPS ☐ NO NR ☐ TRANSFER ☐ DF/NDF NDF ☐ |

SMPTE	SECT		Track 1	Track 2	Track 3	Track 4	Track 5	Track 6	Track 7	Track 8	Track 24
01:00:03:06	Scene 1	EXT DAY	Source Audio	MARY	JOHN						SMPTE
01:01:33:16	Scene 2	EXT DAY									
01:01:58:22	Scene 3	INT DAY	↓	MARY	JOHN	MATT					
01:02:19:27	Scene 4	INT DAY									
01:03:02:19	Scene 5	INT DAY	Source Audio								
01:03:03:21	Scene 6	EXT NITE									
01:03:59:01	Scene 7	INT NITE	↓	JANE	GARY	MATT					↓

Fig. 13.2. The same ADR sections combined.

In this regard, packing the tracks for each scene from left to right provides some organization in that the tracks for additional recording are available in uninterrupted vertical rows.

"Cleaning" Existing Dialog

Occasionally, problems arise with production dialog. These problems range from motor noise generated by a film camera to high levels of electronic noise originating from production equipment. In most cases the engineer has little choice but to use a graphic or parametric EQ to try to "slice out" those frequencies at which the unwanted noise is loudest. This approach, however, usually also affects the tonal quality of the dialog itself, forcing the engineer to choose between too much noise or too much dialog EQ. However, during passages where there is no dialog, a noise gate can be used to minimize noise .

Asynchronous Dialog and Narration

Because only synchronous dialog requires ADR, any asynchronous, or "wild," narration can be recorded from original production tapes in at least two different ways:

• Directly onto the multitrack master

• Directly into a sampling device

Use of the GPI

Recording directly onto the multitrack from the original quarter-inch production tapes can be done in one of two methods: If the synchronizer is equipped with a GPI (see chapter 8), then the ATR playing back the production tapes can be "triggered" into play mode by the synchronizer when a given time code number is received from the master VTR (Fig. 13.3). This process calls for the "cueing" of each individual dialog segment on the original production tapes to the proper position on the ATR's play head (Fig. 13.4). When the GPI activates the ATR's play mechanism, the production tape will start playing from the cued point. In this and all following illustrations any audio is shown going into the multitrack E to E. The reasons for doing this are explained in Chapter 9.

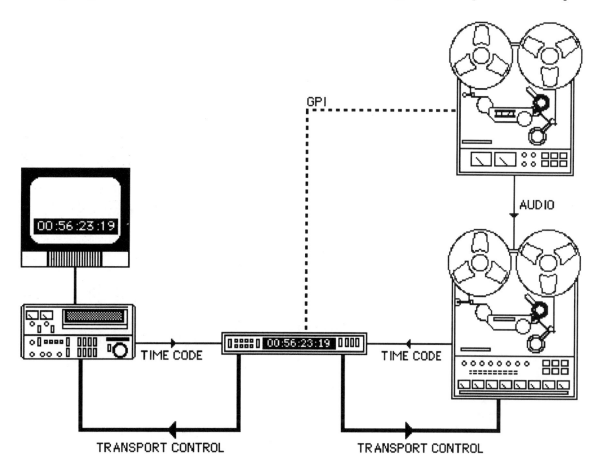

Fig. 13.3. Using the GPI to trigger a two track ATR.

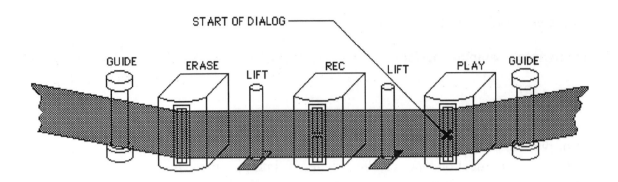

Fig. 13.4. Cueing the start of dialog on an ATR for GPI triggering.

This method is has disadvantages, however. It is not frame-accurate because the playback will start from the cued point, which will not be exact from one attempt to the next. Furthermore, the ATR may delay the playback if its transport electronics do not respond quickly enough to the GPI signal. If that happens, any incorrect takes will have to be re-done, which will require recueing the production tape and readjusting the GPI's time code start number. Despite these drawbacks, however, this method is still an excellent way to trigger sounds that do not require absolute frame accuracy.

Use of a Second Slave ATR

The second method is a more accurate method of playing back original production tapes and uses a second ATR that is synchronized into the system in the same manner as the multitrack ATR. Using the offset function of the synchronizer, the relationship of the multitrack and second ATR can be changed at any time, allowing for precise, frame-accurate recording of dialog.

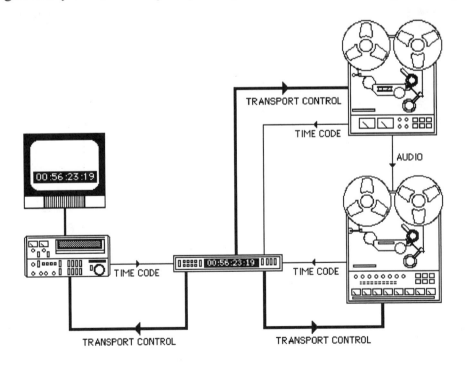

Fig. 13.5. Connection of a second slave ATR.

372

Use of a Sampler and MIDI

An alternative to using a second synchronized ATR is to use a sampler or sampling device, which requires that a computer or other sequencer be locked to SMPTE, which in turn will trigger the sampler with MIDI.

Remember that MIDI carries only data, not audio. To play a given piece of dialog at, say, time code number 00:56:23:19, not only must we instruct the sequencing software to play a "note" at that time, but we must also set up the receiving device, in this case the sampler.

Use of Editor/Librarian Software

An editor/librarian program (discussed in Chapter 12) is used to tailor and manipulate the dialog.

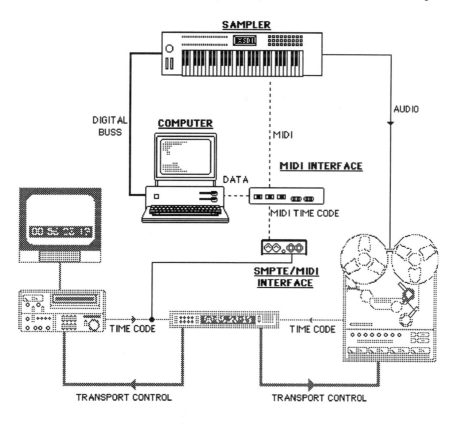

Fig. 13.6

Fig. 13.6 illustrates the basic synchronization system — including a VTR, video monitor, synchronizer and multitrack deck — described over the last several chapters. (In the figure, these elements and any others not being used are faded into the background to simplify the figure.) Added to this basic system are an SMPTE-to-MIDI interface, a MIDI-to-computer interface, a computer and a sampler. The sampler is connected to the computer with both a MIDI cable and a cable for transmitting sample data from the sampler to the computer. (In most cases this connection would go through the MIDI-to-computer interface and be switched at the interface's front panel. However, these connections are omitted for simplification.)

The first step is to sample the dialog required from the production tape by connecting the output of the playback ATR to the sampler's input (Fig. 13.7).

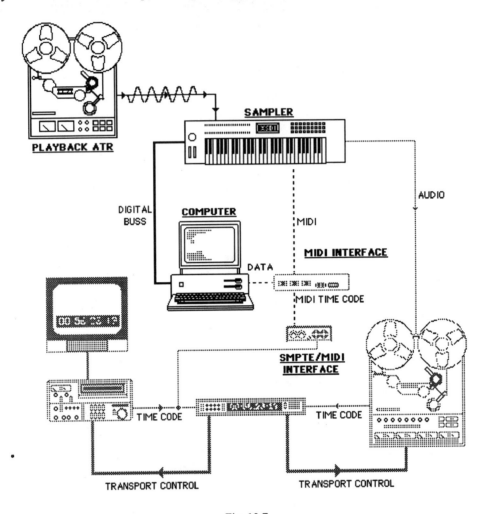

Fig. 13.7

Once the desired line has been sampled, the computer is then instructed to copy the data from the sampler. This data travels over the second cable mentioned earlier (Fig. 13.8).

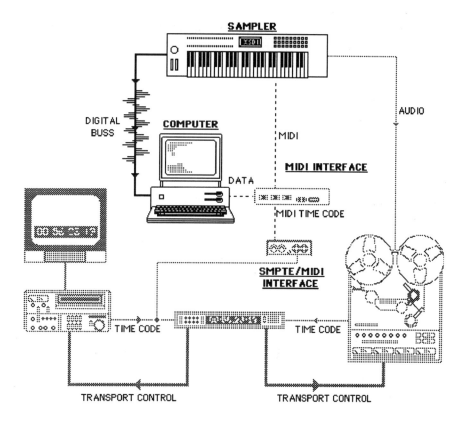

Fig. 13.8. Connection of a sampler to a computer for use with both a MIDI event trigger and sample editing.

With the data is in the computer, the dialog appears on the computer screen and can be manipulated by the engineer (Fig. 13.9):

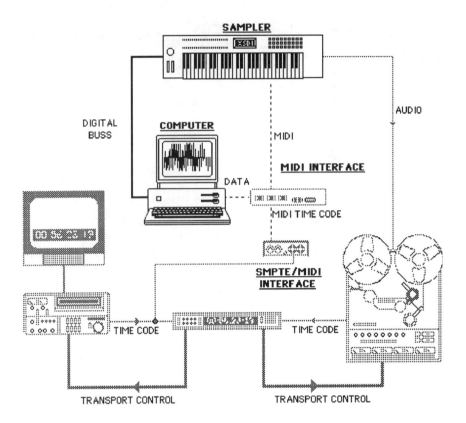

Fig. 13.9. Editing the sample data.

The figures that follow come directly from Digidesign's *Sound Designer*; although the labels "noise", "dialog" and "time" were added by the author. Fig. 13.10 shows the sample as duplicated by the computer. Because we now have the sample in a medium that displays the information visually, we can make some quick edits. For that, several considerations come into play: First, we want to remove as much noise as possible and, second, the dialog must start at exactly zero seconds for accurate triggering later in the process.

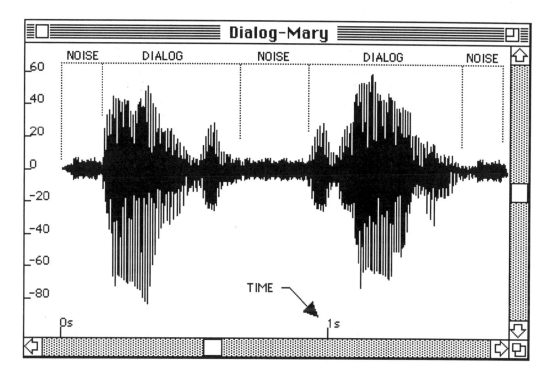

Fig. 13.10. Dialog and noise as displayed by the PC.

Fig. 13.11 represents the same sample after editing. It shows that the noise at the head and end of the sample have been completely removed, allowing the sample to start at exactly zero. In addition, the noise that occurs in the center, where there is no dialog, has been "flattened" to absolute zero amplitude. In other words, no signal occurs at that point.

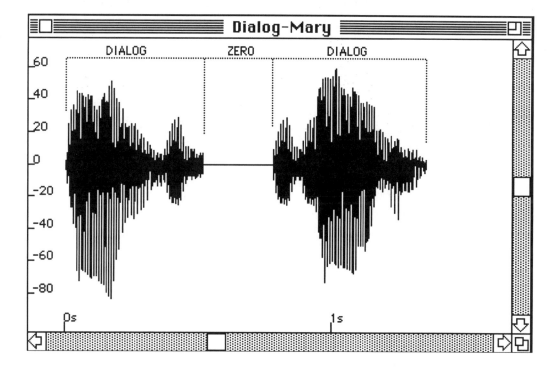

Fig. 13.11. The noise eliminated from the dialog.

Once the modifications are made, the sample is saved within the computer and retransmitted to the sampler. This requires that the sampler's memory be cleared (if no other samples within it are needed) and that a storage location be designated to determine which key or keys on the sampler will activate the samples (see Chapter 10 for keyboard nomenclature). In this particular case, we will designate that key to be C1. The sample data is retransmitted back to the sampler using the same cable (Fig. 13.12):

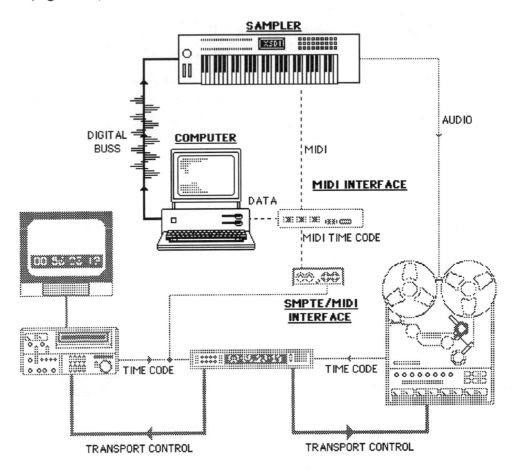

Fig. 13.12. The edited sample data transferred back to the sampler.

Use of MIDI Sequencing Software

Once the sampler is properly set up, all that remains is for the dialog to be triggered at the desired time. To find the desired start point, the slave is disabled from the synchronizer and the VTR, playing the window dub copy, is "jogged" until the proper time code number is determined. In our example, the number is 0:56:23:19.

The next step is to set up the computer as a MIDI sequencer and to synchronize it to time code. The following examples are taken from Mark of the Unicorn's *Performer* software.

Fig. 13.13 illustrates the three basic windows of interest. Clockwise from the top we have the control panel, the tracks window and the counter, which has been set to read in time code frames.

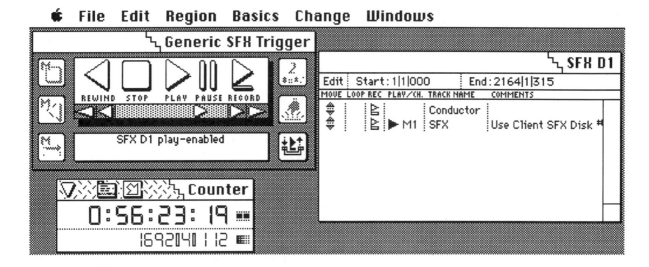

Fig. 13.13. Creating a MIDI event trigger.

Upon opening the tracks window, we instruct the computer to insert a MIDI message. In this case, the message consists of only one note (Fig. 13.14). The parameters of the message that concern us are: the selected note, its placement in relation to time and its duration (how long the note will sound). Because the sampler has been set up so that the dialog is the "note" being played, neither the computer, its software nor the sampler care that the note played is not a musical tone but in fact a dialog line.

In this and similar situations, remember that MIDI and audio are separate. MIDI is the data zipping between various devices. The audio played *always* depends on the receiving devices, a concept that basic to modern post-production techniques.

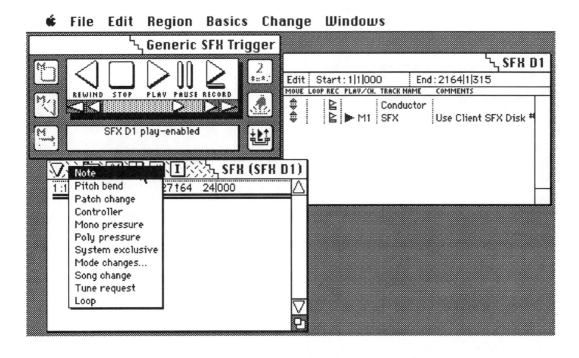

Fig. 13.14. Inserting a MIDI trigger in the form of note on data.

379

Figs. 13.15 and 13.16 show how this information is entered. All that is needed is the note to be selected (i.e., MIDI message) and the information to be typed in on-screen.

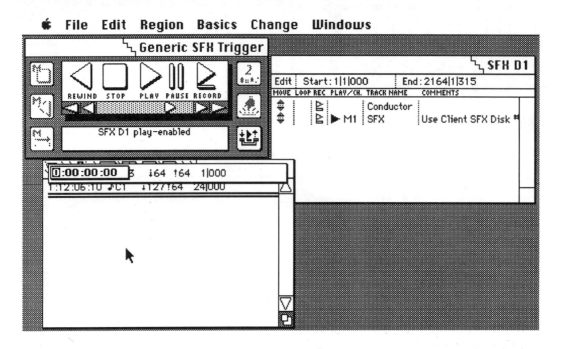

Fig. 13.15. Determining the start time of the MIDI event trigger.

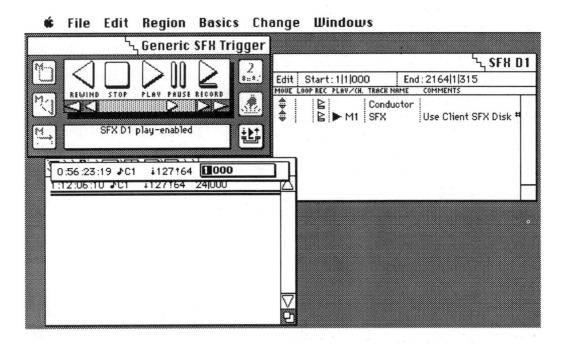

Fig. 13.16. Determining the duration of the MIDI event trigger.

Because the first two message parameters have been specified — which note and when — the last step is to determine the note's duration. Because *Performer* gives a note's duration only in terms of a musical signature (measures, beats, etc.), we choose to select the duration using the application's graphical editing feature.

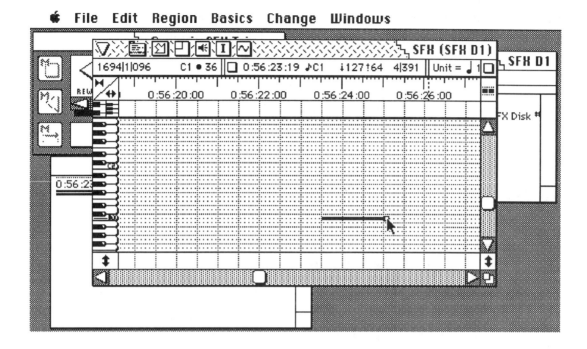

Fig. 13.17. Editing the duration of the MIDI event trigger graphically.

Figs. 13.17 and 13.18 show this feature. The note-duration message is basically an "on-and-off" message specified for a selected time. Therefore, we can change the duration by selecting the note message and extending it while viewing the time code numbers above it. In this example, we have determined that our "out" point is at 0:56:26:00 and so extend the "on" message slightly past that point. For as long as the message is received, the sampler will play note C1 or, in this case, the dialog. Fig. 13.18 shows the modified "on" message:

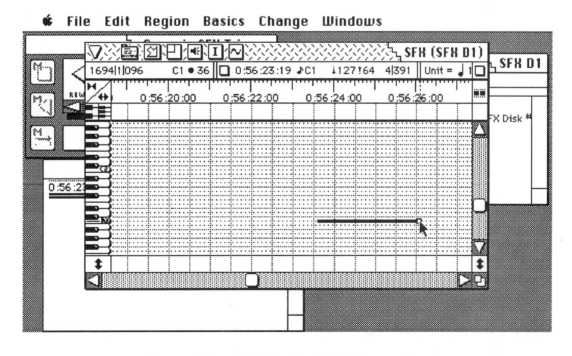

Fig. 13.18. The modified duration of the MIDI event trigger

Once the sampler and sequencer have been set up, all that remains is to slave the computer to time code and for the synchronizer to be given "in" and "out" record points that will be sent to the ATR.

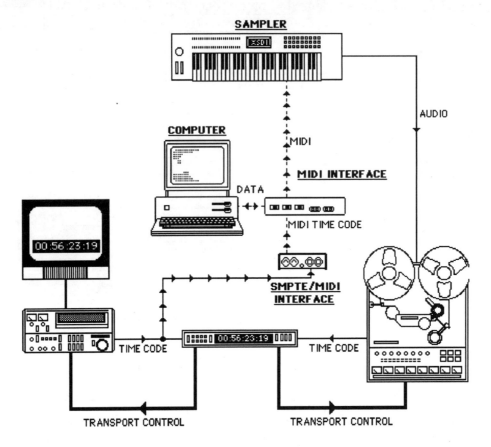

Fig. 13.19. MIDI, transport controls, SMPTE time code, and audio signal paths.

Following the signal paths shown in Fig. 13.19, we see that when the VTR, ATR, and synchronizer play, the prestriped time code will feed both the synchronizer and the computer through its interfaces. So, the dialog occurring at 0:56:23:19 will sound *and be recorded* at that exact number.

Music

Music, as described in Chapter 9, will usually be recorded on the multitrack ATR and can originate from any of two sources:

- Prerecorded libraries

- Music written for the specific production

Scoring, or the art of setting music to film, is a subject that can, by itself, fill a book. Some software is designed specifically for that purpose. The production of cue sheets, the sequencing of events and other features make some packages ideal for the end user. This subject is discussed later in the book.

Prerecorded Libraries

Prerecorded libraries appear most commonly on compact disks as do sound effects libraries. The selection, length of each and musical style are all displayed in a catalog that accompanies the library.

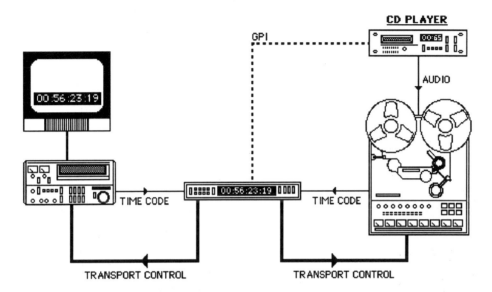

Fig. 13.20. Use of a synchronizer's GPI to trigger a CD player.

If a CD music library is to be used, each selection can be triggered by a synchronizer 's GPI, discussed earlier in this chapter (Fig. 13.20). Also refer to Fig. 9.24, which illustrates the Tascam CD-501 CD player, a device that can be easily interfaced to a GPI. Another system that can be used is the Gefen M&E organizer system, a multidisk system useful in accessing disks from large libraries quickly (Fig. 9.26).

Live and Sequenced Music

Although music from libraries is useful for commercial work, nothing quite equals the effect obtained from music that has been written specifically to picture. There are several approaches to scoring a film. The main consideration is whether the music has to be frame accurate or if it can be recorded somewhat loosely with respect to time. In the latter case, a stopwatch is sufficient to determine the segment's time, with the music written and recorded to fit. However, a piece of music that must be frame accurate requires more extensive measures.

We can take several approaches to writing the music for our imaginary session:

- Live music can be written to specific cues and the players directed by a conductor while viewing picture. This emulates traditional scoring methods and is still used in many feature films. However, it is the most expensive procedure.

- Music can be written with a MIDI system and sequenced with software that locks a computer to time code originating from the videotape. Many composers now use this approach or a combination of live and MIDI-sequenced music. Many directors, producers and composers feel, however, that the combination of live and sequenced music reduces important elements in tonality and rhythm, and that this can be perceived as unnatural.

Furthermore, a given piece of music can be recorded in one of two ways:

• Live onto the post-production multitrack ATR on one or more tracks

• Recorded on a separate multitrack reel and mixed down at a later date. This mix can be recorded onto the multitrack ATR used for post-production or onto a quarter- or half-inch tape and resynchronized to picture. In either case, all of the tapes used must have time code that matches the videotape's original code.

Back to The Session...

Limited ourselves to new post-production technologies, we cover three cases for recording accompanying music :

1. We must record one selection from a known artist's CD (for which we obtained permission)

2. A second piece of music will need to be created, but will not require frame accuracy

3. A third piece of music to be created *will* require frame accuracy

We will use a MIDI sequencing system for (2) and (3) with additional live musicians for (3).

To record the selection from CD, the synchronizer must be given record start and stop times. Also, a time code number must be entered to trigger the GPI (see Fig. 13.20). The CD player is patched directly into the input of the multitrack ATR and the sequence of events is:

• The multitrack ATR starts recording

• The CD plays

• The multitrack ATR stops recording.

Note that additional synchronizer functions, such as loops, can also be set at this time. Most likely, the GPI time code number will have to be adjusted several times to get the exact start time relationship between the CD audio and the picture. The start and stop record times are entered in each instance and correspond to the length of the selection. The stop record time can be determined by adding the start record time to the playing time of the music.

Our next project involves creating and recording the two pieces of music, one of which must to be frame accurate. For this, we use the MIDI system shown in Fig. 13.21:

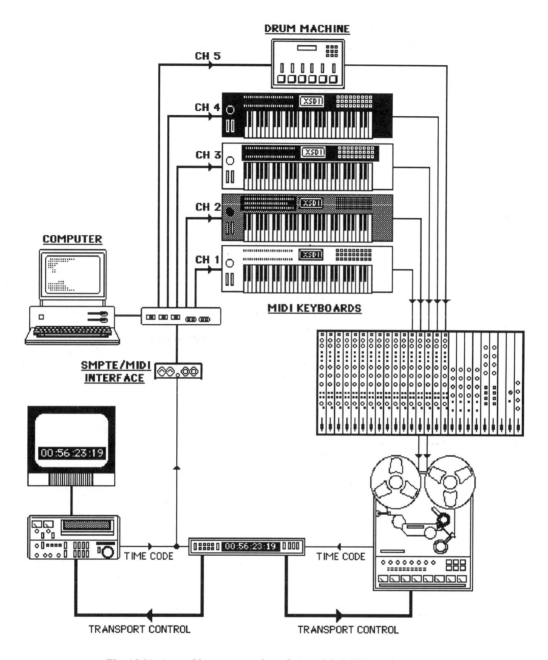

Fig. 13.21. A graphic representation of a possible MIDI scoring system.

Comparing Fig. 13.21 with Fig. 13.19, we see that, although the former is more complex, the only real changes are the addition of three keyboards, a drum machine and a console. The basic setup remains unchanged. Again, because MIDI and audio are separate, the actual audio generated always depends upon the devices receiving the MIDI signal.

Assuming that *Performer* is the sequencing software being used, the tracks window might look like the following (Fig. 13.22):

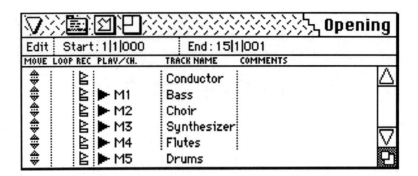

Fig. 13.22. Tracks showing data assignments for various MIDI instruments and voices.

Because the drum machine and each of the four keyboards are assigned to different channels, only the message information contained in the corresponding tracks will be received. For example, the track titled Bass is assigned to channel one, and only the keyboard assigned to channel one will respond to those messages. Obviously, that particular keyboard must be set to playback a bass sound.

The most important concept to understandwhen scoring with MIDI is that the note information (see Fig. 12.19), patch changes, tempo changes, controller information and devices receiving the MIDI messages all combine to form the system that will generate the music. Once this information is locked to time code, the tempo of the music that has been "recorded," or stored, in the computer-sequencer and can be changed to match the desired frames of the picture (Fig. 12.22).

If, for example, we wanted a chord to sound on a given frame to match action — such as a horror reaction — the information could be entered directly and its timing relative to picture corrected on screen.

Sound Effects

Sound effects recorded on the multitrack ATR can originate from any of five sources, as described in Chapter 9:

• Prerecorded effects originating from a commercially available library

• Prerecorded effects originating from a personal library

• Prerecorded effects obtained where the production was shot

• Live acoustic effects created in the studio, similar to Foley work, which are recorded either in sync to the picture or asynchronously.

• Live electronic effects created in the studio that are also recorded in sync to the picture or asynchronously.

All of the techniques described in this and previous chapters are applicable to the recording of sound effects. In fact, the recording of effects by Foley methods is similar to ADR, or looping, because sound is recorded in sync to the picture. However, many methods and their combinations allow for creative and rapid recording of effects. As we continue with our imaginary session, we will explore the many possibilities that can arise and use all five probable sources of effects and many techniques to record them.

Prerecorded Commercial Library and the Use of the GPI

If a CD sound effects library is to be used, each selection can be triggered with from a synchronizer 's GPI in the same way discussed earlier with regard to CD music libraries (Figs. 9.24, 9.26 and 13.20). As before, recording sound effects from a CD system will require that we:

• Enter a location or loop start point into the synchronizer

• Enter both the start and stop record times

• Enter the end or loop end number

• Enter the GPI time code number

Assume that the film we are post-producing requires that we add sound effects to a car crash, and the client wants to precede the crash with an off-screen car horn approaching the scene and terminating in a violent on-screen crash and explosion. However, out of the 18 car horns available from our CD library, none even approach the listener and stop, much less end in a violent crash and explosion. The time code numbers for these particular events are as follows:

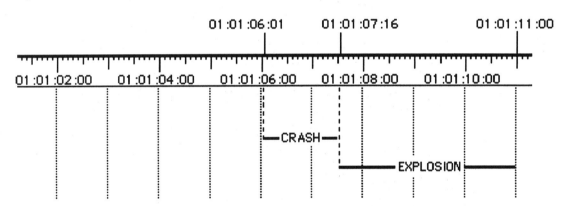

Fig. 13.23. Start and duration times for sound effects as given by time code addresses.

As shown in Fig. 13.23, the crash occurs at 01:01:06:01 and the first signs of explosion appear at 01:01:07:16. At 01:01:11:00 the picture cuts to a new scene and we are told that the sound will end with the edit.

The closest sound we can find is that of a car blaring its horn, coming closer, passing and disappearing as it travels away from us. Because we want to use the section of the effect from its beginning to the height of the Doppler effect (see Chapter 10) we must determine the length of the event and **back time** its start point. Back timing an event requires finding the length of an event, knowing where it must end and calculating its starting position. Because we know that the horn will end precisely at 01:01:06:01, we time the effect from its start to the height of the Doppler effect . This turns out to be slightly over 3.5 seconds. Using the synchronizer's time code calculator, we sub-

387

tract three seconds and 19 frames; that is 00:00:03:19 from 01:01:06:01, which gives us 01:01:02:12, the time at which the event will start (Fig. 13.24):

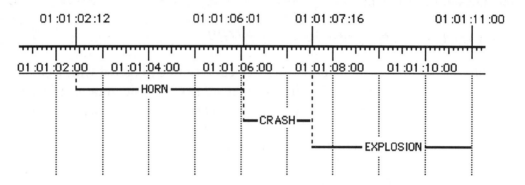

Fig. 13.24 "Back timing" an effect by duration to find its start time.

The start time of the event also yields the GPI time code number. As mentioned, we must enter this and the loop start and end points and the record start and stop numbers. This will produce the following result (Fig. 13.25):

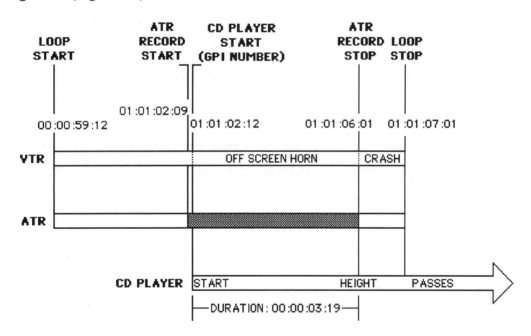

Fig. 13.25. Graphic representation of loop start, punch in, GPI trigger, punch out, and loop stop times.

Fig. 13.25 illustrates the VTR, ATR and CD player relative to each other. Our original crash number of 01:01:06:01 is shown. From this we calculate 00:00:03:19 back to 01:01:02:12, which gives us our GPI number, at which point CD will start. The ATR will start recording several frames before the CD player starts at 01:01:02:09, and the loop will start at least three seconds before the ATR starts recording (this amount will vary among different systems). Our loop will end one second after the ATR stops recording, but the CD player will have to be stopped manually.

Once everything is set up and the CD has been cued, all that remains is to press "play." All of the above functions will then automate the process for recording the car horn.

Use of a Sampler, Editing and Sequencing Software

The next sound effect, that of the crash, proves to be a little more difficult. No car crashes found on the CD library are to the client's satisfaction, so a crash must be built from various components. Each separate sound will be sampled and transferred into a computer using an editor/librarian program and triggered using MIDI sequencing software. The various sounds will be:

- Glass breaking

- Tires screeching

- Woman screaming

- Metal twisting and shearing

- A garbage lid, pots and pans dropping on a hard tile floor

- A gunshot from the CD library

Once stored inside the computer, each sound is processed to some extent. The glass breaking is duplicated, combined with its copy, and offset by a few samples to give it a slightly extended quality and to give the illusion of a large quantity of glass breaking. The tires screeching and the woman's scream are digitally mixed to produce a sound that is initially recognized as a tire screech, but with a strange undertone quality that gives it an ominous nature.

Also, the metal twisting and shearing are digitally equalized to add low frequencies to give the impression that a large object is being demolished. The garbage lid, pots and pans dropping on a hard tile floor are sampled repeatedly and combined. Finally, the gunshot is truncated so that only the initial percussive attack remains.

After processing, each sound is given its own assignment on the sampler so that it can be triggered individually with the sequencing software. The keys colored grey will be the ones used to create the effect (Fig. 13.26). Note that the keyboard nomenclature, discussed at the end of Chapter 10, is used to denote each sound's location:

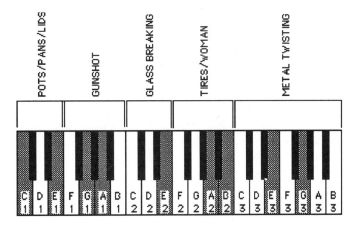

Fig. 13.26. Possible assignment of various samples to specific notes.

When varying pitches of the same sound are used, the effect is equivalent to running an ATR slightly slower or faster, resulting in further alteration of the original sound. If the pitch is dropped by a substantial amount, the original sound may become unrecognizable and a new sound is created. In this case, however, we are copying most of the sounds with the same sounds at slightly altered pitches for even greater dramatic effect.

Once in the sampler, the sequencing software is set to chase time code (see previous examples in this chapter) and to play the sounds in the sampler. However, it will not play them simultaneously, but delay some by a few frames. The following illustrations depict the sequence in both graphical (Fig. 13.27) and note form (Fig. 13.28). Both forms correspond to the keyboard nomenclature illustrated in Fig. 13.26. (Figs. 13.27 and 13.28 were created using Mark of the Unicorn's *Performer*, version 3.3. The dashed lines (**....**), boxes (GLASS (E2)), and arrows were added by the author for the purposes of illustration.)

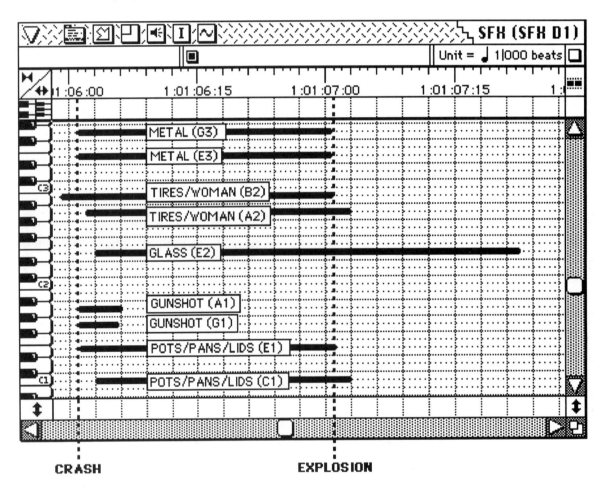

Fig. 13.27. Event triggers for the samples as set up in Fig. 13.26.

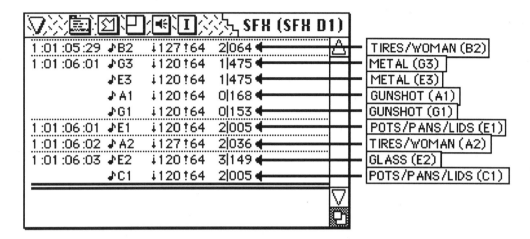

Fig. 13.28. Event triggers data for the samples as set up in Fig. 13.26.

As in all previous examples of this type, the window shown in Fig. 13.27 is a graphical depiction of MIDI note on, note off and duration. The various samples are made to start and stop at different times for the following reasons:

- The initial sound combines the tire screech and scream (B2), which precedes the actual crash by one frame. Bear in mind that a frame lasts only about 1/30th of a second. Perceived only subconsciously, the time difference will contribute a mood of impending disaster and shock. This sound continues up to the explosion itself and remains throughout the crash.

- The second pitch of the screech and scream (A2) is lower than the first and set to start one frame after (B2). The continuation of the sound for less than one frame into the explosion will help to tie the explosion to the crash.

- The next sounds are those of the metal crash (G3) and (E3). The sound, reproduced at two different frequencies, will be magnified.

- The gunshots (A1) and (G1) are reproduced in the same manner as the metal crash. The attack of the sound falls at exactly 01:01:06:01 and, when combined with the other sounds that start at this point, will contribute to the percussion of the car's impact.

- Again, the pots, pans and lids (E1) dropping on the floor also starts at the same point, contributing to the acoustical illusion that metal parts are flying off during the impact. Again, the sound's initial attack is made to coincide with the impact of the crash.

- The second sample of the pots, pans and lids (C1) is made to start slightly after the first (E1), as does (B2). Again, this continuation of the sound into the explosion will help to merge both events.

- Glass shattering (E2) starts slightly after the initial impact, yet continues into the explosion up to 01:01:07:21.05. This sound will be mixed into the explosion itself. There it serves to establish the illusion of glass being shattered by both the crash and again by the explosion. This continuation will also create a "smooth" transition from crash to explosion.

391

Once the MIDI trigger is set up, the individual sounds are assigned to separate outputs of the sampler (see Chapter 10, Fig. 10.27), each of which is assigned to its own console channel (Fig. 13.29):

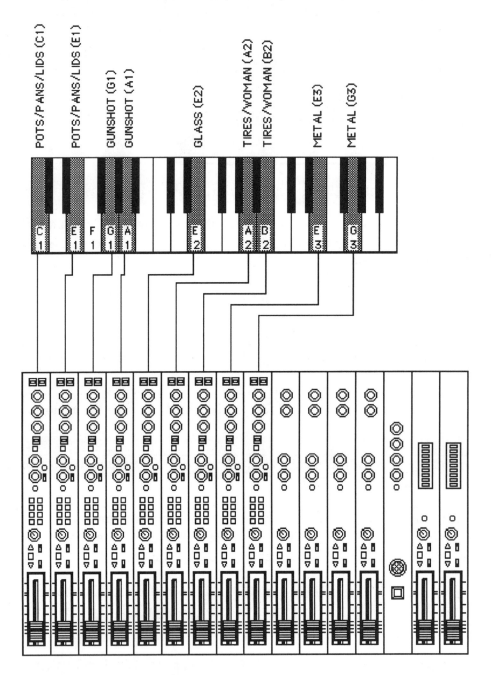

Fig. 13.29. Connection of assigned samples and outputs to console input channels.

The resulting mix is then recorded on one or more tracks of the multitrack ATR.

Prerecorded Personal Library

Immediately following the explosion, the visual cuts to an office interior about fifteen stories above the accident scene. The most important effect will be obtained from our personal library, stored on R-DAT cassette. Naturally, some effects, like typewriters, telephones and other office equipment, will be found on the CD library.

Because the explosion is of titanic proportions — after all, this is film — the sound heard through the office windows is that of a rumble combined with the vibrations of glass. The rumble is obtained by placing a microphone in a vacuum cleaner, turning it on, sampling the sound and digitally eliminating all but the lowest frequencies. This sequence, with the addition of a loop, is created solely with our editor/librarian software. The glass vibrations are added later.

Prerecorded Production Effects and the Use of the GPI

Following the office scene, we cut back to the scene of the accident. The one production effect that must be added is that of a panicked crowd, for which extras were used on a set after the shoot.

The screaming of the crowd was recorded on a standard film-type, reel-to-reel recorder, and is triggered and recorded with the use of the synchronizer's GPI function as described earlier. To increase the size of the crowd, different sections of the tape could be recorded at the same time using the multitrack ATR.

Foley to Picture/Use of Electronic Effects

The last edit takes us to a hospital emergency room, which requires the use of live and electronic Foley work. Live Foley work includes the matching of dropping and lifting of medical instruments, the rustling of papers and so on. Electronic Foley includes the use of a synthesizer to produce a bell tone when the elevator door opens and the beeping of the EKG monitor.

G. MIXDOWN

Once all of the sounds have been recorded, all that remains is to mix these into soundtrack form. For this process, we use an automated mixing system (see Chapter 12). Our primary concern will only be to program the mix. The actual recording will be the final step before layback to film. The system used is illustrated in Fig. 12.30.

The software is the same MIDI sequencing software that has been used throughout the post-production of this film. Once the initial starting levels are set, all fader moves, mutes, effects sends, pans and EQ settings are stored in real time by the computer as MIDI data. As the mix is performed, sections of the film are cycled by the synchronizer and the mix settings for each section are continually updated until the required balances are obtained. Once the mix is programmed, all that remains is to record the mix onto the videotape master and, then, onto an audiotape format for layback to film. The R-DAT audiotape format eliminates or minimizes the generation loss between the multitrack master and the final optical print. However, the original time code on the videotape will be regenerated on one channel and the mix recorded on the second. The end result of the process will be that the client has synchronous audio on both the master videotape transfer and film.

H. LAYBACK

The R-DAT cassette is given to an optical house, which offers two options: The cassette can either be transferred directly to magnetic stock while the dubber is set to run at 23.98 fps and slaved to the time code on the R-DAT cassette. The negative and mag stock are then used to create an optical and answer print in the conventional manner.

The second method bypasses the resolution to mag stock entirely, with the optical print made directly from the time-coded R-DAT cassette. The need for a 0.1 percent speed reduction still applies — that is, the optical printer is set to run at 23.98 frames per second. The end result eliminates generation loss between the multitrack master and the final optical print. The same result could be obtained by mixing directly to optical. With the session completed, our last concern is that the client's check clear the bank.

14
THE FUTURE OF AUDIO POST-PRODUCTION

A. INTRODUCTION

The focus of this book has been to introduce you to the current techniques and basic technologies in the field of audio post-production. But within this field, there is one factor we have not discussed that often confuses clients and frustrates operators and owners of post-production facilities. That factor is the fast pace with which new techniques and equipment become obsolete.

What renders a technology and the techniques derived from it obsolete? There are several factors: First, to stimulate sales, manufacturers introduce products that replace models that were new just six months earlier. Other reasons for this type of marketing involve pressure from competitive products and improvements. In reality, the number of "new and improved" products that revolutionize or greatly improve your ability to post-produce audio is low.

So what becomes obsolete? In my own studio I have an Otari 5050 two-track quarter-inch recorder that is at least twelve years old. It works as well as the day it was purchased. Is it obsolete because it still relies on analog, and not digital, technology? No client has ever complained. At the same time, I also rely heavily on a sampler made by E-Mu systems. Based on much more recent technology, it is superb for creating, storing and manipulating sound effects.

In other words, very few technologies are ever really replaced overnight. The merit of any individual product is determined only by its usefulness in a given context, regardless of its age. Seen in this light, the term "state of the art" is a superficial standard by which to judge anything.

What, then, is the future of audio post-production? Certainly digital technology has increased in importance and will continue to do so. To best answer question, however, consider four products that are ahead of their time and, as such, point to that future.

B. THE FOSTEX D-20 R-DAT

The Fostex D-20 R-DAT is the first digital audio cassette recorder intended for use as a time coded and synchronized deck. It is significant in that existing DAT format tapes can be striped after the fact. In other words, it is possible to build a sound effects library with a portable DAT, stripe the same tapes and use a synchronizer to lock the tape as a second slave ATR. Thus, by entering the proper slave offset, frame accurate sounds can be recorded directly onto the multitrack ATR.

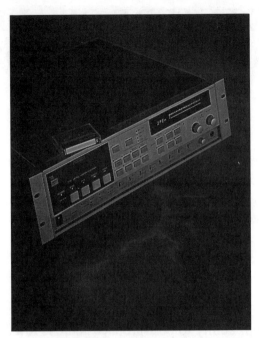

Fig. 14.1. The Fostex D-20 R-DAT center stripe digital audio tape recorder. This deck allows existing DAT tapes to be post-striped with time code.
(Photo Courtesy of Fostex Corporation of America)

The same deck can be used to record a synchronous mix for playback to film or another format videotape (see Chapter 13). Furthermore, sounds recorded in split format production or asynchronously can be digitally interfaced with the Studer Dyaxis system (described in the next section). By using a portable pilot tone and time code generator, sync sound for both film and video can be recorded with dramatically improved results. Thus, the full advantages of synchronous digital audio can be realized for film for less than the cost of conventional reel-to-reel film recorders.

C. STUDER DYAXIS

The Studer Dyaxis system is one of several types of hard disk recorders and editors available in the professional market. It also points to the direction in which post-production audio is headed. (A further description of this system can be found in Chapter 10.)

Fundamentally, the Dyaxis system consists of several rack-mounted units that house hard disk drives. It uses a Macintosh II to control the various recording, playback and editing tasks of signals stored and recalled from those drives. Because the system converts sound to digital data and stores it on a hard disk, it is similar to the sampler and computer setup discussed in Chapter 10. In essence, the Dyaxis hard disk *is* a sampler, but one of immense capacity.

By including a MIDI time code interface, the Dyaxis can read and synchronize with all forms of time code and film tach (pilot tone), enabling a stored signal to be instantly matched to picture. This type of random access audio system (see Chapter 10) allows lockup to picture within 1/10 of a second. As soon as the videotape has "settled" and the VTR is generating stable, legible time code, the audio is interlocked. There is no need for an audio transport to chase, park, play and settle down to speed, as is the case with a mechanical system.

Audio inputs are both digital and analog and can be connected to an R-DAT and Sony's D-1 and D-2 VTRs. This arrangement keeps the audio in digital form from start to finish. Furthermore, the Dyaxis accepts the Sony P-2 editing protocol, allowing the audio signal to be treated as an additional VTR in a video editing system.

In addition to time scaling (see Chapter 10), the signal processing capabilities of the Dyaxis include up to four separate channels of audio storage, enhanced mixing functions, digital equalization, panning, on-screen metering and sampling frequency conversion.

D. THE LEXICON OPUS SYSTEM

The Lexicon Opus is perhaps one of the most astounding audio systems available. It has many of the features found in other random access recording systems but, unlike the others, is totally self-contained. Moreover, the ease with which it can be learned and used and the creative freedom that it provides to the engineer seems remarkable. It must be experienced to be fully appreciated.

The principle physical components of the Opus, simple in appearance, consist of a console and a rack (Fig. 14.2). The rack contains the hard disks that store digital data as well as eight analog-to-digital (A/D) and 12 digital-to-analog (D/A) converters.

 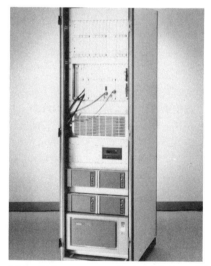

Fig. 14.2. The two components of the Lexicon Opus system are the console, at right, which connects to the hard disk, and the rack, which contains the A/D and D/A converters.
(Photo Courtesy of Lexicon, Inc.)

Ideal for audio post-production, the Opus hard drives store 1.2 gigabytes of data, and are expandable to 4 gigabytes (a gigabyte is one billion bytes). Sampling rates can be set to 44.056 , 44.1 or 48 kHz and 99 tracks are available at any time. At a sampling rate of 48 kHz, the Opus provides 190 track minutes per hard disk. If, for example, two tracks are used, each would have a capacity of 95 minutes (190 mins. ÷ 2 tracks = 95 mins.). If four tracks are used, each has a capacity of 47.5 minutes, and so on.

The console connects to the rack through a RS-422 cable. No analog audio signals of any kind pass through the console. In much the same way that MIDI *controls* audio signals (see Chapter 11), the console controls the functions of the system. The functions themselves are carried out within the rack. The rack contains the A/D and D/A converters mentioned and these can be assigned in any configuration to any combination of tracks. The system accepts up to 32 external sources, for example, ATRs and VTRs. These inputs can also be assigned to any combination of tracks and the subsequent signals recorded digitally within the unit. All patching is accessed by the console electronically and performed by Opus's computer (Fig. 14.3).

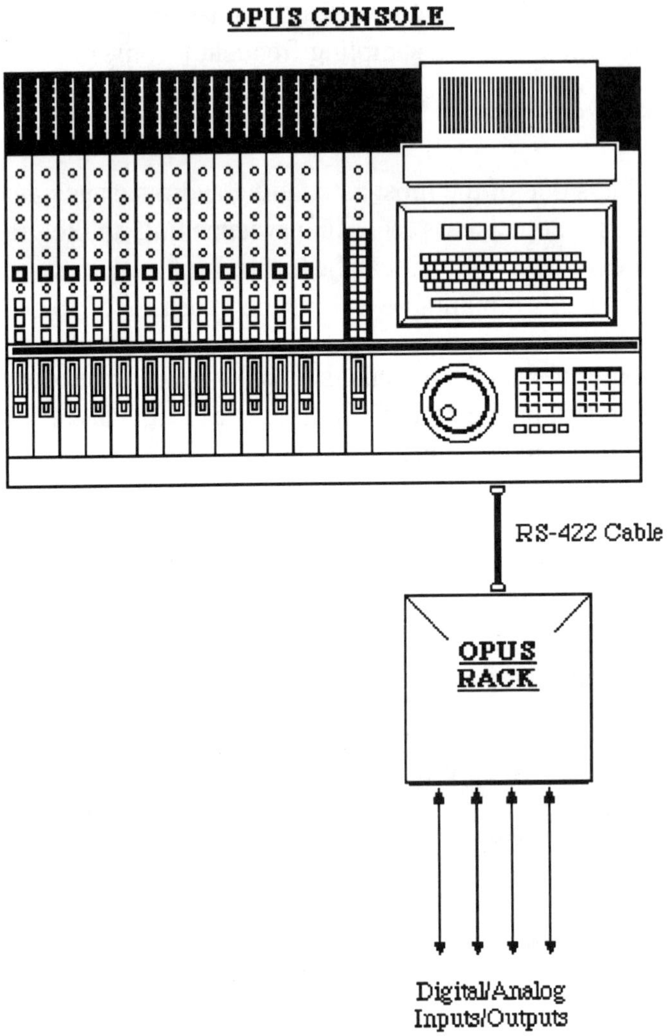

OPUS CONSOLE

RS-422 Cable

OPUS RACK

Digital/Analog
Inputs/Outputs

Fig. 14.3. A simplified view of rack and console connections of the Lexicon Opus system. All audio and sync is supplied to and handled by the rack.

The console, with faders, panpots and similar controls, looks conventional but functions quite differently from conventional consoles. It consists of twelve channels, one equalization module and one master module. Each channel can control signals received from or going to a specific track. The equalization, which is fully parametric, also consists of a notch filter, low and high shelving filters, low and high pass filters, and de-emphasis for transferring material between analog and digital formats. This module can be accessed by any channel or combination of channels. When the EQ is programmed for a channel, that channel retains its EQ information until changed. For example, if channel one is assigned a given EQ setting, channel six can be EQ'd afterwards and each channel's EQ parameters will remain unchanged until updated or canceled by the operator.

Editing and the creating soundtracks are the Opus's main strength. These functions are accomplished primarily by the jogging wheel on the console and operating the buttons located above it (Fig. 14.4).

Fig. 14.4. The jogging wheel and edit buttons of the Opus console.
(Photo Courtesy of Lexicon, Inc.)

After selecting a particular sound, it can be edited using a number functions:

Cut   Removes the selection from the track. It is like instantly erasing an entire selection on a conventional multitrack ATR.

Copy   Copies a particular sound so that the duplicate can be used elsewhere.

Replace   Replaces one sound with another that has been copied or cut. This is comparable to "punching" in and out on a traditional ATR.

Align   Adjusts two sounds so that they occur simultaneously.

Loop   Places visible "markers" at any given point in the track for reference.

"XFade"   Crossfades two sounds in exact proportion to each other. Crossfade time is adjustable in milliseconds from 0 to 99 seconds.

All sounds, tracks and procedures in the Opus system are displayed on a monitor located on the console, as shown in Fig. 14 2. The displays are clearly and sensibly laid out and easy to understand. Fig. 14.5 shows a typical screen: At the top, from left to right, are the job title, reel number and date. The left hand vertical column gives the channel to which each track is assigned, followed by the track number. The sounds are shown as located within the tracks and each is titled, allowing for easy visual identification and placement.

399

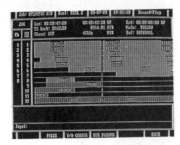 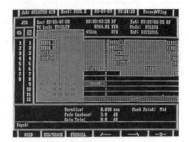

Fig. 14.5. The record-play screen of the Opus. (Photo Courtesy of Lexicon, Inc.)

Fig. 14.6 Editing sounds on the Opus. (Photo Courtesy of Lexicon, Inc.)

Slippage can be easily achieved by selecting the sound and "sliding" it forward or backward on the screen in relation to the current time code position, or by simply cutting and re-locating it. Fig 14.6 shows a group of sounds about to be edited. Note that the location, duration, stop and start times are all indicated.

As with any good hard disk system, synchronization is easy to maintain. All sync parameters can be accessed and the Opus will also lock to film tach, as seen in Fig. 14.7, which shows some of the sync capabilities of the Opus.

Fig. 14.7 The sync parameters screen of the Opus. (Photo Courtesy of Lexicon, Inc.)

As with all hard-disk-based audio systems, lockup to picture occurs as soon as valid time code is received from the VTR, allowing instant audio playback to picture. As discussed, input and output configurations, patching and assignments of the D/A and A/D converters are all controllable from the Opus console. Moreover, these parameters can be saved and recalled later. Fig. 14.8 shows the screen used to display this information.

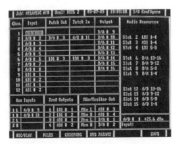

Fig. 14.8 The patching and input/output (I/O) configuration screen of the Opus. (Photo Courtesy of Lexicon, Inc.)

The actual files that represent audio information can be grouped according to a job or client title. The contents of these can be displayed, as can other pertinent information, as shown in the screen in Fig. 14.9. Furthermore, all Opus information can be backed up onto an 8-mm videocassette and from which any job can be retrieved.

Fig. 14.9 The files screen of the Opus.
(Photo Courtesy of Lexicon, Inc.)

In summary, the advantages of the Opus system are many: It is completely self-contained and does not require a synchronizer, ATR or console. The system's $200,000 price tag must be weighed against the cost of these items if purchased separately. In addition, all work is done in the digital domain. The speed with which one can lay in sound effects, music and dialogue to picture is astounding. It is this type of approach to audio post-production that points to where the art is headed in the coming years.

15
THE AESTHETICS OF SOUND

A. INTRODUCTION

All of the audio and sound equipment in the world is useless without competent engineers to operate it. A working knowledge of technology and techniques, when thoroughly understood and practiced over years, becomes second nature. At the same time, aesthetic perceptions and routines must also be developed and these are often harder to grasp. A working professional must understand both techniques and aesthetics to successfully post-produce the audio portion of a film or video.

Consider, for example, how sound changes the way we interpret an image. A series of visuals accompanied by an objective commentary produces a different reaction from one shown with a negative commentary. In addition, sound can be used to shift the viewer's attention. If a character is in the background, a sound can call the viewer's attention to another person or object in the frame.

Sound can also aid or determine the time of a story by relating to the visual image in two ways: viewing time and story time. Viewing time indicates the actual length of the visual; story time is the amount of time assumed to pass during the course of the video or film's action. Introducing sound prior to, during or after a scene can shift the viewer's sense of time.

Today, the trend is to compile more detailed and realistic backgrounds by paying greater attention to acoustic detail. For example, if a refrigerator door is shown to close, the tinkle of glass coming from within will indicate that the refrigerator is full.

Here are general ideas and guidelines:

1. A visual image is not a self-contained frame, but a window on a much broader reality.

2. For most film and video makers, to imagine means to visualize. To realize that visualization, one must also *hear* the production as well.

3. If visuals are the medium of statement, then sound is the medium of suggestion.

Sound accompanying visuals falls into three general categories of dialog (including narration and any spoken material), music and noise. Noise is anything that is not spoken or of a musical origin and includes sound effects and ambiance. The distinctions among the three categories are often blurred, as a particular sound can fall into several categories at once.

B. TRANSITIONS

Sounds can be joined end to end or overlapped, as in a voice-over. Transitions of sounds can range from smooth to abrupt as dictated by the need for effect. An abrupt, jarring transition nearly always wakes up an audience.

C. TYPES OF SOUND

For the sake of analysis, sound can be broken down into several categories. These distinctions in themselves are not as important as their capacity to help us understand how the components of sound relate to an image.

Diegetic Sound

If the source of a sound is an object or person in the story, the sound is said to be diegetic. Character's voices are diegetic sounds. Diegetic sounds can be on- or off-screen.

Nondiegetic Sound

If the source of a sound is not an object or person in the story, the sound is said to be nondiegetic. Music added to a soundtrack to affect the image is a nondiegetic sound. Narration can be either diegetic or nondiegetic.

External Diegetic Sound

The audience assumes that the sound has a physical source; that it is an object or person in the story.

Internal Diegetic Sound

Internal diegetic sound originates from the mind or body of a character in the story. An example is narration produced by a character thinking to himself, which no other character in the story can hear.

Off-screen Sound

Off-screen sound suggests the extension of space beyond the visible action. It can also introduce an element or character by defining its visual source as being off-screen. (Remember that a visual image is not a self-contained frame, but a window on a much broader reality.)

In terms of dialog, off-screen sound can be used to establish a nonexistent character, as in the 1960 movie *Psycho*, where Mrs. Bates, unseen to the viewer until the last portion of the movie, had been alive only in her son's mind.

The separation of sound effects from their visual source can produce suspense. Examples include the footsteps used in *Rear Window* (1954) and mysterious screeches in *The Haunting* (1985).

Asynchronous

Asynchronous sound is when there is a discrepancy between the things heard and the things seen on film. In film, this type of sound is also said to be "wild." For example, footsteps can be recorded by themselves and later synchronized to the picture.

D. CONSIDERATIONS

The nature of a sound must be considered in terms of how it relates the nature of the image. These considerations include the following:

Rhythm

The rhythm, tempo or pace of a visual can be supported or contradicted by its sound. For example, a serene visual accompanied by fast-paced music would lend a tense, suspenseful air to the image. The rhythm of a series of edits can also be taken into consideration. If a chase scene has a series of fast edits, would a slow piece of music be appropriate?

Slow-motion Sound

Slow motion sound is yet another technique, as used in *Rocky II*, that can draw out greater detail. This works particularly well if the visual has been slowed down.

Mono versus Stereo

Monaural sound can only simulate depth, but stereophonic sound can simulate the sideways spread of reverberant or ambient sound, as well as sideways travel of characters and objects.

Space

Just as the camera can move closer to or further from its subject, so can sound be distanced. The specific loudness of a track determines the perceived distance. A louder sound will make the image appear closer. If two people are seen meeting in a fog, the increasing or decreasing loudness of a character's footsteps will suggest the existence of more space than can be seen from the moment.

Aural Flashbacks

An aural flashback can be created by lowering or muting the sound accompanying the visual and by replaying lines that may not have been heard earlier in the picture, bringing the viewer to another location in the story time.

E. SOUND EDITING

There are two general approaches to editing sound for film: the English and Hollywood systems.

English System

This system is also called the horizontal system, as several sound editors are assigned the work of selecting and editing in one or more groups of sounds. One editor, for example, can be assigned the task of obtaining and editing in gunshots. As a result, each editor sees the film as a whole.

Hollywood System

This system is also called the vertical system because one sound supervisor selects all the sounds to be used and determines their placement. The supervisor then delegates the process of physically placing the sounds in the soundtrack to several sound editors, each of which edits in his or her allotted sounds. In addition, each editor can work on only one reel. As a result, no one editor sees the film as a whole. The process is suggestive of an assembly-line procedure.

F. SOUND EFFECTS

It would be possible to write an entire book on the subject of sound effects. More so today, with the trend to compile more detailed and realistic backgrounds. At the same time, a sound track does not have to reproduce every action seen or every noise on the set. It is generally a good idea to avoid redundancy between the sound and the visual image. Is it necessary to hear a faucet dripping because it's shown?

Similar sound can be substituted for effect. For example, the victim's screams accompanying her demise in *Psycho* were not of human origin, but instead were unnaturally high-pitched violins. It is the interpretation of the sound, not its imitation, that is the key element.

The source of a sound is less important than its quality. For example: A viewer might see the horrified face of a character and hear the buzzing of flies. A corpse does not have to be in the frame for the viewer to realize the character's gruesome discovery.

Sound is usually faithful to its source. This, however, has nothing to do with what originally caused the sound in the first place. Few people recognize real gunshots because they almost never sound like movie gunshots.

A comic effect can be achieved by playing with a sound's fidelity. A shot of a woman cutting a loaf of bread accompanied by the sound of a chain saw will imply that she is the world's worst cook. Animated cartoons commonly use this technique.

Sound Effects Design

When designing a sound effect:

1. Analyze the physical nature of its source. How does it move? Is it big and clumsy or delicate?

2. Pinpoint its effects: Is it scary? Astonishing? Serene?

3. Match the pitch of the effect to the camera angle: A high camera angle can suggest a weak, high-pitched sound; a low angle can suggest a bassy, rumbling sound.

4. Some designers see a link between color and sound. Green can denote a bass tone, yellow can suggest high tones and red can suggest shimmering resonances.

A designed sound effect can have one of two approaches: The effect can be layered, where several effects are happening at once, or the effect can be sequential, where several sounds happen in succession.

There are three ways in which to conceptualize a sound effect:

1. The most common method is to go to the original source of the sound. A microphone, however, does not necessarily "hear" the way a person does. The full spectrum of a volcano exploding might be recorded as a tinny, washed out version of that sound.

2. The second method is to use visual analogy. A rainstorm might be interpreted by recording water splashing in the shower.

3. The third and most difficult approach is to select sounds that have no visual congruence at all. For example, a fire approached in this manner might be simulated by crumpling tissue or wax paper.

Creating Sound Effects

If the required sound effects are unavailable from standard sources, they may need to be created. This is one of the most challenging, creative and satisfying processes that can take place in audio post-production. It takes much experimentation, patience and practice. Often, it demands the ability to generate sounds that have no visual congruence to the effect required. The following are several recipes for producing different types of effects:

Arrows in flight: Whip a fencing foil or thin wooden dowel through the air.

Blood spurting: Squirt milk from a water pistol into a wet sponge.

Breaking teeth: Shake a bed spring after the punch.

Demonic chanting: Have a congregation of at least twenty people recite The Lord's Prayer, then play it backwards after removing most of the pauses in the reading.

Gigantic belch: Prerecorded roar of Godzilla played backwards.

Gravel falling: Pour uncooked rice into a wooden bowl.

**Internal organs
(dropping on floor):**   Ready-made pudding dropped onto a flat garbage bag.

**Metal (or ice)
creaking:**   Rub a balloon and play back at a lower speed.

Rain: Pour fine sand onto wax paper or aluminum foil.

Digestive gurgling: Squirt melted Jell-O through a baster or empty dishwashing liquid bottle.

Sword fighting: Hit various pieces of silverware together. Alternate knives, forks and spoons.

Whip: Whip a fencing foil or thin wooden dowel through the air. The hit can be produced by making a loop out of a leather belt or strap, holding each end in your hands and pulling the hands apart quickly. This closes the loop, slapping the two sides of the belt together.

I. MUSIC AND SCORING

The process of scoring is, to say the least, an elusive one for inexperienced film and video producers. Here is some information about the process of working with a composer:

Pre-tracking

In the early stages of editing, a film is sometimes pre-tracked. In pre-tracking, scenes are cut to "stock" music so that the tempo and phrasing of the music lend added structure to the visual. Later, a composer then writes music that is similar to the phrasing and structure of the stock music used. Pre-tracking is done when no original music has been written and a composer has not yet been engaged.

Spotting

The first step in scoring is the process called spotting, which usually takes place in a screening room. Working together, the composer and director decide which scenes should have music, where the music begins and where it ends. Each segment of music in a film is called a **cue**. This session is called the spotting run.

Creating the Breakdown

On a flatbed, the music editor then creates a breakdown or cue sheet (see Chapter 8) by timing each cue with a stopwatch. The feet and frames of the film can be converted to seconds or even hundredths of a second.

Scoring and Recording

The composer then takes the information from the cue sheet and writes the music. When all the cues have been reviewed, the recording session takes place.

When on the stage, the conductor is alerted by a three-foot long scratch in the film called a streamer at the end of which is punched a hole called a punch (Fig. 15.1). When the punched frame passes through the projector, it produces a flash of light, which indicates the start of a cue. Within a given cue there can be additional streamers and punches which alert the conductor to key scenes or events.

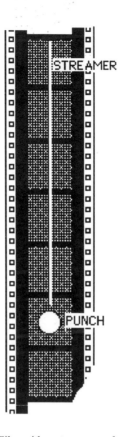

Fig. 15.1. Film with a streamer and punch.

Additional Notes

The trend today is to move away from "catching" the action with music. Instead of having each phrase or note accompany an action, such as chords sounding in synchronization with footsteps, music is simply used to highlight the values in a scene.

There are other terms that deal with scoring. The following are included for reference:

A **long cue** is a piece of music that accompanies a lengthy visual sequence. A **short cue** is a segment consisting of several bars or notes that serve as punctuation for the visual. **Stings** or **stingers** are sustained or momentary chords or notes that accompany the discovery of death, the opening of a door, etc. A **quotation** is a segment of familiar music, such as the national anthem.

Underscoring is music added for dramatic enhancement. It has been said that underscored music it best when it is unnoticed. **Source music** is music that is realistically part of a scene (i.e., a street musician or car radio). A **segue** is a transition without pause from one piece of music to another. This is usually done by an editor, and generally only when the key and tempo of each piece of music are close enough to permit a smooth edit.

GLOSSARY

1/4-INCH TRANSFER
The process in film during which original production audio, recorded onto 1/4-inch stock, is dubbed in sync onto film stock prior to editing.

3/4-INCH VIDEO TAPE FORMAT
A video tape format that uses 3/4-inch wide tape and corresponds to established parameters as described in Chapters 4 and 8.

3/2 PULLDOWN
The process by that one film frame is transferred into three and then two fields. This is done only on older, optical film-to-video transfer systems.

8-MM VIDEO TAPE FORMAT
A video tape format that users media 8-mm-wide film stock and corresponds to established parameters as described in Chapters 4 and 8.

16-MM FILM FORMAT
A film format that uses media 16-mm-wide film stock and corresponds to established parameters as described in Chapter 4

35-MM FILM FORMAT
A film format that corresponds to established parameters as described in Chapter 4

70-MM FILM FORMAT
A film format that uses media 70-mm-wide film stock and corresponds to established parameters as described in Chapter 4

A-ROLL EDITING
See Off-line Editing

A/D CONVERTER
A device that translates analog signals into digital form.

ACADEMY LEADER
A length of film that contains lab references and provides information on synchronization, sound and other details.

ADDRESS TRACK
A third audio track used in some video decks for time code.

ADR
See Looping.

ADSR
The method used to describe the four basic stages of an envelope: attack, decay, sustain and release.

AMPLITUDE
The height or strength of a wave as determined by the difference between the positive and negative peaks of a waveform.

ANSWER PRINT
The combination of an optical print and its negative. The answer print is the copy used for projection on optical systems.

ANTI-ALIASING FILTER
A filter used to eliminate frequencies beyond the digital recording system's tolerance range during sampling.

APPLICATION
Another name for a computer program; software.

ASSEMBLY EDITING
A method of video tape editing in which the audio, video and sync material is assembled sequentially from start to finish.

ASSIGNED
Describes when a signal is sent to the output section of a console. Control of this section is usually through a group of push buttons called the matrix or bus assign. This section determines the destination of the signal leaving the input module.

ASYNCHRONOUS SOUND
When there is a discrepancy between the audio and visual portion of a film, the sound is said to be asynchronous. Asynchronous sound does not rely on a synchronous visual for its origin. In film, this type of sound is also said to be "wild."

ATR
An acronym for audio tape recorder.

ATT
See Trim

ATTACK TIME
A control on an audio compressor that determines the speed with it starts processing a signal.

ATTENUATION
See Trim

AUDIO CHASE
A type of interlock system where only the audio deck is controlled by outgoing transport control signals originating from a controller.

AUDIO HEAD
A device located in the tape path of an ATR that uses electromagnetic principles to generate an electrical current proportional to the magnetism it detects on an audio tape.

AUDIO MONITORS
Loudspeakers in an audio facility.

AUDIO-VIDEO INTERLOCK
The process of having a multitrack deck and a video deck run together in perfect synchronization using SMPTE time code.

AUTOLOOP (SAMPLING)
The ability of a sampler to close the loop of a sample at the two most closely matched amplitudes of the loop point. Otherwise, a played loop may cause an audible "glitch," or a click.

AUXILIARY SEND MASTER
The master level control on a console for the auxiliary mix.

AUXILIARY SENDS
The controls on a console that provide additional mix outputs that may be required for supplemental mixes, signal processing or to feed a performer's headphones in another room. These controls do not affect the signal in the input module.

AUXILIARY TRACK
See Address Track.

BACK TIMING
The process of finding the length of an event, knowing where it must end and calculating its starting position.

BALANCED
A method of transmitting signals by using two conductors and a separate grounding conductor.

BANDPASS EQUALIZATION
A type of equalization that amplifies only a range of fre-

quencies between two predetermined frequencies. All other frequencies higher and lower are attenuated.

BANTAM

A type of audio patch bay. Bantam jacks are roughly half the size of standard 1/4-inch jacks. Consequently, one bantam bay holds twice as many connections as a bay for standard 1/4-inch jacks.

BASIC TRACKS

The initial tracks recorded on a multitrack ATR.

BEAT (MUSICAL)

A musical beat is (usually) a steady and repetitive pulse, determined by the meter; a musical notation for the rhythmic division of the music.

BEATS (MIDI)

A timing system used in MIDI in which pulses are sent out every quarter note.

BEATS PER MINUTE (BPM)

The number of beats that occur in one minute, used for describing the tempo of a musical piece.

BENCHMARK

The position on the fader of a console which is usually located about 2/3 of the fader's travel from its bottom. This is significant because at this point a signal's input amplitude at the fader equals its output leaving the fader. This is level is considered to yield the best possible signal quality.

BETACAM VIDEO TAPE FORMAT

A video tape recording and playback format that corresponds to established parameters.

BIDIRECTIONAL

See Bipolar.

BIPHASE SIGNAL

A signal usually generated by the drive motors of a magnetic dubber. It varies in content and format among machines from different manufacturers. As a result, there are multiple standards in use today.

BIPOLAR

A pattern that picks up sound equally on two sides (90° off axis) or from front to back.

BIAS CURRENT

A high-frequency current of 100 kHz or greater that is combined with the audio signal during recording to improve sound quality. Too little current increases distortion; too much results in the loss of higher audio frequencies

BIASED

Some types of tape work best with specific amounts of bias current, and for this reason some audio decks are sold with their bias current set for a particular brand of tape. In such cases the deck is said to be biased for that type of tape.)

BINARY CODE

Combinations of binary digits ("bits") that indicate a specific event or value.

BIPHASE SIGNAL

The synchronizing reference used by some film equipment. Also called film tach.

BIT

A binary digit and the smallest binary value. A group of bits is a byte.

BLACK BURST GENERATOR

Any device that generates black burst.

BLACK BURST

The signal used in establishing video synchronization.

BLACKING (A VIDEO TAPE)

See Recording Black.

BOARD

See Mixer.

BOOST EQUALIZATION

See Peak Equalization

BOUNCING TRACKS

The process of mixing several tracks on one multitrack deck onto one or more tracks on the same deck.

BPM

See Beats Per Minute

BRAKE ARM

The component of an ATR that maintains tension in the audio tape and lets the transport operate when upright. In the event that the tape breaks or runs out, the brake arm will stop the machine from running. This prevents any tape from spilling from the supply reel should the tape break

BREAKDOWN

See "cue sheet."

BROADCAST CONSOLE

A type of mixer or console specifically designed for use in a radio station or broadcast situation.

BUMPING UP

The process of copying video and audio material from one format to another for the sake of achieving higher quality, as in the case of dubbing from 3/4-inch U-Matic video to one-inch or D-2 video.

BURN-IN DISPLAY

See Window Dub

BUS ASSIGN

See Matrix

BUS SYSTEM

A network that distributes a common set of signals to various devices.

BYPASS SWITCH

Any switch which allows the operator to route a signal around a given circuit for testing and comparison.

BYTES

A unit digital data used by computers and consisting of binary information. One byte is made up of eight bits.

CABLE SYNC

An early method of synchronizing used in film and in conjunction with double system. A cable connects both film camera and audiotape recorder, and carries a sync pulse produced by a small AC generator that is coupled to the camera motor. The cable transmits the pulses from the camera to the deck.

CALIBRATION

The speed at which an ATR records and plays back will change slightly with time. Adjustment of the controls that affect the operation of an ATR is called calibration and is required periodically.

CAPSTAN

The component of an ATR that keeps the tape at a constant linear speed.

CARDIOID
A microphone pickup that has its highest sensitivity at the front end, the 0° axis, and extends from that point in a heart-shaped pattern.

CCD
See Charge Coupled Device

CENTER DRIFT
Occurs when program levels alternate between left and right too rapidly or often. Center drift can create unacceptable surges of audio when played in mono.

CENTER STRIPE
A thin center track of time code between two audio tracks.

CHANNEL ON/OFF
See Mute

CHARACTER INSERTER
A device that inserts time code numbers into a video pictures for a visual display.

CHARGE COUPLED DEVICE (CCD)
A device used in video cameras that produces an electrical voltage proportional to the light it receives.

CHORUS (MUSICAL)
Usually the focal point of a contemporary song.

CLAPSLATE
Essentially a chalkboard with a moving clapper. The individual "take" numbers and other information are written on the slate for each take.

CLIPPING
See Distortion.

CLOSED REEL SYSTEMS
In audio, any type of system in which the tape is enclosed (e.g., an audio cassette).

COAXIAL CABLE
A method of cable construction in which an insulated center conductor is surrounded by a grounding conductor.

CODING
During conversion to digital form, bits are generated as an analog signal reaches or falls below a given quantizing level. Pulses are coded as a binary "1" for on and a binary "0" for off. Specific combinations of these binary digits, called a binary code, represent the voltage level of an analog signal at a particular point in time. The process of generating this code is called coding.

COINCIDENT MIKING
A technique for stereo recording in which two, usually directional, microphones are placed with their elements at different angles. The four accepted angles are 90°, 120°, 135° and 180°. Each angle of miking gives a different result.

COMBINE (SAMPLING)
A sampler's ability to digitally combine two samples to create a new sample.

COMPONENT VIDEO
Video in which the separate components, or red, green, blue and sync signals, are split and carried independently of each other, usually with physically separate cables.

COMPOSITE VIDEO
The result of electronically combining the separate red, green, blue and sync video signals into one.

COMPRESSION RATIO
A compressor setting that describes how much of an increase in the input must be present to create a 1-dB increase in the output.

COMPRESSORS
See Limiters

CONDENSER MICROPHONE
A microphone that translates an audio signal into an electrical one by a varying capacitance.

CONSOLE
See Mixer.

CONTACT MICROPHONES
See Transducers.

CONTINUOUS JAM SYNC
A method of dubbing time code in which the generator copies and regenerates the incoming code exactly (sometimes called reshape, regenerate or transfer).

CONTROL ROOM
The area in an audio facility that contains the console and other equipment. It is here that all recording, monitoring, patching, processing and mixing activities take place.

CONTROL TRACK
The control track in video is analogous to sprocket holes on film. When a video deck records a signal, the deck adds a series of evenly spaced electronic pulses on the tape. During playback, these pulses are counted by video decks and editing systems to recognize a complete frame, or picture, of video.

CORNER FREQUENCY
See Shelving Frequency

CROSSTALK
Crosstalk occurs when the signals on adjacent tracks interfere with each other. This happens when a signal on a one track exceeds a certain amplitude and spills over to an adjacent track.

CRYSTAL SYNC
A film synchronizing method used in conjunction with double system recording. Both camera and deck each have their own crystal-based oscillator to generate a 60-Hz pulse. The pulse from the camera's oscillator regulates the motor speed, ensuring that it runs at a constant rate of 24 frames per second. The tape deck's oscillator has the dual function of regulating the tape-to-camera speed and generating the tone to be recorded.

CUE
An individual segment of music in a film or video.

CUE MIX
A mix derived from an auxiliary send and used in conjunction with a performer's headphone mix for monitoring tracks while overdubbing or recording.

CUE SHEET (FILM)
A detailed listing of the scenes and action in a visual with footage, frame, time code counts or all of these.

CUE SHEET
The written record of the visual material that is compiled prior to scoring and other post-production processes.

CUE TRACK
See Address Track.

CUEING

The act of setting a tape, CD, record or other sound source at a specific point for playback at a specified time.

CUTOFF EQUALIZATION

A type of equalization in which all signals past a predetermined frequency are attenuated in increasing proportion to their frequency.

CUTOFF FREQUENCY

The frequency at which cutoff equalization begins to occur.

CYCLE

The distance between two consecutive and equal points on a wave, usually between two negative or positive peaks.

CYCLES PER SECOND

Once the unit for the measurement of frequency, now called Hertz.

CYCLING

The function of a synchronizer that will "loop" an ATR and VTR. When a specified end point is reached, both transports rewind to a pre-designated start point and begin to play. This process will continue indefinitely until stopped by the operator.

D/A CONVERTER

A device that translates digital signals to analog form.

DAILY

A print of the raw footage returned from a lab for screening. Also called a rush, professional shoots require it for a daily review of the material shot.

DAISY CHAINING

A method of interconnecting instruments and other devices in a linear fashion using MIDI and which relies on the replication of MIDI data in each device.

dB

See Decibel (dB).

DDL

See Digital Delay Line

DE-ESSER

A device specially designed to reduce sibilance, or excessive hissing of "s" sounds.

DECAY TIME

A measure of the amount of time required for the reflections of a reverberation signal to fade.

DECIBEL (dB)

A measure of volume. Generally, the smallest change in volume the human ear can detect.

DECODING

The process of playing back audio with noise reduction.

DEMAGNETIZER

A device that removes any magnetism from the heads and tape path of an ATR.

DESIGNATION STRIP

The paper strip on a patch bay that indicates inputs and outputs.

DIALOGUE REPLACEMENT

See Looping

DIEGETIC SOUND

If the source of a sound is an object or person in the story, the sound is said to be diegetic. Character's voices are diegetic sounds. Diegetic sounds can be on- or off-screen.

DIGITAL DELAY LINE

A signal processing device that is designed specifically to create delay based effects, such as doubling, echo, etc.

DIGITAL VIDEO TAPE FORMAT

A video tape format that corresponds to established parameters.

DIP EQUALIZATION

See Notch Equalization

DIRECT BOX

A device used to transform the line value of an electric guitar or bass to microphone level, allowing for direct insertion of the instrument into the recording system.

DIRECT INSERTION

When an instrument or other signal-producing device is connected directly to a console.

DIRECT OUT

A line-level output from an input module, usually obtained prior to the pan and matrix.

DIRECT SOUND

When sound reaches a microphone by following a straight path without reflection.

DIRECTIONAL CHARACTERISTICS

The aspect of a microphone that describes its pickup pattern. Specifically, the way in which a particular microphone responds to the sound from different directions.

DISTORTION

Distortion occurs when the signal level exceeds the equipment's ability to handle it and the peaks of the signal cycles are actually cut off.

DOMAIN

A group of magnetic particles that have become magnetically aligned.

DOPPLER EFFECT

The effect caused by the compression of air waves ahead of a moving object and their expansion behind it. As the object approaches the listener, the sound rises in pitch; as it passes, the pitch decreases.

DOUBLE SYSTEM RECORDING

The recording of physically separate synchronous field, or location-recorded, audio obtained by having two separate decks for audio and video (or film) recording.

DOUBLE SYSTEM SOUND RECORDING

The separate and synchronous recording of sound and picture. Both sound and picture can each be manipulated and edited separately.

DROP FRAME TIME CODE

The elimination of two frames every minute, or 108 frames per hour, of SMPTE time code. This is done is by having two frames dropped each minute except for every tenth minute. Not having the tenth-minute exception would cause a drop of 102 frames every hour instead of 108. Frame dropping occurs only at each minute's changeover point. For example, when the time code changes from 01:11:59:29, the next number would be 01:12:00:02.

DRY SIGNAL

A signal that is not combined with reverberation.

DUBBER (FILM)

See Mag Dubber

DUBBING (FILM)
See Looping

DUBBING
Copying one tape to another.

DUBBING STAGE, THEATER OR STUDIO
See Looping Stage

DYNAMIC MICROPHONE
A microphone that relies upon electromagnetic induction to produce a mirror voltage of the audio source.

DYNAMIC RANGE
The range of volume, or sound pressure level, that any sound may have, from inaudible (0 dB) to painful (120 dB).

E TO E
See Electronics to Electronics

EDIT CONTROLLER
A device that controls the transport functions of two or more video decks during editing.

EDITING BLOCK
A rectangular block of aluminum with a center channel to hold the tape. Editing blocks are available for every type of recording tape, although the most common blocks contain channels for 1/4-inch and 1/2-inch tape.

EDITING
The process of removing, adding and rearranging sounds or images.

EFFECTS MIX
A mix derived from an auxiliary send and used in conjunction with signal processing.

EFFECTS RETURN
The master level control on a console for the auxiliary mix sent to and returning from a signal processing device, usually a reverb unit.

EIA STANDARD RACK MOUNTING SYSTEM
An industry standard specification for mounting equipment in cabinets having spaces that are 19 inches wide.

EIA STANDARD UNIT
One EIA unit is 1.75 inches high, two units are 3.5 inches high, three are 5.25 inches high and so on.

ELECTROMAGNETIC INDUCTION
A phenomenon that occurs when a wire moves through a magnetic field, generating a voltage on the wire.

ELECTRONICS TO ELECTRONICS (E TO E)
The method of direct transfer of signal in which the output of a playback device is connected directly to the input of the recording device. This provides for a cleaner sound, eliminating the noise introduced by speakers and microphones used to transfer sound.

ELEMENT
The component of a microphone that converts acoustical energy to electrical energy.

EMI
See electromagnetic induction

ENCODING
The process of recording in a way that reduces noise.

ENVELOPE
The overall pattern in which the loudness, or amplitude, of a sound waveform varies.

EQ
See Equalization

EQUALIZATION
The process of amplifying or attenuating frequencies individually or in groups.

EQUIPMENT NOISE
Any unwanted audio signal generated by audio equipment. Typically, equipment noise is a hissing sound with frequencies ranging from about 8 to 12 kHz.

ERASE HEAD
The audio head located in the tape path of an ATR that, among other things, erases any sounds from an audio tape immediately prior to its being recorded.

EVENT TRIGGER
A feature of some synchronizers that allows a user to start the equipment at a given time code number even though that equipment does not use time code. The interface, or output, of this signal is commonly referred to as a GPI, or general purpose interface.

EXCITER LAMP
A photoelectric pickup that reads the variations of light through the track of an optical or answer print and changes them into electrical impulses. These impulses are amplified within the projector and can be heard either through the projector's internal speaker or an external sound system.

EXTERNAL DIEGETIC SOUND
A sound that has as its source an object or person in the story.

FADER
The control on a console's input module that determines the level of signal at the module's output.

FAST FORWARD
The transport mode of an ATR that advances audio tape quickly.

FIELD STORE DEVICE
A device capable of storing one digitized video field, or one half frame.

FILE
A set of computer data created by the user. A file can consist of a video sequence, sound effect, text, etc.

FILM CHAIN
A generic term used to indicate any device for transferring film to videotape.

FILTERS
Devices that attenuate specific frequency bands. The names of the most common types of filters correspond to the different equalization types: shelving, cutoff, bandpass, peak and notch.

FIXED EQUALIZATION
A type of equalization in which only the sound level is variable.

FIXED GUIDES
The fixed components in an ATR's tape path that help guide the audio tape in proper position to the heads and other components.

FLANGES
Flat metal disks, usually 10-1/2 inches in diameter, that have holes and notches that correspond to those in the hub and tape pancake.

FLATBED
A machine used during film editing that displays the pic-

ture in sync with sound. Available in a wide variety of configurations.

FLUX
An area of a magnetic field.

FOLEY STUDIO
A facility where sound effects are recorded live and in sync with the picture.

FORMAT
Parameters that determine a tape's setup. These include: speed, track width, tape width, number of tracks, type of noise reduction, etc.

FORWARD-BACKWARD FILM MIXING
See rock-and-roll film mixing

FPF
See Frames Per Foot

FRAME, IN (OR OUT) OF
A object or person within (or outside) the film or video image.

FRAMES PER FOOT
The number of frames contained in a foot of film. This number will vary according to the format of the film and subsequently to the size of each frame. Larger formats have physically larger frames.

FREEWHEEL MODE
A synchronizing mode used by some synchronizers in the event that time code on one or more tapes used in the interlock process is intermittent or faulty.

FREQUENCY RESPONSE
The measure of the amplitudes of varying frequencies reproduced by a microphone.

FREQUENCY SPECTRUM
A sound's frequency range.

FREQUENCY
The number of times per second a cycle will occur. Frequency determines a sound's pitch.

FULL COAT
Film stock that is covered with one or more stripes of magnetic substance without picture.

FULL TRACK
Single track audio tape format in which almost the entire width of tape is used for a single track.

FUNCTION SELECT
See Track Record Control

GAIN CONTROL
See Fader

GAIN
See Trim

GENERAL-PURPOSE INTERFACE (GPI)
See Event trigger

GENERATION LOSS
When audio signals are rerecorded from one tape to the next, noise is cumulatively added, the signal to noise ratio decreases, the signal is increasingly degraded and successively higher frequencies are lost.

GENLOCK
See Genlocking

GENLOCKING
The synchronization of SMPTE time-code signal to video sync reference information.

GIGABYTE (GBYTE)
1 billion bytes

GOBO
A portable acoustic baffle, usually used in music production studios. The gobo is used to reduce unwanted reflected sound.

GPI
See General-purpose Interface

GRAPHIC EQUALIZER
A type of equalizer that allows for various frequencies to be altered in amplitude, and with the frequency presets are fixed and invariable.

GROUP BUS
The output section of a production console that is usually connected to the inputs of a multitrack ATR.

GUARD BAND
A blank audio track left between the time code track and the highest program material track. Also the blank spaces between head gaps in audio tape formats that contain two or more tracks.

HALF TRACK
A two-track audio tape format in which almost half the width of tape is used for a single track.

HARD WIRED
Connecting one piece of equipment directly to another so that it cannot be accessed via a patch bay.

HEAD BLOCK
The central unit of a tape deck that houses the tape guiding and head assemblies.

HEAD CONFIGURATION
A description of the arrangement of audio heads. In mastering decks this is usually erase-record-play. In multitrack ATRs, it is usually erase-sync-play.

HEAD GAP
The space on an ATR head's surface where the magnetic flux is concentrated. Its length is set by the size of the gap in the magnetic coil.

HEAD STACKS
The heads on a multitrack deck are called head stacks because they are literally composed of magnetic coils stacked upon one another.

HEADS OUT
When an audio tape is wound on the left (supply) reel.

HERTZ
A unit of measure of a signal's frequency; formerly called cycles per second.

HOOK (MUSICAL)
The catchy, repetitive portion of a contemporary song.

HUB
A plastic core around which is wound a 10-inch diameter audio tape "pancake."

HUB ADAPTERS
Accessories used on an ATR that are designed to accept both 10.5- and 7-inch reels.

HYPERCARDIOID
Further increasing the directionality of a supercardioid microphone produces a hypercardioid pickup pattern.

Hz
The abbreviation for Hertz. See Hertz.

IPS.

See Inches Per Second

IEC EQUALIZATION

See NAB Equalization.

IMAGING

The characteristics of a reproduced audio signal.

IMPEDANCE

Resistance to the flow of electrical energy in a circuit; more resistance means higher impedance.

IMPEDANCE-MATCHING DEVICES

Devices specifically designed to convert the line value of one audio system to that of another.

IN POINT

The beginning of a video editing sequence.

INCHES PER SECOND (IPS)

A measure of tape speed. The length of tape in inches that travels past a fixed point in one second.

INERTIA IDLER

A component in an ATR's tape path that is coupled to a heavy flywheel within the machine and helps to maintain the tape's speed and tension.

INPUT SELECT SWITCH

The control on a console's input module that determines the source of signal being supplied to the module.

INSERT EDITING

A method of video editing in which control track remains undisturbed and picture and audio may be inserted independently.

INTEGRATED SYSTEM

A semiprofessional system that combines a multitrack deck and mixer in one package. It is suited for the consumer who doesn't want to be bothered— after buying a tape deck — with the trouble and expense of selecting and connecting a console.

INTERLOCK CONTROLLER

A device that controls an interlock system by means of incoming time code signals and outgoing transport control signals.

INTERNAL DIEGETIC SOUND

Internal diegetic sound originates from the mind or body of a character in the story. An example is narration produced by a character thinking to himself, that no other character in the story can hear.

INTRO (MUSICAL)

A portion of a contemporary song, usually based on the chorus or hook.

ISO BOOTH

See Isolation Booth

ISOLATION BOOTH

An acoustically isolated area, heavily soundproofed that is used to record audio sources. The iso booth minimizes acoustic interference from external sources.

JAM SYNC

See Continuous Jam Sync and One-Time Jam Sync.

JOG AND SHUTTLE

The transport mode on a VTR that allows an operator to search both in fast mode and in frame-by-frame mode.

KILOBYTE (KBYTE)

1,024 bytes.

LARGE HUB 7-INCH REEL

A 7-inch reel with a larger center hub is used when less tape needs to be stored or worked with. The increased diameter of the center core reduces tape tension and handling problems.

LAVALIERE

A type of condenser microphone developed to be unobtrusive, and is clipped or pinned to a performer's lapel or tie.

LAYBACK ATR

A specialized deck with head configurations and specifications that exactly match those of a type-C one-inch VTR. The layback deck allows the one-inch master videotape to be placed directly onto its transport and will treat the one-inch master videotape simply as audiotape. It cannot playback picture information.

LAYBACK

The final phase of audio post-production, during which separated audio and video are joined on one physical media.

LAYDOWN

The post-production phase that transfers the original source audio on a videotape to the multitrack ATR.

LEADER TAPE

Nonmagnetic plastic or paper tape that is used for separating recorded pieces of magnetic tape. Plastic leader is stronger, but cannot be torn like paper leader. Paper is easier to work with if many edits are to be made.

LIMITERS

A device that restricts the dynamic range of audio material.

LINE LEVEL

A standard voltage reference used by the audio industry, referenced to 0 VU.

LINE OUT

See Direct Out

LINE VALUES

The electrical measurement of a given audio system used to transmit signals.

LIVE BOUNCING TRACKS

The process of mixing several tracks on one multitrack deck to other tracks on the same deck while combining live signals with the mix. This process is similar to bouncing.

LIVE MIXING

The process of combining of different audio signals to produce a fixed combined signal as an auditory event is occurring.

LONG CUE

A piece of music that accompanies a lengthy visual sequence.

LONGITUDINAL TIME CODE (LTC)

A type of time code intended for use on an audio track. The most common and economical type of time code, LTC is recorded directly onto an audio track of an audio or video deck as if it were an audio tone. LTC is effectively a square wave consisting of 2,400 bits of information per second (80 bits per frame).

LOOP (SAMPLING)

When a sample is recorded, it has a fixed duration.

However, a loop can be created so that the sample repeats indefinitely between two points.

LOOPING SESSION
See Looping

LOOPING STAGE
Facility where looping takes place.

LOOPING
Traditional film post-production process during which dialog is re-spoken live to picture and recorded in sync.

LOW-WIDTH OPEN REEL FORMATS
Demands for low-priced decks with greater track capacity have led to specific consumer formats, such as eight-track decks using 1/4-inch tape, as well as 16-track decks using 1/4-inch and 1/2-inch tape. These formats, intended only for small or semiprofessional studios, are subject to crosstalk and lower S/N ratios.

LTC
See Longitudinal Time Code

MAG DUBBER
A device that holds magnetic film stock and operates in much the same way as a conventional audiotape recorder.

MAG STOCK
See Magnetic Stock

MAGNETIC MEDIA
Any material capable of storing and reproducing information coded as magnetic impulses.

MAGNETIC REFERENCE TAPE
A carefully prerecorded tape used during the playback calibration of an ATR. Tones of different frequencies are recorded at a laboratory and recorded at exactly 0 VU.

MAGNETIC STOCK
Audio recording media in film.

MAGNETIC STRIPE
Magnetic stripe film works in a similar fashion to audiotape and, depending on the format and application, is integrated into the film stock carrying the picture.

MASTER (AUDIO-VIDEO INTERLOCK)
The transport, usually a VTR, in a synchronized system to which all other decks are synchronized. The time code numbers originating from the master transport are used to determine the relative position of all slave transports in the system.

MASTER BUS
The stereo output section of a production console that is usually connected to the inputs of a mastering ATR.

MASTERING DECK
An audio tape deck, usually stereo, used for recording the separate tracks played by a multitrack recorder and combined through a mixer.

MASTERING
The process of creating a final videotape, analogous to a mixed audio master.

MATRIX
An electronic device, usually located within a console, used to route signals to varying locations.

MEASURE (MUSICAL)
A rhythmic division in music that is determined by its meter.

MEGABYTE (MByte)
One million bytes

METER (MUSICAL)
A musical notation for the rhythmic division of music.

MIDI DELAYS
Delays in the transmission of MIDI data that can occur when four or more devices are arranged in a daisy chain network.

MIDI
Stands for Musical Instrument Digital Interface and is a standardized communication protocol for different makes and models of electronic musical instruments.

MIDI THRU-BOX
A device that duplicates the original MIDI signal into multiple outputs, each of which is an exact duplicate of the original.

MIDI TIME CODE
The use of SMPTE time code converted to MIDI.

MIDI CONTROLLER
A device used as the master data originator that supplies information throughout a MIDI system.

MILS
Unit of measure for audio tape thickness given in thousandths of an inch.

MIX
Any tape that embodies electronically combined audio signals.

MIXDOWN
The phase of audio recording during which multiple pre-recorded signals are synchronously played back and combined. The result is referred to as the mix or mixed master.

MIXED MASTER
See Mixed, Mixing and Mixdown

MIXED, MIXING
The process of combining and recording different audio signals to produce a fixed combined signal.

MIXER
The device used to combine audio signals for mixing.

MODEM PORT
A data port on a computer usually associated with the use of a modem.

MODULES
The separate, usually removable electronic portions of an audio console. This term can also apply to other pieces of electronic equipment.

MONITOR SECTION
The section of a console that allows the operator to monitor signal flow within the console.

MONITOR SELECTION
A control on an ATR that determines where a signal will be monitored. The signal will either originate from the ATR's input or from its play head.

MULT
Multiple jacks on a patch bay wired to each other only. These are used as built in "Y" connectors.

MULTIDIRECTIONAL
Microphone that has two or more selectable pickup patterns.

MULTIPLEXER
A device that transfers film to videotape optically and is

capable of transferring from film and 35-mm slide formats.

MULTISTRIPE

Magnetic stripe film formats used for recording sound.

MULTITRACK DECK

A type of audio recorder that is capable of recording on separate, individual tracks, that may later be played back, combined through a mixer and recorded onto a stereo tape deck called a mastering deck.

MUTE

The control on a console's input module that shuts down the signal exiting the module.

NAB EQUALIZATION

Equalization refers to a deliberate adjustment of the amplitudes of different frequencies that occur in both the record and playback electronics of an ATR. The American standard of EQ is called NAB. The European standard is called IEC. The two are incompatible.

NEGATIVE PEAK

The point in a wave at which the amplitude is lowest.

NOISE GATE

A device that can be set to allow a signal to pass and then to shut down when no signal is present. It prevents unwanted ambient or recurring sound from being heard or recorded.

NOISE

Any unwanted audio signal. Typically, it may be a hissing sound with frequencies ranging from about 8 to 12 kHz. It is unavoidably produced by electronic equipment or magnetic recording tape in varying degrees. It falls under the two categories of equipment noise and tape noise.

NONDIRECTIONAL

See Omnidirectional.

NONDESTRUCTIVE EDITING

The method by which original digital audio data is first copied in the segments that will be used to create the edit. In this way the original data remains undisturbed.

NONDIEGETIC SOUND

A sound that does not come from an object or person in the story. Music added to a soundtrack to affect the image is a nondiegetic sound. Narration can be either diegetic or nondiegetic.

NONDROP FRAME TIME CODE

Continuous, uninterrupted SMPTE time code that uses continuous and consecutive time code numbers.

NORMALED

A type of patch bay connection that allows signals to pass from one point to another unless manually interrupted.

NOTCH FILTER

A type of equalization that attenuates a specific frequency and an extremely narrow range of frequencies to either side of it.

ODD-EVEN PANNING

A panning system in which the signal is panned between odd and even numbered buses. For example, if bus 1, bus 3 and bus 4 are selected, the pan control acts as if bus 1 and 3 are left, and bus 4 is right. Then, left rotation of the pan control will send more signals to bus 1 and 3, and less to bus 4.

OFF-LINE EDITING

The simplest type of video editing system, usually incorporating no more than two decks and lacking computer assistance.

OFF-SCREEN SOUND

The extension of space beyond the visible action. It can introduce an element or character by defining its visual source as being off-screen.

OMNIDIRECTIONAL

A pickup pattern that allows a microphone to pick up sound with equal or almost equal sensitivity from its front, back and sides.

ON AIR CONSOLE

See Broadcast Console

ON AXIS

When sound enters a microphone from the front (at 0°), the microphone is said to be on axis.

ONE-INCH VIDEO TAPE FORMAT

A video tape format that corresponds to established parameters as described in Chapters 4 and 8.

ONE-TIME JAM SYNC

A method of dubbing time code that is similar to continuous jam sync with the exception that the generator does not regenerate the incoming code. Instead, it waits for a time code signal to be received. Once a valid time code number is registered, the generator begins emitting code starting with the number received. The generation of code continues regardless of the continuity of the input device.

OPEN LOOP TRANSPORT SYSTEM

The most common type of ATR tape path.

OPEN REEL SYSTEMS

In audio, any type of system in which the tape is wound on an open reel.

OPTICAL TRACK

Optical track is created photographically during the development of the film at a lab. During playback, the track is illuminated by an exciter lamp within a projector. The photoelectric pickup reads the variations of light through the track and changes them into electrical impulses.

OSCILLATOR

An electronic device that generates pure waveforms.

OSCILLOSCOPE

An electronic display and measuring device that allows an operator or engineer to see a waveform and its components.

OUT OF SYNC

A condition used to describe two or more audio signals played out of time with each other.

OUT POINT

The end of a video editing sequence.

OUTBOARD EQUIPMENT

Equipment that is located outside of, and is independent from, the mixing console.

OUTTAKES

Unused audio takes, usually removed and set aside during audio tape editing.

OVERDUBBING
A method of listening to one or more audio signals while recording another to build a multitrack tape.

OVERDUBS
When additional sound is recorded while simultaneously monitoring the basic tracks on a multitrack ATR.

OVERLOAD
See Distortion

PAD CONTROL
The fixed control on a console's input module that determines the level of the incoming signal.

PAN CONTROL
The control on a console that allows the operator to place a signal in any proportion between two outputs, as in the case of stereo imaging. Pan is similar to the balance control on a consumer sound system.

PANCAKE
A method of tape packaging in which is what is essentially a 10-inch spool of tape is wound around a plastic core, called a hub.

PARAGRAPHIC EQUALIZER
A type of equalizer that incorporates features of both the graphic and parametric types. For example, the bandwidth and frequency are independently adjustable, and the boost and cut controls may take a graphical form.

PARAMETRIC EQUALIZER
A type of equalizer that allows for various frequencies to be altered in amplitude where the frequency presets are variable.

PATCH BAY
A device used to route signals to various locations.

PATCH CORD
A specialized cord made for routing signals through one or more patch bays.

PATCH NUMBERS
An identification system found on most electronic musical instruments that allows the user to access different sounds within each instrument.

PATCH
The connection of one item to another through a patch bay.

PAUSE CONTROL
A control found on older ATRs that brings the tape and heads into contact prior to recording and playback.

CM
See Pulse Code Modulation

PEAK EQUALIZATION
A type of equalization that amplifies a central frequency and a narrow range of frequencies to either side in proportion to their proximity to the central frequency. All other frequencies remain unaffected.

PEAK LED
The indicator on a console's input module that lights up when the level of the incoming signal exceeds specified parameters.

PEAKING
See Distortion

PERFECTONE
A synchronizing signal recorded onto the audio tape dur-ing film production to ensure later synchronization between sound and picture.

FL
See Solo

PHANTOM POWER
An external power supply used in conjunction with condenser microphones. The output voltage is usually 12 to 48 volts DC.

PHASE INVERTER
A device used to correct signal phasing. Such a device may be located within a mixing console or be physically separate.

PHASING
Phasing occurs when different cycles of the same signals arrive at one point and affect the overall sound; the resulting sound quality may suffer from a decreased bass or from stereo imaging with a drifting center.

PICKUP PATTERN
A measure of a microphone's ability to select audio signals by their direction relative to the pickup device, typically a microphone. The measure is based on the amplitude produced by the microphone relative to the position of the audio source.

PILOT TONE
The most commonly used synchronizing signal recorded onto the audio tape during film production to ensure later synchronization between sound and picture.

PINCH ROLLER
A component of an ATR that functions in conjunction with the lifters. In play mode it moves down and presses the tape to the capstan's surface.

PITCH CONTROL
A control on an ATR that allows the tape to be played faster or slower than its normal play speed, usually by as much as 20% either way.

PITCH
The sonic quality of a sound as determined by its frequency.

PLATE REVERB
A type of device that creates reverberations by inducing wave motion in a rectangular steel sheet that is placed under tension and encased in a frame.

PLAY
The control on an ATR or VTR that engages the play mode.

PLAYBACK HEAD
The audio head located in the tape path of an ATR that reproduces the signal from audio tape by converting magnetic to electrical energy.

POLAR RESPONSE CHART
A graphical representation of a microphone's pickup pattern.

POLYDIRECTIONAL
See Multidirectional.

POP FILTER
A device to reduce a microphone's susceptibility to "pops" and other wind noise. The pop filter, usually a foam rubber cover, is found either within the microphone windscreen or as an accessory made to slip over the outside of the windscreen

POSITIVE PEAK
The point in a wave where the amplitude is highest.

POST-DUBBING
See Looping

POST-FADER
A point after the fader in a module signal path. Subsequent changes made to the fader's position will affect a post-fader signal.

POST-PRODUCTION CONSOLE
See Production Console

POST-PRODUCTION
The processes that occur immediately after production. These include editing, looping, scoring, etc.

POST-SYNCHRONIZATION
See Looping

PRE-FADE LISTEN
See Solo

PRE-FADER
When a signal is sent from a point prior to the fader in a module signal path. Changes made to the fader's position will not affect the pre-fader signal.

PRE-ROLL
The practice of allowing a given amount of time before the desired segment of program material starts. This allows time for a synchronized system to properly interlock.

PRESET NUMBERS
See Program Numbers

PRESSURE ZONE MICROPHONE
A type of microphone design that eliminates reflected sound waves reaching the microphone after the direct sound. It appears as a flat plate with a connector attached, and is available with either a directional or hemispherical pickup pattern.

PRINT THROUGH
Print through refers to the transfer of magnetism from one layer of tape to the next and usually occurs when a tape has been stored for a considerable length of time. The result is two signals that play back at the same time, one much weaker than the other.

PRINTER PORT
A data port on a computer usually associated with the use of a printer.

PRINTER'S SYNC
When the soundtrack of a film is placed ahead of the picture by a certain number of frames. This displacement keeps the soundtrack from interfering with the projection of the image. The placement of the exciter lamp for reading the sound track and the projection assembly compensates for this difference. The amount of frames of advance differs with each format.

PROCESSING (SAMPLING)
A term that describes the manipulation of digital audio by means similar to those used in processing analog audio.

PRODUCTION CONSOLE
A type of mixer or console specifically designed to be used in conjunction with multiple signal manipulation.

PRODUCTION
The creation of film, video or music. In film and video, this includes the shoot, going on location, etc.

PROGRAM NUMBERS
An identification system found on most electronic musical instruments that allows the user to access different sounds within each instrument. These numbers are assigned to MIDI devices that contain a specific set of sound-producing or sound-modifying information.

PROPS
The items used for creating or replacing synchronous sounds, such as doors, guns, etc.

PROXIMITY EFFECT
Proximity effect occurs when a directional microphone is placed too close to the sound source, resulting in a relative increase of bass frequencies. (Omnidirectional microphones are not subject to proximity effect.) The resulting boost in bass frequencies causes "boominess".

PUCK
See Pinch Roller.

PULSE CODE MODULATION (PCM)
A process in which digital audio signals are recorded onto audiotape.

PUNCHING IN
The process in which a selection of multitrack tape is rerecorded live on one or more tracks.

QUANTIZING LEVELS
The discrete steps or values into which an analog signal is broken down during the sampling process.

QUANTIZING
The process of breaking down a continuous analog signal into discrete digital levels.

QUARTER TRACK
A four-track audio tape format in which almost one fourth of the width of a tape is used for one track.

QUOTATION
A segment of familiar music, such as the national anthem.

RACK CABINET
A cabinet specifically made for the mounting of EIA standard equipment.

RACK MOUNTED
Equipment that is mounted or capable of being mounted in EIA standard cabinets.

RACK RAILS
Rails manufactured specifically for the mounting of EIA standard equipment.

RADIO FREQUENCY INTERFERENCE
The reception of unwanted radio frequency signals often occurring when a wire acts like an antenna.

RAM
See Random Access Memory

RANDOM ACCESS MEMORY (RAM)
The "volatile" memory of a computer, measured in bits or bytes. The memory capacity of a computer is determined by the number and type of memory chips it contains. Volatile memory, unlike disk-drive memory, "forgets" its data when power is turned off.

RANGER TONE
An obsolete synchronizing signal recorded onto the audio tape during film production to ensure later synchronization between sound and picture.

RAW FOOTAGE

The original footage created during production.

RERECORDING

See Remix.

REAL-TIME ENTRY

A method of recording MIDI data into a sequencer by playing an instrument in real time; analogous to recording on tape. The events that are stored are played back exactly as they were recorded.

RECORD CALIBRATION

See Reproduction Calibration.

RECORD CONTROL

The control on an ATR or VTR that places the unit in record mode.

RECORD HEAD

The audio head located in the tape path of an ATR that creates magnetic fluctuation in audio tape.

RECORDING BLACK

When, prior to insert editing, a video tape being edited is recorded with continuous control track.

RECORDING MODES

Controls on an ATR that, among other functions, determine which head will be used for recording and monitoring.

REEL SIZE CONTROL

The control on an ATR that allows the operator to select the size of reel to be used.

REFERENCE TONE

Recorded sine wave tone of a single frequency at 0 VU that allows the operator to verify that the playback levels are consistent between different ATRs.

REFLECTED SOUND

When sound reaches a microphone by following a reflective path.

REGENERATE

See Continuous Jam Sync

RELEASE TIME

A control on an audio compressor that determines the speed with which the compressor will stop acting on a signal.

REMIX

A process during which the separate, individual tracks of a film's soundtrack are combined through a mixer and rerecorded in combined form.

REPRODUCTION CALIBRATION

The way an ATR records and reproduces will change slightly with time. Adjustment of the controls that affect the operation of an ATR is called calibration and is required from time to time. Specifically, the reproduction functions must be calibrated prior to the record calibration sequence.

RESHAPE

See Continuous Jam Sync

RESOLVER (FILM)

A device that controls the speed fluctuations of the dubber's motors to maintain the frame-to-frame relationship between picture and sound during a 1/4-inch transfer.

REVERB

See Reverberation.

REVERBERATION

A phenomenon in which reflected sound and direct sound reach a listener within closely spaced and consecutive spans of time.

REVERSE (SAMPLING)

A sampler's ability to reproduce a sample from end to beginning, resulting in a reversed sound.

REVERSE TAPE EFFECT

The backwards placement of tape on a tape deck to obtain a segment playing in reverse.

REWIND

The transport mode of an ATR that quickly reverses the audio tape.

RFI

See Radio Frequency Interference.

RIBBON MICROPHONE

A microphone that relies upon the movement of a thin metal ribbon suspended within a stationary magnetic field to produce a voltage that mirrors the audio source.

RIDE THE GAIN

A term that describes the frequent adjustment of the faders to keep the average signal level within acceptable limits.

ROCK-AND-ROLL FILM MIXING

The name by which film mixing is known, because the entire system is "rocked" back and "rolled" forward.

ROLL BACK FILM MIXING

See Rock-and-roll Film Mixing.

ROLLING GUIDE

The moving components in an ATR's tape path that keep the audio tape in proper position to the heads and other components.

ROLLOFF EQUALIZATION

See Cutoff Equalization.

ROLLOFF FREQUENCY

See Cutoff Frequency.

ROUTING SWITCHER

A device, usually having an equal number of inputs and outputs, that switches among each electronically.

RUSH

See Daily.

SAFETY

A duplicate copy of a master tape.

SAMPLING FREQUENCY

The number of times per second that an analog waveform is sampled prior to being digitized.

SAMPLING RATE

The number of times per second an analog waveform is sampled for conversion to digital information. Also called sampling frequency.

SAMPLING

The process by which an analog waveform is read at fixed intervals by a digital device and converted to digital pulses. , 10

SCATTERED WIND

Winding an audio tape using the "fast forward" or "rewind" mode to create uneven tension in the tape, causing some edges of the tape to protrude.

SCORING

The art of composing music specifically for use with a particular visual production.

SCREENING

Viewing prints of the raw footage returned on a daily basis for projection or viewing.

SEGUE

A transition without pause from one piece of music to another. This is usually done by an editor and generally only when the key and tempo of each piece of music are close enough to permit an edit.

SELECTIVE SYNCHRONIZATION

See Selsync.

SELSYNC

The method by which a multitrack tape machine keeps rerecorded and newly recorded signals in time.

SEQUENCER

A devices that allows the user to electronically record and play back events, usually associated with the use of MIDI.

SEQUENCING

The practice of electronically recording and playing back events, usually associated with the use of MIDI.

SHELVING EQUALIZATION

A type of equalization in which all frequencies past a certain point are amplified to a uniform, preset level.

SHELVING FREQUENCY

A designated frequency at which shelving equalization begins.

SHOCK MOUNT

A device that physically isolates a microphone by suspending the entire body in an elastic web, often made of rubber. If any extraneous vibrations reach the mount, they are dissipated by the elastic bands suspending the microphone.

SHORT CUE

A musical segment consisting of several bars or notes that serve as punctuation for the visual.

SHOTGUN

Slang film term for most hyper-, ultra- and super-directional condenser microphones.

SHUTTLE KNOB

The control (usually found on a VTR) that allows for shuttle and jog operations.

SIBILANCE

The accentuation, during recording, of sounds like "s" and "ch" causing an unpleasant signal boost in the 3- to 3.5-kHz range. Sibilance is counteracted by a de-esser.

SIGNAL-TO-NOISE RATIO (S/N)

A measure that compares the amount of signal energy to the amount of inherent or added noise. (Ch. 2, 5)

SINGLE SYSTEM RECORDING

The recording of physically combined synchronous field or location-recorded audio obtained by using one camera that records both sound and picture onto the same medium.

SLATE

The control on a console that routes the output of the talk-back module to the group and master outputs, letting the operator record announcements of take numbers on tape.

SLAVE (AUDIO-VIDEO INTERLOCK)

One or more transport mechanisms, usually ATRs, in a synchronized system and controlled by the relative position of the master transport.

SMALL HUB 7-INCH REEL

The standard type of 7-inch audio tape reel.

SMPTE LEADER

See Academy leader.

SOCIETY LEADER

See Academy leader.

SOLO

The control on a console that allows the operator to selectively monitor various signals without affecting the console's output.

SOUND FILL

Any material used during film editing where no sound is available. It is spliced into the fullcoat stock to preserve synchronization to the picture.

SOUND PRESSURE LEVEL

A description of the amplitude or the pressure generated by an audio source.

SOURCE MUSIC

Music that is realistically part of and originating within a scene (i.e., a street musician or car radio).

SPACED MIKING

A technique used in stereo recording in which two microphones, usually directional types, are placed parallel to each other and pointed toward the sound source. The distance between the microphones may be from several inches to several feet, depending on the situation.

SPECTRUM ANALYZER

An electronic measuring instrument that shows the amplitude of frequencies within a signal.

SPINDLE

The part of an ATR that protrudes through a reel or hub adapter.

SPL METER

An electronic measuring instrument that gives the overall loudness of an audio source.

SPL

See Sound Pressure Level .

SPLICE (SAMPLING)

A sampler's ability to join two or more samples, as in conventional splicing.

SPLICE

The joining of two pieces of tape, film or leader.

SPLICER (FILM)

The device used to splice film.

SPLICING TAPE

Tape used during the splicing of audio tape or film.

SPLIT FORMAT RECORDING

See Double System Recording.

SPOTTING SESSION

The session during which spotting takes place

SPOTTING

The process of creating the cue sheet.

SPRING REVERB

A type of reverb device that works by inducing wave motion in a series of springs encased in a frame.

STAR NETWORKING
A way of connecting a MIDI network in a nonlinear fashion so that each MIDI equipped device receives the signal from the source in an uninterrupted manner.

STEENBECK
See Flatbed.

STEP TIME ENTRY
A method of recording MIDI data into a sequencer by allowing the operator to record a series of events while determining the time value of each event.

STEREO SYNTHESIZER
A device that simulates stereo sound from signals recorded in mono.

STINGERS
See Stings.

STINGS
Sustained or momentary chords or notes that accompany a specific moment in a film or visual.

STRIPING
The recording of the longitudinal time code signal onto an audio track of an ATR or VTR.

STRIPPING
See Laydown.

SUBFRAME ACCURACY
The ability to synchronize in increments of less than one time code frame.

SUMMING BUS
The portion of an audio console that combines separate signals.

SUPER 8-MM FILM FORMAT
A film format that corresponds to established parameters as described in Chapter 4.

SUPER VHS VIDEO TAPE FORMAT
A video tape format that corresponds to established parameters as described in chapters 4 and 8.

SUPERCARDIOID
As the directionality of a cardioid pickup pattern increases, it becomes supercardioid. This type of microphone pattern is preferred when the aural focus is directly in front of the microphone and any ambient or extraneous sounds need to be rejected.

SUPPLY REEL
The reel on the left-hand side of a tape deck that supplies the tape to the machine.

SWEEP EQUALIZATION
See Variable Equalization.

SWEETENING
The process of adding audio to, replacing or enhancing the audio of a completed visual.

SYNC HEAD
The head found on a multitrack ATR that functions as multiple independent heads. During overdubbing, the head may play back some tracks while recording others.

SYNC PULSE
A signal recorded onto the audio tape during film production to insure later synchronization between sound and picture.

SYNCHRONIZATION
To cause two or more media to move or occur at the same time and to coincide perfectly.

SYNCHRONIZER (FILM)
A device used in film to ensure rushes and sound are synchronized and to allow the labeling of both sound and picture reels.

SYNCHROTONE
A synchronizing signal recorded onto the audio tape during film production to ensure later synchronization between sound and picture.

TAILS OUT
When audio tape is wound on the right (take-up) reel.

TAKE
A sequence of exposed film, video tape or audio tape; actions performed and recorded.

TAKE-UP REEL
The reel on the right-hand side of a tape deck that winds the tape from the machine.

TAPE LIFTERS
Components in an ATR's tape path that keep the tape from coming into contact with the heads except during play or record.

TAPE LOOP
The creation of a physically closed loop of tape to be played repeatedly.

TAPE NOISE
Unwanted audio signals generated by magnetic media and audio equipment.

TAPE PATH
The route that tape takes when loaded into a VTR or ATR.

TAPE SATURATION
Clipping or distortion caused by saturation of magnetic recording tape and occurring when the dynamic range of the tape is exceeded.

TAPE SLAP
An effect consisting of a single repeat and obtained by playing back a tape deck recording.

TENSION ARM
A component in an ATR that maintains tension throughout the tape path to ensure proper and consistent contact between the tape and heads at all times.

THRESHOLD
In general, the point at which a device begins to act upon a signal. This point is usually adjustable.

TIMBRE
The tonal quality or color of a sound determined by its waveform.

TIME CODE
A system developed by the Society of Motion Picture and Television Engineers to identify and locate individual frames in a video. Numbers are counted as hours, minutes, seconds and frames, and generated sequentially in ascending order.

TIME CODE ADDRESS
A time code number that consists of a specific hour, minute, second and frame.

TIME CODE CONTROLLER
See Interlock Controller.

TIME CODE GENERATOR
A device that creates and generates the time code signal.

TIME CODE READER
A device that interprets previously recorded time code signal.

TIME SCALING
A feature found in some digital storage systems that permits the shrinking or expansion of a sound segment in time without affecting the pitch of the sound.

TRACK (FILM)
A roll of edited stock that is prepared for a traditional film mix.

TRACK MINUTES
The amount of recording time available in a hard disk system.

TRACK RECORD CONTROL
The control on a multitrack ATR that allows the operator to record selectively on any track or tracks.

TRACK SLIPPING
The process by which sounds can be adjusted to picture by altering the sound's position relative to time code or another sync reference after the initial recording has been made. This is analogous to time code offset, where a sound can be "slid" in either direction until it matches the picture.

TRACKS
A channel created by a head gap onto which audio information can be recorded and reproduced. In film, a track refers to a roll of edited stock that is prepared for a traditional film mix.

TRANSDUCERS
Transducers, also called contact microphones, attach directly to the body of a musical instrument such as an acoustic guitar, piano or violin. Rather than responding to sound pressure transmitted through the air, transducer microphones transform the mechanical vibration of the instrument directly into electrical energy.

TRANSFER (TIME CODE)
See Continuous Jam Sync.

TRANSFORMERS
See Impedance Matching Devices.

TRANSPORT CONTROLS
The group of controls on any piece of equipment that allow access to transport and record functions.

TRANSPOSITION
The manipulation of a sampled sound by altering its pitch.

TRIM
The variable control on a console's input module that determines the level of the incoming signal.

TRUNCATE (SAMPLING)
A sampler's ability to chop off a portion of a sample.

U-MATIC
A 3/4-inch videotape format developed by Sony Corp., now standard worldwide.

ULTRACARDIOID
The ultracardioid pickup pattern is an even more extreme version of the hypercardioid pattern. It has a narrower angle of acceptance than the hypercardioid, but similar rejection characteristics at the sides.

UMBILICAL SYNC
See Cable Sync.

UNBALANCED
A method of transmitting signals by using a single conductor insulated and wrapped with a grounding conductor.

UNDERSCORING
Music added for dramatic enhancement.

UNIDIRECTIONAL
See Cardioid.

UNIPLEXER
A device that optically transfers film to videotape.

VARIABLE EQUALIZATION
A type of equalization in which both level and frequency are variable.

VCA
See Voltage Controlled Amplifier.

VERTICAL INTERVAL TIME CODE
The type of time code that is recorded into the vertical blanking interval of a video signal.

VHS VIDEO TAPE FORMAT
A video tape format that corresponds to established parameters as described in Chapters 4 and 8.

VIDEO MONITOR
Essentially a television without the receiver section that displays only the image supplied to its video inputs.

VITC
See Vertical Interval Time Code.

VOLTAGE CONTROLLED AMPLIFIER
A mixer that operates by controlling the fader amplifier's gain with a voltage.

VTR
The acronym for video tape recorder.

WAVEFORM
The shape of a wave as determined by its components.

WAVELENGTH
The distance between two adjacent cycles in a wave.

WET SIGNAL
A signal returning to a console from a reverb unit.

WINDOW DUB
A video tape with a superimposed display of time code numbers for visual identification of scenes, actions and edits.

WINDOW DUBBER
See Character Inserter.

WIRELESS MICROPHONE
A microphone that uses a radio transmitter and receiver instead of a standard cable to carry the audio signal. Wireless microphones are easily concealed and unconstrained by a cable.

ABOUT THE AUTHOR

Mico Nelson is an audio engineer, instructor and sound effects designer and composer for film. His musical credits include scoring and sound effects for a number of independent films and several spots for MTV.

He has taught courses in basic audio for many years, and has been an audio professional for 15 years.